STO

COMMUNISM AND NATIONALISM IN INDIA

WRITTEN UNDER THE AUSPICES OF
THE RESEARCH INSTITUTE ON COMMUNIST AFFAIRS
COLUMBIA UNIVERSITY

A list of other Institute publications
appears at the back of this book

COMMUNISM AND NATIONALISM IN INDIA

M. N. Roy and Comintern Policy 1920-1939

JOHN PATRICK HAITHCOX

PRINCETON UNIVERSITY PRESS
PRINCETON, NEW JERSEY
1971

LCC 79-120755
ISBN 0-691-08722-9

This book has been composed in Linotype Caledonia
Printed in the United States of America
by Princeton University Press, Princeton, New Jersey 08540

FOR MARILYN,

KEVIN, AND STEFFAN

Table of Contents

List of Illustrations

Acknowledgments

IT IS with considerable pleasure that I acknowledge the assistance I have received from various persons and institutions in the preparation of this book. To Professor Richard L. Park of the University of Michigan I owe the inspiration for writing on M. N. Roy. It was through him that many of my initial contacts in India were made. Professor Robert C. North of Stanford University was generous in sharing the results of his work on Roy with me. A Ford Foundation Foreign Area Training Fellowship made possible an extended period of field research abroad. Further research was supported by a Faculty Research Grant from the Rackham School of Graduate Studies of the University of Michigan. The leisure and financial support required for preparing the manuscript was provided by a Senior Fellowship from the Research Institute on Communist Affairs at Columbia University. I am especially grateful to its director, Professor Zbigniew Brzezinski, for his confidence and encouragement. My task was lightened immeasurably by the cheerful efficiency of the Institute's administrative assistant, Mrs. Christine Dodson, and the competence of my two research assistants, Mr. Edward McGowan and Miss Toby Trister.

But most of all I am indebted to a remarkable group of enlightened Indians, the Royists,* whose kindness, concern, and intelligence made this study possible. They submitted patiently to numerous interviews and generously made available the material, including much private correspondence, at the Roy Archives in Dehra Dun, U.P. Their friendship has enriched my life.

* Members of this group with whom I have consulted are listed in the subsection of the bibliography entitled, "Selected List of Interviews."

Earlier versions of portions of this book have appeared in the *Journal of Asian Studies* (November 1963 and May 1965, copyright by the Association for Asian Studies, Inc.) and in *Modern Asian Studies* (January 1969, copyright by the Cambridge University Press).

COMMUNISM AND NATIONALISM IN INDIA

Abbreviations

AICC	All-India Congress Committee
AIRF	All-India Railwaymen's Federation
AITUC	All-India Trade-Union Congress
CCP	Communist Party of China
Comintern	Communist International
C.P.	Central Provinces
CPGB	Communist Party of Great Britain
CPI	Communist Party of India
CPSU	Communist Party of the Soviet Union Official designations of the Soviet party are as follows: 1898-1918—Russian Social Democratic Labor Party 1918-1925—Russian Communist Party (Bolshevik) 1925-1952—All-Union Communist Party 1952- —Communist Party of the Soviet Union
CSP	Congress Socialist Party
ECCI	Executive Committee of the Communist International
G.I.P.	Great Indian Peninsula (Railwaymen's Union)
GKU	Girni Kamgar Union
Inprecor	*International Press Correspondence*
ITUF	Indian Trade-Union Federation
LCC	Left Consolidation Committee
LRC	League of Radical Congressmen
NFL	National Federation of Labor
NTUF	National Trade-Union Federation
PCC	Pradesh Congress Committee
RPIWC	Revolutionary Party of the Indian Working Class
WPP	All-India Workers' and Peasants' Party
U.P.	United Provinces (before 1947) or Uttar Pradesh (after 1947)

Introduction

THIS STUDY traces the development of communism and socialism in India from the Second Congress of the Communist International in 1920, which dealt with the issue of communism and nationalism in colonial and semi-colonial countries, to the defeat of the left wing of the Indian National Congress, or Congress party, in 1939. The latter date coincides with the outbreak of World War II. It marks the end of an important chapter in the development of the Indian nationalist movement and the beginning of a new phase in which the British government of India was less tolerant of dissent and allowed less scope to nationalist activities.

A conscious effort has been made to concentrate on those areas where there are gaps in the existing literature or where, it is felt, new evaluations are required. The central focus of this work is M. N. Roy, the founder of the Communist Party of India. It is my view that his activities in the 1920's, about which much has been written, have been misinterpreted. Almost nothing is known about his role in the Indian nationalist movement—both in the Congress party and the Labor movement—in the 1930's. Only passing references have been made to the Roy group in accounts of the Indian freedom struggle. This is due in large part to the stand Roy took during World War II in support of the British war effort, which ran counter to Indian nationalist sentiment.

Readers familar with the literature on the development of communism in India will note the ways in which my findings differ from those of previous accounts. These differences are especially evident with respect to the Roy-Lenin debate on colonial policy at the Second Congress of the Communist International, the role of M. N. Roy in the development of the Indian communist movement, Roy's activities in China, and the circumstances surrounding his expulsion from the Comintern. To illuminate subject areas not previously studied in any detail, I have explored at some length such topics as the role of the Royists and the communists in the development of the Indian trade-union movement, the decolonization controversy of the Sixth Comintern Congress, and the efforts of M. N. Roy —following his expulsion from the Comintern—to challenge Stalin's policies in India in the 1930's and to pursue an independent line of action. In this connection the reader will find new material on the influence of Roy and his followers within the Congress Socialist party during its early years, the activities of the Roy group within the Indian nationalist movement on behalf of trade-union unity, and Roy's program to radicalize the Congress party by working within the nationalist organization.

Since the main body of this study deals with Roy after his conversion to communism, the remainder of this introduction will be devoted to showing the evolution of his political thought from the extremist nationalism of his early youth to Marxian socialism. This distinct phase of Roy's life served as the prelude to his sudden emergence at the Second Comintern Congress as the spokesman of Indian communism.

Narendra Nath Bhattacharya, later to be known as Manabendra Nath Roy, was born of Brahmin parentage in the Bengali village of Arbalia, some twenty miles from Calcutta, in the district of 24 Parganas. When he was about nine, his parents moved to the nearby village of Kodalia, where he spent the remainder of his boyhood.[1] The exact date of Roy's birth is unknown—estimates range from 1886 to 1893. The late Ellen Roy, M. N. Roy's widow, although herself not certain, felt that the correct date was closer to the latter.[2]

Even as a young teenager Roy was already participating in the nationalist, anti-British struggle as a member of a terrorist, patriotic society in his native Bengal.[3] He was first arrested in connection with the Howrah Conspiracy Case, but was acquitted in 1911.[4] The following year a number of local groups, which operated in the vicinity of Calcutta and had been loosely associated with the terrorist organization known as Juguntar, were organized into a more tightly knit party under the leadership of Jatindranath Mukherjee. Most of the local units of Anushilan, the other major secret society in Bengal, also merged under Jatin's leadership.[5]

Roy became a member of Jatin's group, which eschewed isolated acts of political assassination in favor of a more ambitious scheme for a province-wide revolt. When the war broke out in 1914, Jatin's group, along with other revolutionary underground organizations in India, sought German support. To secure funds to enable them to contact the Germans, the group executed the Garden Reach and Belliaghat dacoities in January and February 1915. Roy was arrested in connection with the former affair, but was again acquitted.[6]

The following April, Roy was sent to Batavia[a] in the Netherlands Indies to contact the German consul there. In addition to securing funds, Roy succeeded in getting a cargo of arms, bound for Karachi, diverted to Bengal. The arms had been purchased in the United States.

On April 22 the oil steamer *Maverick* left San Pedro, California, bound for the uninhabited island of Socarro, about 600 miles off the coast of Mexico. There it was to rendezvous with the schooner, *Annie Larsen*, which had departed earlier from San Diego laden with arms and ammunition.[7] The munitions, ostensibly intended for shipment to German East Africa, had been purchased by a former Krupp agent in New York and transported by rail to the West Coast.[8]

Roy returned to India in June when plans were laid, in anticipation of receipt of the arms, for a large-scale revolt. The arms were to be stored initially in the Sundarbans.

[a] Now Djakarta, the capital of Indonesia.

From there they were later to be distributed to Calcutta, to Hatia—an island off the coast of Bengal—and to Balasore,[b] where the headquarters of Jatin Mukherjee's group was located. Bepin Ganguly and Roy were assigned to a group which was to seize Port William. They were later to be joined by another group based on Hatia for a march on Calcutta. The city itself was to be cut off from reinforcements by the demolition of three key railroad bridges.[9]

British intelligence soon learned of the conspiracy and in August raided the Calcutta office of Harry and Sons, a bogus firm established as a conduit for German funds. In the meantime, Roy had returned to Java. He arrived there on August 15 to discover that the *Maverick* had already put into port, but without the expected arms.[10] Having waited in vain for the *Annie Larsen* for twenty-nine days on Socarro Island, the steamer had left without its precious cargo.[11]

In Roy's absence, British authorities closed in on the Juguntar conspirators. On September 4, the New Emporium, a branch of Harry and Sons at Balasore, was raided.[12] Not long thereafter Jatin was killed in an armed encounter with the police and military, popularly known as "the battle of Balasore."[13] As a result of this turn of events and because he himself was under indictment, Roy decided not to return to India—at least not in the immediate future. Arriving in Japan via Shanghai, Roy secured a visa to enter the United States.[14]

Roy arrived in San Francisco on June 15, 1916, under the alias of Charles Allen Martin, a bearded Roman Catholic priest from the West Indies bound for Paris for advanced theological studies.[15] The West Coast was then a center of revolutionary activity in behalf of Indian independence. Har Dayal had organized an American branch of the Ghadr party, a Punjabi revolutionary society, in San Francisco in 1913.[16] The party enjoyed wide support among the large Indian community residing in California, such as the pros-

[b] Balasore is now located in Orissa, which constituted part of Bengal until 1911 when it was made into a separate province.

perous Sikh cotton growers in the Imperial Valley. A more important source of funds, however, was the German government which was more then willing to encourage unrest in Great Britain's most valuable colony.

Shortly after arriving in the States, Roy went to Palo Alto, the site of Stanford University, where he was certain of finding a warm welcome. Dhan Gopal Mukherjee, the brother of Jadu Gopal Mukherjee, a leading Bengali revolutionary and friend of Roy's, was there.[17] In addition, there was much sympathy for the Indian cause within the intellectual community at Stanford.

While at Palo Alto, Bhattacharya assumed the name of M. N. Roy. It was here too that he met Evelyn Trent, a bright and attractive graduate student with radical views. When Roy moved to New York a few months later, Evelyn went with him.[18/c] She was a great asset to Roy in his work until their separation in 1926.

In New York, Roy contacted H. L. Gupta, Dr. Chandra Chakraberty, and other Indian revolutionaries who were in league with the Germans.[19] It was here that Roy's transformation from a Bengali nationalist of the extremist school to an international communist began. One evening he attended a socialist rally addressed by the Indian nationalist leader Lala Lajpat Rai, who spoke of the poverty of the Indian people. After the speech, a member of the audience asked what difference it would make if Indians were exploited by "native capitalists" rather than by "foreign imperialists." Lajpat Rai replied that "it does make a difference whether one is kicked by one's brother or by a foreign robber." The reply struck Roy as inadequate, and for the first time he felt that there was something missing in the nationalist blueprint for freedom.[20]

It was at the New York Public Library that Roy first made his acquaintance with the writings of Karl Marx.[21] In his

[c] They were married in New York and resided for a time at 2116 Daley Avenue (U.S. War Department Files, 10640-690. M.I. 5, Report on M. N. Roy's Activities in Mexico by the United States Military Attaché in Mexico in 1918).

gravitation toward Marxism, Roy was no doubt influenced by his wife and the many socialist supporters of India's independence with whom he became acquainted in America. At this time, however, his conversion to communism was far from complete.

In June 1917 Roy was indicted for illegal entry and a warrant for his arrest was issued.[22] Already under investigation because of his association with known Indian revolutionaries and their German contacts, Roy absconded to Mexico with his wife.[23] The following month a federal grand jury returned an indictment against over 100 Americans, Germans, and Indians. The charge was violating American neutrality laws by participating in a nationwide conspiracy, financed by the Kaiser and promulgated through the Berlin Foreign Office, to foment rebellion in India and to aid Germany in the prosecution of the war by compelling Great Britain to divert essential troops from Europe in order to put down insurrection elsewhere.[24/d]

In Mexico, Roy was in contact with German agents who, considering him useful as a contact with revolutionaries in the States, kept him well supplied with money.[e] He lived sumptuously and established contacts with highly placed government officials, some of whom were close to President Carranza. In addition to circulating in Mexican society, Roy began to frequent the meetings of various socialist groups in Mexico City. One of these was a small group called the Mexican Socialist party. One of its members, Manuel Gomez, has admitted that the party "didn't amount to anything" and was referred to as the *cinco gatos* ("five cats").

According to Gomez, Roy "took himself very seriously and considered that his life work was to prepare himself to act

[d] In November over thirty persons were brought to trial in the dramatic Hindu Conspiracy Case in which the purchase of munitions in the United States and their intended shipment to India via the *Maverick* and the *Annie Larsen* played a prominent part.

[e] While in Mexico, Roy used the name Manuel Mendez in corresponding with sympathizers in the States (U.S. War Department Files, 10640-690, M.I. 5).

as a militarist participant in the freeing of India from British rule."[25] Another of Roy's acquaintances in Mexico, Carleton Beals, described Roy as "tall, with long, slim, expressive hands and black-white eyes that flashed frequent wrath out of a very dark face," and as a person with "boundless energy" who mastered enough Spanish in a few months to write pamphlets and speak from the platform.[26]

Roy considered Mexico the land of his rebirth. It was here that he met the Soviet emissary, Michael Borodin, whom Roy credits with having initiated him "in the intricacies of Hegelian dialectics as the key to Marxism" and with having broken down his resistance to Marxist thought.[27] Manuel Gomez was the editor of the English-language section of the newspaper *El Heraldo de Mexico,* and under his influence and that of his associates this page acquired a definite socialist tinge. Some of the material was taken directly from Soviet publications. This came to the attention of Borodin shortly after his arrival in Mexico City in the summer of 1919. Borodin sought out Gomez and through him met Roy. Borodin stayed at Roy's home during the remainder of his stay in Mexico and the two became close friends.[28]

In daily discussions with Borodin on the theory and practice of communism and the philosophical aspects of Marxism, which generally began after dinner and often ran late into the night, Roy sought to resist Borodin's arguments with a defense of cultural nationalism. After listening to Roy's arguments, Borodin would protest, "But it is all subjectivism." He succeeded in convincing Roy that he was attempting to defend a point of view in which he no longer firmly believed. These few months, according to Roy, constituted "the most memorable period" of his life. It was at this time, he later wrote, that "the foundations of my subsequent intellectual development were laid."[29] Thus, shortly after the end of the war and the defeat of Germany, Roy had turned to a new source of support for revolutionary activities in India.

Roy sought to gain control of the Mexican Socialist party, of which he was a member, and convert it into a communist organization. He eventually succeeded in ousting from the party his most serious rival, the American Linn A. E. Gale, but Gale promptly styled his rump group, the Communist Party of Mexico. Having failed to persuade the remaining members of the Socialist party to change its name and its principles, Roy and a small group of followers broke from the party and founded a second Communist Party of Mexico.[30] Roy's small group—described by a contemporary as "six members and a calico cat"[31]—had the blessing of Borodin and consequently won affiliation with the Communist International. Although Roy was to become the doyen of Indian communists, he attended the 1920 Comintern Congress as an official representative of the Mexican party.[f]

[f] Salvador de Madariaga, in *Latin America Between the Eagle and the Bear* (London: Hollis and Carter, 1962), states that Roy returned to Mexico in 1920 as an agent of Zinoviev to establish the Pan-American Agency of the Comintern. His source for this claim is Rodrigo Garcia Trevinso, *La Ingerencia Rusa en Mexico* (*y Sudamerica*) (Mexico City, 1959). I have been unable to substantiate this claim from any other source.

1. The Second Comintern Congress

THE Indian Brahmin Narendra Nath Bhattacharya, alias Manabendra Nath Roy, made his debut in the international communist movement at the Second World Congress of the Communist International (Comintern), which was held in Moscow from July 19 to August 7, 1920.[a] Lenin had prepared in advance a draft thesis on the national and colonial question, which he circulated among the delegates with a request for comments and criticisms. As a result of Roy's response, Lenin invited him to write an alternative draft.[1] Both Lenin's and Roy's theses were later submitted to the National and Colonial Commission for its consideration. In the subsequent debates within the commission, a distinction evolved between different kinds of "bourgeois-democratic movements" in dependent areas —between those of a truly revolutionary and those of a merely "reformist" character—based on differences in their class composition. In countries where "reformist" nationalist movements prevailed, Roy argued before the commission, the Comintern should eschew alliances with nationalist leaders who were bound to desert to the imperialist camp in a revolutionary situation, and should instead assist exclusively "the institution and development of the communist movement" and "the organization of the broad popular masses for the class interests of the latter."[2]

After some modifications were made in the theses prepared by Lenin and Roy, the congress took the unusual step of adopting both.[3] In the revised version of Lenin's thesis, the Comintern was counseled to support only "revolutionary movements of liberation," rather than all "bourgeois-democratic liberation movements," as stated in the

[a] The congress met on the first day in Petrograd, but all subsequent meetings were held in Moscow.

original draft.[4] In this way the distinction Roy made between different types of bourgeois-democratic liberation movements was incorporated into Lenin's thesis. As Lenin explained to the congress: "It was argued that if we speak about the bourgeois-democratic movement all distinctions between reformist and revolutionary movements will be obliterated; whereas in recent times, this distinction has been fully and clearly revealed in backward and colonial countries." Elaborating on this distinction, Lenin continued:

> Very often, even in the majority of cases perhaps, where the bourgeoisie of the oppressed countries does support the national movement, it simultaneously works in harmony with the imperialist bourgeoisie; i.e., it joins the latter in fighting against all revolutionary movements and all revolutionary classes. . . . In the [National and Colonial] Commission this was proved irrefutably, and we came to the conclusion that the only correct thing was to take this distinction into consideration and nearly everywhere to substitute the term "nationalist-revolutionary" for the term "bourgeois-democratic." The meaning of this change is that we Communists should, and will, support bourgeois liberation movements in the colonial countries only when these movements are really revolutionary, when the representatives of these movements do not hinder us in training and organizing the peasants and the broad masses of the exploited in a revolutionary spirit.[5]

It is important to note that this was Lenin's first attempt to formulate in a systematic manner his ideas on the problems of promoting communist revolution in Asia. Robert C. North and Xenia J. Eudin have contended that "Roy ranks with Lenin and Mao Tse-tung in the development of fundamental communist policy for the underdeveloped . . . areas of the globe."[6] This study does not attempt to defend this view, but it does support the position that Roy played a highly significant role in the formulation and conduct of Comintern policy on the national and colonial question in the 1920's.

In the early years of his Comintern career, Roy had felt that a united front policy, which called for communist support for nationalist movements in colonial and semicolonial areas, was inappropriate for India. When he warned of the possible betrayal of "bourgeois-democratic" nationalist leaders, he had the Indian National Congress in mind. Lenin, in contrast, felt that the national bourgeoisie could be a progressive force, particularly in the early stages of the nationalist movement when anticolonialist fervor was strong, but he agreed with Roy that continued alliance with this group, once its revolutionary potential had been exhausted, would be self-defeating.

But how was the point at which communists must abruptly shift from a policy of "revolution from above" to a policy of "revolution from below" to be determined? What would be the sign that the time was ripe for a communist party to break away from the nationalist movement and seek support directly among the workers, peasants, and petty bourgeoisie? Although never clearly formulated, it is evident that such a determination would require an assessment both of the relative strength of bourgeois and proletarian forces and of the class composition of the nationalist movement within the country in question. On both these points Lenin and Roy disagreed with respect to India.

Roy suspected the "reliability" of the leadership of the Indian National Congress. He had left India in August 1915,[7] and this attitude was no doubt conditioned by his early acquaintance with the moderates. The moderates, partisans of British culture and institutions who had faith in the ultimate good will of their British overlords, stressed nonviolent, constitutional methods for securing measured progress toward self-government. The radicals, more firmly rooted in their own culture and more impatient and less trusting than the moderates, felt that extraconstitutional methods were required to secure relief from a repressive raj.[8] At the annual Congress session at Surat in 1907, the two groups came to blows over their differences, but the moderates were able to assert their control over the party. The following year a new party constitution was adopted. It stated that the objectives of the Indian National Congress were "to be achieved by constitutional means, by bringing about a steady reform of the existing system of administration, and by promoting national unity, fostering public spirit and developing and organizing the intellectual, moral, economic, and industrial resources of the country."[9] Party delegates were required to express in writing their acceptance of this creed. In this way the radicals—whose most prominent national spokesman was the Maharashtrian Bal Gangadhar Tilak—were effectively debarred from active participation in the Congress party.

In Bengal, radical nationalists were divided among themselves on the question of violence. Among the extremists were members of a number of secret, patriotic (or, as the British preferred to call them, terrorist) organizations, chief among which were Anushilan and Juguntar. As a youth in Bengal, Roy had participated in the nationalist activities of Juguntar during the period when the radicals were temporarily estranged from the Congress party.[10] They did not return to the Congress fold until late 1915—after Roy left India—when the ban against them was lifted. The year 1915 also marked Gandhi's return to India after twenty-three years in South Africa. In 1918 the moderates, now outnumbered, left the Congress party in a dispute with the radicals over the Montagu-Chelmsford proposals for constitutional reform to form the Liberal party.[11] The following year Gandhi launched his first all-India campaign against British rule. In the course of a few years the Congress party had been transformed markedly from the upper-middle-class debating society with which Roy had been familiar to a broad-based, militant nationalist organization.

In his analysis of class forces in India, Roy greatly exaggerated both the numerical and ideological strength of the Indian proletariat. Estimating that India possessed five million workers, and an additional thirty-seven million landless peasants, he reported to the Comintern that, although the Indian nationalist movement rested for the most part on the middle classes, the downtrodden Indian masses would shortly blaze their own revolutionary trail.[12] In his supplementary thesis, he claimed that "the real strength of the liberation movement is no longer confined to the narrow circle of bourgeois-democratic nationalists. In most of the colonies there already exist organized revolutionary parties."[13]

Lenin did not share Roy's confidence in the strength of the Indian proletariat or peasantry. He lacked Marx's faith in a "spontaneous" development of class-consciousness. He saw, for example, an essential difference between the proletarian and the socialist, i.e., the class-conscious proletarian. Two years earlier Lenin had written that "workers have to work in the factory as if on a chain gang and neither time nor possibility remain for them to become socialists."[14] "Spontaneity" represented for Lenin merely a nonrational opposition to society which might temporarily coincide with the interests of a class, but would in the long run oppose it. Lenin considered the development of genuine class-consciousness dependent upon party organization, discipline, and indoctrination. At the time of the Second World Congress there was no communist party in India. Lenin is reported to have pointed out to Roy that it would take some time before Indian workers and peasants could be mobilized effectively.[15]

Their differing assessment of the Indian situation resulted in contrasting attitudes toward nationalist movements in general. Lenin urged "temporary relations and even unions" with such movements.[16] Roy spoke only in terms of "cooperation" with nationalist movements. Less trustful of the national bourgeoisie than Lenin, he laid greater stress on developing independent communist parties in dependent areas than on supporting existing nationalist movements. Although in his thesis he recommended a modified agrarian program of land reform, he also urged that "peasants' and workers' soviets" be organized "as soon as possible."[17]

In his fervent faith in the class-consciousness of the proletariat, Roy resembled Karl Marx before 1848. Marx had looked forward eagerly and with high optimism to the European revolutions which finally erupted in 1848, but each one failed. Following these events, Marx revised his views concerning the degree to which class-consciousness could arise spontaneously, solely as a result of "objective conditions." He came to realize the necessity of a longer apprenticeship for the proletariat than he had thought necessary heretofore. He also concluded that the development of proletarian class-consciousness should be facilitated by destroying those elements in the "objective" situation which tended to retard its growth.

To achieve this, Marx proposed a minimum program of action.[18] His purpose was to remove all obstacles to the maturation of "bourgeois democracy" and the capitalist system—a stage whose attainment he considered a prerequisite to the advent of communism. It called for the promotion of democratic liberties and privileges, such as universal suffrage, to bring social grievances into the open and solidify class antagonisms. It also involved the exorcism of religious and patriotic sentiments, faith in reform via constitutional means, and other ideas which Marx regarded as ideological blinkers.

In conjunction with the minimum program, a maximum program, which aimed at the ultimate achievement of communism, was also to be pursued. Simultaneously, while working for the development of bourgeois democracy in its purest form, communists were to strive to weaken the bourgeois order by making ideological attacks on the capitalist system and by encouraging rebellions. It can be seen that this two-pronged attack, which sought to strengthen bourgeois democracy as a step in the direction of its overthrow, requires antennae acutely sensitive to a developing situation and a delicate sense of timing. One program must be balanced carefully against the other without aborting the ultimate goal, and the precise moment when the minimum program should be abandoned altogether, must be recognized.

In a sense, the debate between Lenin and Roy on the national and colonial question can be interpreted as reflecting a difference of opinion on the relative weight to be given to the maximum and minimum programs in the formulation of Comintern policy. In 1920 Roy shared the impatience of youth. Like Marx before 1848, he underestimated the task of mobilizing class unrest and forging an effective organizational weapon. Roy wanted to force the pace set by Lenin in order to liberate the masses at once from all oppressive relationships of both foreign and domestic hue.

In his supplementary thesis Roy stated that "the imperialist policy of preventing industrial development in the colonies" had restricted the growth of a proletarian class "until recently."[19] But since the abandonment of this policy, he maintained, Indian industry had grown at a remarkable pace. Roy's stress on "revolution from below" was based on his assumption that India had already attained a stage of capitalist development in which proletarian class consciousness was beginning to solidify. Following the Second Comintern Congress, Roy attempted to buttress his thesis with a Marxian analysis of Indian society. This study was published in 1922, under the title *India in Transition.*[20] A Russian version had appeared the year before.[21] In his book, Roy maintained that as a result of a "spectacular" growth of Indian industry during World War I, the native bourgeoisie was now demanding a much larger share in the exploitation of India's natural and human resources.[22] Moreover, in his view the government of India, to forestall an alliance between the native bourgeoisie and the Indian masses, had been obliged to placate the former by granting them increasingly larger concessions. The Indian bourgeoisie, according to Roy, shared the British fear of mass revolt, and though for a time they would use the strength of the masses to win still further concessions, they would eventually compromise with their rulers and settle for something less than complete independence.[23]

It will be shown in subsequent chapters that Roy's views with respect to the revolutionary potential of the Indian proletariat altered considerably over the years. But the Roy-Lenin debate, nevertheless, has an important historical significance in that it marks the first attempt within the Comintern to formulate a policy which would successfully merge the revolutionary aspirations of nationalist anticolonialism and communist anticapitalism. Disagreement over the degree of support to be given nationalist leaders as opposed to indigenous communist parties has continued to plague the international communist movement to the present day. The 1927 dispute between Stalin and Trotsky, and between Roy and Borodin,[b] over the China policy provided dramatic evidence that these opposing views had not been reconciled at the Second World Congress. Stalin's campaign against Trotsky and the Left Opposition was followed by a struggle against Bukharin and the Right Opposition. Because of the prominent role played by the Russian communists in the Comintern, the struggle for power within the Soviet party inevitably spilled over into the international communist organization. The dispute between the Stalin and Bukharin factions within the party on domestic issues was reflected on the international level in the differences between the Comintern and the International Right Opposition, a group which emerged in 1928, over the attitude to adopt toward socialists in Western countries and nationalists in dependent areas. The opposition of Roy and his group to the strategy and tactics of the Communist Party of India (CPI) in the late 1920's and the early 1930's was a part of this latter controversy.

The conflict today between the Soviet Union and the People's Republic of China over the correct attitude to adopt toward nationalist regimes in underdeveloped areas, such as the Congress government in India, is the latest manifesta-

[b] Borodin was to the right of Stalin, Trotsky to the left. As will be shown in the chapter on China, Roy was not a Trotskyite.

1. M. N. Roy as Father Martin, 1916.

2. M. N. Roy in Mexico, 1917-1919.

3. M. N. Roy in Moscow, early 1920's.

4. Wang Ching-wei, leader of the Left Kuomintang.

5. M. N. Roy (standing fourth from left) with Oriental delegates to the Comintern congress in Moscow, Nov.-Dec. 1922.

6. M. N. Roy and two Russians at Soviet consulate, Canton, 1927.

tion of the long-standing controversy, which dates back to the early days of the Comintern, over how to utilize nationalist movements for communist ends. This is recognized by Indian communists themselves. The communist leader and theoretician, Dr. Gangadhar M. Adhikari, in preparing a critique of E. M. S. Namboodripad's document "Revisionism and Dogmatism in the CPI," found it necessary to review the history of the debate within the international communist movement over the role of the national bourgeoisie. He takes as his starting point the 1920 Comintern Congress and argues that the roots of the present dispute between the Right CPI (the so-called "pro-Moscow" party) and the Left CPI (the so-called "pro-Peking" party) lie in the perennial controversy over the "role of the national bourgeoisie in our country, and in our national democratic revolution in its various phases." It is impossible to understand or evaluate the dispute which separates the two Indian parties without keeping in mind the context in which it is being carried on—the struggle for "national political independence (before liberation)," and its extension, the struggle for "national economic independence (after liberation)." The central problem, the author maintains, has always been, both before and after independence, how to unite with the national bourgeoisie, counteract its "compromising tendency" and, at the same time, build an independent communist party.[24]

2. The Dawn of Indian Communism

THROUGHOUT the 1920's, M. N. Roy made strenuous efforts to organize a communist movement in India. Along with copies of the Comintern organ, *International Press Correspondence*, large quantities of Roy's journal, *The Vanguard of Indian Independence*,[a] were smuggled into India with the aid of Indian seamen, or lascars, specially recruited for the purpose. This literature found its way into the hands of promising Indians, many of whom were also contacted directly through correspondence. During this early period, Roy hoped to penetrate the nationalist movement not only through radical Congress members, but also via the Khilafat movement, the Bengali revolutionary societies, and the trade unions. Roy's efforts with respect to each of these last three groups now will be examined in some detail.

Indian Moslems

In late 1920 an emigré communist Party of India was organized in Tashkent.[1] The party was formed from among Indian *muhajirun*,[b] who had participated in a *Hijarat*, or exodus, from India in protest against the dismemberment of Turkey by Great Britain and her allies following World War I. The ruler of Turkey was also the Caliph of Islam and as such was regarded traditionally as the spiritual head of all Moslems. The harsh terms of the treaty imposed on Turkey were interpreted by many Moslems as a threat to Islam itself. When in March 1924 the Caliphate was abol-

[a] *The Vanguard of Indian Independence* began publication in May 1922. Its name was later changed to *Advance Guard*, and on January 1, 1925 it became *Masses of India*. The journal was discontinued in 1928 (Gene D. Overstreet and Marshall Windmiller, *Communism in India*, p. 448, table XI).

[b] *Muhajirun* are Moslem pilgrims.

ished by the newly proclaimed Turkish Republic, the Khilafat movement in India died a natural death.[2]

In 1920 thousands of Moslems left India to establish their homes in a Moslem country or to join Mustafa Kemal Pasha's rebel army in Turkey. Some of the *muhajirun* found their way across Afghanistan into Central Asia, a turbulent area, parts of which had only recently fallen under Bolshevik control. They had been informed that Soviet authorities would provide facilities for those who wished to proceed to Turkey. In the summer of 1920, a group of about eighty, having crossed the Hindu Kush on foot, were captured by Turks who were in revolt against Bolshevik rule. They were subsequently rescued by Russian troops stationed at the fort in Kirkee and given the option of continuing on their journey to Turkey or going to nearby Tashkent for military training. About half the group chose to go to Tashkent, where, on arrival in late September 1920, they were greeted by M. N. Roy.[3]

Roy had only recently come to Tashkent from Moscow. He had been sent as a member of the recently constituted Central Asiatic Bureau of the Comintern, which was charged with the responsibility for directing revolutionary activities in Asia. Part of his mission was to provide military supplies and financial aid to the turbulent frontier tribes in order to foment rebellion along India's borders with Afghanistan, and to raise from among deserters of the Indian army and other groups a liberation army which would use the frontier area as a base of operation. For this reason he was accompanied to Tashkent by twenty-seven wagons carrying arms, ammunition, and military stores; two wagons of gold coins, bullion, and pound and rupee notes; ten wagons of dismantled airplanes; and the staff of a military training school.

When Roy heard of the arrival of the *muhajirun*, he thought he might be able to recruit some of them for the proposed liberation army. It was for this purpose that he had invited to Tashkent the group that had been rescued near Kirkee. Those who accepted the invitation were joined by other small groups of Indian Moslems. They were all quartered in a building which became known as India House. Most of these men were poorly-educated Moslem zealots, not likely candidates for conversion to communism. A few, however, responded to the political indoctrination offered by Roy and sought permission of the Central Asiatic Bureau to organize a communist party. The request was granted and an emigré party was formed in October or November 1920, with Muhammed Shafiq as its general secretary. Other important members of the party were M. N. Roy and his first wife Evelyn, Abani Mukherji and his wife Rosa,[c] Musood Ali Shah, Abdur Rab, Trimul Acharia, Shaukat Usmani, and Abdallah Safdar.

One of the *muhajirun* at Tashkent, Abdul Qadir Khan, has left a portrait of Roy as he was at this time. In 1930, after he had become a British sympathizer, Khan wrote a three-part series for *The Times* (London) on his experiences in Soviet Russia in which he described Roy as a "tall, slim man with dark Bengali features and burning eyes, rather handsome and with a certain grace. Self-important and ill-tempered in discussion, he was often vehement in seeking to impose his opinions on others." After presenting this somewhat unflattering picture, the author added that

[c] As a youth Abani Mukherji was a member of one of Bengal's secret revolutionary societies. On a mission to Japan he was captured and imprisoned by the British in Singapore. He escaped and, under the pseudonym of Dr. Shaheer, made his way to Europe and finally in 1920 to Moscow, where he attended the Second World Congress of the Comintern as one of the Indian delegates. Although he collaborated with Roy on the book, *India in Transition*, by 1922 he had broken with him and later became one of his chief detractors and rivals in India. His wife, the former Rosa Fitingof, had joined the Soviet party in 1918. When Abani first met her in 1920, she was an assistant to Lydia Fotieva, Lenin's private secretary. She later served as Roy's interpreter on his trip to Tashkent. Abani Mukherji is deceased, but as late as April 1967, his wife was reported living in Leningrad with their daughter (*New Times* [Moscow], April 5, 1967, pp. 10-12). Muzaffar Ahmed, *The Communist Party of India and Its Formation Abroad* (pp. 136-44), contends that Abani was expelled from the emigré CPI in 1922, but was later granted permission to live in the Soviet Union with his wife. He was allegedly arrested in 1937 or 1938 in the Stalin purges.

"Roy, with all his faults, showed himself a courageous and determined man" who kept abreast of developments in India by assiduously reading official British government documents.[4]

The Indian Military School, which had been formally established in Tashkent after the arrival of the *muhajirun*, was short-lived. The failure of the Afghanistan government to allow free passage across its territory which lay between India and Soviet Russia aborted the plans to use the Indian frontier area as a revolutionary base. The trainees who had not joined the communist party were, on the whole, a refractory lot and the Soviet government, not wishing to jeopardize economic relations with Great Britain for the sake of a project with such uncertain prospects, disbanded the school in May 1921.

The Central Asiatic Bureau of the Comintern was also abolished. The attempt to conduct revolutionary activities in the dependent areas of Asia from a base in Central Asia had not proved fruitful and the task was assumed by a newly-created Eastern Commission of the Executive Committee of the Communist International (ECCI), headquartered in Moscow. This body was to be assisted by the communist parties of the Western colonial powers.

Roy had returned to Moscow in January, leaving Abani Mukherji in charge of his affairs at Tashkent. Shortly thereafter, a decision was made to channel all activities in India through Roy, rather than through expatriate Indian nationalists in Europe led by Virendranath Chattopadhyaya. Roy's headquarters were to be in Moscow, where political training would be available to Indians who, on return to India, would help establish a communist party there.[5]

Twenty-two of the graduates of the Indian Military School had accompanied Roy to Moscow for further training at the Communist University of Toilers of the East, which had been established in April 1921.[d] The re-

[d] Writing in the 1950's, Roy stated that twenty-two *muhajirun* were chosen for further training in Moscow (Roy, *M. N. Roy's Memoirs*, pp. 5-8). Ernestine Evans, who was in Moscow in the winter of 1921-

mainder were broken down into small groups and allowed to return to India or to proceed to Turkey, if they wished. In Moscow, those who had come from Tashkent were joined by other Indian groups, and later that year, members of these various Indian groups came together to form a reconstituted CPI. Muhammed Shafiq was again chosen as general secretary and a working committee—consisting of Shafiq, M. N. Roy, and Abani Mukherji—was elected. Some of the other important members of the party were: Shaukat Usmani, Fazl Elahi Qurban, and Khushi Muhammed (alias Muhammed Ali, alias Ibrahim, alias Sipassi).[e]

In April 1922, Roy's center of activities was transferred from Moscow to Berlin. Once there, he lost little time in getting down to work. On May 15 the first issue of his propaganda journal, *The Vanguard of Indian Independence*, appeared. Before the end of the year, he had published three books—*India in Transition*, *India's Problem*

22, wrote in 1922 of visiting a class at the school attended by eighteen Indian students and taught by M. N. Roy's first wife, Evelyn. The instruction on that occasion consisted of reading aloud from Raymond William Postgate's (ed.) *Revolution From 1789 to 1906*. There was a total of 713 students at the school at this time. From the account, it would not appear that the curriculum was very demanding or the intellectual capabilities of the students very high. In the author's words, "it was not a very tidy university" (Ernestine Evans, "Looking East From Moscow," *Asia*, XXII [1922]: 972-76).

One of the Indian Moslems who studied at the University has recalled that the program of studies included such topics as historical materialism, the class war, the French Revolution, the American Revolution, and the evolution of modern capitalism (Abdul Qadir Khan, *The Times* [London], Feb. 26, 1930). Muzaffar Ahmed (p. 78) has provided a list of seventeen of these Indian students: Gawhar Rahman Khan, Mian Muhammed Akbar Shah, Sultan Mahmud, Meer Abdul Majeed, Firozuddin Mansur, Fazl Elahi Qurban, Abdallah Safdar, Shaukat Usmani, Rafiq Ahmed, Habib Ahmed Nasim, Fida Ali Zahid, Abdul Qadir Sehrai, Musood Ali Shah, Abdul Qwayyum, Master Abdul Hamid, Sayeed and Aziz Ahmen. The eighteenth was Abdul Qadir Khan.

[e] Among others who joined the emigré party in Moscow were: Gawhar Rahman Khan, Mian Muhammed Akbar Shah, Sultan Mahmud, Meer Abdul Majeed, Firozuddin Mansur, Abdallah Safdar, Rafiz Ahmed, Fida Ali Zahid, Abdul Qadir Sehrai, Musood Ali Shah, and Rahmat Ali, alias Zakaria (Ahmed, p. 32). Obviously there were some dropouts from the Tashkent group.

and Its Solution, and *What Do We Want?* All of this literature was dispatched to India. From Moscow, fairly efficient channels of communication had linked Roy with North India via Central Asia. But he had found that other regions were more difficult to reach. This was one of the principal reasons his headquarters were shifted to Europe. He was particularly anxious to establish contact with his former associates in the secret revolutionary societies in his home province of Bengal.[6]

Bengali Revolutionaries

As a youth in Bengal, Roy had been a member of a revolutionary group located in the vicinity of Calcutta and led by Jatindranath Mukherjee.[7] Of the two major revolutionary societies in Bengal, Anushilan[f] and Juguntar,[g] Jatin's group was associated with the latter. As a result of his early engagement in political activities, Roy's formal education was limited. He was largely a self-taught man, and his voluminous writings reflect both the advantages and disadvantages of such an education. He sometimes misinterpreted ideas thoroughly explored in the past as personal discoveries derived from experience and private reflection. Unable to gauge the extent of common knowledge, he occasionally belabored the obvious. But his writings were seldom trite, often strikingly original, and always distinctively his own.

[f] The name was derived from the title of Bankim Chandra Chatterji's novel, *Anushilan*.

[g] "Juguntar" means "new life" or "revolution." Because of the association of the Atmonnati Samiti ("soul-developing society") with the newspaper, *Juguntar*, the *samiti* gradually came to be known as Juguntar. The Alipore Conspiracy Trial of 1908 marked the end of this organization. Later a number of revolutionary groups, including the Calcutta section of Anushilan, joined together under the leadership of Jatindranath Mukherjee, to form a federation which was called Juguntar. This new grouping, however, had no organizational continuity with the original Juguntar party (T. N. Lahiri, *Our Patriots of Wax, Iron and Clay: Moderate, Revolutionary and Intermediate Strains in the Indian Struggle for Freedom* [Calcutta: C. K. Bhattacharjee, 1954], pp. 100-104).

Secret nationalist societies first arose in Bengal in the last quarter of the nineteenth century. They were formed by Calcutta students who had been inspired by Surindranath Bannerjea's lectures on Mazzini's "Young Italy" movement.[8] Although Bannerjea himself abhorred violence as a means of achieving national unity, many of his young charges, like Bepin Chandra Pal, did not share his antipathy. It was difficult to separate Mazzini's nationalist zeal from his support of the weapon of political assassination.

Before 1905 a number of Anushilan Samitis, or physical culture societies, were to be found in Bengal. These societies were not simply institutions of physical culture, but were, according to a Bengali who lived through this period, "like the Prussian gymnastic clubs organized by the poet Jahn before the war of liberation against Napoleon, institutions for giving training in patriotism, collective discipline, and the ethics of nationalism, with the ultimate object of raising a national army to overthrow British rule."[9]

In 1905 the Viceroy, Lord Curzon, divided Bengal into two distinct administrative units separated by the Ganges River. The new province to the east of the river comprised the territory of present-day East Bengal and Assam. The new province on the west bank embraced the areas now known as West Bengal, Orissa, and Bihar. This move aroused widespread indignation among Bengalis, who viewed it as an attempt to reduce Bengal's impact on the Indian scene. It was particularly alarming to the *bhadralok*. This common Bengali term may be loosely translated as "respectable people" or "gentlemen"—persons belonging to the educated classes who do not earn their living by manual labor. The *bhadralok* is a status group comprised of the landed and educated among the Bengali Brahmins, Kayasthas, and Vaidyas—three of the highest castes in the province.[10] Before the advent of the twentieth century, this group had enjoyed a virtual monopoly of the most prestigious positions available to Indians in British India by virtue of the fact that, among the inhabitants of the seacoast who received the initial impact of an alien culture, they were the first to recognize the advantages of acquiring an English education. By the turn of the century, however, the socioeconomic status of this group was threatened as English education spread to the interior provinces while, at the same time, their hold on the land was weakened by the pressure of population and excessive subinfeudation.[11] The partition of Bengal seemed calculated to further reduce their influence. In the new province of Eastern Bengal and Assam, the Moslems and Assamese constituted a majority of the population and in dimidiate Bengal they were outnumbered by the Oriyas and Biharis.

Following the partition, revolutionary societies proliferated due to the organizational abilities of Pramathanath Mitter and Pulin Behari Das and the inspiration of Aurobindo Ghose and Bepin Chandra Pal.[12] In the populist doctrine of Ghose and Pal, religious symbols and values drawn from Bengali Hinduism were skillfully employed to fan antipartition agitation and anti-British sentiment. The *bhadralok*'s vested interest in self-preservation was cloaked in an appeal to regional and national sentiment. It was a powerfully effective combination. In Ghose's newspaper, *Juguntar*, Lord Krishna's counsel to Arjuna in the *Bhagavad Gita* ("Song of the Lord") to perform his duty without concern for reward was interpreted as an injunction to patriots to fight for their Motherland without fear of death. Service to the Motherland, symbolized by the goddess Kali,[h] was interpreted as a religious sacrament:

> The Mother is thirsty and is pointing out to her sons the only thing that can quench that thirst. Nothing less than human blood and decapitated heads will satisfy her. Let her sons, therefore, worship her with these of-

[h] The goddess Kali ("the black") is the Bengali version of the goddess Parvati, or Devi, the consort of Shiva in the Hindu pantheon. She is also known in Bengal as Durga, Shakti, Jagaddhatri, and Bhawani. Devi has two aspects—one compassionate, the other fierce. Kali is a representation of her destructive and fearsome nature. She is depicted as a multi-armed, black hag, mounted on a lion and bristling with terrible weapons. A loathsome red tongue extends from her mouth and a garland of skulls surrounds her throat.

> ferings and let them not shrink even from sacrificing their lives to procure them. On the day on which the Mother is worshipped in this way in every village, on that day will the people of India be inspired with a divine spirit and the crown of independence will fall into their hands.[13]

To quell the agitation, the government of India adopted carrot and stick methods. At the Delhi Durbar in 1911, eastern and western Bengal were rejoined by royal command. At the same time, however, the capital of India was transferred from Calcutta to Delhi. Moreover, reunited Bengal was reduced to less than half of its former size by the separation of certain linguistically distinct areas. Both of these moves were regarded by Bengalis as punitive measures on the part of a vindictive government. Later, with the advent of World War I, the Defence of India Act, which provided for the arrest of suspects without trial, was deployed. By the adoption of such harsh measures as these, the revolutionary groups were eventually suppressed, although never completely destroyed.[14] At the end of the war, many of the *détenus*[i] were released. At the prompting of Gandhi and the Bengali leader C. R. Das, they joined the Congress party in large numbers, without, however, abandoning their own revolutionary traditions or beliefs.[15] In Bengal, Ghandian techniques of nonviolence never attained the degree of support they enjoyed elsewhere in India.

Roy hoped to penetrate the nationalist movement through these revolutionaries and sought to capitalize on his former association with them in order to attract them to the communist fold. Most of them, however, were members of the *bhadralok*. With their roots in a tradition-bound, landowning, and rural-oriented gentry, they resembled in some respects the Social Revolutionaries of Czarist Russia. Therefore, it is not surprising that they proved to be more

[i] In Indian parlance this term is reserved for persons detained under emergency measures without trial.

receptive to Comintern aid than to communist ideology.[j] Indian communists, both before and after independence, have frequently been accused of antinationalism, and consequently, to avoid this stigma, they have made exaggerated claims, which have been popularly accepted, about the number of revolutionary nationalists they have converted.

Most of the former associates with whom Roy corresponded communicated to him their distaste for his newfound faith. Although they applauded Roy's critique of Gandhian nonviolence, they bristled at his condemnation of private property and "bourgeois-democratic" nationalism. Others would not forgive him for having abandoned them to join the Comintern.

The choice of Ramcharan Lal Sharma, a former gunrunner and printer for the *Jugantar* press, to serve as a conduit for remittances to the Bengalis complicated Roy's task of soliciting their support. Sharma was chosen primarily because it was assumed that as a resident of the French enclave of Pondicherry he would be immune from arrest. Unfortunately for Roy, Sharma frequently pocketed money designated for use in Bengal. His dishonesty deepened the revolutionaries' distrust of bolshevism.

Despite the many obstacles, Roy did manage to win over a few of the Bengali revolutionaries. One of the most important converts was Jibanlal Chatterjee, a Juguntar leader from Mushiganj district in eastern Bengal. He was arrested, however, in September 1923, along with a number of other Juguntar members, and not released until 1928.[k] During this

[j] An insight into the social backgrounds of the Bengali revolutionaries is provided by an analysis of the 168 Bengalis convicted of revolutionary crimes between 1905 and 1917. Out of this total, 152 were of the Brahmin and Kayastha castes and 13 were of the Vaidya caste. There were 68 students, 42 small landowners and traders, 20 clerks and governmental employees, 14 teachers, 7 doctors, and 5 newspapermen (Banki Bihari Misra, *The Indian Middle Classes: Their Growth in Modern Times*, p. 395).

[k] Jibanlal Chatterjee was given the dubious distinction of being sent to Mandalay prison in Burma, where such Indian notables as Lokmanya Tilak and Lala Lajpat Rai had been incarcerated earlier. In

long period he was out of touch with Roy and the Comintern.[16]

Roy was also able to secure the services of at least three prominent members of Anushilan—Jogesh Chatterjee,[l] Gopendra Chakravarty, and Dharani Mohar Goswami. Gopendra Chakravarty had been recruited by Roy's agent, Nalini Kumar Das Gupta, who made two trips to India, in 1921 and again in 1923, to contact Bengali revolutionaries. Although he had never been a member of any of the terrorist societies, Nalini Das Gupta was acquainted with many of their members. Moreover, his knowledge of bomb manufacturing, acquired in Dr. Kartik Bose's laboratory in Calcutta and in the munition factories in England where he was employed during World War I, assured him a ready welcome among their ranks. While in Bengal, Nalini Gupta was also able to contact Muzaffar Ahmed, later to become an important member of the CPI. On his return to India from Moscow in June 1925, Chakravarty attempted to divert Anushilan activities into bolshevik channels. He concentrated on Mymensingh district, where he achieved a modicum of success.[17]

The third of Roy's converts, Dharani Goswami, was a close associate of Chakravarty. Because of the hostility of the older leaders of Anushilan to communist ideology, these two, together with a few other younger members, were forced out of the secret society. In February 1927 seven members of this group joined the executive committee of the Bengal Workers' and Peasants' party,[18] the origin of which will be discussed below.

The Labor Movement

In addition to Moslem zealots and Bengali revolutionaries, India's fledgling labor movement was an early com-

---

1925 he was joined in prison by Subhas Chandra Bose (Bose, *The Indian Struggle, 1920-34*, pp. 152, 156).

[l] In 1924 Jogesh Chatterjee organized a number of branches of the Hindustan Republican Association in the U.P. He was arrested in October of that year in connection with the Kakori Conspiracy Case (Government of India, Home Department, *Communism in India, 1924-27*, pp. 64-65).

munist target. Throughout the 1920's, Roy assiduously cultivated the secretaries of the important trade unions, sent them copies of his journal, and requested informational reports. In February 1923 Roy established a Labor Information Bureau in Berlin for the purpose of providing a legal channel of communication between Indian and European labor organizations. Until 1929 the All-India Trade-Union Congress (AITUC), founded in 1920, was India's sole trade-union federation organized on a national scale. During its first few years of existence, the AITUC was a loosely structured organization whose chief function was to represent India at various international labor conferences. Its secretary, as well as one of its founders, was Chaman Lal—a member of the Workers' Welfare League of India. This organization, established in 1917, became a communist vehicle for influencing trade-union activities in India. Roy urged British communists to secure the cooperation of Shapurji Saklatvala, the Indian communist member of Parliament, who was both a friend of Chaman Lal[m] and a dominant figure in the league. This scheme met with some success for, in August of the following year, the league was appointed as the AITUC's representative in England. The league, which occasionally sent trained trade-union organizers to India, professed political neutrality, but according to British intelligence, it was "the first foreign agency to introduce Bolshevik principles into the trade-union movement in India."[19] The league, however, was ineffectual. Communist influence in Indian unions was slight during these early years. Until 1927 the AITUC leadership was dominated by nationalists and moderate trade unionists.

As a result of Roy's efforts, there were already several small communist groups in India by 1922. The leaders of these groups were Shripat Amrit Dange in Bombay, Muzaffar Ahmed in Calcutta, Malapuram Singaravelu Chettiar in

[m] This is not to suggest that Chaman Lal was himself a communist. A moderate trade unionist, he seceded from the AITUC in 1929, when this body was captured by the communists and militant nationalists, to help establish a rival organization.

Madras, Ghulam Hussain in Lahore, and Shaukat Usmani in the United Provinces (U.P.).[20] Communists first began to enter the trade unions in 1923 in Bombay and Calcutta under the leadership of Dange and Ahmed respectively. In that same year, Singaravelu Chettiar, Roy's contact in Madras and a venerable Congressman, was elected a member of the Labor Subcommittee of the Congress party.[21] A desire for the formation of such a committee had been expressed in the form of a resolution at the Congress party's annual session in December 1922. Although Congressmen Lala Lajpat Rai and C. R. Das had served as presidents of the AITUC in 1920 and 1924 respectively, the Congress party as a whole had generally ignored the trade-union movement in India and the resolution was an attempt to rectify, at least partially, this deficiency. The activities of these communist groups in India were financed by the Comintern, which in November 1922 had appropriated £70,000 in support of trade-union work in India and £35,000 for party work, as well as £15,000 for Dange's weekly, the *Socialist*.[22]

In addition to Comintern aid, the suspension of Gandhi's noncooperation program in 1922 was a boon to communism in India. Though the Congress party did not then acquire the mass nationalist character it was to obtain in the 1930's, this early campaign did attract a large number of intellectuals into the nationalist movement. Some of these men, frustrated by Gandhi's abrupt termination of the noncooperation movement, proved receptive to communist blandishments. Many of the early communists in the trade-union movement came from this group. For most, however, the transformation from nationalism to communism was not precipitant but gradual and halting.[23]

The Fourth Comintern Congress

At the Fourth Comintern Congress (November 7 to December 3, 1922), Roy continued to warn against the "unreliability" of Indian nationalist leaders, who, he predicted, would eventually "become a counterrevolutionary force."

He classified colonial and semicolonial countries into three types—areas where capitalism and class differentiation were well developed; where capitalism was on a low level and feudalism remained the backbone of society; and where primitive conditions still prevailed and feudal patriarchalism existed. He placed India in the first category. There, not even the successful conclusion of the nationalist struggle, much less the class war, was assured unless close attention was paid to political indoctrination and organization of the workers and peasants, who in the end would have to assume the leadership of the liberation movement.[24]

"The Theses on the Eastern Question," drafted by the Eastern Commission, of which Roy was a member,[25] were adopted unanimously. These theses defined the task of "communist workers' parties of the colonial and semicolonial countries" as a dual one: to "fight for the most radical possible solution of the tasks of bourgeois-democratic revolution, which aims at the conquest of political independence," and to "organize the working and peasant masses for the struggle for their present class interests, and in doing so, exploit all the contradictions in the nationalist-democratic camp."[26]

The theses warned that Asian communist parties, in cooperating with nationalist leaders, must maintain their own political independence and not allow themselves to become helpless appendages of the national liberation movements: "Only when its importance as an independent factor is recognized . . . are temporary agreements with bourgeois democracy permissible and necessary." How these parties would be able to cooperate with nationalists and at the same time expose their "vacillation" and build an independent political base was not spelled out. Although pointing to difficulties, the Comintern continued to assume, despite Roy's misgivings, that support of bourgeois nationalism in dependent areas could never be inconsistent with the strengthening of the communist movement. The theses specifically rejected Roy's view that in the more advanced colonial countries, like India, the national bourgeoisie would eventually betray the nationalist cause. They held that "the danger of an agreement between bourgeois nationalism and one or several rival imperialist powers is far greater in the semi-colonial countries like China or Persia, or in countries which are fighting for their independence by exploiting inter-imperialist rivalries, like Turkey, than in the colonies."[27]

Despite this disagreement, the Comintern officials were pleased with the modest but significant gains made in India under Roy's guidance. The chairman of the Comintern, Zinoviev, reported to the congress that "organized parties have been formed within the last fifteen months in such countries as . . . India. . . . These parties are still weak . . . but the kernel at least is formed."[28] Satisfaction with Roy's work was reflected in his rapid rise in the Comintern hierarchy. In 1922 he was elected a candidate member of the Executive Committee of the Communist International (ECCI).[29] He later became a full voting member. The ECCI, as the official interpreter of Comintern policy, was the leading organ of the Comintern between sessions of the World Congress. It had authority to control the activities of all sections of the Comintern.[30] Roy was also a member of the Eastern Commission. In June of the following year, he was elected to the Presidium.[31] This body, elected by the ECCI, enjoyed supreme authority in the Comintern between sessions of the executive committee.

The Peshawar and Kanpur Trials

It was at this juncture that the government of India decided to crack down on the nascent communist movement. In late 1922, many of the Indian Moslems who had received training in Tashkent and Moscow began infiltrating back into India. Some crossed the rugged Afghanistan border on foot. The remainder came by other routes. These men were promptly arrested by British authorities. Most were convicted on minor charges relating to passport violations. Ten, however, were charged with conspiracy with a view to depriving the King-Emperor of his sovereignty over India and brought to trial in the Peshawar Conspiracy Case of 1923. Nine of the accused were members of the emigré CPI. Of these, seven were convicted. Two—Mian Muhhamed Akbar Shah and Gawhar Rahaman Khan—were given two-year sentences. Five were sentenced to five years at hard labor. They were: Meer Abdul Majeed, Firozuddin Mansur, Rafiq Ahmed, Habib Ahmed Nasim, and Sultan Mahmud.[32]

Most of the Tashkent-trained *muhajirun* foreswore communism on their return to India. A few of the emigré CPI members convicted at Peshawar later joined the party formed inside India in late 1925.[33] Only three made significant contributions to the communist cause in Asia—Shaukat Usmani, Fazl Elahi Qurban, and Firozuddin Mansur. The latter two became members of the Communist Party of Pakistan following the partition of the Indian subcontinent in 1947.[34]

One of the members of the emigré party, Shaukat Usmani, was apprehended too late to be brought to trial at Peshawar. Together with Muzaffar Ahmed, S. A. Dange, and Nalini Das Gupta, he was brought to trial in April and May 1924 in connection with the Kanpur Bolshevik Conspiracy Case. Ghulam Hussain and Singaravelu Chettiar were also arrested, but were not brought to trial. The former turned informant and was released. The latter escaped trial because of poor health and advanced age. M. N. Roy and R. L. Sharma had also been named in the original indictment, but since they were not in a country under British jurisdiction, they could not be apprehended. All were charged with conspiracy to organize a revolutionary organization for the purpose of overthrowing British rule in India. The four defendants were found guilty and sentenced to four years' imprisonment.[35] Nalini Das Gupta[n]

[n] About 1927, Nalini Das Gupta returned to Europe. For a time in the 1930's he owned a restaurant in Berlin. He returned to India at the time of World War II but shunned all contact with his former political associates. He died in 1957 (Government of India, Home Department, *Communism in India, 1924-27*, pp. 33, 64, 68; Ahmed, pp. 114-16).

was released from prison in 1925 because of illness and dropped out of the communist movement altogether. Shaukat Usmani had helped to organize a small communist group in the U.P. shortly before his arrest. After his release from prison in September 1927, he fell out with his comrades and lived quietly for a time in Delhi away from the principal industrial centers where most of the communist activity was taking place.[36] In 1928 he attended the Sixth World Congress of the Comintern in Moscow. He carried false credentials claiming to represent the CPI. After his return to India he dropped out of the communist movement altogether.

The conviction of S. A. Dange[°] and Muzaffar Ahmed of Calcutta removed from the Indian trade-union movement its two principal communist organizers. Their detention, in addition to the more rigorous attitude exhibited by the authorities toward communist activities, resulted in a serious setback to the communist movement in India. Because of the Peshawar and Kanpur trials, and the wide publicity received by the latter, many Indians, no doubt, were discouraged from active participation in the communist movement. To avoid further government persecution, Roy pressed, following the Kanpur trials, for the creation of a dual organization in India—a legal, revolutionary, mass party, which was to be a part of the Indian National Congress, and a separate, underground communist party, which would maintain control over the more broad-based party serving as its legal cover.[37]

[°] In 1964, before the CPI split into two separate parties, the more radical wing of the party, in an attempt to discredit its so-called "revisionist" wing, made public a letter purported to have been written by its leader, S. A. Dange, following his conviction at Kanpur. The letter, dated July 1924 and addressed to the British Viceroy, is said to have been discovered at the National Archives in New Delhi. Dange denies its authenticity. According to the text of the letter released by his political opponents, Dange offered to use his "influential position in certain circles here and abroad . . . for the good of Your Excellency's Government and the Country," if his sentence was remitted (*Current* [Bombay], March 7, 1964, pp. 1-2).

3. The CPI and the Workers' and Peasants' Party

AS EARLY as 1922, Roy advocated the formation of a broad-based legal party in India with an illegal communist nucleus. At a secret meeting of the Colonial Commission, held in Moscow in November 1922, Roy reported that the tactics of the Indian communists should be "to combine the independence movement, the labor organizations and the Kishan Sabhas [Peasant Leagues] into one struggle." The commission approved these tactics. Shortly thereafter Roy dispatched to India a series of letters which directed that the various communist groups there be linked together with the left wing of the National Congress, the left wing of the trade-union movement, the Khilafat movement, and the Sikh movement, to form a radical, all-India party. This legal party, which would be controlled by the communists, was to be formed, if possible, inside the Indian National Congress.[1]

At about the same time, Roy wrote to S. A. Dange in Bombay urging him to build a "mass party of all truly revolutionary elements" and suggesting that it be given some "non-offensive name, such as the 'People's Party.'"[2] He supported Dange's efforts to form an "Indian Socialist Party of the Indian National Congress," but the venture did not bear fruit.

The following May, Roy wrote to Muzaffar Ahmed in Calcutta suggesting a similar course of action. Indian communists were to form a secret communist party. At the same time, they were to develop an open party which would be called either the "People's party" or the "Workers' and Peasants' party." This group, which would incorporate "all the revolutionists and nationalists," was to stress a nationalist, anti-imperialist platform. The issuance of communist slogans was to be postponed until after the attainment of independence.[3]

As we have seen, the 1924 Kanpur trial made the creation of a legal cover for communist activities in India an urgent task.[4] Subsequently, Roy placed increased emphasis on the formation of a broad-based, legal party in India.

The Fifth Comintern Congress

This was Roy's main theme at the Fifth Comintern Congress, which was convened in June 1924. At the congress, Roy maintained that the nationalist movement, for the last few years, had been moribund. Agitation in India during this period had been directed more against native exploiters than against the foreign oppressor. The national bourgeoisie, fearing the wrath of the exploited, was already seeking the protection of British imperialism. In such a situation, he argued, communists must have direct contact only with the most revolutionary classes in India—the proletariat, peasantry, and petty bourgeoisie. The latter, he continued, are "still linked in thought with feudalism and landlordism and are separated from the masses, but if we organize the peasantry and workers, they will force the pace of the petty-bourgeoisie."[5]

Accordingly, Roy approved of that portion of a recent report of the ECCI which called for "restoration of the national liberation movement (abandoned by the big bourgeoisie) as a revolutionary basis"; the "formation of a national people's party which is to comprise the urban petty-bourgeoisie, the pauperized intellectuals, the small clerks, the rebellious peasantry, and the advanced workers"; and the "establishment of a proletarian party."[6] But he objected to a resolution on this report which called for "direct contact" between the international communist movement and "national movements for emancipation."[7]

The latter resolution overturned a procedure that had been established in 1921. In trying to decide whether to channel communist activities in India through M. N. Roy or Virendranath Chattopadhyaya's Berlin Committee, it had been established that only communist groups should be recognized and supported directly by the Comintern. These, in turn, would make contact with various nationalist groups and organizations. Writing at the time to a correspondent in Paris, Roy's first wife, Evelyn, reported: "All work is to be carried on by the Communist party which already exists here (Moscow). . . . The International cannot aid Nationalist causes except through a Communist party as intermediary."[8]

Roy's argument in essence was: if the national bourgeoisie is already abandoning the Indian National Congress, direct support of its program and party either by the Comintern or Indian communists should be eschewed in favor of an indirect approach through the agency of the proposed people's party. Indian communists should join the Congress party, but neither as defenders of its current program, which still reflects the interests of the national bourgeoisie, nor as advocates of a full-fledged communist platform. Instead, they should enter the Congress under the aegis of a multi-class party with a Marxist, minimum program of action. At the same time they should not neglect to strengthen their own independent power base. Only in this way, he felt, would the party of the proletariat be able to capture the nationalist movement.

In his concluding speech on the national question, Dmitry Manuilsky criticized Roy's position that class differentiation within the Indian nationalist movement was well advanced. He conceded that in India there had been "a relative development of the class struggle," but warned against generalizing this fact to all the colonies. "As at the Second Congress," he stated, Roy has "exaggerated the social movement in the colonies to the detriment of the nationalist movement. . . . He goes so far as to say that the nationalist movement has lost its character of the united front of all classes of an oppressed country, that a new period was beginning, in which the class struggle was becoming transported into the colonies." "The truth is," he continued, "a just proportion must be looked for between the social movement and the national movement. Can the right of self-determination be a contradiction to the interests of the revolution?" To resolve the disagreements that had arisen, Manuilsky proposed, at the conclusion of his speech, the formation of a commission—consisting of Stalin, Bukharin, Roy, and himself—to prepare a final thesis on the national question.[9]

The "Theses on Tactics" adopted by the Fifth Comintern Congress held that the task of the Comintern was twofold: "to create the kernel of a Communist Party . . . and to support with all the means at its disposal the nationalist revolutionary movement which is fighting imperialism." The theses also called for "the extension of direct contact between the Executive [ECCI] and the national emancipation movement of the Orient."[10] Roy's qualifications about the manner in which support to nationalists was to be extended had not won acceptance. The debate over whether "the right of self-determination" could be "a contradiction to the interests of the revolution" was revived by events in China in 1927.

The Fifth Congress also declared that there should be "very close contact between the sections in the imperialist countries with the colonies of those countries." To this proposal Roy voiced no objection. In fact, in a speech before the delegates, Roy urged such a course of action. With respect to India, he held that "the task of the British Communist Party transcends the boundaries of the British Isles. . . . The British Party must make its activities 'imperial' in scope."[11]

Significance of Colonial Policy

Extraordinary importance was attached to the deliberations on colonial policy at the Fifth Comintern Congress. When the anticipated revolution in Europe failed to materialize, the Comintern placed renewed emphasis on the East as the key to world revolution.

Lenin had firmly believed that proletarian revolution would begin in industrialized Europe rather than in Asia.

He wrote: "To count on an European revolution is obligatory for a Marxist if a revolutionary situation is at hand."[12] Underlying his colonial thesis, adopted at the Second Congress, was the assumption that revolution in Europe was imminent and that upon it depended the success of world revolution. For Lenin, therefore, the immediate task in Asia was to weaken the imperialist powers by encouraging nationalist revolt. This strategy, it was acknowledged, would benefit the nationalist bourgeoisie in the short run, but it was justified on the grounds that conditions were not ripe for communism in Asia. Moreover, it was deemed necessary to reduce the "super-profits" which were said to be extracted from the colonies. A portion of these excess profits, it was held, was being used to bribe the proletariat of the home countries to stave off revolution. Since it was assumed that European revolution would both preserve communist gains in the Soviet Union and assure, ultimately, communist victories in Asia, Lenin felt that a Marxist, maximum program in dependent areas was for the moment unnecessary as well as inappropriate.

Belief in the imminence of a European revolution soon faded. Lenin found consolation in his disappointment by turning to the East. To Asia was assigned an increasingly larger role in the struggle to promote world communism, and the Comintern devoted a correspondingly larger amount of attention to this area of the globe. But Lenin clung to the belief, nevertheless, that communism's first advance would be in Europe once its colonial empires became a burden instead of a blessing. In his last published work, *Better Fewer, But Better*, Lenin continued to argue that in the West the bourgeoisie is retarding the "development of Socialism" by its ability to exploit the East. He expressed confidence, however, that "the final victory of Socialism . . . [was] fully and absolutely assured" by virtue of the fact that "Russia, India, China, etc.," the countries which constitute "the overwhelming majority of the population of the globe," had been completely drawn "into the struggle for its emancipation."[13]

At the Second Comintern Congress, Roy, in contrast, had taken the position that the East would take precedence over the West on the revolutionary timetable. In his original thesis, Roy had maintained that because "world capitalism is drawing its main resources and income from the colonies," it must be accepted as a "fundamental thesis" that "the destiny of world Communism depends on the triumph of Communism in the East."[14] In the debates before the Colonial Commission, Lenin had declared that Roy had gone "too far" in taking such a position.[15] Consequently, Roy's thesis had been modified. The final version held that "the breaking up of the colonial empire, together with the proletarian revolution in the home country, will overthrow the capitalist system in Europe."[16]

At the end of 1923 the attempt at revolution in Germany had failed. As a consequence, at the Fifth Congress a new appreciation of the role of the East in communist global strategy was expressed. Revolution in Europe now was held to be completely dependent on the fortunes of nationalist, anti-imperialist movements. Manuilsky, reporting on the national and colonial question, reminded the delegates of Marx's warning that English workers could never be free until the Irish were free.[a] This, he said, was even more true today with regard to colonial peoples, who must be freed from British rule before the British workers will be able to liberate themselves. "Do our British comrades," he asked, "think that the revolutionary process begins with the English proletariat liberating itself and then in the capacity of a Messiah carrying deliverance to the colonial peoples? We do not think so."[17]

Accordingly, the congress resolved that in the past "the attention of the Comintern . . . [had] been too much concentrated on the West," and that in the future it would be

[a] In 1870 Marx wrote to Mayer: "I have come to the conclusion that the decisive blow against the English ruling classes . . . cannot be delivered in England, but only in Ireland" (Karl Marx and Friedrich Engels, *Letters to Americans, 1848-95* [New York: International Publishers, 1953], pp. 77-80).

necessary "to devote far more attention than hitherto to work in the East." Henceforth the Comintern would bear in mind that nationalist anti-imperialism was "one of the most important parts comprising the great movement for emancipation which alone can lead to the victory of the revolution, not only on a European, but on a world scale."[18] In 1924 the emphasis was on combatting British imperialism in India and Afghanistan. In a few years attention was to shift to China.

"Appeal to the Nationalists"

In the period following the Fifth Comintern Congress, Roy continued to develop the argument that the formation of a people's party was necessary because neither the government of India, the national bourgeoisie, nor the Indian masses were hospitable to an avowedly communist program. Such a party, he stressed, would provide both a legal cover and a popular platform around which nationalist-minded Indians could rally.[19] This thesis was the subject of his book, *The Future of Indian Politics*, which was published in 1926.

After Kanpur, Roy stressed in his correspondence the importance of penetrating the AICC—the second highest body in the Congress party organizational structure—and called for the creation of a Nationalist party "to rescue the Congress from the present degeneration." Accordingly, Roy issued a manifesto entitled "Appeal to the Nationalists," at the time of the Belgaum Congress session in December 1924. It received wide publicity in the English and vernacular press in India. In this appeal to the Congress delegates, Roy argued that "in India, nationalism is a revolutionary force" and consequently "must pursue a revolutionary course." This the Congress, so far, had failed to do. As a result the country was no closer to *swaraj* than it had been five years before. He accused the party leaders of fearing revolution more than the British government and warned that "constitutional nationalism" was futile. "The nationalist movement," he contended, "can become really powerful only when it is based upon the direct action of the revolutionary masses." The masses are discontent and will rise in revolt if properly led and organized. But this requires "a political party having the confidence of the masses and a revolutionary outlook. . . . The choice has to be made between this revolutionary adjustment of social relations and continued Imperialist domination." Roy concluded the appeal by calling for the creation of a "Revolutionary Nationalist party" with the following program: "national independence; abolition of feudalism and landlordism; nationalization of land, mines, and public utilities; and freedom of religion and worship." Such a program, he felt, would infuse new life into the nationalist movement.[20]

Satya Bhakta's Communist Conference

The first communist party to be organized within India's borders was born in December 1925. At the end of 1924, a resident of Kanpur by the name of Satya Bhakta published what purported to be "the first quarterly report of the Indian Communist party." In this document, he claimed that the party had been formed on September 1, 1924, and had a total of seventy-eight members. Some months later he claimed a membership of 250 for his party. The author's real name is unknown. The name "Satya Bhakta," an obvious pseudonym, was adopted by him as a result of having spent some time at Gandhi's Sabarmati Ashram. Gandhi was noted for his exposition of *satyagraha* ("firm adherence to truth").

In September 1925 Satya Bhakta began to make preparations for a communist conference to be held in Kanpur in December to coincide with the annual Congress session scheduled to be held there. The conference was duly convened during the last week of December with Singaravelu Chettiar serving as president-elect. The chairman of the reception committee was Maulana Hasrat Mohani, a famous poet, who had the distinction of being the first Congress delegate to move a resolution on behalf of complete independence at an annual Congress session. This occurred at

Ahmedabad in 1921. The resolution, to be sure, had been defeated.[b]

The two most important communists convicted at Kanpur were S. A. Dange and Muzaffar Ahmed. The latter was released from Almora District Jail in September 1925 because of poor health, but Dange remained in jail until May 1927. Ahmed did not return directly to his native state of Bengal, but remained in Almora, a popular hill station, to recover his health. While in Almora, Ahmed received an invitation to attend Satya Bhakta's conference and he decided to return to Bengal via Kanpur. S. V. Ghate, J. P. Bergerhotta, and other communists who had long been in contact with Roy and the Comintern also attended. They knew nothing about the convener of the conference, recognized his membership claims as fraudulent, and were suspicious of his motives. At Kanpur a dispute soon erupted between this group and Satya Bhakta and his supporters over the question of the party's relationship to the international communist movement. Bhakta felt that the party should be completely independent of the Comintern and consequently wished to retain the name he had coined, the "Indian Communist Party," to symbolize its distinctively nationalist orientation. His opponents were equally insistent on calling the party the "Communist Party of India" and retaining contact with Moscow. Outvoted and outmaneuvered, Satya Bhakta left the conference.

After Bhakta's departure, Ahmed and his collaborators proceeded to organize the Communist Party of India. J. P. Bergerhotta and S. V. Ghate were chosen as its joint secretaries and an executive committee was elected. This committee, in addition to the joint secretaries, included K. N. Joglekar and R. S. Nimbkar, both from Bombay, Muzaffar Ahmed from Calcutta, Abdul Majid from Lahore, C. K. Iyengar from Madras, and others. At the same time, it was decided to shift the party's headquarters to Bombay to facilitate communications with the Comintern. The party was

[b] Mohani left the communist movement in 1927.

comprised largely of those who, through Roy's efforts, had come to communism inside India, although a few of its members, as mentioned earlier, had first been introduced to communism in Tashkent and Moscow.

In his absence, Satya Bhakta was elected to the executive committee of the newly formed CPI, and in addition was appointed U.P. provincial secretary. He was resentful, nevertheless, of the treatment he had received. Consequently, he resigned from the executive committee and changed the name of his U.P. organization to "Samavadi Dal." In February, Roy wrote to a correspondent in India denouncing Bhakta as a government spy. In April he and his group were expelled from the party. By 1927 Bhakta's provincial organization was virtually defunct.[21]

The Workers' and Peasants' Party

In addition to the formation of the CPI, 1925 witnessed the creation of the predecessor of the Bengal Workers' and Peasants' party. The Labor Swaraj party of the Indian National Congress was organized in November 1925 by persons who evidently had never been in contact with Roy. In addition to the revolutionary poet Quazi Nazruli Islam, the founders of the party were Hementu Kumar Sarkar, Qutubuddin Ahmed, and Shamsuddin Hussain. On returning to Calcutta on January 2, 1926, Muzaffar Ahmed joined the party. The following month its name was changed to the Peasants' and Workers' Party of Bengal. Roy's desire for the establishment of such a party had been met. The change of name also meant that the party no longer was a part of the Indian National Congress.[22] Although in February 1926 a move to that effect was defeated, in March 1928 the party's name was altered to that of the Workers' and Peasants' Party of Bengal.[23]

In February 1927 Gopendra Chakravarty and Dharani Goswami, along with five other former members of the secret terrorist society, Anushilan, joined the executive committee of the Bengal Workers' and Peasants' party.[24] Both of these men, as indicated earlier, had been recruited to the communist fold by one of Roy's agents, Nalini Das Gupta. During the same month, Saumyendranath Tagore joined the party and became its general secretary. Soon thereafter, however, he left for Moscow. Abdur Rezak Khan, a leader of the Calcutta Seamen's Union, succeeded him in the office.[25] Although he never formally held the position, Muzaffar Ahmed served as de facto party secretary throughout this period.[26] Among his responsibilities was the editing of the party organ *Langal* ("Plough")—or, as it was later called, *Ganavani* ("The Voice of the Masses").[c]

Roy congratulated the Indian communists on the formation of the CPI. At the same time he was critical of the fact that its executive committee had been constituted openly.[27] In March he wrote to Bergerhotta warning him that the government of India would not tolerate for long an avowedly communist organization and urging him to "organize the party in such a way that an attack on the legality will not destroy the Party." He suggested that an "illegal organization should be built up side by side with the legal apparatus."

When the party headquarters was transferred from Bombay to Delhi in May, Roy again let his dissatisfaction be known. "The main field of our activity should be Bengal and Bombay," he insisted. "Delhi is the seat of the Parliamentary parties, but the working-class party must be where the working-class is." At the same time relations between Roy and the CPI were further strained over financial matters. Roy was suspicious of the new party because of its connection with Bhakta and funds were withheld. Bhakta's formal expulsion was prompted, at least in part, by the desire to secure increased financial assistance. When party members continued to receive only token amounts, they began to suspect that Roy was diverting money for his own personal use. In July Roy wrote that he regretted that

[c] *Langal* was published between December 16, 1925 and April 15, 1926, when it ceased publication for financial reasons. It reappeared in August under the name *Ganavani* (Government of India, Home Department, *Communism in India, 1924-27*, pp. 69-70).

"an atmosphere of disgust and mistrust towards us prevailed." At the same time, he warned his correspondents not to look upon his headquarters in Europe as "your financial agents." This, he said, would "lead to endless misunderstanding and mistrust." Its main contribution must be political and ideological in nature.[28] The mistrust was due, at least in part, to Roy's agents in India, many of whom, according to British intelligence, were unreliable and dishonest in money matters. The British intelligence contributed to the suspicion by occasionally withholding funds from intended recipients. A large proportion of Roy's dispatches were intercepted. The director of intelligence during this period reported that Roy's correspondence had been "extensively read" and had been "an unfailing source of information of proved accuracy as to the movement of men, money, and literature, and the knowledge derived from it has been used more than once to the discomfiture of our enemies." So accurate was this information, in fact, that when bogus lists of bolshevik agents supposedly operating in India were obtained, British intelligence could conclude only that Roy had intended to deceive the Comintern rather than themselves.[29]

In mid-1926 Roy modified his tactics. He now conceived of a workers' and peasants' party as a temporary alternative to a communist party rather than as a companion organization and urged Indian communists to change the name of the CPI to the Workers' and Peasants' Party. At the same time, he instructed that efforts to form a "People's party" should be continued. Whereas the distinction between the two had previously been blurred, he now observed that a "People's party" and a "Workers' and Peasants' party" were not the same thing: "One is a veiled Communist party, while the other is a revolutionary Nationalist party."[30]

In the past, Roy had been distrustful of nationalist leaders, and he had originally conceived of the People's party as a possible alternative to the Congress party if it proved impossible to organize inside the organization. But as the Congress began to assume, under Gandhi's leadership in the 1920's, a mass nationalist character and to attract members sympathetic to socioeconomic reforms, his views on this matter were gradually transformed. As the left wing of the Congress party continued to gain influence, Roy became increasingly convinced of the possibility of converting the Congress itself into a "People's party." In March 1926 he wrote to Bergerhotta that the political task of the Indian communists was to organize "a Republican wing of the nationalist movement" as the most "suitable way to penetrate into the Congress Party."[31]

In another letter written in December, Roy continued this theme. He noted that there was "a large revolutionary element" in India which was not "ideologically prepared" to join a communist party. Consequently the CPI was bound to remain "a small sect without any political influence unless it can find a broader organizational apparatus through which it can function." This, he said, was the reason why he strongly urged abandoning the CPI in favor of an All-India Workers' and Peasants' party. Such a party, because of its multi-class composition, would not be a real communist party. But communists would form an "illegal fraction" inside the legal party. Their object would be to "develop gradually the Workers' and Peasants' Party into a real Communist Party by means of ideological education and political training connected with action." He continued: "Now that the Communist Party is practically suppressed," it was time "to broaden the Workers' and Peasants' Party of Bengal into a national organization." He suggested that the Bengal party call a conference to organize "a Workers' and Peasants' Party of India."

At the same time, he warned against confusing this task with that of organizing a People's party. There must, he insisted, be two parties in India—one, "a party of the working-class, essentially a Communist Party, but owing to the difficulties of the situation, not with the name of the Communist Party"; the other, "a revolutionary Nationalist Party."[32]

His plan to establish an organizational relationship with the Congress left wing paralleled the attempt of the Chinese Communist party to maintain its alliance with the Kuomintang and later the Left Kuomintang. Both plans necessitated holding in abeyance the more radical communist objectives. Roy hoped that Indian communists would be able to duplicate the apparent success of their Chinese counterparts in working within the Kuomintang. In the November 1926 edition of Roy's journal, *Masses of India,* there appeared an article entitled "From Gaya to Gauhati" which urged the Congress left wing to heed the lessons of the Chinese revolution. "The Kuomintang has been successful in uniting all revolutionary nationalists in the struggle against foreign imperialism. The same thing can be done by the Indian nationalist movement."[33]

The next month, shortly before he was to depart for China, Roy advocated, in the pages of *International Press Correspondence,* bolstering the efforts of "the petty-bourgeois radical elements inside the [Indian] nationalist movement . . . to overthrow the compromising bourgeois leadership," by fusing the former with the proletariat and peasantry into a "united fighting front."[34] British intelligence did not minimize the potential danger of a communist thrust in this direction. The example of Java, where communists earlier had infiltrated Sarekat Islam, served as a warning.[35]

British Emissaries

Roy's enthusiasm for a Workers' and Peasants' party in India was shared by Rajani Palme Dutt, who shortly after graduating from Oxford with first class honors had helped found the Communist Party of Great Britain (CPGB) in 1920. His older brother, Clemens Dutt, was also a member of the British Communist party. Since 1922 Palme Dutt had served continuously on his party's Central Committee and Politburo. In the 1920's he was also editor of the party journals, *Workers Weekly* and *Labour Monthly.* Of Indian

7. M. N. Roy and Louise Geissler, Hankow, 1927.

8. M. N. Roy, unidentified Russian, General Galen (V. K. Blücher), and Louise Geissler (right to left) at railroad station, Hankow, on eve of return to Soviet Union, 1927.

9. Escape from China in 1927, Gobi Desert.

10. Escape from China in 1927, Gobi Desert.

and Scandinavian parentage, he was already in the 1920's his party's chief spokesman on Indian affairs.[36]

Palme Dutt's book, *Modern India*, was published in India in 1926, the same year as Roy's *The Future of Indian Politics*, and it too proposed the formation of a Workers' and Peasants' party in India.[37] In December of that year, Philip Spratt,[d] a young man of twenty-four and only two years out of Cambridge, arrived in India under the guise of a bookseller. An emissary of the British party, he maintained contact with his superiors through the use of letters in which messages were written with invisible ink in a code based on Gray's *Elegy*.[38] One of Spratt's assignments was to set up a labor publishing house as a channel for Soviet funds.[39] His primary mission, however, was to contact Indian communists, scattered in various urban centers, and assist them in establishing a Workers' and Peasants' party on an all-India scale.[40] Such a party, it was hoped, would prove attractive to radical congressmen and was viewed as a possible vehicle for work within both the Congress party and the Indian labor movement.[41]

Spratt arrived in India at the time Roy was preparing to leave for China. This suggests that the British communists might have hoped to take charge of the Indian communist movement in Roy's absence.[e] Spratt, however, denies that the CPGB entertained such an ambition. Both Rajani Palme Dutt and his brother, Clemens Dutt, he has noted, always spoke favorably of Roy. The relationship between Roy and Clemens Dutt, the head of the Colonial Committee of the CPGB, according to Spratt, was particularly warm. For a time, Clemens Dutt served as the editor of Roy's paper, *Masses of India*.[42] Before leaving for India,

[d] Philip Spratt left the communist movement in the 1930's and during World War II became a supporter of M. N. Roy's Radical Democratic party. For many years he served on the staff of the English language weekly, *Mysindia* (Bangalore). He is now editor of *Swarajya*, the organ of the Swatantra party.

[e] For a further discussion of this point, see the section entitled "Emergence of the Left Kuomintang" in Chapter 4.

Spratt was accompanied to Paris by Clemens Dutt and together they had conferred with Roy's chief agent in Europe, Mohammed Ali (alias Sipassi). Roy had helped in making arrangements for Spratt's mission to India.[43] It is doubtful that the Comintern leaders would have considered the CPGB group as a permanent replacement for Roy in India. After the failure of the 1926 general strike in Great Britain, the British party was considered more of a liability than an asset—a costly appendage that had atrophied but would not die.

Roy's group in Europe was directly affiliated with the Comintern and was independent of all other parties. There was always some confusion about its relationship with other European parties.[44] The jurisdictional boundaries of Roy's group and of the CPGB overlapped and the latter sometimes acted on colonial matters without Roy's knowledge. At a meeting of European communists in Amsterdam in July 1925, attended by Roy and representatives of the CPGB, Roy, who alone had direct liaison with Moscow, had asserted his authority over the direction of Indian affairs and questioned certain actions of the British party, which, he complained, had been taken without his advice or approval.[45] In an attempt to clarify lines of authority and ensure the coordination of communist activities in India, the Comintern advised the establishment of a Foreign Bureau of the CPI, to be headed by Roy and in which the CPGB was to be represented. The bureau, when formed, was comprised of three members—Roy, Sipassi, and Clemens Dutt.

Spratt and other British emissaries worked through a series of connected organizations, including the CPGB, the Red International of Labor Unions, the League Against Imperialism, the Welfare League of India, and the Labor Research Department.[f] It was in association with these or-

[f] This was an information service maintained in London by a number of trade unions to collect and disseminate economic data. It was infiltrated by British communists who used it as a cover and an agency for dispensing propaganda (Philip Spratt, *Blowing Up India*, p. 22).

ganizations and the Foreign Bureau of the CPI in Europe that they conducted their work in India.[46] Three British communists had preceded Spratt to India. As a result of a request from Roy to the CPGB for the dispatch of an agent to India to arrange for the reception and transmission of communist propaganda, Charles Ashleigh[g] (alias Nanda Lal) arrived in Bombay on September 19, 1922. Before reaching India, his departure had been detected and his passport canceled. While awaiting deportation, however, he managed to contact several persons, including S. A. Dange.[47] In February 1925, Percy E. Glading (alias R. O. Cochrane), a prominent member of the British Bureau of the Red International of Labour Unions,[h] had traveled to India with credentials from Roy. His primary mission was to make a study of Indian labor conditions. While in India he helped organize a Labor party with the noted Indian nationalist Lala Lajpat Rai as president. The party proved abortive,[i] however, and having accomplished very little in his short three-month stay, he returned to England in April. On his return, he presented an unfavorable report on the progress of communism in India.[48]

In Bombay, Spratt met a former Scottish coal miner named George Allison (alias Donald Campbell) who had been in India since April. He had been sent to India by the Profintern to develop a left wing inside the All-India Trade-Union Congress. The two men worked together for a short time, but on January 23 Allison was arrested on a

[g] Charles Ashleigh had been deported in 1922 to England from America, where under the name of Ashford he had served a ten-year prison sentence in connection with labor riots.

[h] Otherwise known as the Profintern, this organization was established by the Comintern in July 1921.

[i] In Chapter 3 of *The Future of Indian Politics*, Roy noted that all attempts to form an Indian Labor Party had failed. In October 1928, Glading came to national attention in Great Britain when he was dismissed from his job at Woolwich Arsenal by the Admiralty because of his membership in the CPGB (*The Times* [London], October 23, 1928, p. 16). Glading was subsequently reinstated. In 1938 he was convicted of espionage on behalf of the Soviet Union while employed at the Arsenal (Spratt, *Blowing Up India*, p. 30).

false passport charge.[49] He received an eighteen-month sentence and was later deported to England.[j]

In September Spratt was joined by another emissary of the CPGB, Benjamin Francis Bradley.[50] The two formed an effective team until their arrest in March 1929, in connection with the Meerut Conspiracy Case. In September 1928 they were joined by Hugh Lester Hutchinson. It was not certain under whose auspices he had come to India. Spratt only knew that he was not a member of the British party[k] and suspected that he had been in touch with Roy, who was by then already at odds with the Comintern. While in Berlin, however, on his way to India, he had been in contact with Virendranath Chattopadhyaya, a joint secretary of the League Against Imperialism and an early rival of Roy's for the leadership of communist activities in India. Hutchinson's attentions were largely confined to the *New Spark*,[51] a Bombay labor journal which he edited, to various youth organizations, and to Chattopadhyaya's sister, Mrs. Shushani Nambier,[l] an Indian communist with whom he had an affair.[52] He also served as a vice-president of the Girni Kamgar Union (GKU), a communist-dominated union which played a prominent part in the 1928 general strike of cotton mill workers in Bombay.[53]

Though his knowledge of India was slight, Spratt had "jumped" at the opportunity to go there. "I hastily read up two or three books for background," he has recorded, "fixing firmly in my mind that Bombay is on the west coast and Madras on the east, not vice versa."[54] At the time he arrived in Bombay, Indian communists had not yet recovered from the serious setback they had received as a

[j] In 1931 Allison was sentenced to a three-year prison term on a charge of attempting to provoke mutiny in His Majesty's Navy (Government of India, Home Department, *Communism in India*, 1935, p. 114).

[k] Hutchinson served as a member of Parliament for Labour from 1945 until 1950.

[l] Mrs. Nambier's elder sister was Mrs. Sarojini Naidu, the famous Indian poetess and the most distinguished woman member of the Indian National Congress.

result of the Kanpur Conspiracy Case convictions. He soon discovered that the CPI, formed in 1925, had only fifteen to twenty nominal members. Only in Bombay and Calcutta had there been any substantial activity. In Bombay there were five active members: S. V. Ghate, J. P. Bergerhotta, Firazuddin Mansur, R. S. Nimbkar, and K. N. Joglekar. S. A. Dange was in prison. Ghate and Bergerhotta, it will be remembered, were joint secretaries of the CPI. In early 1927 Bergerhotta was suspected of collaborating with the British and was dropped from the communist movement altogether.[55] In addition to these members, there were a few others who were not formally members of the party but were regarded practically as such. These included: S. S. Mirajkar, I. K. Yagnik, and S. V. Deshpande.[56]

Spratt felt that the Indian communists had not taken full advantage of the opportunity provided by the Congress party's relative neglect of the trade-union movement.[57] He immediately set out to energize the small band of Bombay communists who had been floundering for want of adequate leadership. In January 1927, at the prompting of Spratt and his colleague Allison, a Bombay Workers' and Peasants' party was organized. S. S. Mirajkar was chosen as party secretary, and S. V. Ghate, K. N. Joglekar, and R. S. Nimbkar were elected to the executive committee. The noncommunist labor leader, D. R. Thengdi, was given the largely honorific post of party president.[58] In February 1925, Thengdi had been elected president of the AITUC.[59] Both S. A. Dange, after his release in May, and Benjamin Bradley, upon his arrival in September, were co-opted to the executive committee. Most of the members of the Bombay Workers' and Peasants' party were Congressmen and some held important posts in the Bombay Provincial Congress Committee.[60] As Congressmen they were members of the Labour Group, an organization which had been formed within the Congress party at the instigation of George Allison. Joglekar, Thengdi, Ghate, and Mirajkar were all members of this group.[61]

In March 1927 the executive committee of the CPI, meeting in Delhi, reviewed Roy's request that the party be disbanded and replaced by an All-India Workers' and Peasants' party. The committee members decided that, in view of their party's inactivity, formal dissolution of the CPI was not required.[62]

Two months later, a meeting of the party was held in Bombay at which time the CPI was reorganized and a constitution ratified.[m] Although delegates had been invited from various provinces, all but two present when the conference convened on May 31 were from Bombay. S. V. Ghate was elected secretary general, a post which he held until March 1929; Muzaffar Ahmed, K. S. Iyengar, and S. A. Dange (the latter out of prison only a week) were elected to the party's presidium. The conference resolved that the CPI should organize within the Congress party a "strong left wing" in cooperation with the "radical nationalists." In the "annual report," issued at the time of the conference, it was stated that "our movement . . . is neither imported from abroad nor a group maintained by Russia for its propaganda in India."[63] This was merely a ruse to avoid persecution. In December of that year, at a secret meeting held in Calcutta, the CPI decided to apply for affiliation with the Comintern.[64] But for tactical reasons such affiliation was not granted formally until 1930.[65]

Before leaving London for India, the Comintern representative there, D. Petrovsky[n] (alias A. J. Bennet), had directed Spratt to write a pamphlet urging the Indians to

[m] Ralph Retzlaff, "Revisionism and Dogmatism in the Communist Party of India," in Robert A. Scalapino, ed., *The Communist Revolution in Asia: Tactics, Goals and Achievements* (Englewood Cliffs, N.J.: Prentice-Hall, 1965), p. 337, mistakenly dates the founding of the CPI as December 1928. Muzaffar Ahmed claims that the founding of the CPI should be dated either from the formation of the Indian emigré party in Tashkent in late 1920 or from its reorganization in Moscow the following year. He maintains that the emigré party and the party later formed inside India were constituent and inseparable units of one and the same party (M. Ahmed, *The Communist Party of India and its Formation Abroad*, pp. 33-34, 64-65, 84-87).

[n] Petrovsky served in England for several periods between the years 1924 and 1928. He had his own personal staff and reported directly to

follow the example of the Kuomintang. Spratt diligently carried out the assignment. The issuance of the pamphlet, which he entitled *India and China,* resulted in his arrest in August 1927 on the charge of sedition. Approximately three months later, however, he was acquitted by the Bombay High Court.[66] Both before and after his arrest Spratt traveled extensively throughout northern India in an attempt to organize workers' and peasants' parties. In June he was in Lahore where he stayed with the labor leader Diwan Chaman Lal. There he met the Punjabi communists —all former *muhajirun.* He found them to be "all very charming fellows, but disinclined to do anything."[67] As a result of his continued efforts, however, the Punjab Kirti Kisan (Workers' and Peasants') party was formed at a conference at Lyallapur in September 1928. The next month the inaugural conference of the U.P. Workers' and Peasants' Party was held at Meerut.[68] Puran Chandra Joshi was chosen as the provincial party's general secretary and Chaudhuri Dharamvir Singh, a Swarajist member of the U.P. Legislative Council, was elected vice-president.[69] Before the end of the year there were four parties in India— in Bombay, Bengal,[o] the Punjab, and the U.P.—and plans were being laid for the formation of an All-India Workers' and Peasants' party at a conference to be held at the end of the year. Because of the fear of prosecution most of the work of the Indian communists during this period was conducted through these multi-class parties.

Moscow on the activities of the CPGB (Henry Pelling, "The Early History of the Communist Party of Great Britain, 1920-29," *Transactions of the Royal Historical Society,* VIII [1958]: 50).

[o] The Bengal Workers' and Peasants' party, as noted earlier, had been formed before Spratt's arrival in India.

4. The China Episode

The Seventh Plenum of the ECCI

IN THE mid-1920's the Comintern focused its attention on China, where it was now believed the first significant advance of communism in the East would occur. It had already been declared at the Fifth World Congress in 1924 that world revolution was dependent on revolution in Asia. Once China becomes communist, it was now held, all of Asia—and by implication, the entire globe—would inevitably follow suit. In July 1925 Zinoviev, the chairman of the Comintern, wrote:

> The events in China will doubtless have a tremendous revolutionizing significance for the other colonies and the countries dependent on imperialist England. Just as in its day the Russian revolution of 1905 had the greatest revolutionizing influence on Turkey, Persia and China, the present great movement in China will, without doubt, have a tremendous influence in Indo-China, India, etc. The enormous contingents of oppressed humanity who live in the East, numbering hundreds of millions, will greedily seize on every item of news from revolutionary China and will concentrate their thoughts on how they themselves can organize and revolt against the oppressors, the imperialists. . . . China has revolted today: tomorrow Indo-China and India will rise.[1]

China was seen as a steppingstone to India, Great Britain's most important colony. At a session of the Colonial Commission, held in March 1925, Zinoviev reported that Persia and Afghanistan had been replaced by China as "the central starting-point for action in India." China would not only provide moral inspiration for Indian revolutionaries, but also serve as a strategic base to provide direct assistance. The Comintern slogan was now: "Via revolutionary China to the Federal Republic of the United States of India."[2]

The Seventh Plenum of the ECCI (November 22 to December 16, 1926), which was convened principally to consider the China problem, met at a crucial period in the history of the Chinese communist movement. On March 20 Chiang Kai-shek had staged a coup against his Russian advisers, the Chinese Communist party (CCP) and the left wing of the Kuomintang (National Peoples' party). Chinese communist leaders and their Russian advisers had been arrested. Wang Ching-wei, the head of the Kuomintang and of the eight-month-old National Government of China, had been forced into exile in Europe. As a result of the coup, all political, governmental, and military power had devolved into Chiang's hands. A reconciliation between Chiang and the Chinese communists had been effected, but at a price. The influence of the CCP in the Kuomintang was severely curtailed. Communist members of the Kuomintang were forbidden to criticize party principles, to hold more than a third of the membership of any party committee, or to serve as head of any party or government department. In July, Chiang, as commander-in-chief of all the expeditionary forces, had embarked on a military campaign against northern militarists and the legal government in Peking. His communist allies had participated by arousing the sympathies of workers and peasants behind the enemy lines, but it was now feared that the communists might have become victims of their own success. Chiang had already given evidence of his displeasure at this latest display of their growing strength. In late July martial law had been declared in the Kuomintang capital of Canton and all labor and peasant agitation had been proscribed for the duration of the northern expedition. Both labor and peasant organizations in the territory under Kuomintang control had been subjected to attack by various conservative groups, with the government's silent consent.[3] In October, Stalin had telegraphed instructions to the CCP directing them to restrain the peasant movement to avoid antagonizing Kuomintang army officers, most of whom had been recruited from the landholding class.[4]

A vast amount of scholarly effort has been expended in seeking an explanation for the debacle of the Chinese communist movement in 1927. These studies, on the whole, emphasize the confusion surrounding the event. However, to understand the principles underlying the defeat of the CCP, it is necessary to keep in mind that the Comintern's principal aim in China at this time was the elimination of imperialist influence, especially British influence, rather than the promotion of communism. Comintern strategy for China was devised from the point of view of the Soviet Union's world-wide struggle against Western, imperialist powers. This is clearly evident in the resolution on the China question adopted by the Seventh Plenum, which states that "the Chinese revolution—by the mere fact of its anti-imperialist character—is an inseparable part of the international revolution."[5]

In the Comintern's view, the northern militarists and the Peking government were the pawns of the great powers in China. Consequently, the victories of the Kuomintang and the Canton government were hailed as contributing to the reduction of imperialist influence. The northern advance of the Nationalist Army was worthy of support insofar as it served to undermine imperialist domination. This conviction was incorporated within the China resolution. It states: "The Canton government is revolutionary primarily because it is anti-imperialist. . . . The Chinese Revolution and the government created by it must strike at the root of imperialist power in China."[6]

It was recognized that the imperialist interests in China were inextricably bound up with the interests of both landlord and militarist and it was impossible to strike against one without striking against all three. According to the resolution:

> The power of Chinese militarism lies in its support by foreign imperialism on the one hand, and native land-

> owners on the other. . . . Overthrowing the imperialists, abolishing all survivals of the old feudal relations, national liberation, the revolutionary reforms of internal and social relations—these tasks are organically connected with each other and represent the one task of the Chinese Revolution.[7]

Since it was held to be self-defeating for the CCP to take on all the forces of reaction simultaneously, it was necessary for the party to make compromises to enlist the support of, or at least to neutralize, a segment of the landholding and military classes and the native bourgeoise in the interests of the main struggle against imperialist influence. In concrete terms, this meant restraining peasants and workers to prevent a rupture between the CCP and the Kuomintang. With respect to the peasant movement, Stalin justified this policy on the grounds that truly radical reforms must await, in any event, the final elimination of imperialist forces. "Imperialism," according to Stalin, was "the force in China that supports . . . the feudal powers. . . . The feudal survivals in China cannot be smashed and abolished without waging a determined struggle against imperialism."[8]

The resolution on China adopted at the Seventh Plenum reflected Stalin's bias in favor of the anti-imperialist aspect of the Chinese civil war. The policy of maintaining the alliance between the CCP and the Kuomintang was reconfirmed. Though the resolution expressed, in general terms, the necessity for a "radical agrarian program," its concrete proposals were fairly modest. The resolution did not call for the wholesale confiscation of landlord's property, but only of "monasterial and church lands and lands belonging to the reactionary militarists, compradores, landlords, and gentry who are waging civil war against the Kuomintang."[a] With respect to other landholders, all that was demanded

[a] In André Malraux's novel, *Man's Fate* (New York: Random House, 1934), a Chinese communist, upon hearing that land belonging to officers and relatives of officers were not to be touched, comments, "We are all relatives of officers. Is there a single piece of land in China whose owner is not a relative of an officer?" (p. 118).

was the reduction of land rents and the granting of perpetual leases to tenant farmers on the land they cultivated. Instead of peasant soviets, the creation of peasant committees was proposed and the arming of "poor and middle peasants."[9] In the interest of the CCP-Kuomintang alliance, the implementation of even these relatively moderate proposals were dependent upon the consent of the Kuomintang government. As a result, it was later admitted, these promises which were held out to the peasant existed "chiefly on paper."[10]

Emergence of the Left Kuomintang

It was in 1926 that Roy reached the apogee of his career in the international communist movement. In February of that year he was appointed to the editorial staff of the *Communist International*, the authoritative multi-language journal which had been published since the birth of the Comintern. At the time of the Sixth Plenum of the ECCI (February to March 1926), Roy was elected to the Presidium and named chairman of the Eastern Commission.[11] He was also a member of the ECCI Orgburo and Secretariat.[12] Following the Seventh Plenum, he was elected to membership of the British and Agrarian Commissions, and he and Petrov[b] were chosen to serve as joint secretaries of the Chinese Commission.[13] Shortly thereafter, he joined the Political Secretariat of the ECCI, when it was formed by combining the functions of the Orgburo and the Secretariat.[14] Thus, by the end of 1926, Roy had attained membership on all four of the official policy-making bodies of the Comintern—the Presidium, the Political Secretariat, the ECCI, and the World Congress.

Following the Seventh Plenum, Roy was dispatched to China as a representative of the Comintern to help implement the policy in whose formulation he had shared.[15] He

[b] Petrov was a member of the Central Committee of the Chinese Communist party. The Slavic name was apparently a pseudonym (Leon D. Trotsky, *Problems of the Chinese Revolution*, 3rd ed. [New York: Praeger, 1966], p. 413).

was also charged with the responsibility for promoting disaffection among Indian troops stationed in China. In this connection he was to work closely with agents of the Ghadr party and other Sikh groups already operating in China. The activities of these groups were not without result. Writing in 1927, the Director of the Intelligence Bureau of the government of India observed: "The anti-British agitation among Indians in China is of an extent and intensity that cannot be regarded without some anxiety."[16]

Roy had wanted to go to India, but was sent to China instead. In his absence, agents of the CPGB were dispatched to India to guide communist activities there. On this basis Overstreet and Windmiller, in their study of Indian communism, conjectured that Roy "may have been sent to China in order to remove him from Europe and thus from participation in Indian affairs."[17] This suggestion, however, is not a plausible one.[c] If Stalin was dissatisfied with Roy's work, how does one account for his recent promotions within the Comintern? Would it have been likely, under such circumstances, that Stalin would have sent him, of all places, to China, where for the moment the Comintern had placed all its hopes? Furthermore, Stalin must have known that if he allowed Roy to return to India and his presence was detected, he would have faced almost certain arrest and imprisonment. Roy was under indictment in connection with the Kanpur Bolshevik Conspiracy Case; whereas the British emissaries had the advantage of British citizenship and, until the promulgation of the Public Safety Ordinance in April 1929, could operate in India with relative impunity.

Roy was accompanied on the trip to China by an International Workers' Delegation consisting of Tom Man from England, Earl Browder from America, and Jacques Doriot from France. Sydor Stoler, a Russian, accompanied the delegation as its secretary. This group planned to attend the Pan-Pacific Labor Conference, which was eventually

[c] For additional comments on this point, see section entitled "British Emissaries" in Chapter 3.

held in Hankow, May 20–27, 1927. One of the purposes of the conference was to establish direct contact between Chinese communists and radical trade-union leaders and their counterparts in India and elsewhere. Consequently, Roy was eager for an Indian delegation to attend. Several Indian delegates were chosen, but they were denied their passports by the government of India.[18]

Roy and his traveling companions arrived in Canton in February 1927. The previous December, the seat of the national government had been transferred from Canton to Hankow, which was located close to the cities of Hanyang and Wuchang at the junction of the Han and Yangtze rivers. The three cities were known collectively as Wuhan. Roy planned to travel to Hankow by plane. The plane's arrival in Canton, however, was delayed. When it did arrive, engine trouble developed. After waiting impatiently in Canton for about two weeks, Roy engaged some bearers and set out overland. It was a strenuous journey and another three weeks passed before he finally reached Hankow.[19]

At about the time Roy arrived in Hankow, the situation with respect to which the China resolution had been formulated was altered dramatically. In March, Nationalist forces, with the assistance of the communists acting through the instrument of the General Labor Union, captured Shanghai from the militarist Sun Ch'uan-fang. On April 12, Chiang launched a coup d'état against his communist allies which resulted in the death of thousands. Events in Shanghai were duplicated in several other major Chinese cities. The Chinese communists had been urged to support Chiang's northern expedition with the argument that the revolution should first be broadened before it was deepened, and the fall of Shanghai, which Bukharin had labeled "the workers' Petrograd for China,"[20] had seemed to justify this position. But Shanghai was not only the site of a powerful labor organization under communist control, but also China's chief center of banking, commerce, and industry. With the city in his hands, Chiang was able to strike a deal with the representatives of its Western and native-owned banks, firms, and commercial associations. In return for their financial support, he agreed to strike a blow against the communist movement—which was viewed as a threat to their common interests.[21]

Following the coup, Chiang called a meeting of his supporters in the Central Committee of the Kuomintang. This meeting, held in Nanking, signaled a break between Chiang and his followers on the one hand, and Wang Ching-wei, the Kuomintang left wing in Wuhan, and its communist supporters on the other hand.[22] Wang had recently returned from exile. The Wuhan faction of the party, now known as the Left Kuomintang, reacted on April 17 by "expelling" Chiang Kai-shek from the party. At the same time, however, plans were laid for a military advance toward Peking to be able to bargain with Chiang at a later date from a position of strength.[23]

The Eighth Plenum of the ECCI

In May 1927, the Eighth Plenum of the ECCI was convened to reconsider the China policy in the light of the most recent developments. The resolution on the Chinese question, adopted at the plenum, declared that "recent events have entirely confirmed the point of view of the Communist International concerning the Chinese Revolution, and are a brilliant confirmation of Lenin's predictions as to its international role." Chiang's coup d'état and the establishment of a separate government at Nanking by the right wing of the Kuomintang were interpreted as the inevitable desertion of the "united national revolutionary front by the bourgeoisie." Although it was acknowledged that the "bourgeois revolutionary coup" represented at least a "partial defeat of the Chinese revolution and a real acquisition of strength by the counter-revolution," it was claimed that this was more than offset by the fact that the revolution had advanced to a "higher stage of development." The CCP was advised to preserve its alliance with the Hankow government and the Left Kuomintang, which was characterized as "a revolutionary bloc of the urban and rural petty-bourgeois masses with the proletariat." The Comintern held out the hope that the CCP might be able to secure the hegemony of the Left Kuomintang by entrenching itself among the peasantry through the pursuance of a more radical agrarian program in the territories of the Hankow regime. The program included "the abolition of rent paid to the rich, the redistribution of land, radical reduction of taxation . . . [and] the mass arming of the workers and peasants."[24]

This agrarian program, however, was to be pursued under the aegis of the Left Kuomintang government, not in defiance of it. Otherwise "the policy of close cooperation" between the Left Kuomintang and the communists—without which, Stalin declared, "the victory of the revolution" would be "impossible"—would have been jeopardized. For the same reason the CCP was enjoined from establishing soviets of workers, peasants, and soldiers, a policy advocated by Trotsky. The establishment of a parallel government in this way, Stalin argued, would be a direct challenge to the authority of the Wuhan regime and would inevitably precipitate a break with the Left Kuomintang and correspondingly strengthen the position of Chiang Kai-shek. What was required for the present, according to Stalin, was the formation of peasant committees and peasant leagues and the constitution of peasant armed units—groups which could be made to serve as the nucleus of future soviets.[25]

Although acknowledging the possibility of "betrayal by various generals . . . or individual political leaders," the framers of the China resolution at the Eighth Plenum insisted that to divorce the class struggle in China from the national liberation movement was to invite its defeat. The consent of the military to agrarian reforms, it was felt, could be won "by guaranteeing . . . the security of their property and the land belonging to the soldiers of the national army."[26]

The Eighth Plenum directed the Chinese communists to

preserve the alliance with the Left Kuomintang and, at the same time, to pursue a more radical program in the countryside. This was an impractical policy as events in China were already proving. In April the second northern expedition, under the command of General T'ang Shêng-chih, had gotten under way. The Chinese communists and their Russian advisers in Hankow decided to support the expedition. Borodin felt that such a course of action was necessary to avoid a split with the Left Kuomintang. Moreover, he supported the view that the revolution could not be defended in the relatively industrialized South,[d] where imperialist and Chinese bourgeois forces were strong, and he felt that, consequently, a new center of communist activity should be established in the northwest provinces.[27]

Once troop movements had begun, the Wuhan government adopted a policy of "restraining" the peasant and labor movements in the interests of united support to the revolutionary army. Borodin's attitude to this policy was one of acquiescence. Roy disagreed. Rather than declare a moratorium on workers' and peasants' demands, he wanted to intensify the revolution in the area under the control of the Wuhan government. Such a policy, he argued, would force the resignation of the more reactionary of the military and political leaders in Wuhan and smooth the way to the goal of capturing the nationalist organization.[28] Borodin obviously felt that what would be left would not be worth capturing. Among the Russian advisers, only General Oberst Galen (Vasili K. Blücher) supported Roy's position.[29]

At first the majority of the Central Committee of the CCP sided with Roy. On April 16 this body resolved that "military operations aimed at territorial expansion to the North must be preceded by a consolidation of the base of

[d] It is interesting to note that the Fifth Comintern Congress rejected this "inadmissible . . . tendency to abandon . . . the existing base under the pretext of expansion" on the grounds that this relatively well-developed area should not be left to the bourgeoisie ("Theses on the Political Situation and the Tasks of the Chinese Communist Party," translated in Robert C. North and Xenia J. Eudin, *M. N. Roy's Mission to China*, p. 248).

the revolution in those regions which are already under the control of the Kuomintang . . . in accordance with the suggestions made in Comrade Roy's speech."[30] But two days later the resolution was retracted and assurances of immediate support were extended to the military expedition.[31]

The Fifth Congress of the CCP

The conflict between Roy and Borodin[e] over revolutionary tactics was again in evidence during the proceedings of the Fifth Congress of the CCP, which commenced on April 27, 1927. The "Theses on the Political Situation and the Tasks of the Chinese Communist Party," adopted at this meeting, reflect an effort to compromise their differences. The resolution stated that:

> The rapid territorial expansion of the revolution must be accompanied by intensification of the revolutionary base in territories under nationalist occupation. . . . If radical agrarian reform . . . is postponed until the final conclusion of the Northern Expedition, the bourgeoisie, screening behind a false banner of nationalism, will consolidate its power in the occupied regions. . . . Without underestimating in the least the necessity of the further territorial expansion of the revolution . . . the Fifth Congress, at the same time, sets before the Communist Party as its principal task in the immediate future the ruthless struggle against the reaction in those provinces where the revolution has been partially achieved; namely, in Kwantung, Fukien, Chekiang, Kiangsi, Hunan, Hupeh, and Kwangsi.[32]

[e] Harold R. Isaacs, in *The Tragedy of the Chinese Revolution* (p. 218), remarked on the absence of any contemporary documents which would substantiate the claim, later made by Roy, that "he had fought hard to get the Chinese Communist Party to pursue a bolder revolutionary course even if it meant a break with the Left Kuomintang." With the discovery of the 1927 documents of the CCP, cited above, this observation is no longer valid. It should be added that Roy never expressed a wish to "break" with the Left Kuomintang, but rather to split it. Whether or not this was a reasonable expectation, Roy anticipated the continuance of the Left Kuomintang-CCP alliance, following such a split, with a minority going over to Chiang Kai-shek.

This resolution paralleled that of the Eighth Plenum. It called for supporting Wuhan's military ventures and preserving the alliance with the Left Kuomintang, on the one hand, and creating a mass base through the support of peasant demands and the arming of peasants, on the other hand. Under the circumstances, these were contradictory goals. On May 21, a few weeks after the Fifth Congress had adjourned, a Wuhan general staged a coup d'état at Changsha, the capital of Hunan, replaced the provincial government and suppressed local communist organizations with a display of great brutality and inhumanity. In the following days the repression spread throughout the province. An estimated 20,000 persons were killed before the terror had run its course.[33] Under the direction of local communist leaders, preparations for a counteroffensive were made. A peasant army was hastily assembled with a view to storming Changsha. The Central Committee of the CCP, however, succeeded in calling off the attack in favor of a personal investigation of the affair by the commander-in-chief of the Wuhan forces, acting under the auspices of the Wuhan government.

The Unequal Alliance

Roy had called for a test of strength between the armed peasantry and the military at Changsha and disapproved of Borodin's efforts to secure a negotiated settlement.[34] Rather than capitulate to the will of the Left Kuomintang leaders, he felt it was now time for a confrontation. He referred this question to Moscow. Stalin's telegraphed reply arrived in Hankow on June 1. Like the resolution of the Eighth Plenum of the ECCI and the Fifth Congress of the CCP, it tried to reconcile the irreconcilable by striking a balance between the views of Roy and Borodin. The Chinese communists were advised to support T'ang's military offensive and, at the same time, to develop the revolution in the territories of the Wuhan government.[35] Both Roy and Borodin knew that this was not possible.[36] For each step forward in support of the nationalist, anti-imperialist revolution, it was necessary for the CCP to retreat two steps from the social revolution.

At this point it is instructive to review the Comintern's general assessment, which evolved gradually over the years in the debates and discussions on the national and colonial question, of the revolutionary potential, in dependent areas, of various social classes—"feudal remnants" and militarists, compradores, the national bourgeoisie, and the petty bourgeoisie. Compradores were defined as that segment of the native bourgeoisie whose economic interests are closely interwoven with those of their foreign rulers, e.g., merchants and bankers who serve as intermediaries in foreign trade. Together with the "feudal remnants" and militarists, they were considered to be unredeemable reactionaries. The national bourgeoisie, in contrast, was regarded as a potential ally in the early stages of the nationalist movement, but it was held that in the final stages of the nationalist revolution this group would compromise with their colonial overlords should the social revolution be sufficiently advanced to frighten them. If faced with the choice, they would prefer continued ignominy under the familiar foreign rule to possible extinction under the dreaded proletarian dictatorship. The petty bourgeoisie was a broad category which embraced several groups: artisans, small traders, and poor intellectuals; so-called servants of the capitalist system—clerks and the like; and small owners of private property. Peasant proprietors were included among the petty bourgeoisie as well as, in a certain sense, all peasants inasmuch as they were all said to aspire to own land. Although the petty bourgeoisie was regarded as tending toward conservatism, it was felt that the class, if given a sufficiently firm lead, could be induced to support at least the initial, minimal demands of the communists.[37]

In agrarian societies, the radicalization of nationalist politics requires at least a minimal response to the demands of the peasantry for land and for relief from the most burdensome exactions of the landlord and usurer. Consequently, it can be seen that should a nationalist movement become the plaything of the feudalists and militarists, any attempt to develop it in the direction of a radical social revolution inevitably would be frustrated. This was the situation in China in 1927, although it was not recognized either by the CCP or by its foreign advisers until it was too late.

Both the Kuomintang and the CCP sought to use each other for their own ends. The important question was who would come out ahead. Comintern leaders had hoped that the Kuomintang could be captured eventually by the communists,[38] but they were wrong. The alliance with the Kuomintang and later with the Left Kuomintang was purchased by the CCP at a ruinous price. Such an alliance, as Trotsky put it, was "an unequal alliance," analogous to that imposed on China by Western powers against which the Comintern had persistently inveighed. When the Russian agent, Vologin, in Malraux's novel *Man's Fate* stated that the communists have been using the Kuomintang "unceasingly—every month, every day," his comrade Kyo retorted, "As long as you have accepted its aims: not once when it was a question of accepting yours. You have led it to accept gifts which it was dying to get: officers, volunteers, money, propaganda. The soldiers' soviets, the peasant unions—that's another matter."[39]

The Debacle

When Stalin's telegram arrived, the situation was already desperate. Chiang's coup in April 1927 had already tipped the balance decisively against the communists. The Wuhan government was little more than an empty shell, beset on all sides by economic stagnation, military rebellions, peasant and labor agitation, and pressures of foreign powers, whose gunboats had been arrayed along the approaches to its harbors. Roy felt that the only hope of preserving the Wuhan regime as an independent political entity, and with it the Left Kuomintang–CCP alliance, lay in unleashing the power of the estimated three million members of the peasant unions and playing on Wang Ching-wei's political ambitions. With this end in view, Roy showed the telegram to the Left Kuomintang chairman. In the telegram Stalin not only supported an intensification of the agrarian revolution through the seizure of land, but also urged the immediate formation of a workers' and peasants' army. Roy suggested that this army could be placed under the command of a general upon whom Wang could rely. In this way, Roy hoped to detach Wang from the influence of the fuedal, military aristocracy. He felt that Wang's position did not depend entirely on the good will of the military but was based, at least partly, on his popularity as "the chosen successor of Sun Yat-sen."[40] He thought that there was a good chance that his proposal might appeal to Wang insofar as it offered him an opportunity of reestablishing his leadership in the Wuhan government.

But the proposal had come too late. The Comintern and the CCP had neglected for too long the essential task of building an independent power base. The CCP was unwilling to make a bold bid for peasant support for fear of incurring the wrath of the Wuhan regime. At a meeting of the Central Political Bureau of the CCP held in June, Roy urged that the party propose to the Wuhan government the policy of land expropriation. Members of the bureau were unanimous in rejecting this advice on the grounds that to make such a proposal to the Left Kuomintang "was like playing a lute to entertain a fox."[41] For this they were later rebuked by the Comintern.

A few weeks after this episode, Wang is reported to have said:

> The communists propose to us to go together with the masses. But where are the masses? Where are the highly praised forces of the Shanghai workers or the Kwantung or Hunan peasants? There are no such forces. You see, Chiang Kai-shek maintains himself quite strongly without the masses. To go with the masses means to go against the army. No, we had better go without the masses but together with the army.[42]

Roy considered Wang "the leader of petty-bourgeois radicalism,"[43] but perhaps "opportunist" would have been a more fitting description.[f] In July a reunification of the Wuhan and Nanking governments was effected on the basis of a purge of all communists within the Left Kuomintang and its army.[44] Their Russian advisers, including Roy and Borodin, were obliged to return to Moscow. Roy left Hankow in early August. Together with a small party, he traveled by car across the Gobi Desert to Lake Baikal, where he took the Trans-Siberian Railway to Moscow.[45]

The Two Revolutionary Streams

In an interview with Mao Tse-tung, Edgar Snow asked the Chinese communist leader who he thought was most responsible for the failure of the CCP in 1927. In his response Mao placed the greatest share of the blame on Ch'ên Tu-hsiu, the general secretary of the CCP at the time, for indecisive leadership. The man next most responsible for the debacle, according to Mao, was Borodin, who "was ready to do everything for the bourgeoisie, even to the disarming of the workers, which he finally ordered." On Roy's role, Mao remarked that he "stood a little to the left of both Ch'ên and Borodin, but he only stood." According to Mao, "he could talk," but he failed to offer "any method of realization." Snow summed up Mao's opinions in this way: "He thought that Roy had been a fool, Borodin a blunderer, and Ch'ên an unconscious traitor."[46] Diverting as it may be, any attempt here to apportion blame for the temporary eclipse of Chinese communism can be only a sterile exercise. Earl Browder, one of the members of the Workers' Delegation that accompanied Roy to China, has recorded that in his opinion the situation in China when he arrived there was "hopeless." He disliked Roy from Moscow days and had little regard for his political sagacity; whereas he was befriended by Borodin, whom he admired, while in

[f] Wang Ching-wei's opportunism was again in evidence in 1940 when he accepted the presidency of the Japanese puppet regime established at Nanking. He died on November 10, 1944.

China. Nevertheless, in retrospect, Browder felt, that "probably the cleverest proposals would not . . . have changed the overall outcome."[47]

Both Roy and Borodin wished to preserve the nationalist alliance. They differed only on the price they thought would have to be paid. Borodin excused his concessions by reference to the anti-imperialist aspects of the nationalist revolution. Roy, in contrast, placed more emphasis on radicalizing the Left Kuomintang. In the context of conflicting advice neither of these approaches was given a fair trial, but one can be fairly certain that neither approach would have facilitated communist assumption of power under the conditions then existing in China. The success of communists in colonial and semicolonial areas is dependent on their ability to reconcile the Comintern's two aims—personified by Roy and Borodin—with respect to such areas, namely, both the strengthening and radicalizing of nationalist, anti-imperialist movements. The Comintern's China policy faltered in the late 1920's not because of the failure of Roy and Borodin to compromise their differences, but because of the conditions which made compromise impossible. In the China context, the national cause was irreconcilable with the interests of the indigenous class struggle. Communists have come to power in dependent areas only under circumstances in which these two interests have coincided[g]—in China at the time of the Japanese invasion, in Yugoslavia during World War II, in North Vietnam, and in the Indian state of Kerala.[48] The fate of South Vietnam is still uncertain. Because of the peculiar nature of the nationalist movement in China, the CCP started on the road to victory only when in 1934, acting independently of the Kuomintang, it developed under its own leadership a mass nationalist struggle against the Japanese invader. The suc-

[g] The interests of anti-imperialism and local class struggle are often dealt with as though belonging exclusively to the sphere of Soviet foreign policy and the Communist International respectively. Such a bifurcation, which obscures their interrelationship and suggests a permanent opposition, is highly misleading.

cess of the CCP cannot be attributed to its post-1935 united front with the Kuomintang. The front virtually ceased to exist after the New Fourth Army incident of January 1941. Moreover, communists expanded into Japanese-occupied territories and not into areas where the façade of united front was still maintained, such as in Hankow. Peasant nationalism, as developed in China in the 1930's and the 1940's, represented the union of these two potentially revolutionary forces.[49] For a policy which had as its aim the promotion of such a union, Roy later coined the term "Twentieth-Century Jacobinism."[50]

It is at the conflux of these two revolutionary streams of nationalist and local class struggle that the greatest opportunities are offered for communist advancement. The existence of a mass national movement[51]—a nationalist movement which has actually secured the support of an overwhelming majority of the people which it claims to represent—is a precondition for the joining of these two revolutionary streams; for such movements are necessarily sympathetic toward meeting the most pressing needs of the peasantry, who constitute the bulk of the population in underdeveloped areas of the world, and are likely to be receptive to communist demands if they are couched in minimal terms. Neither the Kuomintang nor the Left Kuomintang was a mass nationalist party. The membership of both was largely confined to the intellectual and urban middle classes. Both were dependent on the good will of militarists resolutely opposed to agrarian reform. Nationalist sentiment did not arise among the Chinese peasantry until the Japanese occupation of 1937.[52] The Comintern policy for China failed in 1927 because the nationalist, anti-imperialist stance of the Kuomintang and the Left Kuomintang could not be translated into mass nationalist terms.

Trotsky and Roy

The Comintern policy in China was one of the central issues in the power struggle between Stalin and Trotsky. At first glance, it might appear that Roy's position on China more closely corresponded to Trotsky's than to Stalin's views. Both Roy and Trotsky would have preferred to deepen the revolution before broadening it. Both favored strengthening the agrarian revolution in Wuhan to extending the territory under Left Kuomintang control. Finally, both saw the Chinese civil war primarily as an opportunity to promote communism in Asia; whereas for Stalin, China was another battleground in a world-wide contest with the Western powers.

Despite Trotsky's later claim that he had opposed forming a bloc with the Kuomintang "from the very beginning, that is, from 1923,"[53] Conrad Brandt, from a study of the letters and memoranda at the Trotsky Archives at Harvard, has concluded that Trotsky originally supported forming a bloc with the Kuomintang. His study shows that it was not until after the CCP gained substantial support among urban workers in the May 30 movement in 1925, that he felt the alliance no longer served any purpose. It was not, however, until a few days before Chiang's coup that Trotsky first made public his misapprehensions. Even after the coup he consented to communist participation in the Wuhan government and it was not until June 1927 that he openly demanded that the communists leave the Left Kuomintang.[54] Despite his tardiness in declaring his reservations, it is clear that from mid-1925 Trotsky seriously doubted the wisdom of the alliance with the Chinese nationalists. Roy, in contrast, expressed no such reservations. For him the alliance with the Kuomintang, and later the Left Kuomintang, was valuable in that it served as a bridge to the petty bourgeoisie and the peasant masses. Although he wanted to split the nationalist ranks, he did not want the CCP to break away altogether from the Chinese nationalist movement.

Trotsky advocated the creation of workers', peasants', and soldiers' soviets in China. To meet the objections of those who feared that this would lead to an immediate rupture with the nationalist forces, Trotsky argued that it was "nonsense, nonsense, nonsense" to believe that the creation of soviets would precipitate such a break.[55] Both Stalin and Roy, it should be noted, opposed Trotsky on this issue. Instead of soviets, they advocated at first merely the creation of peasant committees.[56] Later, following Chiang's coup, Stalin called for "the mass arming of workers and peasants,"[57] but hoped to gain the consent of Wang Ching-wei's government for such a policy. As we have seen, Roy supported this position. Though Roy contemplated a split in the Left Kuomintang, he did not wish to frighten the party wholesale into the camp of counterrevolution.

Roy's expulsion from the Comintern in 1929 was related to Stalin's offensive against Bukharin and the Right Opposition rather than to Trotsky's demise.[58] Although persons close to Roy at the time have indicated that Stalin was displeased with Roy's work in China,[59] it is not correct to conclude, as at least one authority has done,[60] that this was the principal cause of his expulsion. Roy has maintained that a joint commission of the Presidium of the ECCI and the Political Bureau of the Soviet party, "appointed to receive a report of the happenings in China" on his return, "passed a resolution which did rather credit to me." It is not possible to check the veracity of this claim, but his challenge "to produce one single sentence from any official document of the Communist International" censuring his role in China has never been met.[61]

After China, it might well have been possible for Roy to continue to serve the Comintern, albeit in a less major role, had it not been for subsequent events. It should be remembered that although Borodin returned from China in disgrace, he managed to salvage his career. He later served in a succession of government posts—People's Commissar for Labor; deputy head of *Tass*, the official Soviet press agency; manager of the paper industry; and, from 1932, editor of the *Moscow Daily News*.[62] He retained the latter position until 1945, when he fell victim to Stalin's postwar purge.[h]

[h] Borodin was given a life sentence in a concentration camp. He died in 1951, presumably while serving his sentence in a Siberian labor camp.

Turn to the Left

Publicly Stalin defended his China policy against the charges of Trotsky and his allies that the Wuhan defection had been the direct result of a misguided policy framed in Moscow. As a result of his strategy, Stalin argued, the petty-bourgeois leaders in China had been discredited in the eyes of their people. "Is it not clear," he asked, "that only a correct policy can lead to such results? Did anyone ever say that the revolutionary bloc with the Wuhan government was to last forever? Are there such things as eternal blocs?"[63] He placed the blame for the catastrophe in China entirely on the shoulders of the Chinese communists for allegedly failing to implement Comintern directives urging them to promote agrarian revolution.

Although Stalin was forced to defend his China policy against its critics, the Chinese debacle was a major influence contributing to Stalin's change of policy in the late 1920's. This will become evident in our discussion of the Sixth Comintern Congress held in 1928. Although the reasons for the Comintern's turn to the left at this time are complex, three factors were undoubtedly of major significance: Stalin's factional struggle with Bukharin, the failure of the Anglo-Russian trade-union unity committee in June 1927, and the turn of events in China. The Stalin-Bukharin feud within the Soviet party will be discussed in a later chapter. It relates to Stalin's doctrine of socialism in one country, his preparations for introducing the First Five-Year Plan, and Bukharin's opposition to it. Since the doctrine of socialism in one country had profound implications for the international communist movement and since Bukharin, a leading member of the Soviet party, held the highest office in the Comintern, international policy could not be isolated from domestic policy.

The trade-union unity committee was the result of an alliance formed in 1924 between the British Trade-Union Congress and the Russian trade-union movement. With the failure of the general strike in England in 1926, the British group was eager to disassociate itself from the discredited communists, and in June of the following year, after the rupture of diplomatic relations between London and Moscow over China, they withdrew from the committee.[64]

Most decisive of all, however, was the failure of the united front in China. It will be shown in the next several chapters that despite the signs of a desire on the part of a growing section of the Congress party to forge a political weapon by championing the cause of India's peasants and workers—i.e., by going to the masses—the Comintern, under the influence of Stalin, failed to make a distinction between strategy and tactics appropriate for China and those appropriate for India and other dependent countries. This failure resulted in inestimable harm to the international communist movement.

5. The Radicalization of Indian Politics

Return to Moscow

ACCOMPANIED by a number of Russian advisers to China, including Oberst Galin (Vasili K. Blücher), Roy returned to Moscow in September 1927.[1] The reception was far from hospitable. Roy had been certain that he could explain his actions in China to Stalin, but he was denied the opportunity. Stalin refused to receive him. Friends were few at the moment Stalin's favor was withdrawn. Those who stood by him included the British communists Rajani Palme Dutt, his brother Clemens Dutt, Hugh Rathbone, and outside the Comintern, Borodin,[a] who, himself in disgrace, discovered anew his friendship for Roy.[2]

While in Moscow, Roy was also confronted with charges that he had misrepresented the strength of the CPI and misappropriated funds intended for use in India.[3] These claims were made in an interview with Osip Piatnitsky, the Comintern treasurer, by Saumyendranath Tagore, a grandson of the elder brother of the noted Bengali artist, writer, and musician, Rabindranath Tagore. Only the previous February, Tagore had been elected the general secretary of the Workers' and Peasants' Party of Bengal, which he had joined in January 1926 when it was known as the Labor Swaraj party. He was also a member of the CPI. Tagore had arrived in Moscow in June and remained to attend the tenth anniversary celebrations of the Russian revolution, so that his stay in Moscow coincided with Roy's.

There was some question, however, about his credentials and the credibility of his report. He had left India in April

[a] It was Borodin who, more than any other single person, had been responsible for Roy's conversion to communism (M. N. Roy, "An Emissary of the International," and "End of the Mexican Sojourn," in *Radical Humanist* [Calcutta], XVIII, 32 [1953]: 379 and 35 [1953]: 414-16).

without consulting with any of the leaders of the Bengal party or informing the Central Committee of the CPI. Moreover, he had a personal motive in minimizing the influence of Roy and the communist movement in India. He hoped to play a larger role in communist activities in India and undoubtedly saw his chance when he heard of Roy's political difficulties. His bias is strongly evident in his booklet, *Historical Development of the Communist Movement in India,* a work which casts considerable doubt on the reliability of its author's testimony. In it he attacked Roy as one who "always served the man in power" and as "the most servile agent of Stalin." Among its many errors are the assertions that as late as 1927 a communist party had not been formed in India and that it was not until after his expulsion from the Comintern that Roy began to raise objections to Stalin's policies.[4]

Tagore's aspirations never materialized. He never had a place in the communist movement, and outside of Bengal he had little acquaintance with communist activities in India. Moreover, during his absence from India, he was named a defendant in the Meerut Conspiracy Case and to avoid prosecution he did not return to his homeland until 1934. In the interim he toured Europe on behalf of the League Against Imperialism. After returning to India, he did not resume his activities in the CPI, but instead formed a rival Trotsky-oriented organization, the Revolutionary Communist Party of India, whose influence in India has been minuscule.[b] As a "renegade," he is regarded with considerable disdain by Indian communists, who mock him for his studied eccentricity, aristocratic airs, and dilettantism.[5]

It is doubtful if Tagore's report would have endangered Roy's position within the Comintern had it not been for de-

[b] Tagore severed his connection with the Revolutionary Communist Party of India some time ago. After his break, the party gained some notoriety in India when it was involved in a case in which the English manager of the Jessup Engineering firm in Calcutta was thrown alive into a furnace.

velopments within the All-Union Communist party (Bolshevik).[c] Piatnitsky was head of the Comintern's organizing bureau, commonly referred to as the Org-Bureau, which had the responsibility for overseeing the activities of member communist parties. In the course of performing this duty, he developed a contempt for the parties under his jurisdiction and made a practice of publicly criticizing their leaders and juxtaposing party claims with facts and figures, presumably to goad them to greater effort.[6] As the dispenser of "red gold," he was one of the most feared and flattered men in the Comintern and he used his influence to bribe, buy, and blackmail support of non-Russian communists for the Stalinist faction in the Russian ruling party.[7]

Because of Roy's stand, after his return from China, in favor of the continuation of a united front policy, his political fortune became enmeshed with that of Bukharin and other "rightist" opponents of Stalin within the Soviet party. This argument will be developed presently. Tagore's report, regardless of its reliability, must have been welcomed by Piatnitsky for several reasons: it was grist for his mill, and it might be useful in the forthcoming campaign to discredit Bukharin's ideological comrades within the Comintern. Furthermore Piatnitsky and Roy had never been on good terms. However, no public charges were ever made against Roy on the basis of Tagore's allegations. When Roy later joined the Communist Opposition this became unnecessary.

Roy was neither saint nor sinner. He had many admirable qualities and some human weaknesses as well. In his Comintern days, he struck many as brilliant, but arrogant, a fact which is regarded as incomprehensible by his associates in India, who knew him only after he had mellowed considerably. Nor was his personal conduct always above reproach. Until his marriage to Ellen Gottschalk in 1936,

[c] This was the official designation of the Soviet party from 1925 until 1952 when its name was changed to the Communist Party of the Soviet Union.

11. M. N. Roy at St. Moritz, 1928.

12. Brajesh Singh, one of Roy's early associates in India, in the 1930's, and the late common-law husband of Stalin's daughter, Svetlana Alliluyeva.

13. M. N. Roy on his first visit to Bombay after release from jail in 1936. In the photo can be seen (left to right beginning with the fourth person from left) K. F. Nariman, S. K. Patil, Maniben Kara, M. N. Roy, Yusuff Meherally, and Leelavati Munshi.

his refusal to be bound by the legal restraints of monogamy or the moral inhibitions of fidelity caused considerable suffering in the lives of several women who had been attracted to him. In his political activities, he was often guided by the maxim that the ends justify the means. Thus, he was not fastidious about his source of funds as long as it supported causes in which he believed. This was to create a serious political problem for him in 1944, when it was revealed to the public that his labor organization, the Indian Federation of Labor, had accepted a subsidy from the government of India in support of its efforts on behalf of war production.[8]

Inflation of party figures, as Piatnitsky's reports from 1924 to 1934 indicate, was common practice, due in part to revolutionary zeal and in part to a desire to make a good impression. It must be presumed that Roy was not immune to this temptation. Tagore's charges of misappropriation of funds is another matter and difficult to sustain. Roy did not equate revolutionary zeal with abstention, parsimony, or asceticism. His tastes were as cosmopolitan as his outlook. When times were good, he lived well—within the limits imposed by a life devoted to conspiratorial activities. But even then he had few possessions besides his books and clothes. From his current expenses, which were heavy, he set aside nothing so that from the moment of his break with the Comintern he was without resources of his own, but was dependent upon the support of his friends in Berlin.[9] Moreover, when the occasion required it, he was capable of great sacrifice in the interest of principles and causes he held dear. Thus, in late 1930 he returned to India despite the warnings of his friends that this meant almost certain arrest and imprisonment. After his release from jail, he never achieved any degree of affluence, as visitors to his Dehra Dun residence can attest. The house at 13 Mohini Road, in which he lived with his wife Ellen from 1936 until his death in 1954, was not owned by himself, but by the Indian Renaissance Institute, an organization formed by Roy and his close political associates.

The Ninth Plenum of the ECCI

Roy left Moscow for Berlin on October 3, 1927, but returned to Moscow the following February to attend the Ninth Plenum of the Executive Committee of the Comintern (February 9-25). In his absence there had been an "unofficial conference of all the experts" on the China question[10] and this was to be one of the main items on the agenda of the Plenum. Although he had been warned in Germany against entertaining such illusions, Roy evidently still felt that he could vindicate himself in the eyes of Stalin.

Arriving on February 4, he found the atmosphere "somewhat strange."[11] At first he felt that Heinz Neumann would bear the brunt of the Comintern's displeasure for leading the December putsch in Canton which had resulted in a wholesale disaster for the CCP and put an end to communist influence within the Chinese labor movement.[12] He reported that Neumann, who had pleaded with him in vain for support, was "politically . . . in a hole."[13] Apparently Roy was unaware that Neumann's action had aided Stalin in a decisive moment in his struggle against the left communists, Trotsky, Zinoviev, and Kamenev, who had charged Stalin with being insufficiently revolutionary. Neumann's cable, announcing the apparently successful uprising, arrived happily while the Fifteenth Congress of the Soviet party, which excluded Zinoviev and Kamenev and endorsed Trotsky's expulsion, was in session.[14]

The advent of the sectarian policy the Comintern was to pursue until 1933-35 under Stalin's direction was signalled by the decisions of the Ninth Plenum. The communist parties of both Great Britain and France were directed to inaugurate united front "from below" tactics. The British communists were to abjure any further attempts at affiliating with the Labour party. In France the communists were forced to abandon their practice of entering into electoral agreements, on the second ballot, with other left-wing parties.[15]

The plenum was more than half over before the China problem came up for discussion. Roy, contrary to his expectations, was not allowed to present his views on the question and several days before the end of the plenum he was bedridden with grippe, fever, and a severe pain in the left ear.[16]

With respect to China, the plenum declared that "the first wave of the broad revolutionary movement" had subsided with the "heavy defeats" suffered by the workers and peasants "in several revolutionary centers."[17] But it was indicated that this was only a temporary recession which soon would be followed by another revolutionary upsurge. This ingenious formula, devised by Bukharin, satisfied Stalin's needs. The notion of a temporary lull in revolutionary activity was consistent with the leftward direction in which Stalin now intended to take the Comintern. At the same time, it was sufficiently sanguine to avoid the appearance that he had been forced, belatedly, to agree with his political adversary, Trotsky, who had proclaimed shortly after the break with the Left Kuomintang that China was entering an indefinite period of revolutionary inaction.

At the plenum, Ch'ü Ch'iu-pai, who among the Chinese communists had played a prominent role in the events at Canton, was censored for his tendency to "play with uprisings."[18] But the Canton insurrection, in which the Comintern representative Neumann, as well as Ch'ü Ch'iu-pai, had been involved, was exempt from criticism. It was not referred to as a "putsch," which would have suggested a premature uprising, but was described in laudatory terms as a "heroic attempt on the part of the proletariat to organize Soviet power in China." Heinz Neumann salvaged his political career for the moment. In 1937 he was to meet his death before a firing squad in Moscow.

Roy, in the meantime, was bedridden. The intense pain in his left ear was diagnosed as mastoiditis and to relieve the abscess it became necessary to punch a small hole behind the ear. The operation brought some relief, but it was only temporary.[19] By mid-March there had been no improvement in his condition and it was decided that he must be hospitalized to undergo a more delicate operation.[20] Instead of being sent to the Kremlin hospital, where members of the Comintern were usually treated, Roy was consigned to a small hospital outside Moscow.[21]

Shortly after entering the hospital, Roy wrote to a friend in Europe that he would prefer "to go outside somewhere, and be sick there, but it can't be done. I tried this from the beginning. The doctors won't permit [it]. I like it less here than ever before. I hate the idea of your coming back with the risk of getting somehow entangled."[22] Because of the possibility of censorship, Roy had been forced to be circumspect in his correspondence. Consequently this message, though vague, was interpreted by its recipient as a confirmation of her fears that Roy was in political difficulty. It is doubtful that Roy felt his life was in danger. It was too early in Comintern history for that. More likely he suspected that he would be detained in Moscow for an indefinite period during which he would be deliberately isolated from developments in India. An assignment in Moscow or in some insignificant corner of the world was the usual practice at the time for dealing with those who had fallen from favor in the Comintern.[d]

Roy's correspondent, a Swiss woman who had accompanied him to China in 1927, hastened to Moscow. There she enlisted the aid of Borodin, and together they moved Roy, who was unable to walk, from his hospital bed to a room at the Hotel Lux. Arrangements were then made to get him out of the country. Piatnitsky, the head of the Org-Bureau, refused to return Roy's passport on the pretext

[d] One year later members of the right wing of the American Communist party met a similar fate in Moscow. Benjamin Gitlow was asked to accept an assignment with the OGPU, the Soviet intelligence agency, in Latin America. Bertram Wolfe, who, unlike Gitlow, knew Spanish, was asked to go to Korea, then considered the Comintern's "Siberia." Jay Lovestone, after ten weeks of detention, was finally able to secure his passport and a visa with the help of friendly connections and escape, undetected, by plane to Europe (Theodore Draper, *American Communism and Soviet Russia: The Formative Period*, pp. 425-28).

that he would be arrested at once in Germany. After two weeks of pleading with Piatnitsky, she then turned to Bukharin. Stalin's campaign against Bukharin had only just begun and he still retained sufficient influence in the Comintern to pry the passport from Piatnitsky's office. With some difficulty the necessary visas were also secured. Through personal connections with the director of the Russo-German Airline, Deruluft, she was able to secure two seats on a flight to Berlin without going through the required registration procedures. She and Roy departed without incident but there was great relief when the plane finally touched down in Berlin.[23] Although he was not aware of it at the time, Roy was never to return to Moscow.

Roy was quite ill when he returned to Berlin in April. Puss continued to concentrate in his ear, which gave him great pain, and he had lost his sense of equilibrium so that he was unable to walk unaided. He also suffered from enlargement of the heart. A doctor advised that he undergo another operation, but due to his generally weak condition this was postponed. In the interim he went to St. Moritz, where the high altitude helped him to regain his health.[24]

Roy utilized this period of relative inactivity to work on his book *Revolution und Konterrevolution in China*,[25] which he wrote to justify his policies in China. He also continued to observe the Indian political scene and to contribute articles to the *International Press Correspondence* urging the continuance of a united front policy for India.

As we have seen, Roy helped to formulate, as early as the Second Comintern Congress, a distinction between different types of nationalist movements—between those of a truly revolutionary and those of a merely reformist character. As a result of the deliberations on the national and colonial question at the Congress, Lenin had concluded that the policy of supporting nationalist, anti-imperialist movements was to be followed only in situations where it did not hinder the development of class struggle.[26]

Because of a preoccupation with the anti-imperialist aspect of the Chinese revolution, however, this principle was violated in 1927 by a determination to maintain the CCP's alliance with the Left Kuomintang, even at the expense of the class struggle if necessary. This was the basis of Roy's basic charge that the Chinese debacle had resulted from making a fetish of the alliance with the Left Kuomintang.[27] Roy placed the blame for the setback in China on Borodin and the CCP leadership. He never acknowledged Stalin's responsibility in the affair even though it was he who had placed particular emphasis on the nationalist content of the Chinese revolution. Furthermore, as his feud with Trotsky developed, Stalin was forced to stand by his China policy, at all cost, in the face of Trotsky's opposition to it.

Roy did not see in the China episode any cause to abandon the united front policy in India. To him there was a clear distinction between the political situation in China and that which prevailed in India. The CCP–Left Kuomintang alliance, he felt, had been undermined by "feudal-militarists," a group which had no counterpart in the Indian nationalist movement. Consequently, on his return from China, Roy continued to support a four-class united front policy for India, his recent experience with the Kuomintang notwithstanding. He praised the Workers' and Peasants' party and contrasted its accomplishments with the relative inactivity of the CPI, which, he held, had been hampered by "imperialist terror" and the "hostility of the national bourgeoisie."[28] He was encouraged by the progress of the Workers' and Peasants' party in the Indian trade-union movement, and by the radicalization of the Indian National Congress.

The Indian Nationalist Movement

There was good reason for cautious optimism on Roy's part. A sizable sector sympathetic toward the idea of radical socioeconomic reform and eager to step up the struggle for complete independence was clearly discernible within the Congress party by 1927. Its spokesman was Jawaharlal

Nehru. In February of that year, Nehru traveled to Brussels to attend the Congress of Oppressed Nationalities as the Congress party's sole delegate. It was at this time that the League Against Imperialism was founded.[29]

This organization was the inspiration of the German Comintern agent, Willi Muenzenberg,[e] the patron saint of the "fellow traveler." It was he who organized the Communist Youth International and the highly successful International Workers' Aid, which became the prototype for all subsequent communist front organizations. According to its statutes, the league was to serve as the "union of all persons and organizations which, disregarding their own particular aims, are prepared to lend support in the struggle against Imperialism and for the political and social liberation of all peoples." Because of its broadly-stated objectives the league was able to attract the support of a large number of noncommunist nationalists, not all of whom were altogether ignorant of its source of financial support.[30]

Nehru played a prominent role in the proceedings of the conference. In a speech to the delegates he stated that the Congress party had been inspired by the "noble example" of Chinese nationalists and hoped "as soon as possible . . . to follow in their footsteps."[31] He was elected a member of the organizing committee of the league and later served on its nine-man executive committee.[32] Although not well-versed in Marxist literature, it was at this juncture in his political career that Nehru began to employ socialist phrases. It was he who drafted the Congress's resolution on India expressing the hope that "the Indian nationalist movement" would "base its program on the full emancipation of the peasants and workers of India, without which there can be no real freedom."[33]

[e] Muenzenberg was expelled from the German communist party in 1938. He died under mysterious circumstances in 1940. Some attribute his death to one of Stalin's agents (Branko Lazitch, "Stalin's Massacre of the Foreign Communist Leaders," in Milorad M. Drachkovitch and Branko Lazitch, eds., *The Comintern: Historical Highlights, Essays, Recollections, Documents* [New York: Praeger, 1966], p. 145).

In November 1927 Jawaharlal Nehru and his father, Motilal, journeyed to Moscow on the invitation of the Society for Cultural Relations to Foreign Countries to attend the Tenth Anniversary Celebration of the Bolshevik Revolution.[34] The brief four-day visit made a deep impression on the younger Nehru. On his return to India, a series of his "random sketches and impressions" appeared in the Indian press. These articles were later published as a book under the title *Soviet Russia*, which constituted as a whole a panegyric to the Soviet system. There were, however, occasional expressions of reservations, which were to assume a greater significance in Nehru's estimation of communism in later years.

Shortly after returning to India, Nehru attended the annual Congress party session in Madras, at which he sponsored a number of fairly radical resolutions. Potentially the most important and far-reaching of these was a resolution on the political objective in which it was stated unequivocally, for the first time, that the party's goal was the attainment of complete independence rather than dominion status or some other form of relationship with Great Britain. Among Nehru's other proposals was a call for association with the League Against Imperialism and a resolution on war danger which was inspired by the Comintern's then current denunciations of Great Britain for allegedly harboring aggressive designs against the Soviet Union. Much to Nehru's surprise, according to his own account, they were all adopted.

In an article in *International Press Correspondence*, Roy interpreted the sponsorship of such a resolution as a favorable sign, but characterized its passage as "a mere stage show. . . . Not a word," he noted, was said about "how the goal was to be attained." The resolution, he argued, had been conceded to the "petty-bourgeois elements" within the Congress party to deflect "their deviation towards revolutionary alliance with the masses."[35]

Although the resolutions themselves represented a radical departure from previous Congress policy, Nehru was under no illusion that their adoption actually represented a change of direction on the part of a majority of the Congress delegates. He attributed much of his support to the influence of the ordinary delegate, who, he felt, regarded his resolutions as academic exercises to be voted on and gotten out of the way in order to proceed to more important business.[36] Gandhi did not participate in the deliberations of the Madras session, but he later vehemently opposed the independence resolution. He charged angrily that the "Congress stultifies itself by repeating year after year resolutions of this character when it knows that it is not capable of carrying them into effect." He concluded that "we have almost sunk to the level of a schoolboy's debating society."[37] The opposition of Gandhi and the conservative old guard was soon to render the resolution meaningless. Jawaharlal Nehru preferred to judge the temper of the Congress by another resolution which it endorsed proposing that an All-Parties Conference to draft a constitution for India based on common agreement be convened.[38] It was well known at the time that no party, other than the Congress, contemplated complete independence as its goal. The decision of such a gathering to opt for dominion status, instead of complete independence, was a foregone conclusion.

The radicalization of Indian politics proceeded apace during the course of 1928. In February, the Indian Statutory Commission—or, as it was more popularly known, the Simon Commission, after its chairman, Sir John Simon—arrived in India to gauge Indian opinion on the question of constitutional reform. It was greeted with violent demonstrations and a nationwide boycott by all political parties, except the Justice Party of Madras and a dissident section of the Muslim League under the leadership of Sir Muhammed Shafi.[39] Public indignation had been aroused against the committee because it did not contain a single Indian representative. It was widely felt that Indians should have a greater voice in determining the shape of their own future constitution. The presence of the committee in India throughout the year served to quicken nationalist, anti-British sentiment. During this period, Roy, from Berlin, contacted all the parties participating in the boycott and urged them to issue a joint declaration that the right of framing a constitution belonged exclusively to the Indian people acting through their representatives in a constituent assembly.[40] Roy helped to popularize the slogan of constituent assembly within the Congress ranks in succeeding years.

The secretary of state for India, provoked by the controversy surrounding the appointment of the Simon Commission, had challenged Indian leaders to come up with a proposal for constitutional reform upon which they all could agree. The All-Parties Conference was their response. This body delegated the task of formulating a constitution to a sub-committee representing various shades of nationalist opinion both within and without the Congress party and chaired by Jawaharlal Nehru's father, Motilal Nehru. The Nehru Report, authorized principally by its chairman and Sir Tej Bahadur Sapru, provided for a constitution envisioning dominion status for India within the British Commonwealth of Nations. When the All-Parties Conference, convened in August to consider the Report, approved a resolution endorsing dominion status as their common objective, Jawaharlal Nehru led a group of about thirty delegates who disassociated themselves from that particular measure. He announced that the group would support the All-Parties' Report in the interest of nationalist unity, but at the same time he informed the conference that "we propose to carry on such activity as we consider proper and necessary in favor of complete independence."[41]

Such activity first assumed organizational form in Madras at the instigation of S. Srinivasa Iyengar. President of the Congress party the previous year, he alone among Congress leaders had refused to participate in the All-Parties Conference because of his opposition to dominion status. Later, a group of Congress members, under the leadership of Subhas Chandra Bose, issued a manifesto and a provisional program for a proposed Independence for India League. This program was adopted by groups in Bombay and elsewhere, and in November 1928 the All-India Independence for India League was formed to press for the reinstatement of the goal of complete independence as adopted by the 1927 party conference at Madras. Iyengar was president of the League, Bose and Jawaharlal Nehru were joint secretaries. The League, which enjoyed the support of a number of prominent members of the Congress party, operated as a pressure group within the nationalist movement. It never developed a well-articulated organizational structure or a mass following of its own. Its appeal was largely to young members of the Congress party. When in December 1929 the Congress party once again declared complete independence to be its goal, the League, always a loose organizational structure, died along with its major *raison d'être*.[42]

The League's program was divided into three parts, entitled "political democracy," "economic democracy," and "social democracy," and was clearly modeled after Dr. Sun Yat-sen's tripartite program—"nationalism, socialism, and democracy." On domestic issues, the program urged Congress members to adopt a policy in favor of the introduction of a socialist state. It called for such measures as the removal of social and economic disparities, nationalization of key industries and transport services, introduction of a uniform system of land tenure with annulment of agricultural indebtedness, and the "abolition of landlordism by indemnification."[43] At the time, it was the most radical proposal ever put forward by a nationalist group in India.

The sole item under the heading, "political democracy," was the demand for "complete independence." Today it is difficult to understand the controversy that raged in India at this time over the question of dominion status unless it is recalled that the concept itself was not defined until the Imperial Conference of 1926 and not formally embodied in law until 1931 by the Statute of Westminster.[f] Until then, there was a great deal of ambiguity concerning what dominion status actually entailed. Long after 1931, suspicion as to the relationship between Great Britain and her dominions remained until experience and custom gave it final form.

The Independence League opposed dominion status on the grounds that it was something less than complete independence. It was felt that full equality with other members of the Commonwealth would be denied to India because of the racial prejudice prevalent in Great Britain and her dominions. Moreover, it was argued, India should not associate herself with British imperialism. Great Britain, it was said, was committed to extending her influence in Asia; whereas India was anxious to free Asia from colonial rule.[44] Although his views on the subject were to change in later years, Jawaharlal Nehru insisted, at this time, that India must sever all ties with the British Empire, for, he argued, "the British Commonwealth, in spite of its high-sounding name, does not stand for . . . international cooperation and in its world policy has consistently stood for narrow and selfish ideals and against the peace of the world."[45]

At the annual Congress party session held in Calcutta at the end of the year, Jawaharlal's father, Motilal Nehru, answered the criticism directed at dominion status by the Independence League and socialist-inclined members of his party. To the objection that other members of the Commonwealth would not grant perfect equality to India, he replied simply: "We shall not take anything less." To the

[f] At the Imperial Conference of 1926, Great Britain and her dominions were held to be "autonomous communities within the British Empire, equal in status, in no way subordinate one to the other in any aspect of domestic or external affairs, though united by a common allegiance to the Crown and freely associated as members of the British Commonwealth of nations."

These principles were embodied formally in law by the 1931 Statute of Westminster, under the terms of which dominions enjoyed legislative autonomy, the right of their ministers to direct access to the crown, and the right of representation in international bodies as separate states—except Newfoundland—(*Encyclopædia Britannica*, VII [London: William Benton, 1963]: 575).

characterization of the Commonwealth as "an imperialist combine," he replied by denying that a dominion is required to participate in the exploitation of other nations. He conceded, however, that the question of whether or not dominions were obliged to join Great Britain in "her wars" was open to debate.

Motilal Nehru assured the British government that dominion status, if granted, would not be used, as some feared, merely as a stepping-stone to a complete break with the empire. At the same time, however, he warned that the time was fast approaching when nothing short of complete independence would be acceptable. Obviously, he hoped to utilize radical voices within Congress to win political concessions. It is equally clear from his speech that the demand for complete independence put forth the preceding year had been intended by moderates within the party as a bargaining counter. He stated:

> Dominion status involves a very considerable measure of freedom. . . . I am therefore not against an exchange of abject independence with whatever measure of freedom there is in full dominion status, if such an exchange is offered. But I cannot make dominion status my goal as it has come from another party over whom I have no control. The only way I can acquire such control is by working in right earnest for complete independence. I say in "right earnest" because I know mere bluff will not take me far; it is only when complete independence is in sight that the party in power will be inclined to negotiate for something less. Empty bluff will not carry into that stage. Solid work and ungrudging sacrifice alone will do it.[46]

He sympathized with young party members who were impatient for freedom and social reform. He expressed admiration for their idealism and spirit of self-sacrifice. But he also counseled: "You cannot curse exploitation and imperialism out of existence and the way to do it is a long and dreary one." The left wing, he felt, took little heed of either the party's weaknesses or the strength of the enemy and was willing "to dash out full steam ahead on unchartered seas." Such idealism, divorced from realities, he said, had no place in politics and was "but a happy dream which must sooner or later end in a rude awakening." He warned against allowing differences within the party to stand in the way of common action. To avoid paralysis, party members should concentrate on immediate and minimum goals, on which all can agree, and offer the foreign oppressor a "united front."

The All-Parties Conference, which had agreed on dominion status, he noted, had represented many political, labor, religious, communal, and commercial organizations. The Congress party could not spurn its recommendations without giving up its claim to speak for all of India. Moreover, the party should not make any demands without developing a sanction. "Whatever the ultimate goal, we must be prepared to traverse the same thorny path to reach it. If we are not so prepared, independence will ever be an idle dream and dominion status an ever-receding will-o'-the-wisp."

Despite Motilal Nehru's eloquent plea for moderation, pressure from the left wing was too strong to be ignored. A compromise resolution was adopted. The British government was given one year to grant dominion status. If there was no response by the end of the year, the Nehru Report proposals would be withdrawn and the demand for complete independence reinstated. The Congress party had one year to prepare for a direct confrontation with the British raj. It was also decided at the Calcutta Congress session that the party would take up the organization of workers and peasants as part of the constructive work program, which was viewed as a necessary prelude to the launching of noncooperation.

The Workers' and Peasants' Party and Indian Labor

Indian workers, although small in number, were a potentially significant force in pre-independence India as, indeed, they remain today. They occupied critical areas in the economy—in organized industry, transport, mining, plantations, and commerce. Moreover their concentration in a relatively few urban areas invited organizational efforts.[g]

Although a few of its leaders had taken an active interest in the All-India Trade-Union Congress (AITUC), the Congress had generally ignored the Indian labor movement despite its potentiality as a political weapon. Gandhi hoped to avoid, as far as possible, the mixing of politics with trade-union activity, and he abjured the use of strikes as conducive to violence and therefore in violation of the principle of *ahimsa* ("nonviolence").[47] He confined his labor activities to the Ahmedabad Textile Workers Union, which refrained from joining the AITUC. A minority within the party, led by Jawaharlal Nehru and Subhas Chandra Bose, wished to link the aspirations of the workers and other impoverished groups with the nationalist struggle.

Indian communists saw their opportunity. It has already been noted that Spratt, shortly after his arrival in India in late 1926, helped to organize workers' and peasants' parties in Bombay, the U.P., and the Punjab. In Bengal, such a party, under various names, had been in existence since November 1925. It was hoped that such broad-based parties would serve both as a legal cover for communist activities in India and as a means of penetrating the Indian labor movement.

The communists had gained an early foothold in the AITUC with the election of the communist sympathizer D. R. Thengdi as its president in 1925. The Kanpur trial, however, had removed some of the most able of the communist trade unionists and frightened away many of the others, and communism had been unable to make much headway in the trade-union movement.

All of the members of the Bombay Workers' and Peas-

[g] At this point the reader may wish to review the sections entitled "The Labor Movement" and "British Emissaries" in Chapters 2 and 3 of this book.

ants' party had been associated with labor activities in the Bombay area. With this base Spratt and his colleagues set out to widen communist influence in the labor movement. In March 1927 Spratt and a few other communists, with the help of the Parsi labor leader S. H. Jhabwala, attended the AITUC session in Delhi as delegates, though they were not entitled to such status.[48] Although the meeting was addressed by the communist member of Parliament, Sharpurji Saklatvala,[49] Spratt's group had little impact on the decisions taken.

Soon thereafter, however, the Indian communists were able to capture a number of trade unions and to secure a measure of influence within the AITUC beyond their most extravagant expectations. Their success was due to a number of factors in addition to the Congress party's general neglect of the labor field. First, they had the support of those nationalist-oriented leaders who were active within the labor movement and who shared the communists' aim of associating the AITUC with the anti-British struggle.[50] Even moderate trade unionists, like N. M. Joshi, who favored a neutral policy on political matters, initially welcomed the communists as collaborators in the trade-union field. Second, they were helped by the deplorable conditions in the textile industry, which will be discussed below. Finally, the recently passed Trade-Unions Act of 1926, which went into effect on June 1, 1927, served as a stimulus to trade unionism by providing for the registration of unions that met certain specified requirements and granting such unions immunity from criminal and civil suits for actions taken in furtherance of labor objectives.[51]

At the eighth annual session of the AITUC held in Kanpur, November 26-28, 1927, communists were elected to several high offices within the organization. S. H. Jhabwala was made organizing secretary, S. A. Dange was chosen as one of the assistant secretaries, and the communist sympathizer D. R. Thengdi became one of the three vice-presidents. The moderate trade unionists C. F. Andrews and

N. M. Joshi were, however, elected president and general secretary respectively.[52]

Communist and left-wing influence can also be seen in the various resolutions which were adopted at the session. The delegates resolved to boycott the Simon Commission and to appoint a subcommittee to draw up a "Labor Constitution of the future government of India." Among its nine members were Philip Spratt (convenor), S. A. Dange, S. H. Jhabwala, and D. R. Thengdi. Other resolutions were passed which condemned imperialism as "a form of Capitalist Class Government, intended to facilitate and perpetuate the exploitation and slavery of all workers"; congratulated the U.S.S.R. on its tenth anniversary; expressed support of workers and peasants in China who were frustrating "the aggressive designs of the United Imperialist Powers"; deplored the failure of the Anglo-Russian Unity Conference; and condemned the action of the government of Bombay in prosecuting Philip Spratt and congratulated him on his acquittal. Finally a Council of Action was created for the purpose of organizing "a mass movement of the workers and peasants of India." Chaman Lal and S. H. Jhabwala were elected president and secretary respectively. Spratt, Jhabwala, and R. L. Bakhale were chosen to represent the province of Bombay on the Council.[53]

It was among the cotton mill workers of Bombay that the Bombay Workers' and Peasants' party made its most significant gains. The Bombay Presidency, where approximately two-thirds of the country's mill operatives were employed, dominated the cotton textile industry in India. Within the province, eighty percent of whose workers were mill hands, the principal center of the industry was Bombay and its environs, where over half of the labor force worked in the cotton mills.[54]

During World War I, Indian industry, including the cotton mills, thrived. Indian troops serving abroad had to be supplied with clothing and munitions. Belligerent countries were hungry for India's raw materials. At the same time, imports of manufactured goods into India were severely curtailed due to the unavailability of transport.

At the conclusion of the war, euphoria gradually gave way to the specter of unemployment and retrenchment as the armed forces were demobilized, munitions works closed, demand for manufactured goods declined, and prices fell. Accompanying the outbreak of militant nationalist agitation were widespread strikes which occurred throughout 1920 and 1921. By 1923 economic depression had set in. It was to continue, interspersed with short intervals of revival, until the middle of 1934.

The difficulties of the Indian textile industry were compounded by severe competition from Japanese producers. Indian mill owners had been preoccupied with short-run profits and consequently had made little effort to operate their factories efficiently. In the Bombay mill industry particularly, corruption, inefficiency, and speculation were rampant.[55] To survive, Indian mill owners began to seek ways to cut production costs. When the Bombay Mill Owners Association in 1925 sought to reduce wages by eleven and one-half percent, a three-month strike ensued which was resolved in favor of the workers. In lieu of reduced wages, the government of India gave relief to the employers by removing the excise duty of three and one-half percent on Indian cotton manufactures.

From 1925 until 1927-28 relations between workers and employers were relatively calm. With the decline in prices which had begun in 1929, real wages had in fact improved. In 1927, however, Indian cotton manufacturers, because of world market conditions, found it necessary once again to reduce production costs. Instead of seeking to reduce wages, as they had done earlier, mill owners sought to introduce a rationalization scheme, or more efficient methods of production, in order to increase output per worker and permit a reduction in the total work force. In July 1927, Bombay mill owners asked spinners to operate more spindles and weavers to operate more looms in return for a small compensatory increase in wages. At the same time, large numbers of workers were to be laid off.[56] As a result of this action, the average daily number of persons employed in the Bombay cotton mills declined during the period 1927-28 from 145,000 to 118,500.[57]

This period coincided with the entry of the communists into the trade-union movement in India. Although textile unions had been formed in Madras and Ahmedabad at a comparatively early date, no effective organization of cotton mill workers existed in Bombay until 1926. In January of that year the moderate trade unionists N. M. Joshi and R. L. Bakhale founded the Bombay Textile Labor Union.[58] As indicated earlier, the Bombay Workers' and Peasants' party was formed in January 1927 to promote the organization of trade unions and to influence the budding labor movement. Its members had belonged to the Labor Group of the Congress party, but had been unable to win acceptance for their ideas within the nationalist party. In May, the Workers' and Peasants' party began publication of a Marathi-language paper, *Kranti* (*Revolution*). Suspended at the end of the year for financial reasons, the paper was resumed during the 1928 general strike of cotton mills in Bombay.[59]

When the management of the Sasson Group of Cotton Mills in Bombay on January 3, 1928 announced the introduction of a rationalization plan, the workers struck. Members of the Bombay Workers' and Peasants' party took an active part in the strike, but were unsuccessful in their attempt to expand it into a general strike embracing all cotton mills in the city, owing largely to the opposition of Joshi and the Bombay Textile Labor Union. The strike ultimately failed and the strikers were forced to return to work on the company's terms.[60]

In addition to the Bombay Textile Labor Union, another union of cotton mill workers, the Girni Kamgar Mahamandel, had preceded the formation of the Bombay Workers' and Peasants' party. This union had been formed in August 1925 under the leadership of A. A. Alve and D. R. Mayekar, who served as its president and secretary respectively.[61]

The call of the Bombay Workers' and Peasants' party, seeking to capitalize on the widespread fear of unemployment, for a general strike precipitated a split in the Girni Kamgar Mahamandel. Alve, as a member of the Bombay Workers' and Peasants' party, supported the plan for a general strike; whereas Mayekar rejected the proposal as bolshevik-inspired. A contest ensued between the two for control of the union. Alve's point of view prevailed, and on February 28, 1928, the union passed a resolution condemning Mayekar for attacking its president and resolved to support a general strike. The following month, Mayekar was removed from his post as secretary.[62]

At about the same time, S. H. Jhabwala, a vice-president of the Bombay Textile Labor Union, broke with the predominantly moderate leadership of his union. With the encouragement of the Bombay Workers' and Peasants' party, he and some of his followers, in March, formed a separate organization, the Bombay Mill Workers Union.[63]

When the mills operated by Currimbhoy Ebrahim and Sons sought to introduce a rationalization scheme in April, the communists were prepared to take advantage of the opportunity. The Bombay Workers' and Peasants' party called for a strike, which began on April 16. A Strike Committee was formed on the initiative of the Workers' and Peasants' party to coordinate the strike. It was comprised of representatives of the Girni Kamgar Mahamandel, the Bombay Mill Workers Union, the Bombay Workers' and Peasants' party, and nonunion mill workers.[64] The Bombay Workers' and Peasants' party was represented by S. H. Jhabwala, A. A. Alve, S. A. Dange, S. S. Mirajkar, R. S. Nimbkar, D. R. Thengdi, and Benjamin Bradley. On April 12 an Inner Council of six members was formed consisting of Alve, Nimbkar, Dange, Mirajkar, Ghate, and Jhabwala—all members of the Bombay Workers' and Peasants' party.[65]

On April 23 an incident occurred in which the police opened fire on a procession, killing one person and wounding several others. The next day the Strike Committee proclaimed a general strike of all the cotton mills in the city. Within a few days all but two of the Bombay mills were struck. Sixty-eight cotton mills, two silk mills, and one bleaching mill in the city were involved in the strike.[66]

The moderate trade unionist, N. M. Joshi, of the Bombay Textile Labor Union, had initially refused to join the Strike Committee unless his union was given fifty percent of the seats on the committee. On May 2, however, after prolonged negotiations a new Joint Strike Committee was formed consisting of twenty workers and five representatives each from the moderate and radical wings of the trade-union movement. The latter group nominated Jhabwala, Dange, Mirajkar, Nimbkar, and Bradley to serve on the committee.[67] A negotiating subcommittee was also appointed, comprised of Joshi and Ginwala of the Bombay Textile Labor Union, Alve of the Girni Kamgar Mahamandel, Jhabwala and Dange of the Bombay Mill Workers Union, and three workers.[68] The reconstituted Strike Committee issued a statement listing seventeen demands of the workers.[69] The mill owners, however, refused to bargain with any group other than Joshi's union and insisted that workers would not be allowed to return to work except under the same terms as before the strike.[70]

In the course of the strike, the communists gained control of the Girni Kamgar Mahamandel. Before the end of April an advisory board consisting of members of the executive committee of the Bombay Workers' and Peasants' party was in charge of the union's affairs. However, Mayekar, after being deposed, appropriated the union's name by fraudulently registering his new union under that title with himself as president. Consequently the communist-dominated section of the Girni Kamgar Mahamandel joined forces with Jhabwala's newly formed Bombay Mill Workers Union. This reconstituted union, known as the Bombay Girni Kamgar (Mill Workers) Union (GKU), was registered on May 23, 1928. Its executive was comprised entirely of the extremist labor leaders of the Bombay Workers' and Peasants' party. Alve was president; Dange, the general secretary; and Ghate, the treasurer. Bradley, Hutchinson, Nimbkar, and Jhabwala served as vice-presidents of the union.[71]

The Bombay Workers' and Peasants' party revived its paper, *Kranti*, and through its publications and ceaseless activity succeeded in the course of the strike in winning the loyalty of a large section of the Bombay labor force. Within the first few months of the strike, claimed membership of the GKU rose from 324 to 54,000 members.[h] Although this figure was probably exaggerated, the GKU almost overnight had become the largest labor union in India.[72]

The strike continued for nearly six months—a laudable achievement considering the poverty of the workers and the inadequacy of provisions for strike relief. The strike, which had resulted in the loss of 21,000,000 working days, was called off on October 4 when an agreement was reached between representatives of the mill owners and the Joint Strike Committee at a conference convened by the governor. Pending a final settlement to be based on the results of an inquiry into labor conditions by a committee appointed by the government of Bombay (later known as the Fawcett Committee),[i] workers were to return to their jobs at the rates paid in March of the previous year. This meant that, for the time being at least, there

[h] V. B. Karnik, *Indian Trade Unions* (pp. 39-40) claims that the membership of the GKU eventually reached 70,000. These membership figures should not be taken as authentic. In India it is difficult to check the veracity of union membership claims, which are often exaggerated, due to inadequately maintained registers, lack of a check-off system, and the absence of periodical inspections of registers and records (Government of India, Department of Labor, *Report Regarding the Representative Character of the All-India Federation of Labour*, by S. C. Joshi, Chief Labour Commissioner [Simla: Government of India Press, 1946], pp. 8, 30-31). These factors, combined with the low rate of subscription dues, make it possible for any group commanding relatively modest financial resources to increase their voting strength in the national labor federations by filling in the names of known workers on the union rolls and paying the nominal fee involved.

[i] The chairman of the Committee of Enquiry was Sir Charles Fawcett, Judge of the High Court of Judicature, Bombay.

would be neither a reduction in wages nor the introduction of efficiency methods.[73]

The Royal Commission on Labor, reporting on labor conditions in India at the time, stated that the absence of a strong organization of cotton mill workers, combined with the mood generated by prolonged strike, allowed a few communist leaders "by an intense effort to capture the imagination of the workers and eventually to sweep over 50,000 of them into a communist organization."[74] In Bombay, communist influence also spread among municipal, oil installation, transport, and dock workers.[75] As a result of the influx of membership in the communist dominated unions, trade-union membership in Bombay increased seventy percent in the four-month period preceding December 1, 1928.

Indian communists did not confine their trade-union work to the city of Bombay. They were also active among the textile workers of Sholapur and Kanpur, the iron and steel workers of Jamshedpur in Bihar, the jute workers near Calcutta, and the railroad workers throughout northern India. During this period the Great Indian Peninsula (G.I.P.) Railwaymen's Union[j] was organized with Jhabwala as general secretary, Bradley as vice-president, and Joglekar as organizing secretary.[76] By 1929 it claimed a membership of 41,000.[77] Communists were successful in organizing workers in other areas of the economy as well. British intelligence reported:

> By the end of 1928 . . . there was hardly a single public utility service or industry which had not been affected, in whole or in part, by the wave of Communism which swept the country during the year. Transport, industrial, and agricultural workers of every description, clerks, policemen, colliers and even scavengers were amongst the many who were subjected to, if they did not fall under, the baneful influence of this whirlwind propaganda campaign which promised them the sweets of

[j] This line is now known as the Central Railway.

revolution if they would but raise their hands to grasp them.[78]

On the basis of their new strength in the labor unions,[k] communists made a determined effort to capture the AITUC when it held its ninth annual session at Jharia, Bihar, December 18-20, 1928. The delegates were addressed by the American J. W. Johnstone as a representative of the League Against Imperialism. He compared the exploitation of Indians by the British with that of the negro by American capitalists and "the chauvinism of the white worker." He argued that there could be little improvement in the conditions of Indian labor under British domination and urged the AITUC to strengthen its cause by affiliating with the League Against Imperialism.[79] Johnstone, who had been under close police surveillance since his arrival in India on November 22 and had been served orders to leave the country shortly before the Jharia session convened, was arrested immediately after the close of the open session. After spending sixteen days in prison, he was deported.[80]

The communist candidate for the presidency of the AITUC was D. B. Kulkarni, a railroad clerk. To block his election the moderates sponsored the candidacy of the well-known nationalist leader, Jawaharlal Nehru, for the office. Nehru, who was attending the session, won[l] by only a narrow margin.[81] Kulkarni and the communist, Muzaffar Ahmed, along with three others, subsequently became vice-presidents of the AITUC. Thengdi, Bradley, and Spratt

[k] The GKU had applied for affiliation with the AITUC but had not been accepted by the time of the Jharia session because of the requirement that a union must be in existence for at least one year before joining the federation (*All-India Trade-Union Bulletin* [Bombay], v, 6 [1928]: 42).

[l] The communists were not entirely displeased with Nehru's election for they felt that he would be sympathetic to them. They were quick to note, however, that temperamentally he was not one of them. They became quite annoyed when Nehru angrily rebuked a communist delegate charging that "communists make a cult of working class crudeness" (Philip Spratt, *Blowing Up India*, p. 109).

were elected to the ten-man executive committee and Dange was chosen as one of two assistant secretaries.

The resolutions adopted at Jharia, like those of the previous year, reflected the increased strength of the left wing within the labor movement. The delegates voted in favor of condemning the arrest of Johnstone; reaffirming their opposition to imperialism as "a form of Capitalist Class Government" and promoting international class solidarity; urging the All-Parties Conference to draft a constitution for India based on labor's demand for a "Socialistic Republican Government of the Working Classes" and the nationalization of industries and land; and castigating the British Labour party for betraying the Indian working class. As a form of protest against the arrest of Johnstone, the AITUC decided to affiliate with the League Against Imperialism for a period of one year and elected D. R. Thengdi and K. N. Joglekar as fraternal delegates to the forthcoming world conference of the League.[82]

A British intelligence report paid the following tribute to Spratt's and Muzaffar Ahmed's industry and effectiveness during this period:

> To him [Spratt] and Muzaffar Ahmed is due in very great measure the striking success which attended the party's efforts during 1928 and the spring of 1929. . . . Spratt in particular was ubiquitous. He worked in 1927 mainly with the Bombay group, in 1928 with the Bengal party. He played a large part in uniting the Punjab groups into one party and in the formation of those in the United Provinces into another. And all the time he was carrying on correspondence with the conspirators on the Continent and in England, informing them of the progress of the work, discussing difficulties, receiving instructions. . . . Second only to him was Muzaffar Ahmed, who, however autocratic he may have been, managed by voluminous correspondence to keep in touch not only with the workers abroad but also with all the other workers in India and saw to it that none was idle.[83]

6. The Sixth Comintern Congress

ON MAY 25, 1928 the Program Commission of the ECCI adopted a "Draft Program of the Communist International," which foreshadowed the strategy and tactics which would be adopted at the Sixth Comintern Congress. This document reflected a marked change of attitude toward the nationalist bourgeoisie. It was now held that in dependent areas this group had "already crossed over into the camp of the avowed counterrevolution or is crossing over." Consequently workers and peasants must be organized in their independent organizations and "liberated from the influence of the nationalist bourgeoisie." Henceforth, only "temporary agreements" with the nationalist movement were to be sanctioned. In India, Gandhism, to which Lenin had attributed a revolutionary role, was now regarded as an "openly reactionary force" which must be "resolutely combatted."[1]

The ECCI later issued a report in which even "the petty-bourgeois left wing" of the Congress party, which was soon to assume the organizational form of the Independence for India League, was condemned for leading the workers and peasants away from revolutionary goals toward socialist noncooperation without violence. "The nationalist left wing," it was held, "with its slogans of independence, social equality, and socialism, had evolved into an instrument for the penetration and vicarious leadership of the broad working masses," impeding their development into "an independent political force."[2] While acknowledging that the newly formed Workers' and Peasants' parties had achieved "remarkable results," Indian communists were criticized for attaching more importance to collaborating with the "left nationalists" than "to its independent role as a party." The Workers' and Peasants' parties, it was argued, could never develop into truly revolutionary parties unless they freed themselves completely "from the influence of bourgeois politicians" and developed an independent political organization. At the same time, Indians were warned against regarding such two-class parties as a substitute for a communist party, the organization of which was considered "absolutely necessary." This was a repudiation of Roy's earlier advice to disband the CPI.[3]

At the Sixth Comintern Congress (July 17 to September 1, 1928) Nikolai I. Bukharin presented the ECCI report. In dealing with colonial and semicolonial areas he acknowledged that the CCP had "suffered a severe defeat." But, he contended, it was not "the main line of tactics" which had been at fault, but "the political actions and practical application of the line" on the part of the Chinese communists. After thus defending Stalin's policies in China, he argued against applying the same line in India, where the situation was entirely different. In China the bourgeoisie had conducted an armed struggle against the imperialists, but it was inconceivable that the Indian bourgeoisie would play a comparable role. They would maneuver against the British rulers, but this was "a far cry from armed struggle." Moreover, he predicted, "they will desert to the camp of counterrevolution at the first manifestation of the mass movement." Hence, Indian communists must "come out against the bourgeoisie" and expose their half-heartedness.[4]

Otto V. Kuusinen,[a] in presenting his report on the revolutionary movement in the colonies, continued to develop the theme that it was time for the Comintern to reappraise its efforts in the colonies. To protect Stalin against Trotsky's charges, he contended that the ECCI had "of course paid

[a] The son of a Finnish tailor, Kuusinen was one of the founders of the Comintern. Before his death in May, 1964, at the age of 82, he had shared with former Premier Khrushchev, Mikhail A. Suslov, and Frol Kozlov, the honor of membership on both the Secretariat and the Presidium of the Communist Party of the Soviet Union (CPSU). His daughter, Herta, is a leading figure in the Finnish Communist party (*New York Times*, May 18, 1964, p. 2).

considerable attention to all questions connected with the Chinese movement," but he held that the ECCI, in the past, had not paid sufficient attention to colonial questions. As a result, it was necessary "in many important colonies" to "begin our work from the beginning." He deplored the fact that "in most colonies and semi-colonies, even in the important ones, we have as yet no real Communist parties." And, in part as a rebuke to Roy, he stated that "for a time some comrades considered the advisability of peasant and labor parties as a substitute" for communist parties, but that such forms were "not to be recommended." Such multi-class parties, with their large petty-bourgeois component, might actually serve as a barrier rather than as a channel of communication between communists and the downtrodden classes:

> It would be an easy matter for the labor and peasant parties to transform themselves into petty-bourgeois parties, to get away from the communists, thereby failing to help them to come in contact with the masses. To consider such parties as a substitute for a real Communist Party, would be a serious mistake. We are for a bloc with the peasantry, but we will not have anything to do with fusion of various classes.

He concluded that "the foremost practical task" in dependent areas was the formation of communist parties.[5]

Decolonization

Roy did not attend the Sixth World Congress. In his absence, he was denounced by Comintern leaders. Shortly after his return from China, he had drafted a resolution on decolonization in which he had analyzed British economic policy in India. This document was the basis for the attacks made on Roy at the Sixth Congress. Since it was ostensibly on an analysis of British colonial policy that the new Comintern line on dependent areas was based, it is important to understand the controversy which was waged over the concept of decolonization at the Sixth Congress. This, in turn, necessitates a brief review of the history of the term.

The Sixth Plenum of the ECCI (February 17 to March 15, 1926) had characterized the general economic situation in the capitalist countries as one of "tottering stabilization."[6] With respect to Great Britain, it had declared that a decline of British capital was leading to a strengthening of native capitalism. But it had been carefully pointed out that "economic concessions to sections of the native bourgeoisie" did not entail political concessions, but on the contrary, were accompanied always by a policy of increased political oppression.[7]

At the Seventh Plenum, held later in the year, Roy had expressed a similar point of view. He had maintained that the days of "classic imperialism" had passed. Great Britain, no longer able to export capital, was compelled "in the more advanced parts of the colonies, such as India" to adopt a new policy which called for the development and utilization of "inner capital resources." Britain, he had argued, "hopes that by keeping the entire capitalist structure under the financial domination of London, it will be able to utilize the available capital resources of the colonies to help British capital." But, he had predicted, this policy would serve only to postpone temporarily the collapse of the British capitalist system and with it the British Empire; for India's potential wealth was so great that money eventually would be available for export. He had concluded, "the little child that Britain is nursing may begin to kick before very long." Roy's comments, by implication, had gone beyond the Sixth Plenum resolution. In speaking of the dominions, he had held that Great Britain could not hope to maintain political control in the face of declining export capital.[8]

In the following year, while Roy was in China, Saumyendranath Tagore had submitted a report to the Political Secretariat of the ECCI on the economic situation in India, in which he had maintained that modern industry was developing rapidly. In discussing the report, Bukharin had remarked that it would appear that a process of "decolonization" had begun in India. Subsequently he appointed a special commission to look into the question.[9] It is important to note that the term "decolonization," which was later to be considered an anathema, had been included within the terms of reference of the commission. In connection with this project, Hugh P. Rathbone, a member of the CPGB, began collecting research materials for a study of "Industrial India."[10]

On his return from China, Roy had been asked to draft a statement on the basis of the preparatory work of the commission. He was assisted in this task by Hugh Rathbone. While Roy was confined to his bed in Moscow in early 1928, Rathbone was a frequent, almost daily, visitor.[11] Later, when Roy returned to Berlin, the two collaborated in the preparation of a book which was to have been entitled *The Decline and Fall of the British Empire*. Work on the project continued until Roy left Europe for India. The materials, which were packed and left in the office of a communist publishing firm, presumably were burned in a fascist raid.[12]

It was as the author of this document, prepared at the request of Bukharin, that Roy was condemned at the Sixth Congress. In it he employed the term "decolonization" in describing the process of gradual industrialization which he suggested might lead to dominion status. He wrote that

> the implication of the new policy is gradual "decolonization" of India which would be allowed eventually to evolve out of the status of "dependency" to Dominion Status. . . . The unavoidable process of gradual "decolonization" has in it the germs of the destruction of the empire.

However, Roy had contended that such an eventuality would benefit only the native bourgeoisie and would result in increased exploitation for the bulk of the Indian people. His main point had been that since the national bourgeoisie, under the given circumstances, could not be expected to continue to lead the struggle for national freedom "completely outside" the British empire, it was necessary to unite all the progressive forces in an effort to capture the leadership of the Congress party.[13] This point becomes quite clear when all of Roy's writings during this period are taken into account.

In articles published in *International Press Correspondence* in early 1928, Roy appeared to have second thoughts about the possibility of India achieving even dominion status by constitutional means. In these articles he took care to align himself with the position of the Sixth Plenum by making a clear distinction between economic concessions leading to a process of decolonization or industrialization and political concessions leading to dominion status. He argued that in spite of economic concessions to the Indian bourgeoisie, "more than a parliamentary fight must take place before even self-government within the Empire is granted."[14] He stated explicitly that the "fundamental principle of imperialist policy . . . is economic concession but political repression."[15]

At its Ninth Plenum (February 1928) the ECCI reversed itself on the question of British colonial policy. The leading Comintern economist, Eugene Varga, presented a thesis which held that Great Britain was now attempting to arrest industrial growth in India. The next month an entire issue of the *International Press Correspondence* was devoted to a long article by Varga entitled "Economics and Economic Policy in the Fourth Quarter of 1927," in which his thesis was set forth in some detail. Half of the sixteen-page article dealt with the topic "India, the Focus of the British Empire." The article summarized the new line on British colonial policy. Formerly it had been held that Great Britain had embarked on a long-range policy of industrialization in India at the time of World War I. Now it was suggested that this was merely a temporary policy created by emergency wartime conditions and that Great Britain had resumed its general policy of treating India as an agrarian appendage—as a source of raw materials and as a market for British export industries. The basis for this hypothesis was a marked decline in British capital exported to India since 1924.[16]

Varga's thesis was challenged by the British and Indian members of the Indian Commission when it came before that body in March and April. They acknowledged the arrest of capital exported to India, but contended that this was due to the economic depression resulting from the reorganization of the industries in Great Britain and the restoration of the gold standard. As such, it represented merely "a temporary deflection" of Britain's general policy of encouraging economic development in her colonies, rather than a permament resumption of economic restraints.[17]

The CPGB, in the weeks preceding the Sixth Congress, openly criticized Varga's thesis. In support of their own position they cited the 1922 Fiscal Commission Report, which had emphasized the advantages of India's industrial development—e.g., the creation of new sources of wealth and the enlargement of public revenues. They insisted that since the war Great Britain had pursued this aim as a "permanent economic policy," as evidenced by the imposition of tariffs, the provision of bounties to the iron and steel industry and the suspension, in 1925, of the cotton excise duty. The creation of the Agricultural Commission in 1926, they argued, was not to be interpreted, as Varga had, as a move counter to the policy of industrialization, but as a corollary to it. The purpose of the commission was to raise agricultural productivity by the introduction of modern agricultural methods, to provide an expanded home market for further industrial development.[18]

The spokesman for the ECCI position at the Sixth Congress was Kuusinen. In his speech he incorporated Varga's economic analysis. He minimized the economic concessions which Great Britain had made to Indian industry since the war. Conceding that in the period 1921-23 almost a quarter of the capital exported by Great Britain had gone to India, he argued that this flow had diminished drastically in recent years. Even at its height, he contended, most of the amount was in the form of government loans. Only ten per-

14. M. N. Roy and Ellen Roy with Congress party workers in the U.P., 1938.

15. M. N. Roy in his study at his home in Dehra Dun in the early 1950's.

cent at the most was invested directly in Indian industry. The British delegate, Robin Page Arnot, later asked what happened to the ninety percent of the capital exported to India in the form of loans. "You don't suggest that they buy champagne with it and drink it at Simla! Not at all!" That ten million pounds, he asserted, is invested in the Indian economy.[19] Kuusinen was careful to point out, however, that he was not asserting that a "complete throttling of industrial development in India" was occurring. This would be impossible. Industrial development would continue, despite Britain's opposition, although "very slowly."

Kuusinen attacked the views of Roy and certain members of the CPGB—he mentioned specifically Palme Dutt and Hugh Rathbone—on the question of British economic policy. They had held out the prospect of "a decolonization of India by British imperialism." "This," he said, "was a dangerous term." As examples of this point of view, he quoted passages from Palme Dutt's book, *Modern India*, and from the draft resolution on the Indian question prepared by Roy the previous October.[20]

Either out of ignorance or for other reasons, a number of speakers at the congress misrepresented the views of the proponents of the decolonization thesis by equating it with the Social Democratic belief in the progressive and liberating role of imperialism in the colonies. The "revisionists," headed by Bernstein, had first postulated such a role for advanced industrial countries as early as the 1890's. This theory was later adopted by the Second International at Brussels. At the time of the Sixth Congress, it was reflected in the theory of "gradualism" espoused by the British Labour party. According to this view the progressive modernization of the Indian economy would result in a steady rise of the standard of living of the Indian worker, which in turn would encroach gradually upon the margin of "super-profit" until imperialist exploitation ceased to exist.

Stalin designated the Social Democrats with their beguiling theories as the communists' most dangerous enemy. Kuusinen, in his concluding speech before the congress, stated that "perhaps we have spoken too much about the decolonization theory," but warned that an error on this question would have grave consequences. He recalled a recent article by "the Austrian social imperialist, Renner—a dangerous enemy"—in which he had held forth the perspective of the entire world becoming industrialized. In his conception, according to Kuusinen, the socialist world revolution would be postponed until after the proletariat had become a majority everywhere, including the colonies. "This," he said, "was the socialist conception against which we must carry on a sharp struggle and the falsity of which we must prove to every worker."[21]

It was feared that the concept of decolonization, if allowed to stand, would have a devitalizing effect on colonial nationalist movements. Not only did it come dangerously close to the views of the European Social Democrats, but it also supported moderating influences in India which sought political advancement either by constitutional or, at least, by nonviolent means. For psychological reasons, if for no other, the term and all it suggested was to be avoided. This motivation was clearly evident in one of Kuusinen's speeches in which he stated:

> If any of the Indian comrades have doubts as to the anti-industrialization tendency of the British policy in India, I would like them to make up their minds on this question once and for all. It depends a great deal on this if the immediate main task of the Communist Party of India is correctly understood, namely the task of relieving, by Communist agitation, the mass of the Indian peasantry and the proletariat of the illusion that the policy of British imperialism can make the decolonization of India a reality, or even bring it nearer. . . . Every Indian worker must realize that the British sahib is a robber and will never carry out the decolonization of India. The liberation of India is a mission for which history has destined the Indian proletariat and peasantry. The Communist Party of India is to play a leading role in this struggle, and its foremost task in the preparation of this liberation

> struggle is to dispose of any illusion in regard to decolonization through imperialism, and to expose and combat any illusions of this kind spread . . . before the eyes of the masses.[22]

The Sixth World Congress is noteworthy as the last meeting of a Comintern body in which debate was allowed and oppositional views published in the official press organ, the *International Press Correspondence.* The debate, however, was not entirely free. Some chose to remain silent; others felt it necessary to strain logic to support the "official" position. Fighting for his own political life, Bukharin sought to free himself from those groups in the international communist movement who had looked to him for support. He denied that he had ever made reference to the "decolonization of India." Although he admitted having pointed to "the large investments of foreign capital" to be found there, he now observed a marked decline in the flow of capital to India.[23] He went so far as to state that the greatest danger to the communist movement came from the right, although he did not think that the remedy lay in purges.[24]

The British Delegation

The majority of the British delegation proved to be recalcitrant. They continued to voice their opposition to the Varga thesis. D. Petrovsky (alias A. J. Bennet), although a Comintern agent, was a member of the British delegation and it was he who opened the attack. He referred to the term "decolonization" as "the famous bogey." He denied that the concept as employed by certain delegates to the congress bore any relationship to the theories of the Social Democrats. "I am prepared to become a target for any possible attacks," he said, "yet I prefer to speak about 'decolonization' rather than to join in the description of India as a village hinterland of the British Empire." Kuusinen, in presenting the ECCI position, had held that "the colonies in their relationship to the so-called 'motherlands' are always transformed into an agrarian hinterland for the industrial city, an agrarian appendage to the vastly bloated body of the capitalist big industries." Petrovsky remarked sarcastically that Kuusinen must have had in mind the end of the last century. The thesis, he said, flies in the face of the widespread industrial unrest in India involving thousands of workers.[25] If India is an agrarian appendage, there would be no prospect for the development of class struggle. Instead of increased numbers of workers, there would be only hordes of pauperized peasants. Later in the debate, Petrovsky defended certain British and Indian delegates who had been the targets of "uncalled-for attack," for acknowledging decolonization in the sense of industrialization. He referred to an earlier statement of the British delegation which held that "no matter what words are used, it never can mean a process of withdrawal, of automatic 'decolonization,' of peaceful liberation, etc. The leech does not withdraw its suckers till it is forced from the body of the victim."[26]

Petrovsky's attack on the Varga thesis may appear strange in view of his relationship to the Comintern. But it should be noted that he supported Stalin's known position on colonial policy. Industrialization, he said, would result in a compromise between the Indian bourgeoisie and its British counterparts. Indeed a large part of this group was already acting "in a coalition with British imperialism." He objected to the notion that the Indian bourgeoisie still had a revolutionary role to play: "Everyone who speaks of any shadow of a possibility of the national bourgeoisie playing any positive active role in the nationalist revolution is spreading illusions."[27]

Andrew Rothstein continued the theme begun by Petrovsky. He characterized Varga's views on Indian economic development as "a travesty of the actual situation."[28] Clemens Dutt also participated in the debate. Although he was officially a representative of India, he was a leading member of the CPGB. Dutt objected to the frame of reference of certain Russian delegates in the debate. They seemed to think there were two sharply opposed views in question—that it was the policy of Great Britain either to industrialize India "by leaps and bounds" or to keep her in economic bondage. Neither of these alternatives was correct. He would prefer to say that "the development of capitalist industry is inevitable and that British imperialism seeks to control it in such a way to receive the maximum benefit." He did not draw the same conclusion, however, as had Petrovsky. Although the Indian national bourgeoisie was extremely unreliable, this did not mean that communist tactics should consist of "attack and onslaught all along the line." It was still possible to utilize the "nationalist reformist oppositional struggle." He also objected to the summary dismissal of the Peasants' and Workers' party. He held that it constituted "an important route through which the Communists are finding their way to the masses," but he agreed that it should not be allowed to become, in practice, a substitute for the CPI.[29]

The tone of the polemics may be gauged by a statement which Andrew Rothstein made on behalf of the members of the British delegation. In it he protested against "all the accusations, which unfortunately are becoming almost a mechanical reaction, against those who dare to criticize a thesis put forward in the name of the ECCI." He rejected "with contempt" the insinuation that certain members of the British delegation had suggested that Great Britain was playing a progressive role in her colonies. On the contrary, he argued, these persons were of the opinion that "imperialism heightens the class contradictions and class oppression."[30]

Kuusinen yielded to the force of the criticisms and acknowledged that the ECCI draft theses contained errors "of a fundamental nature." As a result of the discussions, he felt that the word "decolonization" had been "killed." He conceded that most of the British delegates in their more recent articles and statements had clearly differentiated their position from that of the Social Democrats. No such consideration, however, was given to Roy. Overlooking Roy's current articles on the subject, Kuusinen accused him of propounding the view that "British imperialism will lead the Indian people by the hand to freedom" and denounced him as a "lackey of imperialism."

Kuusinen observed that the development of native capitalism was not being denied altogether in the theses. However, he characterized such economic growth as "an undesired by-product of the imperialist exploitation," which had occurred "in spite of the hampering tendencies on the part of imperialism." He conceded that in India industrialization "forges ahead," but, contradicting himself, he continued, "even if it proceeds with great difficulty, and at a retarded pace." Obviously Kuusinen was having great difficulty defending Varga's thesis before its critics.

He next proceeded to discuss the political implications of the above analysis. He disagreed with Petrovsky that the Indian national bourgeoisie had gone over completely to the opposition, but he warned that a part of this class already was drawing close to the camp of counterrevolution. The Comintern must never forget, he said, that the colonial bourgeoisie will ultimately play "the role of the executioner, the same as the Chinese bourgeoisie has already played."[31]

The theses as moved by Kuusinen were adopted with the reservation that they would serve, not as a final authority, but as the basis of the colonial theses to be elaborated by a specially appointed Colonial Commission. The British delegation—with the exception of four members—voted against such a move and tabled an amendment to the theses. They were responsible, they said, only for what they themselves had written, not what Roy or others might have said about decolonization. They agreed with the ECCI that there could be no decolonization, "in the real sense of the word," without a revolution. At the same time, they insisted that there could be no communist revolution without industrialization and felt that the theses had underestimated the strength of the proletariat in India. The ECCI, they charged, had drawn a "fantastic picture of the policy of finance capital as a kind of deviation from that of capitalism as a whole." The theses violated an important distinction made by Lenin "between the classical era of capitalism and the era of finance capital, when it is the search for higher rates of profit, and not the requirements of industries in the metropolis, that is the determining factor." Finally, they made an "emphatic protest" against "the tone and method of polemics" employed by Kuusinen and others. Before a final decision is reached, questions should be debated "freely, frankly and fearlessly. . . . The method of hurrying to tie labels on comrades who hold different opinions," they predicted, would destroy independent thought and make a sham of the Comintern.[32]

Theses on the Revolutionary Movement in the Colonies

A special commission was duly appointed. It included, among others, Bukharin, Kuusinen, Clemens Dutt, and Petrovsky. The latter two were the sole representatives of the CPI and the CPGB respectively, although Dutt was not a native of India, nor was Petrovsky a native of Great Britain.[33] Ten days later, Kuusinen reported that the Colonial Commission had completed its task. The portion of the theses dealing with tactical questions, he said, had been amended to apply only to China, India, Egypt, and Indonesia—"certainly the most important colonial countries." He maintained that the commission had been in complete agreement "with the fundamental line" of the former draft concerning the character of "imperialist colonial policy." He added, however, that a good many addenda had been elaborated "to make the subject clearer." The tactical line had not been changed at all.[34]

The "Theses on the Revolutionary Movement in the Colonies and Semi-Colonies" in their final form, as adopted by the Sixth Comintern Congress, maintained that British imperialism had returned to its policy of "hindering the industrial development of India." "All the chatter of the imperialists and their lackeys about the policy of decolonization," it stated, "reveals itself as nothing but an imperialist lie." As a consequence, the growth of class consciousness among the workers had been retarded and the work of systematic agitation among them made more difficult.[35] However, the theses on "The International Situation and the Tasks of the Comintern," adopted by the same congress, gave an entirely contradictory picture of the Indian proletariat. There, the wave of industrial unrest that had swept India in the past year was fully acknowledged.[36]

The "Theses on the Revolutionary Movement in the Colonies and Semi-Colonies" reveal the extent of the influence of the China episode on the Comintern's colonial policy and, more specifically, on its attitude toward the Indian National Congress. In a review of the Comintern's experience in China, it was observed that the alliance of the Chinese communists with the Left Kuomintang had served more to screen the counterrevolutionary activities of the Left Kuomintang leaders than to advance the communist cause. If such an alliance had led the Chinese communists astray, how much greater was the danger in India, where political class consciousness was even less developed due to the infancy of Indian industry, the rapid turnover of her small labor force, the high rate of illiteracy, and the prevalence of religion and caste prejudices.

However, the Sixth Congress did not call for a complete break with the nationalist parties. In colonial countries, the trading bourgeoisie, or compradore bourgeoisie, together with "feudal landlords" and high-ranking native officials, were defenders of foreign rule. But "the remaining portions of the bourgeoisie, especially the portion reflecting the interests of native industry," were said to manifest "a special vacillating compromising tendency, designated as nationalist reformism." Although in China the national bourgeoisie had already joined the "camp of counterrevolution," it was held that in India and Egypt there still existed, "for the time being, a typical bourgeois-nationalist movement—an opportunistic movement, subject to great vacillations, balancing between imperialism and revolution." In India the native bourgeoisie continually compromised with imperialism, but it would not abandon the nationalist movement, "as long as the danger of class revolution . . . has not become immediate, acute and menacing."

The resolution on colonial policy reflected an uneasy compromise between those who, like Stalin, wished to make a pronounced shift to the left and those who, like Bukharin, wanted to avoid a drastic change in policy. It was held that an underestimation of the "national reformist" tendency of the national bourgeoisie may lead to "an insufficiently accurate political and organizational delimitation of the proletariat from the peasantry" and to the blurring of revolutionary slogans, such as those of agrarian revolution. This was said to have been the fundamental error made by the Chinese communists. To avoid this error, Indian communists were advised to concentrate their efforts on organizing a "single, illegal, independent, and centralized Party." The formation of workers' and peasants' parties, which could fall too easily under petty bourgeois influence, was "not recommended."

At the same time, an underestimation of the "national revolutionary" tendency of the national bourgeoisie, which enjoys widespread support among the people, may lead to "a sectarian policy and to the isolation of the communists from the toiling masses." Any attempt to "skip over" the present stage of the revolutionary movement would be especially harmful in India, where much work remains to be done in strengthening the communist party and trade-union organizations and in "liberating" the people from "the influence of the national reformist bourgeoisie." Moreover, the Indian nationalist leaders were said to be still playing a revolutionary role. Demonstrations of opposition against foreign rule, "even if they do not have any deep foundation," help to awaken political consciousness among "the wide masses of toilers." Consequently, Indian communists were instructed to utilize every conflict and to "broaden their significance." Although they were to eschew "any kind of bloc" with nationalist organizations, they were authorized to establish "temporary agreements" with them, as long as they did not hinder "agitation among the masses."

Although the CPI was warned against actions which could lead to political isolation, this advice was largely negated by the heavy emphasis the theses placed on attacking nationalist leaders. Communists, it was stated, must know how to take advantage of nationalist struggles and at the same time conduct "the most relentless ideological and political struggle against bourgeois nationalism and against the slightest signs of its influence inside the labor movement." However, no instructions on how this was to be achieved were offered.[37]

The Indian Delegation

The CPI had originally been allotted ten votes at the Sixth Comintern Congress, but the party was unable to meet its quota. The Indian delegation consisted of only seven members—Clemens Dutt, Shaukat Usmani, Saumyendranath Tagore, Ghulam Ambia Khan Luhani, Mohammed Shafiq, and Masood Ali Shah. Habib Ahmed Nasin also attended the conference, but was officially a delegate to the Communist Youth Conference, which was also being held in Moscow. The delegation had three decisive votes and three advisory votes.[38] Clemens Dutt and Shaukat Usmani exercised full voting rights. It has not been possible to determine the third person in this group. Probably, however, it was Mohammed Shafiq who, as the first general secretary of the émigré CPI, must have been accorded a special place in the Indian delegation. Muzaffar Ahmed claims that neither Luhani nor Tagore were allotted voting rights at the congress. He also states that Masood Ali Shah, an ex-administrative officer in the U.P. government, was under suspicion as a British spy before he left to attend the congress.[39] On the basis of this information, it may be conjectured that it was Luhani, Tagore, and Shah who held consultative votes.

It was a strange delegation. Clemens Dutt was a member of the CPGB, not the CPI. Tagore was a representative of the All-India Workers' and Peasants' party, rather than of the CPI.[40] Luhani was one of Roy's protégés in Europe. He had left India about 1913 and gone to London. Later he had joined Virendranath Chattopadhyaya's Berlin Committee.

In 1921, however, he defected from this group and joined forces with Roy. Before his assignment to Roy's headquarters in Europe, he had worked for a time in the Information Department of the Comintern at Moscow.[41]

Shaukat Usmani had been refused credentials by the CPI, and he and his three companions—Mohammed Shafiq, Masood Ali Shah, and Habib Ahmed Nasin—had traveled to Moscow with forged letters of introduction.[42] In reply to a query from London before the Sixth Congress was convened, Philip Spratt had reported that Usmani and his group did not represent the CPI.[43] Having joined the émigré party in Moscow in 1921, Usmani was one of the founding members of the CPI. He was also one of the *muhajirun* who had been recruited by Roy in Tashkent. "Shaukat Usmani," a name he had adopted when he left India to begin his pilgrimage, meant "the glory of the Usmanias." The Moslem Caliph, the Sultan of Turkey, was a descendant of the Usmania dynasty. Usmani's given name was Maula Bukhsh.[44] A devout Moslem, he became an equally devout communist, but after his release from prison, following his conviction in the Kanpur Conspiracy Case, he had fallen into disrepute among his communist colleagues in India.

On the question of supporting bourgeois nationalism, Tagore's views, as expressed at the Sixth Congress, were more radical than the ECCI draft resolution. He objected to the formation of even "temporary agreements" with the Indian national bourgeoisie which, he contended, was conducting "absolutely no revolutionary program at all" against their British rulers.[45] In this respect, Tagore's position foreshadowed the tactics the Comintern was to adopt the following year. He also disagreed strongly with Varga's analysis of British colonial policy. It was the industrialization of India, not the retardation of this development, as Varga had maintained, that was pushing the Indian bourgeoisie into the camp of counterrevolution. He stated: "We find that to the same degree as the hindrance to the way of capitalist development of India has been removed by British imperialism, the bourgeoisie is sliding more and more toward cooperation and one group after the other is capitulating to imperialism."[46]

A representative of the All-India Workers' and Peasants' party, Tagore vigorously defended this type of two-class party against its critics at the congress. "Some comrades," he said, are "scared with the nightmare, which is the result of their own irrational fantasy, that the Workers' and Peasants' Party is a substitute for the Communist Party." Apparently unaware of Roy's earlier instructions to the Indian communists on this matter, he insisted that nobody had ever put forward such a proposition. After recounting the accomplishments of the party, he protested, "now we are told to liquidate all these Workers' and Peasants' Parties. This is pure and simple professional dogmatism against which Lenin warned us so many times."[47]

Because of his association with Roy, G.A.K. Luhani was preoccupied at the congress with defending himself on the question of decolonization. His position must have been an uncomfortable one. At one point in the proceedings, he found it necessary to issue a declaration stating that he had "nothing whatever to do with the so-called 'decolonization of India' theory," as presented by Kuusinen and others. Their interpretation of the theory, he asserted, was a "complete travesty and misinterpretation" of the views of those who, like himself, had used the term "decolonization" in a provisional sense. He protested that the report of the special commission on the subject, against which so much had been said, had not been made available to the delegates. This "method of controversy," he charged, was, "to put it mildly, unfair" both to the delegates and to those whose views were being questioned.[48]

Shaukat Usmani, unlike Tagore and Luhani, supported Stalin on every issue connected with colonial policy. He endorsed Varga's thesis, attacked Roy and the members of the British delegation for their views on decolonization, urged a cautious approach to the national bourgeoisie, and criticized the All-India Workers' and Peasants' party.[49] Usmani's arguments were so strained, so illogical, and so innocent of elementary Marxist-Leninist theory that he must have been, at times, a source of embarrassment to those he sought to support. On decolonization he admitted that "it would be un-Marxian to say that there was no industrial development in India." He went on to declare, however, that only those industries that were profitable to Great Britain, rather than to India, were being developed. These he identified as "the hydro-electric and aviation industries," which, he claimed, constituted "a market for the British-produced machinery and materials necessary for aviation and hydro-electric works."[50]

In the 1850's Karl Marx had written a series of articles on India for the *New York Daily Tribune*. In these articles, he had depicted Great Britain as "the unconscious tool of history."[51] Though intent only on exploitation, he had argued, Great Britain had sown unwittingly the seeds of India's future regeneration. India's railway system, constructed for the exclusive purpose of extracting raw materials at the least expense, was "the forerunner of modern industry"; for once railroads were introduced into a country possessing iron and coal, it would not be long before such raw materials were utilized in fabricating railroad equipment and in "all those industrial processes necessary to meet the immediate and current wants of railway locomotion, and out of which there must grow the application of machinery to those branches of industry not immediately connected with railways." Marx had warned that the industrialization of India would be a painfully slow process: "The work of regeneration transpires through a heap of ruins." But, in a mood of cautious optimism, he wrote that "nevertheless, it has begun."[52]

In contrast to Marx's writings on the subject, Usmani contended at the Sixth Congress that industrialization was a corollary of the development of railroads in imperialist countries only. In India the railway system been built solely for extractive and "military-strategic" purposes. Consequently, according to him, it could not possibly lead to the industrialization of the country. It was not a very convincing argument, to say the least. Usmani characterized the position of those who believed that Great Britain was playing a progressive role in the colonies as "nothing more than an open defence of imperialism."[53] In an obvious reference to Roy, he charged that "comrades who have been here [in Moscow] for about ten years cannot properly deal with the situation. They therefore grope in darkness and formulate such absurd theories as 'decolonization.'"[54]

Usmani dismissed the Workers' and Peasants' parties as having already fallen into the hands of "the philanthropic petty-bourgeoisie."[55] It was imperative that the Comintern assist Indian communists in organizing a strong communist party. Such work, he charged, had been neglected in the past.[56] For his allegiance to Stalin, Usmani was elected to the Presidium of the Comintern along with such notables as Stalin, Bukharin, Kuusinen, Manuilsky, and Molotov. J. T. Murphy, one of the four members of the CPGB who had voted in favor of the colonial theses, was similarly rewarded.[57]

Usmani's apotheosis, however, was short-lived. He returned to India in December 1928, but the three Indians who accompanied him to Moscow were detained. A few months later he was arrested in connection with the Meerut Conspiracy Case. While in prison undergoing trial, he was put forward as a candidate for Parliament by the CPGB to oppose Sir John Simon. In late 1932, shortly before a verdict was reached in the extraordinarily lengthy Meerut trial, he learned that two of his traveling companions—Masood Ali Shah and Habib Ahmed Nasin—had been shot in Moscow as British agents. On receipt of this news, he suffered a nervous breakdown. Already at odds with the CPI for his unauthorized trip to Moscow, he was subsequently expelled from the party. Mohammed Shafiq, who had also gone to Moscow with Usmani, returned to India in 1932, but played no further role in the CPI.[58]

The Tenth Plenum of the ECCI

By the time of the Tenth Plenum of the ECCI (July 3-19, 1929), Stalin had consolidated his power further and consequently he was able to compel the Comintern executive to adopt a tough "ultra-left" policy. Tactical agreements with Indian nationalists, which the Sixth Congress had condoned, were to be abandoned in favor of a policy of "ruthless struggle against the Indian bourgeoisie."[59] Subsequently, the CPI was instructed to sever all ties with the nationalist movement and to attack all sections of the Congress party, including the left-wing group led by Jawaharlal Nehru.[60] The Independence for India League was characterized by the Russian leaders as a "vague organization of intellectuals," some of whose leaders—the reference here was to Subhas Chandra Bose—were "inclined toward fascism."[61] Both Mahatma Gandhi and Jawaharlal Nehru were condemned for attempting "to stifle the rise of the revolutionary movement" and channel it toward moderate "bourgeois-reformism."[62]

Members of the CPGB who had failed to support the Varga thesis did not escape retribution. Compelling the British party to conform to ECCI directives had always presented a special problem to the Russian leaders. Unlike communist parties elsewhere, which were divided along factional lines, the British party presented a solid front against outside interference. Manuilsky complained at the Tenth Plenum that "the fundamental problems" of the Comintern which were being passionately debated in other parties had failed to stir the British party. He continued:

> The German comrades carefully weigh every word spoken by everybody. They allow no deviation from the line, they attack the least deviation, respecting no persons. . . . Yet in the British party there is a sort of special system which may be characterized thus: the party is a society of great friends.[63]

Following the failure of the 1926 general strike in Great Britain, CPGB membership had declined precipitously from a height of 12,000 in late 1926 to a low of 3,200 by the end of 1929. This slump, which had been aggravated by the new Comintern policy of "class against class," provided an excuse for intervention on the part of the ECCI. At the Tenth Plenum, British party leaders were criticized sharply for their "errors." They were compelled by the ECCI to convene a special party congress to elect new officers. At the congress, which met in November 1929, Campbell was removed from the party Politburo. Andrew Rothstein and Tom Bell, among others, were dropped from the Central Committee. Harry Pollitt and Rajani Palme Dutt, with Stalin's blessing, emerged as the new leaders of the British party.[64]

Roy's Expulsion from the Comintern

After returning to Berlin from Moscow in March 1928, Roy eventually joined forces with the Communist Party of Germany (Opposition). He met frequently with two of its leading members—August Thalheimer and Heinrich Brandler. Other members of the group included Paul Böttcher, Jakob Walcher, Rosi Wolfstein, and Arthur Rosenberg.[65]

Roy became an admirer of Thalheimer whom he later regarded as one of his two political gurus—the other being Borodin.[66] Both Thalheimer and Brandler had long been advocates of a united front policy. As a result of his experience in the abortive Kapp putsch in 1921, Brandler had been converted to a "gradualist" approach and had publicly declared, a few months later, his belief in the possibility of a nonviolent revolution in Germany due to the maturity and size of its working class. In 1923, as head of the Communist Party of Germany, he and his chief lieutenant, the party theoretician Thalheimer, proposed an alliance with the left wing of the Social Democratic party with a view to forming a coalition government in the provinces of Saxony and Thuringia, where together the two parties constituted a majority. The left-wing socialists, with the support of the communists, had already formed governments in these two provinces and now it was proposed that they share power with the communists. Trotsky initially opposed the plan but eventually gave it his support after converting it into the preparatory stage of a far more radical scheme involving a general uprising throughout Germany. It was anticipated that the government of the Reich would intervene and that the resistance of these provinces would spark the German revolution. When the communists entered the Saxony government in October, the Reichswehr promptly entered the province and deposed the ministers. Contrary to expectations, neither the left-wing socialists nor the workers offered any resistance. As was to happen later in the case of the CCP, the debacle of the German Communist party became an issue in the power struggle between Stalin and Trotsky. As a consequence, the entire responsibility for the failure of the October revolution was laid at the door of Brandler and his followers and of Karl Radek, the Comintern emissary in Germany at this time, although the plans had been devised in consultation with the Comintern officials in Moscow. Brandler was charged with weak and indecisive leadership. A majority of the members of the German Communist party concurred. The left-wing leaders, Maslow and Ruth Fischer, then assumed the helm of the party only to be replaced two years later, on the intervention of Moscow, by the more pliable Ernst Thälmann. In 1928 the Brandler group was expelled from the party.[67]

Roy's move into the camp of the Communist Opposition was a gradual one. It was not until over a year after his arrival in Berlin that he openly aligned himself with this group by contributing an article to their press criticizing the German Communist party for having called a general strike, which had seriously miscarried,[b] for May Day, 1929.[68]

[b] Only the workers of a single candy factory responded to the call for a general strike (Franz Borkenau, *World Communism: A History of the Communist International*, p. 340).

The proceedings of the Tenth Plenum left little doubt that Roy's expulsion from the Comintern was but a matter of time. He had already been removed from the ECCI the year before.[69] When Kuusinen in his address mentioned that "comrade Roy" had contributed to the press of "the Brandlerite renegades," he was interrupted by delegates who shouted "he is no longer our comrade."[70]

While in Berlin Roy had continued to contribute articles to the *International Press Correspondence*. Between the Sixth Congress and the Tenth Plenum, no less than five of his articles had appeared in the journal. In them he had implicitly rejected the new Comintern line, especially as it was applied to India.[c] Alluding to these writings, Kuusinen noted at the Tenth Plenum that Roy could not forgive the Comintern leaders for forsaking an alliance with the Independence for India League. Mocking Roy's concern that certain members of the League might return to the fold of the "bourgeois capitulators" as a result of the Comintern line, Kuusinen explained that the loss of "the more wobbly leaders of the petty-bourgeoisie" would be no cause for grief.

Solomon A. Lozovsky, the head of the Red International Trade Union, blamed Roy—the Comintern's main link with Indian communists—for the weakness of the CPI. Roy, he charged, was a menshevik, who would be content to hang on to the coattails of the national bourgeoisie. The ECCI, he concluded, must assist the CPI in the task of "purging it from every variety of overt and covert Mensheviks."[71]

G.A.K. Luhani, who had defended himself and others associated with the decolonization theory the year before, used the platform of the Tenth Plenum to recant his former position.[d] He avowed that although he had been in error in the past, he was now in complete accord with the Sixth Comintern Congress on the question of British colonial

[c] The content of these articles will be discussed in more detail in the next chapter.

[d] Luhani never returned to India. He died at an advanced age in the Soviet Union.

policy. Just as he once had abandoned Virendranath Chattopadhyaya, he now repudiated Roy, whom he charged with betraying the Indian revolution and deceiving the Comintern with "double political bookkeeping." He equated Roy with Jawaharlal Nehru—"an agent of the reformist national bourgeoisie." Roy was characterized as "a Nehru" with wider European experience and greater skill in masking counterrevolutionary programs with "pseudo-radical phraseology."[72]

M. N. Roy was expelled from the Comintern in September 1929.[73] That same month he began a series of articles on the topic "The Crisis in the Comintern" which appeared in the Brandler journal, *Gegen den Strom*[74]—the theoretical organ of the German Oppositionists. The following December, a formal announcement of Roy's expulsion appeared in the *International Press Correspondence*. The cause given for this action was his contribution to the press of the Communist Opposition group in Germany. The announcement read in part:

> In accordance with the resolution of the Tenth Plenum of the ECCI on the international situation and the tasks of the Communist International, Paragraph 9, and the decisions of the ECCI of 19 December, 1928 according to which adherents of the Brandler organization cannot be members of the Communist International, the Presidium of the ECCI declares that Roy, by contributing to the Brandler press and supporting the Brandler organizations, has placed himself outside the ranks of the Communist International and is to be considered as expelled from the Communist International.[75]

In the 1930 edition of the *Bolshaia Sovetskaia Entsiklopediia*, Roy was officially designated a "renegade."[76]

Thus, after years of warning the Comintern against the dangers of alliances with anti-colonialist nationalists, Roy somewhat ironically found himself opposing "left-sectarianism." Some have charged Roy with political inconsistency. Certainly his views were modified as his experience widened and his knowledge deepened. But Roy, with considerable justification, has claimed that it was not he so much as his political milieu that had changed. He would have quoted with approval André Malraux's reply to similar charges: "It is not I who have evolved, but events."[77]

Roy fell from Stalin's grace as a result of his actions in China.[78] But, as it has been shown, neither this fact nor the charge laid against him by Saumyendranath Tagore is sufficient to account for his expulsion from the Comintern. Roy's downfall was related to the power struggle within the CPSU and to his penchant for voicing dissent at a time when Stalin was bent on acquiring absolute and unquestioned authority both within the CPSU and the Comintern. Roy himself has provided a clue to understanding the reasons underlying his political demise. In the mid-1930's he wrote that he had been

> the victim of some internal intrigue, the history of which had better not yet be written publicly. The desire of the Communist Party of Great Britain to establish its protectorate over the Indian communist movement had a good deal to do with it. The internal struggle of the Russian communist party also contributed to my victimization.[79]

As indicated earlier, the British party was too weak to be anything but a tool in the hands of Piatnitsky, himself the willing instrument of Stalin. As for the second charge, it might appear that Roy was referring here to the rivalry between Trotsky and Stalin, especially since Stalin's China policy, in which Roy was directly involved, was a subject of bitter dispute between the two. But, as we have seen, this was not the case. Roy differed with Trotsky's views on China and did not support them.

It was Roy's freely expressed views on India, not China, that clashed with Stalin's post-1927 colonial policy and placed him, inadvertently, in the camp of Nikolai Bukharin and other opponents of Stalin within the CPSU. Roy's influence in Moscow was not linked with the political fortunes of Trotsky but of Bukharin, the chief Russian spokesman within the Comintern and the Soviet Union's leading Marxist theoretician. Bukharin, A. I. Rykov, chairman of the Council of People's Commissars (Premier), and Mikhail P. Tomsky, head of the Russian unions, were the leaders of the Right Opposition group within the Russian party. This group opposed Stalin's First Five-Year Plan (1928-32) which called for forcing the pace of industrialization and collectivization of the land, regardless of the human costs involved.[80]

Roy's views had coincided with those of Bukharin throughout the 1920's. Under Lenin, Bukharin had been the leader of the "Left Communists," who had disagreed with Lenin's policy of seeking to utilize nationalist sentiment for revolutionary ends. On domestic issues this group had opposed Lenin's gradualist approach as typified by the New Economic Policy.[81] During this period, Roy, too, was known for his radical views. He was attracted to the "Left Communists" and particularly to Bukharin, whom he once described as "the most lovable of all the Bolshevik leaders."[82] Both Bukharin and Roy modified their views considerably in the mid-1920's, so that when Stalin adopted a middle position in 1926-27, they represented, for this brief period, the dominant viewpoint in the Comintern. This corresponded with Bukharin's elevation to the number one position in the Comintern after Zinoviev was forced to resign the chairmanship in November 1926.[83] Both Bukharin and Roy continued to modify their views in response to external changes, so that after Stalin veered to the left in 1927, they found themselves, for the first time, in the right wing of the communist movement.[e]

[e] This analysis, which indicates a gradual evolution of Roy's views throughout the 1920's, contrasts sharply with that of Gene D. Overstreet and Marshall Windmiller in their book, *Communism in India.* They hold that at about the time of the Sixth World Congress, Roy abruptly abandoned the position he had held for years just when the Comintern was moving toward it (pp. 132 and 142). The authors imply, without specifically charging, that this was done by Roy in order to dissociate himself from Trotsky, who had been defeated by

After securing the defeat of Trotsky and the Left Opposition, Stalin began an offensive against Bukharin and his group,[84] which represented the last remaining challenge to his authority in the communist party. Because of Bukharin's paramount position in the Comintern, Stalin's campaign against "right deviationists" could not help but spill over into that organization as well. Manuilsky revealed the equation which was made between Stalin's critics within the Soviet party and within the Comintern when he remarked:

> The underestimation of the forces of the proletariat by the opportunists in the international communist movement is closely connected with the right-wing elements in the Soviet Union who underestimate the forces of the working class of the Soviet Union in the struggle against the remnants of capitalism in the country. . . . The opportunist elements capitulate before capitalism by overestimating its strength. The tendency amongst certain circles in the Soviet Union not to place too much pressure upon the Kulak is the counterpart of the tactics of the right-wingers in the capitalist countries based upon a more or less peaceful parallel existence of the Social Democracy and the Communists in the international working class movement.[85]

The attack against "right deviationists" within the Soviet Union coincided with a purge of all of Bukharin's supporters within the international communist movement. A case in point was the Lovestone faction of the American Communist party. Jay Lovestone, as one of the chief supporters of the legal Workers' party, had been in line with

---

Stalin (pp. 98-100). This suggestion disregards the fact that Roy's and Trotsky's views on China, as noted earlier, were not identical. Moreover, Roy shared Bukharin's distrust of Trotsky, who, as the organizer of the Red Army and an advocate of a conscripted labor force, was suspected of "Bonapartism" (M. N. Roy, *M. N. Roy's Memoirs*, pp. 494-98). Because of their association of Roy with Trotsky, the authors were unable to find a satisfactory explanation for Roy's expulsion from the Comintern. The final answer, they concluded, "must await the opening of archival materials in the Soviet Union" (p. 144).

Comintern policies until 1927. He was the author of the theory of American "exceptionalism," which held that the crisis in world capitalism predicted by Varga would not occur in the United States—a view which had the same implication in relation to the most prosperous nation in the world as Bukharin's and Roy's theory of decolonization had in respect to the colonies; namely, that the time was not ripe for the adoption of an extreme course of action. When, in December 1928, Lovestone openly declared his support for Bukharin, with whom he agreed on international matters, he was summoned to Moscow.

Lovestone complied, but not before his faction had secured an overwhelming endorsement at the Sixth Convention of the American party (March 1-9, 1929). His group won ninety percent of the contests in the election of convention delegates. Against the known wishes of the Comintern, the convention elected Benjamin Gitlow as party secretary. The pro-Lovestone group also obtained a decided majority in the Central Executive Committee, the Political Committee, and the Secretariat. Arriving in Moscow in April, the Lovestone delegation was denounced as "opportunists" and asked to concede their errors. Of the ten members of the delegation, all but two refused. By the end of June, Lovestone, Gitlow, and Wolfe had been expelled from the party.[86]

Roy's expulsion coincided with the eclipse of Bukharin's influence in the communist movement. In addition to supporting the more moderate forces within his party, Bukharin tried to protect the right dissidents in communist parties abroad. He was opposed to the suppression of opinion either within the Soviet party or the Comintern, and reminded his fellow party members of the words which Lenin had once addressed to him and Zinoviev: "If you are going to expel all the not very obedient but clever people, and retain only the obedient fools, you will most assuredly ruin the party."[87]

Without Bukharin's assistance, it should be recalled, Roy would not have been able to leave Moscow in 1928. The fact that Roy's articles, attacking the leftward trend in the Comintern, continued to appear in the official organ of the Comintern, the *International Press Correspondence*, until as late as March 1929, can be attributed to the support he received from Bukharin. It was in February that Bukharin was removed from his post as editor of *Pravda* and censured in a party resolution for supporting "the conciliationist elements in the Comintern" who would "revise the decisions of the Presidium . . . on the expulsion of the rightists from the German Communist Party."[88]

Delegates to the Tenth Plenum, acting in accordance with the above decision of the Soviet party, voted to relieve Bukharin of his membership on the Presidium of the ECCI. Bukharin's errors, it was declared, in regard to the policy of his party, were "inseparably connected with his erroneous line in international policy." Bukharin was found guilty of contravening the decisions of the Sixth Congress by "slipping over to the opportunist denial of the fact of the ever-growing shakiness of capitalist-stabilization." Such a theory, it was held, served as "an ideological basis for all the Right elements in the Comintern" and was, in substance, a "reformist ideology" on the order of Hilferding's theory of the "recuperation of capitalism." Bukharin was accused of attempting "to discredit" the "healthy" and "absolutely necessary" process of "purging the Communist parties of social-democratic elements." His "lamentations" about the consequent disintegration of the Comintern were derided as simply a "cowardly" method of defending "Right elements."[89] Vyacheslav Molotov succeeded to his position as the chief Soviet spokesman in the Comintern. The following November, Bukharin was expelled from the ECCI and the Soviet Politburo.[90]

After Stalin began to move cautiously to the right once again in 1933, Bukharin was able to recoup, at least partially, his losses. In 1933, he was named a member of the Collegium of the People's Commissariat of Heavy Industry. The next year he became editor of *Izvestia* and in 1935 was appointed to the commission which was to draft a new constitution for the Soviet government. In the mid-1930's he was one of the few Soviet officials to speak out against Hitler and to warn that his regime was communism's mortal enemy, with whom there should be no compromise.[91]

The International Communist Opposition

The German Communist Opposition, which in 1929 claimed a dues-paying membership of 6,000, had fraternal organizations in the United States, France, Austria, Sweden, Czechoslovakia, and elsewhere. Collectively, they were known as the International Communist Opposition or Right Opposition.[92] The American group, which called themselves the Communist Party, USA (Majority Group), was composed of the former Lovestone faction of the American Communist party. The name of the new organization was inspired by the fact that between 1925 and 1928, with Stalin's blessing, its members had dominated the American party. The name was a misnomer, however, since most of the support it had enjoyed was withdrawn following the expulsion of its leaders from the Comintern in 1929.[93]

The International Communist Opposition objected to Stalin's abandonment of the united front in the wake of events in China. They felt that in Europe, instead of denouncing the socialists as the Comintern now instructed, communists should cooperate with all available progressive forces in a combined effort to stem the rising tide of fascism.[94] With respect to the colonial and semicolonial areas of the world, they held that, until complete independence was assured, communist groups should cooperate with all anti-imperialist forces, rather than, as Stalin demanded, dissociate themselves altogether from nationalist movements, which were growing steadily in strength.

There was no desire on the part of the opposition communists to emulate Trotsky's attempt to form a permanent organization in rivalry with the Comintern. They wished only to win support for their position within the international communist movement by propagandizing their views among the communist rank and file and by, in Roy's words, "flooding" the "official apparatus" with "new shareholders" enlisted by them.[95] By this means, it was hoped, the way would be left open for an eventual reconciliation with the Comintern as their views were corroborated by the unfolding pattern of events.[96] "The idea of opening a new shop in these days of depression," Roy held, would be not only "foolish" but "an unpardonable crime."[97]

If our hypothesis is correct, Roy declined in 1935 to reveal the nature of the factional struggle to which he had fallen victim because its final chapter had not yet been written. As long as Bukharin maintained a foothold in the Soviet hierarchy, there was some basis for hope that the "Right Oppositionists" abroad might be reinstated in the Comintern, and Roy, no doubt, did not want to compromise Bukharin's position by laying bare old wounds. With the arrest of Bukharin two years later, however, the Right Opposition was crushed. In March 1938 he was the chief defendant in the trial of the "Anti-Soviet Bloc of Rights and Trotskyites"—a reference to an alleged conspiratorial alliance which the two groups were charged with having formed in 1932-33. Bukharin and Rykov, along with sixteen others, were executed for treason. The remaining three of the accused were given long prison sentences. The third leader of the "right communists," Tomsky, had committed suicide in 1936.[98]

There is much to be said for Roy's assertion that his chief offense had been his "claim to the right of independent thinking."[99] Underlying Roy's attachment to the "right communists" and his subsequent expulsion was his critical mind and independent spirit which refused to be bound by the dictates of a rigid party discipline. Under Lenin he had acquired the reputation of being an "historical leftist." As the Comintern changed course under Stalin, he gravitated toward the right. Roy sought to justify his behavior on the grounds that "the duty of a revolutionary sometimes transgresses the narrow limits of arbitrary discipline."[100] But as Stalin consolidated his power, the margin of tolerance narrowed. As one who knew Roy intimately during this period, but for personal reasons had no cause to exaggerate Roy's virtues, wrote to the author:

> If he could not play the role he was able to, it was also due to this fact. He never kept quiet if it would have been wise to do so for his career. He never made a compromise on this field. He was till his sad end an idealist for the cause of humanity. Don't think me emphatic, this is my earnest belief.[101]

Roy remained in contact with members of the Communist Opposition and continued to contribute articles to their press until 1937. One of the principal reasons for his break with the group at this time was his defense of Stalin.[102] Only the year before he had written to them that he was still "a personal admirer" of Stalin, "who used to pride over our racial affinity, and called me 'gold.' Now, he won't appreciate me even as copper! But I have the weakness of giving the devil his due. And in my account his due is very considerable."[103] Despite his criticism of Stalin's policies and his expulsion from the Comintern, Roy retained a deep admiration and personal attachment for Stalin, whose friendship he had enjoyed until the China episode.[104] In India he loved to regale his friends with personal anecdotes about the Soviet leader.

Although Roy became increasingly critical of the policies of Stalin and the Soviet Union in later life and finally abandoned communism altogether, he never developed a personal revulsion to Stalin's regime nor to communism such as experienced by Arthur Koestler. Roy refused to believe accounts of Stalin's worst excesses and refrained from excusing the disappointing performance of Soviet communism by placing all responsibility for its failures, as Khrushchev was later to do, on a single personage. Roy remained too much of a Marxist to interpret historical events in terms of the will of individuals. To him greatness could be achieved only in the service of inexorable historical forces. On the occasion of Stalin's death in 1953, Roy eulogized him as "the most maligned man of our time." He felt that his iron rule had been required by the necessity to safeguard and consolidate the gains made by the Russian revolution. He wrote:

> No great man has ever been an angel. Greatness is always purchased at the cost of goodness. Stalin did not do anything worse. . . . Stalin was undoubtedly the tallest personality of our time, and as such is bound to leave his mark on history.[105]

The International Opposition was moribund by 1937. In America, Lovestone had erred in expecting that he would be able to retain his majority support in defiance of the Comintern. Stalin knew better. When Gitlow, defying a request to recant, had declared in Moscow that when he returned to the United States he would fight against the Comintern's decisions, Stalin retorted, "the only ones who will follow you will be your sweethearts and wives."[106] Figuratively speaking, he was correct. Only about two hundred of its members, or two percent of the membership, left the "official" communist party to join Lovestone's Opposition party.[107] For a time the German Opposition, strengthened by the adherence of veteran communist trade unionists, enjoyed a modest measure of success. But their bid for public support in the first provincial elections was rebuffed.[108]

The attempt of the International Opposition to gain reinstatement in the Comintern met a similar fate. Encouraged by the Comintern's gradual shift to the right, Opposition communists in 1934 formally requested permission to attend the Seventh World Congress with a view to effecting a reconciliation.[109] In reply, they were informed that this was a matter which should be decided on an individual basis by the various national sections. Discussions subsequently were held but these were abortive and their bid to rejoin the Comintern ultimately was rejected.[110]

Whatever hope still remained that Stalin might eventually welcome back those who had defied him in the past evaporated with the arrest of Bukharin in 1937. Disillusioned and demoralized, members of the opposition groups drifted apart. In America, some went into various anti-Stalinist radical groups such as A. J. Muste's American Workers' party.[111] Many eventually found places in the noncommunist labor movement. After altering its name to the Independent Labor League of America, the Opposition party lingered on until 1940, when it was dissolved.[112] In India, Roy's group of dissident communists and allies joined the Indian National Congress. After the outbreak of World War II, they formed their own political party, the Radical Democratic Party of India.

7. The Decline of Indian Communism

THROUGHOUT 1929 the Congress party made preparations for the lauching of a civil disobedience campaign against the British government. The year was climaxed by the declaration at the annual Congress session in Lahore of the goal of complete independence. The anti-government campaign, when it was launched the following April, met with an enthusiastic response by an aroused Indian public.

Indian communists, however, were unable to take advantage of the upsurge of nationalist, anti-colonialist sentiment that Gandhi had unleashed. Furthermore, the initial advantage that they had secured in the labor movement was soon dissipated. Ordinarily it would have been expected that communist influence would have increased during this turbulent period, but, in fact, after a short period of dynamic growth in 1927-28, communist strength declined precipitously. This failure can be attributed to three causes: the ultra-left course prescribed by the Sixth Comintern Congress, the anti-communist campaign launched by the government of India in 1928, and the Indian communists' own mistakes in the trade-union field. Following a discussion of the civil disobedience movement, each of these factors will be examined in turn.

The Civil Disobedience Movement

At its Calcutta session in December 1928, the Congress party had given the government of India an ultimatum: either dominion status was to be granted in one year or the party would return to the demand for complete independence to be followed by a campaign of nonviolent noncooperation. Throughout 1929 preparations were laid for launching a civil disobedience campaign against the government. In July the Working Committee resolved to advise Congress members to resign their seats in the legislatures should the *swaraj* (freedom) movement be launched.[1] In September the presidency of the Congress party passed symbolically from Motilal Nehru to his son Jawaharlal.

In an attempt to strengthen the position of the moderates within the Congress party and to forestall the threatened civil disobedience campaign, the viceroy of India, Lord Irwin, on October 31, 1929, one month before the Congress was to convene at Lahore, declared that it was the opinion of the British government "that the natural issue of India's constitutional progress" was the attainment of dominion status.[a] The viceroy also announced the convening of a Round Table Conference at which British and Indian representatives would confer on India's constitutional advancement.[2] This, too, was an attempt to conciliate Indian opinion, which had reacted strongly against the absence of any Indian members on the Simon Commission. It was the first time that the British government had conceded to Indians the right to share in the shaping of their own constitution.

In response to the viceroy's statement, leaders of the Congress party and several other political parties conferred at Delhi on November 1 and 2 and issued a manifesto accepting the invitation to participate in the Round Table discussions provided certain conditions were met. One of these provisos stipulated that discussions at the conference must be on the basis of full dominion status and that immediate changes must be made in the conduct of the government of India to approximate such status.[3] Some Congress leaders had evidently chosen to construe Lord Irwin's phrases as implying the extension of dominion status to India in the near future and to regard the forthcoming conference as the occasion for the drafting of such a law. When on November 11 the British prime minister assured the

[a] The Simon Commission Report issued the next year reflected a more conservative outlook. It contained no reference to the possible attainment of dominion status by India.

House of Commons that the viceroy's declaration did not imply any change in government policy,[4] these illusions were shattered.[b] Following this disclosure the Congress party withdrew its support of the manifesto.[5]

In December Jawaharlal Nehru presided over the emotionally-charged Lahore Congress session. The delegates were in no mood for conciliatory gestures. A few days earlier an attempt had been made to assassinate Lord Irwin. A resolution introduced by Gandhi deploring the incident and congratulating the viceroy and Lady Irwin on their escape was almost defeated. On a division vote, it passed by the narrow margin of 904 to 823.[6]

Nehru in his presidential address counseled Congress that those who wish to play for high stakes must dare to act boldly. "If we seek to achieve great things," he said, "it can only be through great dangers."[7] A few days later he wrote, "Who lives if India dies? Who dies if India lives?"[8] When the one year ultimatum expired at midnight on December 31, 1929, the Nehru Report was declared to have elapsed and a resolution was passed interpreting *swaraj* as complete independence. The Congress announced its intention to prepare for civil disobedience and an immediate boycott of the Central and Provincial Legislatures was proclaimed. At Madras independence had been declared as a distant goal; at Lahore it became an immediate objective. At Gandhi's insistence, however, the door was deliberately left open for a peaceful settlement of issues. The independence resolution stated that "nothing is to be gained *in the existing circumstances* by the Congress being represented at the proposed Round Table Conference." (Italics mine.)

[b] Dr. Saifuddin Kitchlew, Chairman of the Reception Committee, in his welcoming address at the Lahore Congress session reminded the delegates that the recent speeches in the British Parliament had made it "pre-eminently clear . . . [that] India is not going to get Dominion Status today or in the near future—in fact at this rate not for a long time—not for centuries to come." (Indian National Congress, *Report of the 44th Annual Session*, p. 17).

Subhas Chandra Bose's[c] efforts to delete the qualifying phrase in this sentence were defeated.[9]

On January 26, 1930, Indian nationalists celebrated their first Independence Day by the reading of the Lahore independence resolution and the hoisting of the national flag in public gatherings throughout India.[10] The event marked the beginning of a momentous year for the Indian nationalist movement.

Before embarking on the civil disobedience campaign Gandhi issued an eleven-point ultimatum, whose satisfaction alone, he declared, could forestall direct action. His principal demand was for the abolition of the salt tax, which he described as "the most iniquitous of all [taxes] from the poor man's standpoint."[11] Although it amounted to less than three annas (approximately four cents) per person per year, this tax constituted half the retail price of a basic necessity of life. It was a ready symbol, with which all sectors of Indian society could identify, of colonial oppression.

The remaining demands appealed to the special interests of various groups in India, but not to the industrial workers. For the peasants, already restless due to a sharp decline of agricultural prices resulting from world-wide depression, there was the demand for the reduction of land revenue. Other requests, such as the imposition of a protective tariff on foreign cloth, were attractive to the business community. The call for a reduction in the expenses of the administration had often been expressed by the middle classes. The demand for an amnesty for political prisoners appealed to radical nationalists.[12]

Accompanied by eight volunteers, Gandhi began his

[c] Bose also sought vainly to amend the independence resolution by calling for the establishment of a parallel government in India and the proclamation of general strikes in addition to a civil disobedience campaign. Gandhi in response stated that such a program was too ambitious in light of the fact that "the Congress flag does not at present fly even in one thousand villages" (*Report of the 44th Annual Session*, pp. 93, 127).

famous salt march from his *ashram* in Sabarmati, Gujarat, on March 11. From there he proceeded to Dandi (Surat) on the seacoast in order to commit a technical breach of the Salt Law, which prohibited the manufacture and sale of salt by private individuals. The government, hoping that the campaign could be contained, hesitated to act. But each day public interest and support grew. When Gandhi reached the sea on April 6 and performed his symbolic act, the response exceeded his expectations.[13] Throughout the country, Indians courted arrest by emulating his deed. Alarmed, the government arrested Gandhi and attempted to suppress the movement, but it was too late. Gandhi's arrest precipitated widespread defiance of civil authority. Within a short time the nationalist movement was broadened. Countless thousands of Indians, including peasants and women, participated for the first time in the independence struggle.[14]

The civil disobedience movement, once it was underway, did not long remain nonviolent. But this time, unlike 1922, Gandhi did not call off the campaign on this account. In Bengal, nationalist-revolutionary activity was revived. Most of the members of the province's secret societies, who had been arrested in the earlier terrorist campaign, were released by 1927-28. In April 1930, when the Congress party began its nonviolent campaign, a force of a hundred men attacked the police and military armories of Chittagong, killing eight of their defenders and escaping with a large quantity of arms and ammunition.[d] Following this incident a wave of terrorism, which was to last until 1934, spread throughout Bengal and the provinces of the U.P. and the Punjab as well.[15]

In the wake of civil disobedience, riots broke out in India's major cities and numerous confrontations were reported between local demonstrators and the police. Two of the most serious threats to British authority occurred in Bombay Presidency and the North-West Frontier. In May,

[d] All were later killed or captured.

the textile workers of Sholapur, a textile center in Bombay, managed to establish their own regime for a few days.[16] In the strategic city of Peshawar in the Frontier large-scale civil disobedience erupted on April 23. Two platoons of the Eighteenth Royal Garhwal Rifles refused an order to proceed to the scene on the grounds that they would not fight their own brethren. On the following day British troops were forced to abandon the town and for ten days local residents, under the leadership of the Gandhian disciple Khan Abdul Ghaffar Khan, "the frontier Gandhi," and his organization, the Khudai Khitmatgars (Servants of God), were in control. In June, a force of 1,500 tribal Afridis invaded the Peshawar district. Despite the support of the local populace, they were expelled by the British in a two-day battle, only to return, their number doubled, two months later.[17] To maintain control of the area local authorities felt it necessary to impose martial law for a five-month period.

Faced with a challenge of unprecedented magnitude, the government of India was compelled to make large-scale arrests. It has been estimated that by the summer of 1930, 60,000 congressmen, including many of the party leaders, were in prison.[18] Despite the absense of Congress leaders, however, the civil disobedience campaign continued on its own momentum. Although government officials in reviewing the events of 1930 were later to note a slackening of the movement toward the end of the year, they continued at the time to be alarmed by the course of events.[19]

The CPI Turns Left

The inaugural conference of the All-India Workers' and Peasants' party (WPP) was held in Calcutta, December 21-24, 1928, and was attended by representatives of the Workers' and Peasants' parties of Bombay, Bengal, the U.P., and the Punjab. A national executive was chosen, ten of whose sixteen members were either members of the CPI or avowed communists. Each of the four provincial parties was represented on the executive by four members.

Although highly critical of the Congress party, the Sixth Comintern Congress had stopped short of demanding a complete break with the Indian nationalist movement. The Calcutta conference of the WPP faithfully reflected this shift in line while at the same time failing to take into account the Comintern's discussions on decolonization and the criticisms directed at workers' and peasants' parties in general. The political resolution adopted at Calcutta accused the Congress party of retreating to "a timid Liberal programme of constitutional demands and communal conciliation." This was in reference to the Nehru Report, which was characterized as a "bourgeois-democratic scheme of a not very advanced type." The WPP declared that it could no longer entertain the prospective of capturing the Congress party because of its reactionary policy. Party members were forbidden to accept office in the Congress organization except with special permission. Temporarily, members of the WPP would be permitted to remain within the nationalist party, but only for the purpose of "exposing its reactionary leadership" and splitting off its "revolutionary sections." It was made clear that the WPP would attempt to play an independent role as soon as it felt strong enough to do so.

The Independence for India League, ironically, came under heavier attack in the resolution than the Congress party. The League, some of whose members were called "fascists" and "counterrevolutionaries," was defined as a "bourgeois organization" whose object was to impede the development of an independent mass movement. Its economic demands, such as the eight-hour day and unemployment compensation, it was claimed, were "calculated to bring Indian industrialism into line with modern bourgeois practice." Although they did not have to leave the Congress party immediately, members of the WPP were instructed not to join the League. The way was left open, however, for the party as a whole to join with the League in united front efforts.[20]

A few days after the WPP conference, Indian communists who had gathered in Calcutta met to discuss the new Comintern strategy. They decided to adopt the Colonial Thesis of the Sixth Comintern Congress as the basis for their work. Subsequently, a revised party constitution appeared which described the CPI as a section of the Comintern. The next meeting of the CPI was convened in Bombay, March 17-19. The Bombay meeting was attended by Dr. Gangadhar Moreswar Adhikari, who had only recently returned to India (on December 10) from his engineering studies in Berlin, where he had come under communist influence. At the meeting Dr. Adhikari outlined his proposals, which were accepted, for the reorganization of the party in order to meet the criticisms of the Comintern concerning its method of operation. Apparently no decision was taken at this time on the future of the WPP. A subcommittee was appointed to work out the details of Dr. Adhikari's suggestions, but before it could meet, the majority of its members were arrested in connection with the Meerut Conspiracy Case.[21]

At the Tenth Plenum of the ECCI in July 1929, Indian communists were criticized for failing to carry out the instructions of the Sixth Congress concerning workers' and peasants' parties. The existence of such parties, it was said, could "obliterate the bounds of the communist organization" and "drown the Communist party."[22] In India, Kuusinen reported, communists were expending their energies in building up workers' and peasants' parties—against the Comintern's advice—with the result that their "greatest weakness" was the lack of a "firmly established" communist party. To make matters worse, he charged, the so-called Workers' and Peasants' party had failed to take cognizance of the deepening agrarian crisis and had done almost no work among the peasantry.[23] Following the Tenth Plenum, communists in India were directed to disband the WPP and to eschew all relations with both the Congress party and the Independence League.[24] In line with the Comintern's new policies, Clemens Dutt in mid-

1929 criticized the WPP as too weak to "fulfill the needs of the proletariat" due to "the mixture of semi-reformist and class-conscious elements" represented within it. He predicted that the multi-class party would eventually collapse and be replaced by a "more firmly based revolutionary Communist party."[25] At the same time he declared that the Independence for India League, which had been launched "with such a flourish of trumpets," was virtually dead. He characterized Nehru's utterances on behalf of social change as a form of "feudal socialism" and as "the same sort of radical claptrap as is talked about independence."

As head of the International Secretariat of the League Against Imperialism, Virendranath Chattopadhyaya wrote to Nehru from Berlin at the end of the year accusing him of a "betrayal of the Indian masses" in signing the Delhi manifesto.[26] Nehru was incensed. His relationship with the League became progressively more strained and he was eventually expelled from it.[e] As president of the Indian National Congress he directed the following April that his party sever all connections with the League Against Imperialism.[27]

In December 1929, shortly before the Congress party adopted the independence resolution at Lahore, Clemens Dutt wrote that the fear of "advancing Indian workers and peasants" had led to reaction within the Indian nationalist movement. He claimed that since the Calcutta Congress session had adopted its one-year ultimatum, nothing had been done to strengthen the anti-imperialist struggle, and he predicted that at Lahore "the question of action against British imperialism, except perhaps in the most limited and unreal form, would once again be shelved." Noting that Congress membership had increased fourfold within the past year, he held nevertheless that "the mass following of

[e] Chattopadhyaya was replaced by Clemens Dutt as head of the League's International Secretariat in August 1931. The headquarters of the Secretariat were moved from Berlin to Paris and then to London following the Nazi putsch in March 1933 (Government of India, Home Department, *Communism in India*, 1935, p. 172).

the Congress" would soon begin to "fall away." Consequently, he said, the time was "ripe" for the Indian proletariat to assume the leadership of the struggle for both national and social emancipation. Unfortunately, he continued, the CPI was neither properly organized nor sufficiently developed to allow the Indian proletariat to play its historical role, and he called upon Indian communists to correct this deficiency.[28]

Rather than welcoming the civil disobedience movement when it got underway in 1930, the Comintern dismissed it as merely an "oppositional manoeuvre" forced on a reluctant Congress by the "pressure of the masses."[29] At the end of the year a document was published in *International Press Correspondence* entitled a "Draft Platform of Action of the C.P. of India," which called for the denunciation not only of Gandhi but of "left nationalist reformists" such as Jawaharlal Nehru and Subhas Chandra Bose, who were now considered to be "the most harmful and dangerous obstacles to victory of the Indian revolution" and whose exposure was held to be "the primary task" of the CPI. Indian communists were directed to work independently of the Congress party for the "violent overthrow of British rule" and "the establishment of a Soviet Government . . . an Indian Federal Workers' and Peasants' Soviet Republic."[30] The draft platform became the subject of heated discussion within the CPI. Although it gave pause to many, it was eventually adopted by the party as the basis of its program.[31] No better program could have been devised to lead Indian communists down the road to political isolation.

Government Offensive

Alarmed at the rapid growth of communist influence in India, especially within the labor movement, the government of India took the offensive in mid-1928. In an effort to dramatize the dangers of communism in India and to prepare the public for stern measures to come, in August the government released to the press the contents of a letter dated December 30, 1927, which Roy had written to the

Central Committee of the CPI and the WPP. This document later became known as the Assembly Letter after passages from it were read out in the Legislative Assembly on September 10 during the debate over the Public Safety Bill.[f] In it Roy urged the CPI to formally affiliate with the Comintern and the WPP with the League Against Imperialism. The letter was useful to the government in its anti-communist crusade because it revealed not only the international aspect of the communist conspiracy but also the attempt to use the WPP as a legal cover for communist activity in India and the extent of financial assistance and direction from Moscow via Roy's Foreign Bureau in Europe.[32]

The government's first targets were the British communist agents, who had been operating with such remarkable effect, within India. Under existing laws British nationals were immune from arrest and deportation unless they violated the common law. When the autumn session of the Indian Legislative Assembly was convened in September, the government of India, to tighten their defenses against communism, introduced the Public Safety (Removal from India) Bill.

The bill was energetically opposed within the Assembly by congressmen under the leadership of Motilal Nehru, nationalists under Lala Lajpat Rai,[g] and independents under Sir Purshotamdas Thakurdas.[33] Questions were raised concerning its constitutionality and the ultimate purposes which the measure was intended to serve. The elder Nehru argued that the bill violated the rights of Englishmen and was therefore repugnant to that section of the Government of India Act which denies the Indian Legislature the right to make laws affecting the unwritten constitution of the United Kingdom. The bill did not specifically

[f] On the same date the letter itself, said to be in Roy's own handwriting, was shown to members of the Assembly to counter denials of its authenticity.

[g] Lala Lajpat Rai died on November 16, 1928, as a result of injuries received in a *lathi*-charge by police while leading a boycott against the Simon Commission in Lahore.

refer to "communists," but provided for the expulsion of foreigners who advocated the overthrow of the government by force or violence and sought to foment or utilize industrial or agrarian unrest to that end. Consequently, Nehru predicted that it would not be long before the bill was applied to Indian communists and nationalists as well.[34]

Despite denials of any ulterior motives on its part, the government failed to secure passage of the bill. It was defeated 62 to 61 when the president of the Assembly broke a tie to vote against its adoption.[35] Revised to empower the government to seize money sent from abroad to finance communist agitation, the bill was resubmitted when the legislature was convened again in January. Motilal Nehru, predicting that the new clause would be used to cut his party from its sources of overseas support, argued that the bill was aimed as much against the Congress party as the CPI. "After all," he observed, "we are all revolutionaries." Both parties sought the subversion of the British government in India. The only difference between congressmen and communists, he continued, was on the question of method—whether violence was to be employed.[36]

The budget session of the Indian Legislative Assembly also considered and subsequently passed the Indian Trade Disputes Act (1929), which was designed to prevent lightning strikes, which had plagued the cotton mills of Bombay. The Royal Commission on Labor later criticized this measure for placing undue emphasis on the need for public order to the detriment of the labor movement.[37]

The debate over the Public Safety Bill might well have continued indefinitely and the measure allowed to die if it had not been for an act of violence perpetrated within the Assembly itself. When V. J. Patel, the president of the Assembly, rose to give a ruling in connection with the bill on April 8, two bombs were thrown at the government benches from the visitors' gallery by Bhagat Singh and Butukeshwara Datta, members of the Hindusthan Socialist Republican Army.[38] No one was killed, but several persons were injured. Although essentially a patriotic organization, definite links had been established between this secret society and the communist movement. Consequently this deed strengthened the resolve of government officials, already alarmed by the threat of mass civil disobedience, to stem the growth of communist influence in India. A few days after the incident, the viceroy, acting under the authority of a section of the Government of India Act which enabled him in case of emergency to promulgate ordinances for the peace and good government of British India, issued the "Public Safety Ordinance, 1929," which granted the government the same powers it had sought to secure through the legislature.[39]

The controversy over the Public Safety Bill helped arouse nationalist consciousness, as the Simon Boycott had done earlier. It also generated sympathy for the Indian communists, the momentary targets of the hated government's wrath. The debate in the Assembly over the bill's passage had shown that in face of the impending battle with the British *raj* the nationalists were willing to consider the communists as their allies. But the latter, out of deference to the new Comintern line, were unable to grasp the hand extended to them.

The government never found it necessary to employ the unpopular ordinance and it was withdrawn before the end of the year. In the meantime, other means had been found for dealing effectively with the communist challenge. Before the promulgation of the ordinance, officials had been challenged in the Assembly to use their existing powers against the communists and this was the course that was adopted. On March 20, 1929, thirty-one persons, including almost all of the important communist leaders and a number of trade unionists were arrested under warrants issued by the District Magistrate at Meerut under Section 121A of the Indian Penal Code of conspiring to deprive the King of His sovereignty of British India.[40] All of the leading members of the WPP—including the entire executive committee of the Girni Kamgar Union (GKU)—were detained.[41] Among the prominent members of the CPI and WPP arrested were: Alve, Bradley, Dange, Ghate, Jhabwala, Joglekar, Mirajkar, Nimbkar, and Spratt of the GKU; P. C. Joshi, secretary of the U.P. and Delhi Workers' and Peasants' party; Muzaffar Ahmed, Gopendra Chakravarty, Dharani Mohan Goswami, and Gopal Basak of the Bengal Workers' and Peasants' party; Abdul Majid and S. S. Josh of the Punjab Kirti Kisan party; Dr. G. M. Adhikari, who had joined both the Bombay Workers' and Peasants' party and the CPI after returning to India from Germany; and Shaukat Usmani, a newly-elected member of the Comintern Presidium.[h] In June the number of defendants was increased to thirty-two with the arrest of Hutchinson. A warrant was also issued for the arrest of Amir Haidar Khan, a member of the CPI, but he absconded before he could be brought to trial.[i] Most of the men were from Bombay and Calcutta. The remainder came from Allahabad, Dacca, Poona, Lucknow, Meerut, and other locations.[42]

The case was heard by a Special Magistrate, who, after lengthy hearings which lasted until mid-December, concluded that all of the accused, with the exception of Dhamavir Singh, should stand trial as charged.[43] Although Singh was a vice-president of the U.P. Workers' and Peasants' party, the court accepted his plea that he had never

[h] During the trial, Alve and Jhabwala, explaining they had joined the WPP because they shared its objective of working for the amelioration of working conditions, denied that they were communists and severed their connections with the communist movement. Nimbkar and Usmani were later expelled from the CPI. Gopal Basak was not formally admitted to the communist party until 1934, but he, too, was subsequently expelled. As noted elsewhere, Spratt left the CPGB in the mid-1930's. Hutchinson, never a member of the British party, returned to England and joined the Labour party after his acquittal by the Appeals court in 1933 (*The Times* [London], April 19, 1929, p. 16; Nov. 28, 1929, p. 13; and Jan. 16, 1930, p. 11; and Muzaffar Ahmed, *Communist Party of India: Years of Formation, 1921-1933*, pp. 34-35).

[i] Khan escaped abroad but returned to India in March 1931. He was engaged in trade-union organization in Madras when he was apprehended the following May. He was tried and sentenced to thirty months rigorous imprisonment. After his release he was under arrest again within a month on an additional charge (Government of India, Home Department, *Communism in India*, 1935, p. 179).

been a communist and as a follower of Gandhi was opposed to communist objectives and methods.[44]

The Meerut Conspiracy Trial before the Sessions Court, which began in late January 1930, was not concluded for another three years. The inordinate length of the Meerut trial, the longest in the history of British India, was due to the prosecutor's lack of discrimination in the presentation of evidence and the calling of witnesses,[j] the cumbersome nature of the Indian legal process, and the use of the trial for propaganda purposes by the defendants. The trial made political martyrs of the communists and gave them a powerful platform for the dissemination of their views. Elaborate statements of communist theory and practice were read by the accused and punctiliously recorded by the court. Because of intense public interest in the trial, not only in India but abroad as well, these exegeses were given widespread circulation in the press and later appeared in book form in England.[45]

The government prosecutor sought to drive a wedge between the communists on trial and the Indian nationalists who were rallying to their support. In his opening speech at the preliminary trial, he contended that the defendants were not seeking a "national revolution" but an "anti-national revolution." He pictured the communists as persons who were opposed to God, country, and family alike, and hence not spiritually akin to India. He warned that they had nothing but hatred and contempt for the country's nationalist leaders: they scorned Motilal Nehru as a "dangerous patriot," Jawaharlal Nehru as a "tepid reformist," Subhas Chandra Bose as a "ludicrous careerist," and Gandhi as a "grotesque reactionary."[46]

The effects of the Meerut Conspiracy Case on communism in India were ambiguous. In the short-run, the arrests were disastrous for the party. With all of its leaders in jail, the WPP became defunct. Although the organization was never formally disbanded, the controversy over its future,

[j] 320 witnesses were examined and 2,500 exhibits filed (*The Times* [London], Nov. 14, 1929, p. 13).

which was to continue for some time, was in fact settled. The remaining communists were soon divided into a number of quarrelsome factions, and, burdened with an unfortunate policy, floundered hopelessly and by their actions rapidly dissipated the good feeling toward their party generated by the trial. The prosecutor's effort to fault the CPI in the eyes of nationalist India proved to be unnecessary. From a longer perspective, however, there were compensations. Because of the publicity the party received, large numbers of radical youth were attracted to communism.[47] Judgment was pronounced on January 16, 1933. Of the thirty-one accused, Shibnath Bannerjee, Kishorilal Ghose, and B. N. Mukherji—Bengali trade unionists who belonged to neither the WPP nor the CPI—were acquitted. D. R. Thengdi, president of the Bombay Workers' and Peasants' party, had died during the trial. The remaining twenty-seven persons were found guilty. The sentences were unusually severe. Muzaffar Ahmed was sentenced to transportation for life.[k] The others received the following terms: S. A. Dange, S. V. Ghate, K. N. Joglekar, R. S. Nimbkar, and Philip Spratt—twelve years; Benjamin Bradley, S. S. Mirajkar, and Shaukat Usmani—ten years; S. S. Josh, Abdul Majid, and Dharani Goswami—seven years; Ayodhya Prasad, Dr. G. M. Adhikari, P. C. Joshi, and M. G. Desai—five years; Shamsul Huda, A. A. Alve, Kasle, Gaurishankar, and Khadam—three years; and Gopendra Chakravarty, Gopal Basak, Lester Hutchinson, R. R. Mitra,[l] S. H. Jhabwala, and Saigal—four years.[48]

All the convictions were appealed before the High Court of Judicature at Allahabad. The verdict was rendered on August 13. Hutchinson and eight others were acquitted. The Appeals Court, taking into consideration that the defendants had already been confined for more than four

[k] Several others were sentenced to transportation for various terms, but the effect of the convictions was imprisonment under hard-labor conditions.

[l] Neither Desai nor Mitra were members of either the WPP or the CPI, but were avowed communist sympathizers.

years, decided to be lenient. The sentences of Joshi, Basak, and Adhikari were reduced to the time they had already served and they were released immediately. The sentences of Muzaffar Ahmed and Shaukat Usmani were reduced to three years, Spratt to two years, Bradley and nine others to one year, and Chakravarty to seven months.[49] By the end of 1933, all but Ahmed, Dange, Spratt, and Usmani had been released.[50]

Split in the Labor Movement

The 1928 general strike in the Bombay cotton mills had been ended when representatives of management and labor had agreed on a resumption of work under terms which existed before the introduction of rationalization schemes pending the results of an inquiry into the dispute by a government-appointed committee. The agreement, however, did not bring peace to the labor movement. It was regarded by the GKU as a temporary truce and the union's leaders immediately began to prepare for a new strike to be launched within six months. In the interim, the mills were subjected to a series of lightning strikes.[51] In February a serious riot in which 149 persons were reported killed erupted in Bombay in connection with an oil strike. An officially-appointed Riots Enquiry Committee blamed the incident on a series of inflammatory speeches made by leaders of the GKU.[52]

In March, a few days after the Meerut arrests, the Fawcett Committee issued its report. Soon thereafter the Joint Strike Committee and the Bombay Mill Owners' Association entered into negotiations to be based on the committee's recommendations. The discussions, however, soon broke down. With the arrest of the top leaders of the WPP, younger, less experienced communist trade unionists had come to the fore. The GKU charged that union leaders were being systematically victimized by the mill owners, and largely on this basis the new leaders of the union, B. T. Ranadive and S. V. Deshpande, broke off the negotiations and issued a call for a second general strike which was begun on April 26.

The government of Bombay appointed a Court of Enquiry[m] in July to investigate the dispute. This body, after a careful study, issued a report the following September in which officials of the GKU were accused of failure to negotiate in good faith with the mill owners and of irresponsible behavior including incitement to riot, intimidation of non-strikers, lightning strikes, and "invidious propaganda." The report concluded that the blame for the continued labor unrest in Bombay lay "wholly at the door of officials of the union [the GKU]."[53]

On the basis of these findings the GKU could have been declared an unlawful association under the Criminal Law Amendment Act of 1908, but it was felt unnecessary to take action against the union, which, disrupted by the arrest of its most prominent leaders and the consequences of an ill-considered strike, had already ceased to be an effective force.[54]

Moderate trade unionists had opposed the strike from the beginning. The workers, having recently sustained a six-month strike, were not prepared to undergo another round with their employers. Moreover, the mill owners, faced with a market glut, were in a strong position to withstand a prolonged work stoppage.[55] By mid-September the strike had collapsed. The strikers returned to work on September 16 without having made any gains. Discredited by the failure of the general strike and the findings of the Court of Enquiry, the Bombay communists lost the support of the workers.[56] As a result membership in the GKU declined from approximately 54,000 members in December 1928 to not more than 800 by the end of the next year.[57]

Although the communists had sustained heavy membership losses in their two largest unions, the GKU and the G.I.P. Railwaymen's Union, they were able to dominate, with the support of militant nationalists within the trade-

[m] The Court of Enquiry was chaired by H. G. Pearson, a judge of the High Court, Calcutta.

union movement, the tenth annual session of the AITUC, which was held at Nagpur, November 30 to December 1, 1929. When the executive committee met on the twenty-ninth, moderate trade unionists challenged the membership claims of the GKU, which had applied for affiliation. They observed that neither of the two major communist-controlled unions had submitted audited statements of accounts as required by AITUC rules. A resolution of affiliation estimating the strength of the GKU at 54,000 members was at first carried by 51 to 50 votes, but was subsequently defeated 52 to 48 on a recount. The moderates suggested a figure of 6,000 members, but a vote was finally taken on an amendment to the original resolution which put the GKU membership at 40,000. The vote was a tie, but the president, Jawaharlal Nehru, voted in favor of the amendment and the GKU was admitted to the AITUC.

This was an important decision for voting at the open session was on a proportional basis according to the size of the affiliated unions. Out of a total of 930 votes, the GKU and the G.I.P. Railwaymen's Union, with a claimed membership of 45,000, were allotted 350. The militants were in control. With the continued support of the nationalists, the communists were able to obtain the endorsement of a number of resolutions opposed by the moderates. Some of these called for affiliation with the League Against Imperialism, the establishment of a "Socialist Republican Government of the Working Classes" in India, and the boycott of the Royal Commission on Labor and the forthcoming Round Table Conference.[58]

N. M. Joshi had accepted appointments to both the Labor Commission and the Round Table Conference. Interpreting the passage of the resolutions as a wholesale repudiation of their views and objectives, Joshi, Chaman Lal, and other moderates withdrew from the AITUC to form the Indian Trade Union Federation (ITUF) with V. V. Giri as president and R. L. Bakhale as general secretary.[59] The new federation's motto was "legitimate trade-unionism free from Moscow influence."[60]

Thirty unions with a total claimed membership of approximately 96,000 joined the ITUF. The AITUC, now controlled by the nationalists and communists, retained twenty-one unions with an overall claimed membership of 93,000,[61] but almost half of this number represented the alleged membership of the GKU which, as previously noted, was reduced to less than a thousand members as a result of the failure of the 1929 general strike.

Following the secession, a nationalist, Subhas Chandra Bose, was elected president of the AITUC, but the communists won a majority of its important offices and captured the executive committee. S. V. Deshpande, secretary of the GKU, became general secretary. Muzaffar Ahmed, Mohammed Abdul Majid, president of the GKU, and D. B. Kulkarni were chosen as vice-presidents. Philip Spratt and Benjamin Bradley, on trial in Meerut, were elected to the executive committee.[62]

The rupture of the labor movement and the marked decline in Indian trade unionism which followed were clearly due to the extremist tactics of communist labor leaders combined with the deepening economic crisis. As a result of the communists' uncompromising stance, organized labor in India was divided and its strength seriously reduced. In 1930, sixty-one, and in 1931, seventy percent of all strikes failed.[63] Employers took advantage of labor's disunity and disarray to impose wage cuts, demotions, and a general retrenchment. Nationalist trade unionists became increasingly disenchanted with their communist allies within the AITUC, and in 1931 a second split, to be discussed below, occurred within the organization.

8. The Foundations of Royism in India

Exile in Germany

BERLIN in the late 1920's was a haven for foreign students who were attracted to economically-depressed Germany by the quality of its universities and its low living costs. Berlin was also at this time a center for political refugees from colonial countries. Germany was not a major colonial power and consequently its government adopted an attitude of benevolent neutrality toward anti-colonialist groups. Among communist and other radical groups in exile there, the aspiration of linking the anti-imperialist struggle with the left wing of the workers' movement of the major western powers was widespread.[1]

After his escape from Moscow in April 1928, Roy enlisted to his cause a number of Indian students in Berlin. His principal recruits were Tayab Ali Shaikh, Brajesh Singh, and Dr. Anadi Bhaduri. The most important of these was Shaikh, a young construction engineering student, who was to perform a large share of the organizational work for Roy in India in the 1930's. Before going to Europe in 1928 he had already been active in the Indian nationalist movement. A member of the Congress party, he had participated in the Bardoli No-Tax Campaign and, as a member of the executive committee of the Bombay Youth League, he had helped organize demonstrations against the Simon Commission.[2]

Shaikh came from an area of India which is now a part of the state of Gujarat. He was a member of the small community of Ismailian Shiahs—descendants of the Assassins of twelfth-century Persia—known as Khojahs, who, except for a small group in the Punjab, recognize the Aga Khan as their spiritual leader.[3] At an early age, Shaikh rebelled against the strictures of his Moslem sect.[4] Having cut himself free from the moorings of a traditional society and religious orthodoxy, Shaikh, as a student in Germany, was searching for some philosophy that would give purpose and direction to his life. After meeting Roy, Shaikh readily committed his life to Roy's service and the cause he represented. Throughout the 1930's he served Roy with single-minded purpose, devotion, and unbounded zeal. A good speaker and organizer, he soon became Roy's right-hand man. Without his services Roy would not have been able to make the progress he did on his return to India. In appreciation, Roy wrote to a friend in 1930: "Give me a dozen Shaikhs and you will see results before long."[5]

By the late 1930's, however, Shaikh had become a detriment to Roy. As a result of constant pursuit and harassment by the police, interspersed with long periods of confinement, Shaikh suffered a mental breakdown. His gradual replacement as Roy's chief lieutenant by the Bombay labor leader, V. B. Karnik, was also a contributing factor. Shaikh began to distrust the motives not only of strangers but even of some of his political associates. Among the Royists his suspicions focused on his rival, Karnik. As a result of factional activities designed to discredit Karnik and his supporters, Shaikh was temporarily relieved in 1940 of all party responsibilities.[6] He was subsequently reinstated, but because of his continued disruptive tactics, Roy reluctantly decided in 1942 that, as he put it, "the diseased limb should be cut off,"[7] and Shaikh was expelled from the Royist group.[8]

Brajesh Singh, who has lately come into prominence as the late common-law husband of Stalin's only daughter, Svetlana, was a brother of the Raja of Kalakankar, a village located near Lucknow, U. P. It was he who financed Roy's convalescence at St. Moritz[9] and later underwrote the expenses of his trip to India. In a few years he was to return to the orthodox communist fold.

Sundar Kabadi's association with Roy was also short-lived. It was through his indiscretion, the Royists suspected, that the authorities came to learn of Roy's presence in

India.[a] The late Dr. Bhaduri had been a member of Virendranath Chattopadhyaya's Berlin Revolutionary Committee.[10]

In May 1930 a meeting of the executive committee of the Socialist Labor International (the Second International) was convened in Berlin. It was attended by members of the British Labor Cabinet, including the prime minister, Ramsay MacDonald. Roy addressed an open letter to the executive committee of the International protesting that the British party had failed to honor an earlier pledge to support the struggle of colonial peoples for liberation.

Shaikh had become the secretary of an Indian organization in Berlin known as the Hindustan Association of Central Europe. Roy wanted this organization to utilize the meeting of the Labor International to stage a demonstration on behalf of the Indian nationalist movement. Out of loyalty to the Comintern, however, some of the communist members of the organization refused to associate themselves with a scheme devised by a "renegade." Others were chary of inviting the displeasure of the German Foreign Office. When a majority of the Association's members voted against holding the demonstration, Shaikh and those who chose to follow Roy's lead resigned and formed the Group of Oppositional Indian Communists. On May 10 this organization picketed the meeting of the Labor International with placards bearing such slogans as "Down With Imperialism," "Long Live the Constituent Assembly," and "Long Live the Revolution." Shaikh was arrested for his part in the affair.

Shaikh was also connected with the League Against Imperialism and had been a delegate of the Indian youth movement to the World Anti-Imperialist Youth Congress. His organization, the Group of Oppositional Indian Communists, contacted Jawaharlal Nehru, who was also active in the League at the time, with a view to joining forces with

[a] He was later a Paris correspondent for the Calcutta daily, *Amrita Bazar Patrika.*

the Indian nationalist movement. The group eventually won recognition as a German affiliate of the Congress party.[11]

At Roy's instigation, the International Communist Opposition, of which Shaikh's group was a part, actively supported the Indian nationalist struggle. In 1930 this body issued a manifesto entitled "For Freedom of the Indian People," which was signed by communist oppositional groups representing India as well as several other countries.[12] On May Day of that year, its American affiliate, the Communist Party of the USA (Majority Group), sponsored a demonstration in front of the British consulate in New York City during which signs were displayed reading "Stop the Murder of Indian Workers" and "Hail the Indian Revolution." On May 10 a meeting was held at Columbus Circle under the party's sponsorship to protest the recent arrest of Mahatma Gandhi.[13] Speakers included Bertram D. Wolfe and Charles Weber of the American Civil Liberties Union. In June, Wolfe and Sailendranath Ghose, president of the Indian National Congress of America, were the principal speakers at the founding meeting of an organization which was called the Labour Friends of India's Independence.[14]

Roy's Program

As noted in the last chapter, Roy opposed the sectarian policy of the Comintern in a series of articles which appeared in the *International Press Correspondence* in 1928-29. In India he saw a continuing process of "class differentiation inside the nationalist ranks and a resulting radicalization of the nationalist movement."[15] Pointing to the activities of Jawaharlal Nehru, Srinavasa Iyengar, and the Independence for India League, he reported that the petty bourgeoisie, previously "allied with religious and social conservatism," was "rapidly outgrowing the leadership of the big bourgeoisie."[16] Socialism, which only a few years ago had been practically unknown in India, he said, was now professed by "all the petty-bourgeois subsidiary organizations of the National Congress." The left nationalists, however, he predicted, would undoubtedly either move back into the arms of the "big bourgeoisie or develop into a Social Democratic party," unless they were met halfway and guided in a revolutionary path. This was the historic task of the WPP. But, he noted, its members had inexplicably adopted a hostile attitude toward the Independence for India League: "When the petty-bourgeois left radicals are trying to oust the bourgeois leaders from the leadership of the nationalist movement, they are not supported; on the contrary they . . . [are] condemned as the enemies of the workers and peasants."[17]

Roy later contended that the Comintern policy formulated in 1928-29 had alienated the petty bourgeoisie just when that class, in the form of the Independence for India League, was coming toward the workers and peasants. He felt that if the united front policy had not been abandoned, the League might have been "transformed . . . into a powerful weapon to develop the revolution."[18] Roy, unquestionably, exaggerated the revolutionary potential of the League, but in a larger sense, he was correct. As a result of the new Comintern directives, the CPI isolated itself from the Indian nationalist movement, just when the time seemed most propitious for establishing some form of *modus operandi* with it. Communists have come to power without the support of Soviet troops only in those countries where they have been at the forefront of nationalist forces—never while snapping at the heels of its leaders.

After his expulsion from the Comintern, Roy sought to dissuade Indian communists from following the new Moscow directives. He condemned the CPI's attempt to swim against the nationalist tide as suicidal. "In India," he contended, "the way to Communism lies through the National Revolution," rather than in opposition to it. Before Indian communists can hope to nationalize the land, he argued, they must work to "nationalize" their country.[19]

Roy became increasingly restive in Germany. He felt that Indian communists were missing a unique opportunity, but felt powerless to do anything about it from a distance.

Moreover, he was convinced that the CPI leadership was inept, and that if Stalin were given a choice between the present Indian party and a more astute group, he would disinherit the sick child and adopt the stronger.[20] Consequently, Roy decided to return to India.

Roy's friends in Germany tried to dissuade him from undertaking such a venture. He had been convicted *in absentia* in the 1924 Kanpur Conspiracy Trial for conspiring to organize a communist party in India with the object of overthrowing British rule, and was consequently subject to arrest anywhere within the Empire. Brandler was the most insistent among those who argued that the game was not worth the candle. From his point of view the situation in India was still quite "immature" and nothing could be achieved before a solid foundation were laid through quiet preparatory work. But this objection only served to strengthen Roy's resolve. What could I have done, he later wrote to a friend, if I had continued to sit "thousands of miles away? The problem is so complicated that it could not possibly be tackled except on the spot."[21]

Before leaving Europe in 1930, Roy spent several weeks relaxing and recuperating from his ear operation at a resort hotel at Merano in the Rhaetian Alps of northeastern Italy. From there he left for India. Traveling via Istanbul and Bagdad, he arrived in Karachi on December 11. By December 17 he was in Bombay.[22] Until his capture seven months later, Roy employed a number of disguises and aliases to avoid detection, but most frequently he went about as a "Dr. Mahmud," dressed as an orthodox Gandhian in khadi.[23]

Roy dispatched four agents to India to prepare the ground for his arrival—Tayab Shaikh, Brajesh Singh, Sundar Kabadi, and Dr. Anadi Bhaduri.[24] Shaikh and Kabadi are known to have reached India in August 1930. They brought with them a manifesto prepared by Roy and dated July 1930. In the manifesto, which was addressed to the "Revolutionary Vanguard of the Toiling Masses of India,"

Roy attacked the new Comintern line and urged Indian communists to reject it. He argued that

> the Communist Party cannot advocate that India will immediately be a Soviet Republic. That will be running after a Utopia. The Soviet State is the organ of the dictatorship of the proletariat. The conditions in India are not at all ripe for such a State. . . . The workers becoming class conscious cannot be expected to join the Communist Party if it is organized only with a maximum program which appears to have little relations to prevailing conditions. They must be shown that the solution of the problems actually before them, concerning the minimum demands of the toiling masses, come within the purview of the Communist Party. There is no other way to free an essentially revolutionary movement for national independence from the leadership of the bourgeoisie. . . . In India, the way to Communism lies through the national revolution. . . . To this end it [the Communist Party] must work through the national mass organizations—the National Congress, Youth League, student organizations and volunteer corps.[25]

In this manifesto Roy argued that the Marxian minimum program, rather than the maximum program, was most suitable to Indian conditions. He stated:

> The attempts to organize a Communist Party only with a maximum programme of Communism is bound to fail in India. . . . In addition to its maximum programme, the Communist Party in a given situation must adopt a minimum programme of National Revolution. . . . In India the forces of production are still far below that level of development in which the struggle for the realization of the maximum programme of Communism becomes a necessity.[26]

Roy was proposing that Indian communists should join with the nationalists to confront their common adversary with a united oppositional front and that to accomplish this objective they must temporarily eschew their ultimate objectives. He was not suggesting that the maximum program be abandoned altogether, but merely deferred. He regarded nationalism as a temporary *amicus usque ad aras*.

One of the themes stressed in Roy's manifesto—the demand for a constituent assembly—was to become virtually synonymous with "Royism" in India. The theme first appeared in a lengthy article entitled, "The Lessons of the Lahore Congress," published in the Indian journal *Vanguard*[b] in 1930 under the signature of Tayab Shaikh and several others.[27] Following the passage of the Lahore independence resolution, leaders of the Congress party had decided to boycott the Round Table Conference, which had been conceived as a meeting of British and Indian representatives to discuss the next step in India's constitutional progress. The article was an exhortation to Congressmen to give positive content to the boycott by raising the counter-demand that Indians be allowed to frame their own constitution through the agency of a constituent assembly and by preparing their countrymen to assert this right through the development of partial struggles over local economic issues. It was argued that an abstract declaration for independence such as was made at Lahore would not find any response unless combined with a program which met the immediate demands of the Indian people.

Roy patterned his program and tactics closely on the model of the French Jacobins. Since he felt that in India a communist maximum program would arouse little enthusiasm, his plan to work within the nationalist framework did not call for the raising of offensive socialist slogans, but rather of slogans appropriate to a Jacobin, bourgeois-democratic revolution. Indian communists, he held, should "raise the banner, not of Communism, but of Jacobinism."[28]

Roy maintained that Indian communists should imitate their Jacobin forebears, whom he characterized as "the Marxists of their time" and hold their materialist creed in

[b] *The Vanguard* was published by the Socialist, Yusuff Meherally. The article also appeared in *Revolutionary Age* (New York) in 1930.

abeyance not out of conviction as in the case of Robespierre, but as a matter of expediency. "Nationalism," he warned, "will not swallow the whole of Marxism—such as materialism." Marx himself, he recalled, had condemned Babeuf for going beyond the Jacobin program and talking of socialism.[29]

Roy sought to replace the radical demand of the official communists for the creation of soviets in India with the Jacobin slogan of constituent assembly, which he felt would appeal to a much broader spectrum of political opinion. When he urged Congressmen to adopt a demand for the convening of a constituent assembly to draft a constitution for free India, he was in reality "aiming at the Jacobin Convention which represented the forces of petty-bourgeois radicalism."[30]

It should be noted that although legal authority in revolutionary France had rested nominally in the Jacobin Convention, power was actually exercised by the Committee of Public Safety, under the chairmanship of Robespierre, the bureaucracy, and a network of local Jacobin clubs.[31] Similarly, Roy anticipated that the Indian Constituent Assembly, ostensibly a slogan of democratic revolution, would be convened "not as an organ of the bourgeois-democracy, but of democratic dictatorship." According to his own admission, the plan was one of deception—to utilize slogans of a "democratic nature so formulated as to be convertible to more radical slogans" at the appropriate moment.[32]

If the leadership of the Congress party, he reasoned, could be put into the hands of "petty-bourgeois radical elements (Jacobins)," it would be possible to convert the constituent assembly into a democratic dictatorship of the proletariat and peasantry under proletarian hegemony.[33] Although the social composition of the Jacobin leadership must be largely petty bourgeois, Roy felt that it would be possible "under the conditions of the contemporary world," for such a leadership to be "decisively influenced by Marxism."[34] For Roy the nationalist revolution was to be merely the prologue for the establishment of a democratic dictatorship which would assume many features of the "proletarian Socialist revolution." It would be democratic in the sense that it would represent an overwhelming majority of the population, but it would be a dictatorship in that it would "suppress a section of the population," namely landlords and capitalists.[35]

Roy's scheme shunned direct elections to the constituent assembly. After coming to power in Russia in 1917, Lenin had convened a constituent assembly elected on the basis of universal adult suffrage with the result that the bolsheviks received only 24.7 percent of the vote.[36] Lenin was forced to dissolve the assembly on the grounds that "the health of the revolution is the supreme law"—a maxim devised earlier by Plekhanov. Seeking to avoid this experience, Roy advocated a Soviet system of indirect elections in which the constituent assembly would be elected by the local units of the Congress party, the primary Congress committees.

In France, the radical Montagnards had been able to defeat the moderate Girondists by securing control over key Jacobin clubs, which gradually assumed governmental functions in the confusion of revolutionary events.[37] Later, the bolsheviks in Russia had used the soviets as a springboard to power. In both cases radical groups had been able to assume power by virtue of their control over an extralegal or parallel government. Similarly Roy hoped to capture the Congress party and the proposed constituent assembly by working through the local party units. To this end he sought to increase the importance of primary Congress committees in party decision-making by supporting democratic reforms in the party constitution.[38]

Roy was confident that the local Congress committees, which he felt had been badly neglected and existed more in name than as functioning bodies, could be "easily captured by those who are prepared to put in quite [a bit of] work."[39] If only they would "go into the village and do a little work," he counseled his followers, they could get hold of the entire Congress organization.[40]

Roy wanted to convert the local party units into a "country-wide network of democratically elected local committees," which would serve as a parallel government and would form the basic units of a post-revolutionary state.[41] Therefore he sought to persuade Congressmen to adopt the plan whereby the call for the elections of a "National Constituent Assembly" would be "the signal for insurrection"—for the final struggle against British rule. At that moment, local Congress committees throughout the country would be directed to destroy organs of power such as police stations and law courts. The insurrection would begin with the slogan of "all power to the Congress Committees," and in the ensuing crisis, the "local revolutionary committees" would assume the functions of government in their respective localities and elect representatives to a constituent assembly.[42]

August Thalheimer of the German Right Opposition objected to Roy's plan to reach rural India under the aegis of the Congress party. He proposed instead that Roy "organize the workers on a revolutionary basis and through them lead the peasants." In place of the constituent assembly he urged Roy to work for the establishment of soviets "of workers, peasants, small merchants," and other non-exploitative groups.[43] Roy answered that Indian workers were too backward politically to play a completely independent role and that such a course as Thalheimer prescribed would only serve to isolate them from the anti-colonialist struggle. Only through the Congress party, he insisted, was it possible to come into contact with the Indian masses, which consisted largely of "the decisive factor of the peasantry." To Thalheimer's characterization of the Congress party as a bourgeois and petty-bourgeois organization, Roy replied that it was a mass nationalist movement and as such was not "objectively" the party of any particular class.[44]

Formation of the Royist Group

Within a few months after their arrival in India, Shaikh and Kabadi had obtained the signatures of about one hundred active members of Congress and the nationalist Youth Leagues to Roy's manifesto.[45] By November, Shaikh had obtained an interview with Jawaharlal Nehru, who later had made a public statement in support of Roy's program and his concept of the constituent assembly.[46]

When Roy reached Bombay he found that Shaikh and Kabadi had already made considerable headway in establishing a basis for his work there.[47] They had gathered the nucleus of a group, later known as Royists, who were to remain faithful to Roy and his ideas, as they evolved from communism to a form of noncommunist Marxist humanism, until his death in 1954. One of the first recruits was a young student leader, V. B. Karnik,[48] who later became an important labor leader in Bombay and who eventually replaced Shaikh as Roy's right-hand man.[c] Others in this early Roy group were Dr. C. Y. Chitnis, Miss Maniben Kara, Charles Mascarenhas, A. N. Shetty, and Dr. M. R. Shetty. Maniben Kara was a young woman from a wealthy Gujarati family. When first contacted by Shaikh, she had recently given up her work in a social institution she had founded, Siva Mandir, a combination nursery school and clinic where free medical care was available for women and children, to take charge of the Bombay Municipal Workers' Union.[49] Mascarenhas, a Goan, was secretary of the Bombay Seaman's Union and later became one of the founding members of the Congress Socialist party.[50] Dr. Shetty was one of the founders of the Bombay Transport and Dock Workers' Union.[d] A. N. Shetty, who was affectionately known as "Pathan"—a reference to his unusual height—was also active among the dock workers.[51] When Dr. G. M. Adhikari returned to India from Berlin in late 1928, he had brought with him a letter of introduction from Roy. It had been rumored for a time that he had come to establish a Roy group within the CPI, but, although he corresponded with

[c] In a speech in 1939 Roy praised Karnik as one "who has contributed to . . . [my] work perhaps more than I could do myself" (*Hindustan Standard* [Calcutta], June 24, 1939).

[d] This Union owes its present strength to the subsequent leadership of the late P. D'Mello.

Roy until his arrest the following March,[52] he never engaged in factional activities.[53] After Roy's dismissal from the Foreign Bureau of the CPI, he apparently cast in his lot with the official communists and has remained a faithful and influential member of the Indian communist movement to this day.

Roy recognized that his dissident communist group would remain a small minority within the Congress party, but he felt that it could successfully carry out his plan of action if its members were welded together into a tightly-knit organization capable of providing sufficient controls to ensure ideological integrity and unity of purpose. To this end he proposed the formation of two groups—a broad-based party of the proletariat, peasantry, and petty bourgeoisie to be organized within the Congress party, and a more select, secret group to be formed outside the nationalist organization.[54] This was a modified version of his earlier call for the formation of an open workers' and peasants' party and an underground communist party.

In accordance with this plan a small but active group of Royist Congressmen, known at first as the Committee of Action for Independence of India and later as the League of Indian Independence, was formed largely as a result of Shaikh's zealous efforts, before Roy's arrest.[55] Its largest unit, with a membership of about thirty-five, was in Calcutta. Other units were in Bombay, Ahmedabad, and several other locations.[56] Roy at one time had hoped that this three-class coalition would eventually, as he put it, oust the "traitorous" bourgeoisie, hiding behind the cult of Gandhism, and inherit the Congress apparatus and name.[57] Within a short time, however, the League of Indian Independence was abandoned on the principle that the division of Congressmen into separate parties would weaken the nationalist organization.[e]

At the same time that the League was being formed on the basis of a bourgeois-democratic platform, efforts were also

[e] The idea of a Royist league within the Congress party was revived in 1939 with the formation of the League of Radical Congressmen.

made by the Royists to form a secret, communist organization in opposition to the official communist party. A number of scattered local committees were soon established, but further progress was slow, and it was not until 1934 that representatives of these units from Bombay, Calcutta, Baroda, Benares, Poona, and a few other places, acting on instructions from Roy, met together to form the Revolutionary Party of the Indian Working Class (RPIWC).[f] The new party adopted the call for a constituent assembly as their slogan and Roy's manifesto, which had been published in 1932 by the Bengal Committee of the RPIWC under the title, *Our Task in India,* as their basic document.[58] Roy counseled that neither membership lists of the party nor the composition of its executive committee should be publicly revealed and that open agitation should be conducted in the name of legal organizations in which members of the group were active.[59]

The Revolutionary party[g] was intended to serve two main purposes—to act as a splinter group within the newly founded Congress Socialist party[h] and to serve as the vanguard of the working class which, it was hoped, would come to the fore in the final stages of the nationalist revolution to force a reluctant Congress onto the path of democratic dictatorship.[60]

The Royists were inveterate pamphleteers. Maniben Kara once remarked, half in jest, that she suspected that she had been invited to join the Royist group because of her ownership of a printing press.[61] Before Roy's arrest, *Independent India,* under the editorship of Charles Mascarenhas, was founded to serve as the organ of the League of

[f] Roy had earlier rejected a proposal made by some of his followers that the new organization be called the "Communist Party Opposition."

[g] Meetings of the RPIWC were conducted in a romantic, conspiratorial atmosphere—at night, behind drawn curtains, by candlelight, and with papers arranged so that they could be quickly destroyed in case of an unexpected interruption (interview with K. K. Sinha, Dehra Dun, May 19, 1962).

[h] The activities of the Royists within the Congress Socialist party will be discussed in Chapter 9.

Indian Independence. Roy was a regular contributor to the journal and managed to send in a weekly column even when he was standing trial.[62] Publication of the paper, however, was eventually suspended for financial reasons. It was revived on April 4, 1937, after Roy's release from prison, with V. B. Karnik serving as editor. In 1943 its name was changed to *Vanguard.* After independence it was published from Calcutta under the title, *Radical Humanist.* In 1969 the paper was moved to New Delhi.

Other Royist journals started at this time included: *Masses* (Calcutta), a counterpart of Roy's earlier journal published from Europe, *Masses of India;*[63] *Roy's Weekly* (Bombay); *Workers' Age* (Calcutta), an English language weekly; and *Sranjibi* ("Labor")—a Bengali paper published in Calcutta. In addition, numerous articles published by Roy, Sundar Kabadi, Tayab Shaikh, and others appeared in various Indian journals, such as the *People* (Lahore), *Independent* (Bombay), *Bombay Chronicle* (Bombay), and Yusuff Meherally's *Vanguard* (Bombay).[64]

Roy worked prodigiously during the brief seven months that he was at large in India and made considerable headway in promoting his program. After several years of relative inactivity in Germany, it was exhilarating to be engaged in concrete political work once again. "It was a real joy," he wrote at this time, "to be doing things, however small, with your own hands. So I am satisfied."[65]

He was helped in his efforts by the disunity and disorganization in the official communist camp. There were serious differences among Indian communists over the implementation of the Comintern's "Draft Platform of Action" for the CPI. Disapproval in some instances took the indirect form of questioning the document's authenticity.[66] In Bombay, S. V. Deshpande and B. T. Ranadive quarreled bitterly over the question of party policy with the latter taking an even more militant stance than the former.[67] On December 18, 1930, the two came to blows while leading processions of their followers in front of a cotton mill in Bombay.[68]

In an article which appeared in *Gegen den Strom* in February 1931, Roy dismissed the CPI as of little consequence and of hardly existing outside of Bombay and Calcutta. He reported that the party consisted largely of students and functioned more as a student group than anything else. Its influence among the workers, he said, was declining and it had almost no contact with the villages.[69] In letters composed during this period, he wrote that the official party line was sheer romanticism. "It was a crime," he said, "for the Comintern to play with this material as they did in the last two years."

At the same time, Roy was surprised at the authority he commanded in various circles. He found that nationalists and trade unionists welcomed his help and cooperation. He hoped that the "Draft Platform of Action," which he reported had "staggered even the very orthodox," would result in some defections to his side from the CPI. To his delight, he found that all but one or two of the Meerut prisoners were "very friendly."[70]

Alarmed that Roy might be making serious inroads within the official communist ranks, the Comintern sent several emissaries to India to check his influence. One of the most successful of these was an American, Henry G. Lynd, who arrived in Bombay in February 1931 and was deported the following December. He was largely responsible for the issuance of a pamphlet entitled "Programme of the Communist Party of India," which was based on the Draft Platform of Action. He also made a number of suggestions for the wholesale reorganization of the party.[71]

Royists and Indian Labor

It was in the trade-union field that the Royists made their greatest gains. Although Roy in his early years in the Comintern had been enthusiastic about the revolutionary potentiality of the Indian proletariat, he gradually adopted a more realistic position toward them. After the Comintern's change of policy in 1928-29, he criticized its attitude and that of the CPI as overly romantic. Without denying the fact of widespread labor unrest in India, he felt that it was "sheer political ignorance to read class-consciousness in every worker ready to throw stones."[72]

Whatever illusions Roy may still have nurtured were quickly shattered after returning to India. A few days after reaching Bombay he confided to a friend that even his modified position toward Indian labor, which he had held before leaving Europe, had overestimated "the maturity of the [Indian] movement. The power of smelling a situation, which the older comrades[i] have acquired in long revolutionary experience," he admitted, had proved to be correct.[73] In an open letter which Roy later wrote to the Comintern, he acknowledged that the Indian proletariat was "not only weak numerically," but also "formed but partially as a class." Echoing Lenin's views on the "spontaneity" of proletarian class-consciousness, Roy wrote that strikes in India were the manifestations of an "elementary revolt" against intolerable living conditions rather than of "revolutionary class-consciousness." There were very few workers, he argued, who understood "the rudimentary ideas of class struggle" or were "consciously inclined toward Communism."[74]

Because of these views, Roy sought to win the support of Indian labor by championing their concrete demands for higher wages, increased benefits, and improved working conditions. At the same time he hoped to unite the labor movement with the nationalist cause. To do this, however, it was first necessary to oust the communists from the AITUC.

This proved to be a less difficult task than he had anticipated. As the communist attack on "left-nationalist reformists" mounted, the two groups within the AITUC became increasingly estranged from each other. The disruptive tactics of the communists in forming rival trade unions when

[i] The reference is to Heinrich Brandler and August Thalheimer who had stressed the weakness of the Indian proletariat in trying to persuade Roy to remain in Europe.

they were unable to control the existing unions provided an additional irritant.[75]

This gave the Royists their opportunity. They shared the interest of the Congress Labor Committee in securing the assistance of the labor movement in the nationalist cause.[j] By working within this committee, the Royists were able to form an alliance with nationalist trade unionists for the purpose of combating the CPI's influence within India's labor force.[76]

With the cooperation of the nationalists and the active assistance of G. L. Kandalkar, president of the GKU and a vice-president of the AITUC, the Royists were able to capture the former stronghold of militant trade unionism in India, the GKU, much to Deshpande's discomfiture.[77] At a general meeting of the GKU, held on October 12, 1930, a resolution was passed expelling Deshpande, its former secretary, from the union.[78] With the communists out, the Royists gradually assumed control. Shaikh, who by 1931 had become the secretary of the Bombay branch of the AITUC[79] and was a popular figure among the city's mill-workers,[80] played a major role in this development. Deshpande and his followers, in response, established a parallel union under the same name.

The Royists steadily made gains elsewhere as well. On December 31, 1930, they secured control of the Bombay Dockworkers' Union.[81] They also made inroads in the G.I.P. Railwaymen's Union. Deshpande had called a strike on the line for February 4, 1930, which was to lead to a general strike, but by April the strike had collapsed and the workers had returned to work largely on their employers' terms.[82] Soon thereafter the Royists, with the support of moderate and nationalist trade unionists, set out to oust the communists from the union. The result of the strike and the internecine struggle among its workers was the decimation

[j] During Bombay's "Labor Week" in 1930, the Royists advanced the slogan, "The workers and peasants are the arms and feet of the National Congress" (V. Basak, *Some Urgent Problems of the Labour Movement in India*, p. 14).

of the union, which had once boasted a membership of over 40,000.[83]

Deshpande, the communist general secretary of the AITUC, anticipated that as a result of the communists' reverses in the labor field, they would be outvoted at the next annual session of the AITUC and, consequently, refused to convene the meeting which had been scheduled for February 1931.[84] When the AITUC finally met in Calcutta the following July at the insistence of its president, Subhas Chandra Bose, Deshpande's worst fears were confirmed. The nationalists and the Royists united to force the communists out of the organization.[85]

Bose led the attack. Charging that the CPI was playing into the hands of the British by attempting to divide the nationalist ranks, he castigated them as "anti-nationalists."[86] Roy did not attend this session but his followers who were present joined in the condemnation. They distributed a pamphlet among the delegates to the session, under the signature of the "Committee for the Organization of a Revolutionary Party of the Indian Working Class,"[k] in which the communists were accused of weakening the labor movement by their action at the last AITUC session at Nagpur. It urged the delegates to remove the delinquents from office and called for reuniting the ITUF unions with the AITUC, which, it was held, should not be regarded as "the organization of the revolutionary vanguard of the proletariat . . . [but as] the platform of the entire working class engaged in the elementary forms of class struggle."[87]

When the executive committee of the AITUC met in Calcutta on July 3, two rival groups appeared—a Royist and a communist contingent led by G. L. Kandalkar and S. V. Deshpande, respectively. Each claimed to represent the GKU. The question was referred to the Credentials Com-

[k] By this title, Roy sought to take advantage of the fact that the CPI was not yet formally affiliated with the Comintern. He hoped that Stalin would eventually recognize his group rather than the existing communist party (Muzaffar Ahmed, *Communist Party of India: Years of Formation, 1921-1933*, pp. 36-37).

mittee, which ruled in favor of the Royists.[88] In addition, Bose announced that unions which had failed to pay their affiliation dues would be ineligible to participate in the executive committee proceedings.[89] This ruling was clearly aimed at the G.I.P. Railwaymen's Union, seventy-five percent of whose members on the AITUC executive belonged to Deshpande's group. Bose was later forced, however, to compromise on this issue.[90]

When the executive committee met again, Bose ruled that the first order of business would be the question of representation of the GKU. Realizing that this would result in a loss of communist strength on the executive, Deshpande objected and Ranadive introduced a motion of censure against the president. With Bose himself voting against the motion, it was barely defeated 26 to 24. When the question of the GKU was again raised, Deshpande proposed an adjournment. This maneuver having failed, hired "goondas" entered the room and succeeded in breaking up the meeting.[91] Bose adjourned both the executive meeting and the open session *sine die* on the grounds that it had not been possible to determine which of the two GKU delegations was entitled to vote.[92]

On the following day, Deshpande convened a separate meeting—attended by about a dozen unions, many of which had failed to secure recognition from the AITUC Credentials Committee—at which the Red Trade Union Congress (TUC) was formed. S. V. Deshpande was chosen one of its three general secretaries and D. B. Kulkarni was elected president.[93] The Red TUC never became a significant force in the Indian trade-union movement. Not once in its three-year existence were audited accounts or membership figures of its constituent unions made public.[94] A few days after its formation, Roy remarked that "the Linie" had "committed suicide."[95]

Following the secession of the communists, the open session of the AITUC was held on July 7 with about thirty unions attending.[96] R. S. Ruikar, the leader of the anti-communist faction within the G.I.P. Railwaymen's Union, and S. Mukundar Lal of Calcutta were elected president and general secretary, respectively. Two of the four vice-presidents chosen—G. L. Kandalkar and J. N. Mitra—were Royist sympathizers. Tayab Shaikh became one of the four secretaries of the AITUC. Bose was elected treasurer.[97] At the session, a motion was passed which criticized the stewardship of the outgoing general secretary, Deshpande, and demanded that he submit audited accounts to his successor within a month.[98]

The Royists and the nationalists, aided by the inexperience and errors of the communists themselves, had accomplished their aim of breaking the CPI's control over India's largest trade-union federation.[99] The way was now clear for an attempt, initially led by the Royists, to unite the non-communist labor federations—the AITUC, the ITUF, and the All India Railwaymen's Federation—into a single national organization.

The Karachi Congress Session

Shortly after Roy's return to India, the civil disobedience campaign was suspended. The viceroy, Lord Irwin, resolving on a course of reconciliation, released Gandhi, Nehru, and twenty-six other imprisoned Congress leaders on January 26, 1931. A few days later Gandhi initiated a correspondence with the viceroy which resulted in a series of six meetings between the two men during the months of February and March. An agreement was finally reached on March 4, subject to endorsement by the Congress party at its forthcoming annual session in Karachi.[100]

When the terms of the settlement, which became known as the Delhi Pact or the Gandhi-Irwin Pact, were made public the following day, there was bitter disappointment in the nationalist camp. The Congress party was to agree that the civil disobedience movement would be "effectively discontinued," and this phrase was expressly interpreted to preclude no-tax campaigns and other activities involving the defiance of law. Most importantly, Gandhi had consented to participate in the second Round Table Conference under terms which had been agreed upon at the first Round Table Conference. The Congress party had boycotted the first conference at which the Indian representatives had agreed to the principle of federation as the basis for India's constitution as well as the imposition of constitutional safeguards in the interest of defense, the protection of minorities, and the discharge of obligations.

In return for an end to the civil disobedience movement the viceroy agreed to a number of concessions on behalf of the government. These included: the withdrawal of all special ordinances promulgated in connection with the civil disobedience campaign; the rescission of the ban on the Congress party; the release of all political prisoners who had not been engaged in violent activities; the remission of fines not already collected and the return of attached property not already disposed of; and the granting of permission to persons residing in areas adjacent to salt deposits to collect salt, but only for domestic consumption.[101]

To many nationalists, the government's concessions were far too limited for the price paid. They were quick, for example, to note that the terms of the amnesty excluded the Meerut Conspiracy Case prisoners or the Bengal terrorists and few felt that any substantial modifications had been made in the Salt Acts, the ostensible target of Gandhi's march to the sea.[102] The greatest disappointment, however, centered on the question of India's future constitution. Nehru, in common with other radical Congressmen, was dismayed when he learned the terms of the agreement. He considered the pact a political defeat and predicted that it would result in the complete demoralization of the nationalist movement.[103] The acceptance of the principle of federation meant the political abandonment of the millions of Indians living in princely states. Moreover, Gandhi's acceptance of constitutional safeguards, he felt, nullified the 1929 independence resolution adopted at Lahore. "Was it for this," Nehru asked rhetorically, "that our people had behaved so gallantly for a year? Were all our brave words and deeds to end in this?"[104]

To compound Gandhi's difficulties, Bhagat Singh,[l] Raj Guru, and Sukh Dev, three members of the Hindustan Republican Association, were hanged for the 1928 murder of an assistant superintendent of police at Lahore. The execution occurred a few days before the 1931 Congress session was scheduled to be convened at Karachi. Gandhi had attempted to intercede on behalf of Bhagat Singh and his companions but had failed to secure commutation of their sentences. Following their execution, a wave of indignation swept the country. The assassinated police official had been popularly regarded as responsible for the death of Lala Lajpat Rai, and Bhagat Singh's act as just restitution for the nationalist leader's death. Bhagat Singh had been lionized as a symbol of national honor and his execution resulted in his martyrdom. Members of the Central Legislative Assembly staged a walkout and demonstrations erupted throughout India.[105]

The principal question to be resolved when the Congress delegates assembled in Karachi was whether to ratify the Delhi Pact or to resume the civil disobedience campaign. Although the pact had already received the endorsement of the Working Committee, there was some doubt as to the outcome of the Karachi deliberations. It was generally believed that Bhagat Singh's execution had weakened Gandhi's hand somewhat, for many felt that he had not made a sufficiently determined effort on his behalf. Vallabhbhai Patel, the president of the session, could be expected to support Gandhi, but none were certain what Jawaharlal Nehru or Subhas Chandra Bose would do.[106] Nehru, regarding the Pact as a *fait accompli*, had not actively opposed it, but he had seriously considered disassociating himself from it.[107] Indian youth had been particularly disenchanted with the discontinuance of the civil disobedience program. Two youth conferences were scheduled to be held simultaneously with the Karachi Congress session—a

[l] This was the same Bhagat Singh who had been involved in the bomb throwing incident in the assembly hall at Delhi during the debate over the Public Safety Bill.

Students' Congress and a Conference of the All-India Nau Jawan Bharat Sabha (New Youth of India League) under the presidency of Nehru and Bose respectively.[108] It was reported that young radical Congressmen would attempt to block the endorsement of Gandhi's action.[109]

On his way to the session, Gandhi got down from his train at a small station some thirteen miles distant from Karachi to avoid possible hostile demonstrations. He was met there, nevertheless, by an angry delegation of the Nau Jawan Bharat Sabha, who greeted him with shouts of "Down with Gandhi," "Hail Bhagat Singh," and "Down with the truce."[110] The following day a youth contingent handed him a bouquet of artificial flowers made of black homespun cotton for his "efforts" on behalf of Bhagat Singh and his comrades. This mock presentation was accompanied by taunts such as "Gandhi go back."[111]

The CPI, in accordance with its new policy of remaining aloof from the Congress party, was sponsoring a separate Workers' and Peasants' Conference at Karachi and was both unwilling and unable to exploit this situation.[112] Roy, in contrast, attended the Karachi session in his guise of Dr. Mahmud[113] as, in his own words, "a semi-official guest of the Congress bosses."[114] On a trip to the province of U.P. he had called on Jawaharlal Nehru, who had befriended him and taken him on a tour of some villages—in order "to show off his glory,"[m] as Roy had later caustically remarked.[115] When Nehru invited him to attend the Karachi Congress meeting, Roy, deciding to take the "bull by the horns," had accepted.[116]

Roy, who was opposed to the Delhi Pact, was under no illusion that by his presence at Karachi he could prevent its adoption. His object was simply to magnify the voice of radical dissent and to ensure that an alternative to Gandhi's proposals would be placed clearly before the delegates. In this manner he hoped to capitalize on the prevalent dis-

[m] Roy added that although Nehru had been "very friendly," he was "politically hopeless."

content within the Congress ranks to promote his own program.[117]

In the debates before the Subjects Committee on the resolution calling for the endorsement of the Gandhi-Irwin settlement, Tayab Shaikh and the moderate labor leader, Jamnadas Mehta, served as Roy's spokesmen. Mehta told the committee that if anyone other than Gandhi had been responsible for the agreement he would have been thrown into the sea,[118] and offered an amendment to the official resolution. In the amendment, written by Roy but proposed on behalf of "a well-organized left wing group,"[119] the Delhi Pact was described as "a betrayal of India by the bourgeoisie"[120] and as inconsistent with the Lahore independence resolution. It maintained that any "safeguards" to independence to which the Congress party was being asked to give its consent could only be at the cost of independence, which, Mehta added in his remarks, had been given so many varied interpretations by Gandhi in the past several months—from complete independence to the substance of independence and finally self-rule through self-control—that not even an Aristotle could now understand what exactly independence entailed.[121]

Tayab Shaikh followed Mehta with an impassioned speech. Where, he implored, were the shouts of "Inquilab Zindabad"[n] which had resounded so incessantly at Lahore? The audience is reported to have responded with loud shouts of "Inquilab Zindabad." "The Round Table Conference," he continued, "was arranged to suck the blood of the poor. We want the rule of the poor and the peasants, not the rule of the capitalists." Despite the enthusiastic reception accorded Shaikh's speech, Roy's amendment was ruled out of order as a negation of the original resolution.[122]

Gandhi was more than a match for his adversaries. Once the delegates assembled at Karachi, there was no doubt as to the outcome. From Karachi, Roy lamented that Gandhi was as popular as ever and that "any voice raised against

[n] "Long live revolution."

him" was "doomed to be drowned in an indignant chorus of protest. . . . There was not," he said, "the ghost of a chance of overthrowing the god."[o] The delegates had come to pay Gandhi homage, not to challenge his authority.[123] In the end, the Subjects Committee endorsed Gandhi's action by the overwhelming majority of 300 to 2,[124] and he was subsequently chosen as the Congress party's sole delegate to the second Round Table Conference.

Gandhi persuaded Nehru to move the resolution endorsing the pact before the open session. Nehru had at first refused the request, but at the last minute consented.[125] In this way, the acquiescence of a large sector of radical Congressmen was assured. Consideration of the pact was preceded by a resolution on Bhagat Singh, deploring his deed but condemning his execution. This was widely interpreted as a maneuver to mollify radical opinion.[126]

The behavior of both Nehru and Bose in Karachi was motivated by a desire to preserve nationalist unity. While presiding over a conference of the Nau Jawan Bharat Sabha, held simultaneously with the Congress session in Karachi, Bose inveighed against the Delhi Pact as a betrayal of India. However, instead of urging his followers to vote against an endorsement of the pact, Bose counseled moderation. He cautioned his audience to avoid a conflict with the Congress leadership which would only serve to "weaken the people and strengthen the Government."[127] Later before the Subjects Committee, he suggested that the execution of Bhagat Singh and his accomplices had been deliberately timed to disrupt the party. Interpreting the Gandhi-Irwin settlement as merely a temporary truce, he urged his fellow-Congressmen to avoid the "cleverly laid" trap and to maintain a united front under Gandhi's leadership while preparing to resume the struggle.[128]

[o] Roy was amazed at the atmosphere surrounding the Congress encampment. "This is a fair–no political gathering," he reported. "If our C.I. [Communist International] *welt-kongresses* were anything like this, Piatnitsky would not have more than one in a century."

The Karachi session was also noteworthy for the passage of the resolution on Fundamental Rights and the National Economic Program, in which, for the first time at an annual meeting, the Congress party committed itself to a policy of socioeconomic reform. The resolution was the precursor of the sections on Fundamental Rights and on the Directive Principles of State Policy of the present Indian Constitution. It provided for state ownership of key industries and transport and included important provisions in the areas of labor rights and agrarian reform.[129]

The resolution was the subject of heated debate at Karachi. The original draft of the proposal was endorsed by the Working Committee following a prolonged six-hour discussion.[130] Later it was recast by a specially appointed subcommittee consisting of Nehru and three others. To appease conservative opinion, a clause was added at this time which provided for subsequent amendments to the resolution by the AICC[p] if "not inconsistent with the policy and principles thereof."[131]

When the amended resolution was debated before the Subjects Committee, considerable opposition was voiced to it. Several delegates expressed the fear that its passage would alienate the landowning classes. Contending that the time was not yet ripe for socialism, Nehru remonstrated that the present proposals could not possibly be regarded as a socialist program. The resolution was finally adopted by the Subjects Committee by a vote of 91 to 50 and subsequently endorsed by the open session.[132]

British intelligence suspected that Roy's influence had been decisive in Nehru's sponsoring of the Karachi resolu-

[p] In accordance with this clause, the Working Committee appointed a special committee in mid-April to solicit the views of various Pradesh Congress Committees (PCC's) and other interested parties on the question of revising the resolution. On the basis of the committee's report, the AICC in August amended the resolution on Fundamental Rights with the view to reassuring landowners and businessmen that the Congress party did not contemplate the large-scale expropriation of property (*Tribune* [Lahore], April 14, 1931, p. 1). For the text of the resolution as amended by the AICC, see Pattabhi B. Sitaramayya, *The History of the Indian National Congress*, I, pp. 779-82.

tion on Fundamental Rights, which they noted was remarkably similar to Roy's minimum program.[133] It is certain, however, that they exaggerated the role Roy played in this regard. Roy, who had the ear of Nehru at this time, undoubtedly discussed the resolution with him and pressed for the adoption of a program aimed at improving the lot of workers and peasants. When Roy expressed his displeasure at an early draft of the resolution, Nehru revised it more in the direction of a socialist line.[134] However, Nehru has denied contemporary press reports that "a certain mysterious individual with communist affiliations" had been the author of the resolution. In his autobiography he characterized such accounts as government-inspired "tales of mystery and imagination."[135] Both Nehru and Gandhi have testified to the effect that it was composed largely by the former in consultation with the latter.[136]

Roy was not at all pleased with the final version of the resolution. In an article written a few months after its passage, he charged that this "confused resolution" had compromised on the two vital preconditions for the attainment of true freedom in India—the overthrow of foreign imperialism and native feudalism.[137] In a manifesto composed in 1934 and entitled "Whither Congress?" Roy criticized the Karachi resolution as an "instrument of deception," which had raised false hopes in the Congress left wing and concealed the party's retreat from the path of revolution.[138]

The U.P. Agrarian Crisis

The Congress party, despite the limited concessions it had won in the Delhi Pact, emerged from the latest confrontation with the British government with increased authority and prestige. By entering into negotiations with Gandhi, the government of India, for the first time, had implicitly conceded the party's claim to speak for all of the Indian people. This gain was clearly recognized in London where Sir Winston Churchill declared that it was "alarming and also nauseating to see Gandhi, a seditious Middle Temple lawyer, now posing as a fakir of a type well-known in the East, striding half-naked up the steps of the Viceregal palace . . . to parley on equal terms with the representative of the King Emperor." He lamented the fact that the viceroy, by negotiating with "this malignant subversive fanatic," had raised the status of the Congress party to that of a dominant and recognized power in India.[139]

Nehru, Bose, and other radical Congressmen were quick to take advantage of their newfound status. They had never accepted the Delhi Pact in the same spirit as Gandhi. For them it was merely a short truce which would provide time for preparing the ground for the next round with the enemy. Moreover, they interpreted the viceroy's willingness to enter into a covenant with the Congress as a license for the party to establish itself as an intermediary between the government and the Indian people. In the process, they hoped to strengthen further the Congress party's authority within the country, particularly in the rural areas.

This effort centered on Nehru's home province of U.P., where peasant conditions were particularly severe. There, the greater part of agricultural land was cultivated by some five to six million tenants, most of whom paid their rent to landlords in cash at fixed rates, rather than in kind as a percentage of the produce.[140] Consequently, they were especially hurt by the decline in agricultural prices resulting from the worldwide economic depression. The hard-pressed peasantry in U.P. were in an angry mood.

This provided an opportunity for the Congress left wing. As general secretary of the AICC, Nehru issued a circular on March 10 to all provincial Congress units urging them to strengthen the party organization in the countryside in preparation for a renewal of the struggle with the British. Strenuous efforts were made in the U.P. to implement this directive. A large number of party volunteers were sent into the villages. They promised tenants that the local party office, on request, would intercede on their behalf for the purpose of reducing rents. Similar offers were made to landlords with respect to the payment of land revenue. Subsequently the party decided that rents should be reduced by a certain fixed rate throughout the province and tenants were instructed not to pay in excess of that rate.[141]

The control of rents and land revenue is ordinarily considered a function of government, not of a political party. There were more direct attempts to supplant local governmental authority in certain isolated areas within the province. In Muttra district, efforts were made to create a parallel government. The Congress party appointed its own *tahsildar*[q] for the district and established a police station and court. A prominent Congressman circulated in Bara Banki district an elaborate scheme for the creation of a parallel government based on the traditional village *panchayats*.[r] By April the government was facing a serious challenge to its authority in rural U.P. The operation of revenue courts was being obstructed, crops attached on judicial decrees were being forcibly removed, and law enforcement officials subjected to attack. The government and the Congress party were accusing each other of violating the terms of the Delhi Pact. At the same time the provincial Congress party was championing the peasants' demand for land. Nehru held forth the prospect of Congress rule under which all land would be owned by the tiller. Other Congressmen were speaking in terms of a workers' and peasants' republic in which parasitic landlords would find no place.[142]

Roy spent part of March, April, and May in U.P. Both before and after the Karachi session, he was active in the peasant agitation there. On occasion he stayed at Brajesh Singh's ancestral home in Kalakankar near Lucknow.[s] It has already been noted that Roy accompanied Nehru on a tour of villages in the province in early March. Before the end of the month he had traveled, according to his own account, "over 2000 kilometres" and had visited scores of towns and villages.[143] After returning from Karachi, he re-

[q] A *tahsildar* is one who collects the land revenue, as an agent either of the government or the landlord.

[r] A *panchayat* is a traditional council or court of a village or caste.

[s] Singh's brother was the Raja of Kalakankar.

ported that the peasant movement was developing rapidly under "our leadership," but that "the apple" was "too large for our tiny hands" with the result that he and his helpers were overworked and not able to accomplish as much as they would have liked.[144]

In an article which appeared in *Revolutionary Age* (New York), in April 1931, Roy wrote that the Congress party had sought to exploit the agrarian crisis but had been unable to control the forces it had unleashed. He revealed that he and his group were attempting to provide Congressmen in the villages with a concrete program of action which did not directly conflict with Congress policy, but which would nevertheless intensify the class struggle and eventually force a break with the party leadership. The extent of Roy's influence among local Congressmen is uncertain, but it is known that he was one of the guiding forces behind the Central Peasants' League, an organization which worked closely with the Congress party and whose efforts met with considerable success in various parts of the province.[145]

The U.P. government was alarmed by the propagation of communist ideology in the course of the peasant agitation. The governor, Sir Malcolm Hailey, referring to this aspect of the campaign, reported to the provincial legislature that

> tenants . . . were told that landlords were parasites and that their only hope for the future is in a peasants' and workers' republic which will abolish landlords and that landlords who resist Congress now will be 'swept beyond the seven seas.' . . . Certain newspapers [reported] . . . that landlords habitually perpetuate nameless horrors on tenants, that in order to force the payment of rents they have habitually been burning villages, maiming peasants, and raping their women.[146]

Roy could not have but rejoiced at developments in the U.P. The broadening of the base of the Congress party, its development into a semilegal organization, and the radicalization of its lower echelons had been his declared aims since returning to India. He felt that the Indian countryside was "in the throes of a mighty peasant revolt" due to the worldwide fall in agricultural prices, and he was confident that the Congress left wing could capture the nationalist organization by championing the demands of the peasantry and the petty bourgeoisie.[147]

In U.P. the interests of the nationalists and the Royists had happily coincided. Both groups had been eager to strengthen the grass-roots support of the Congress party, but for different reasons. Except for its left-wing minority, the former group saw the party as an organizational weapon to be used, in the manner of the Irish Sein Fein, in the struggle against foreign domination. The latter, with the example of the Jacobins and the bolsheviks in mind, envisioned the party as a tool to be used against both the common enemy and their more conservative compatriots.

As a result of the disturbances, the provincial government announced certain reductions in rent, which were implemented before the autumn harvest. Considering the remissions inadequate, the U.P. PCC, under Nehru's guidance, launched a no-rent campaign in December in five districts within the province.[148] British intelligence reported that Roy's spadework had apparently encouraged Nehru to take such action.[149] The British promptly responded to this new challenge with the promulgation of drastic emergency ordinances not only in the U.P. but in two other centers of militant nationalism, Bengal and the Northwest Frontier Province. Before the end of the year, both Nehru and T.A.K. Sherwani, president of the U.P. PCC, were imprisoned.[150]

In traveling between Karachi and the U.P., Roy visited the Punjab. His attempt there to secure the cooperation of the Kirti Kisan party was unsuccessful, but he did manage to win the support of a youth organization associated with it, the Nau Jawan Bharat Sabha.[151]

Arrest, Trial, and Imprisonment

After approximately seven months of strenuous efforts to advance his own program in India, Roy's activities were cut short by his arrest in Bombay on July 21. Apprehended on the same day were ten others—including Tayab Shaikh, Sundar Kabadi, Dr. M. R. Shetty, A. N. Shetty, and Charles Mascarenhas—on the charge of harboring a fugitive.[152]

Seldom had the Indian police worked as hard to capture a man as in the case of Roy. Within a few days after his arrival in India, the authorities had suspected his presence.[153] By late March, Roy was reporting that "the atmosphere" was "getting hot" and that consequently he "must always be on the run."[154] A few days later, he wrote from Karachi that "the secret is completely out," thanks to the services of the official communists[t] who consider it their revolutionary duty to exterminate the "danger" by whatever means necessary.[155] At the same time the CPI was attacking Roy as a "renegade" and as a man who had diverted "Bolshevik gold" to his own personal use.

Despite the determined efforts of the police, Roy managed to elude them for several months while at the same time making creditable progress toward the realization of his goals. A contemporary press report noted that on several occasions he had narrowly averted capture and that "but for his amazing cunning, Roy would have been in custody within a week after his arrival."[156]

Contributing to Roy's difficulties was the arrival of a woman who had accompanied him on his escape from China in 1927 and had helped him flee Moscow the following year. This time, however, she could be of little help, but she was apparently determined to be near Roy, even if, under the circumstances, their meetings would be difficult to arrange. From the moment of her arrival in Bombay on July 1, she was under close police surveillance.[157] Despite

[t] Later the Royists suspected that Sundar Kabadi had also betrayed, perhaps unwittingly, Roy's whereabouts to the police.

the risks involved, Roy managed to meet with her briefly on two occasions. Although she did not lead them to their quarry, as the police had hoped, through her a number of Roy's followers and sympathizers were identified.[158]

Not wishing to create any further difficulties for Roy, she eventually left Bombay to stay with Brajesh Singh at Kalakankar Palace.[159] On July 22 she and Brajesh Singh were arrested by the local police. Released on bail, she returned to Bombay to help make arrangements for Roy's defense, but was arrested there under the Foreigners Act[u] and deported as an undesirable alien.[160]

British authorities had made strenuous efforts to capture Roy for, as one intelligence officer later told him, he was considered to be "the only man who could make communism a real danger in India."[161] An intelligence report, reviewing communist activities in India during this period, acknowledged that Roy had managed to do "very considerable mischief, despite the fact that the police were continually hot on his heels." During the brief seven months at his disposal, he had gained many supporters for his views—including important Congressmen—in various parts of the country. "Roy, ever the realist," the report continued, "stands out heads and shoulders above all other Indian communist leaders with the possible exception of Dr. G. M. Adhikari, and his continuous exhortations to 'eschew the dangerous ultra-left policy,'" would have won more converts to communism "in the end" than the CPI's sectarian policies. "His conviction," it was felt, had "removed from the political arena a dangerous enemy of capitalism, landlordism and imperialism and [had] struck another blow at Indian communism in general."[162]

Roy was sent to Kanpur to stand trial on a warrant issued in 1924 in connection with the Kanpur Conspiracy Case.

[u] In an effort to block her deportation, one of Roy's followers offered to marry her on the theory, later rejected as false, that if married to an Indian she could not be considered an alien. Warned by her that he would then be unable someday to marry the woman he loved, he replied gallantly, if not too diplomatically, "For Roy I would go to the gallows!"

The charge was that between 1921 and 1924 he had conspired to deprive the King-Emperor of his Sovereignty of British India by means of violent revolution. On October 15 Roy was committed by a magistrate to Sessions.[163] After several postponements, his trial in the Court of Sessions began on November 3 and was concluded on December 16.[164] Judgment was reserved until January 9, when Roy was sentenced to twelve years' transportation.[v] The severity of the sentence came as a shock to Roy, and he immediately began to lay plans for an appeal to the High Court and to the Privy Council if necessary.

Soon after his conviction Roy was transferred to Bareilly, U.P., and his classification was reduced from that of a "Class A" to a "Class B" prisoner. This meant that he would have had fewer privileges than before. He was allowed to receive and send only one letter a month.[165]

Since all of Roy's friends, except Brajesh Singh, lived in other parts of the country, he was given the sole responsibility for making arrangements for the appeal. Unfortunately for Roy, several months before the appeal was to be heard, Brajesh Singh renounced Roy's doctrines and returned to the orthodox communist fold.[166] By the end of 1932 he had returned to Europe.[167] With Singh's sudden departure Roy was crippled in his effort to prepare for the hearing. It proved difficult to assemble the papers of the case, which had been in Singh's care. Most of Roy's loyal supporters as well as many left-wing nationalists, who had come to his defense, were in jail. As late as April 23, eight days before judgment was to be delivered, Roy had not been able to engage a lawyer.[168/w]

On May 2, 1933, Mr. Justice Thom of the Allahabad High Court dismissed Roy's appeal, but reduced his sentence to six years' rigorous imprisonment. Speaking from the dock in his own behalf, Roy had admitted that he had preached

[v] In effect, this sentence meant twelve years of rigorous imprisonment.

[w] He was able, at the last minute, to obtain the services of the eminent Indian lawyer and politician, Dr. Kailash Nath Katju.

the doctrine of violent revolution. He had contended, however, that the government of India was an "enormous tyranny" and had quoted Hume and Bentham in defense of a people's right to take up arms against an oppressive regime. The judge was not persuaded by Roy's arguments. Commenting on Roy's statement, he observed in his judgment that the writings of Hume and Bentham were "irrelevant to the present issue," however weighty their opinion might be "in academic matters." The appellant, he said, should have referred "not merely to the attractive doctrine of political philosophers but to the mundane matter of fact provisions of the Indian Penal Code."[169]

Still hopeful for leniency in view of the recent remissions of the sentences of the Meerut Conspiracy Case prisoners, Roy contacted Sir Stanford Cripps and other prominent Englishmen in a vain effort to get his case before the Privy Council. An appeal to the U.P. government for executive clemency met with a similar fate. Roy was not released from prison until November 20, 1936, after serving all but eight months of his six-year sentence.[170]

Throughout this long period of confinement, Roy was able to maintain close contact with his followers through an extensive correspondence. He also composed letters addressed to Congressmen, including the founders of the Congress Socialist party. His letters to socialists will be discussed in the next chapter. One of his most important statements addressed to members of the Congress party was composed in 1934 and entitled "An Address to the Congress Rank and File."[171] Some of his writings during this period were published in book and pamphlet form. These include: *My Defence* (1932), *Congress at the Crossroads* (1934?), *On the Congress Constitution* (1936), and *Letters by M. N. Roy to the Congress Socialist Party* (1937). In addition, a large number of his articles appeared in Royist journals and in the Indian press.[x] All of this was possible

[x] For example, a series of articles by Roy appeared in 1934 under the title "From a Critical Congressman" in the *Independent* (Bombay).

due to the complicity of Roy's jailers, many of whom were nationalist sympathizers.[172]

In addition to politics Roy's mind turned to philosophical questions during this period. He read works on the history of materialism, including the writings of Marx and Engels on the subject, as well as books on biology and the theory of relativity.[173] When he left prison he brought with him nine unfinished manuscript volumes,[174] tentatively entitled "Philosophical Consequences of Modern Science."[y] He sought in the social and physical sciences for the patterns and motivations of human behavior in politics and society. As Roy's political fortunes declined in later years he was to turn more and more to philosophy as a solace.[z] Eventually he was to eschew communism altogether in favor of a philosophy of radical humanism, which sought to reconcile materialism with individual freedom and free will. In the process he was also to abandon party politics in favor of a system of decentralized political power and a cooperative economy, the establishment of which, he felt, was necessary to ward off the danger of dictatorship from either the left or the right.

Roy's arrest did not mean the end of Royism in India. Although his work did not go forward with the same momentum as before, his followers continued to operate at his behest. Although a few defected, there were others who took their place.

[y] Roy later published a three-volume study under this title.

[z] Roy's philosophical ideas, as well as the evolution of his political thought, are reflected in some of his later writings, such as: *Scientific Politics* (Dehra Dun: Indian Renaissance Publishers, 1947); *Science and Superstition* (Dehra Dun: Indian Renaissance Publishers, 1940); *Materialism: An Outline of the History of Scientific Thought* (Dehra Dun: Indian Renaissance Publishers, 1940); *Heresies of the Twentieth Century*, 2nd ed. (Bombay: Renaissance Publishers, 1943); *New Orientation* (Calcutta: Renaissance Publishers, 1946); *New Humanism* (Calcutta: Renaissance Publishers, 1947); *Science and Philosophy* (Calcutta: Renaissance Publishers, 1947); *Radical Humanism* (Eastern Economist pamphlet No. 14); *Reason, Romanticism and Revolution*, 2 vols. (Calcutta: Renaissance Publishers, 1952-55); and *Politics, Power and Parties* (Calcutta: Renaissance Publishers, 1960).

The Royists were helped by the widespread sympathy toward Roy aroused by his arrest and incarceration. Prominent nationalists, including Nehru, joined his defense committee. During his confinement Roy's health deteriorated. His weight dropped. Colds brought complications resulting from his old ear infection. In the summer of 1932 he had serious trouble with his heart, resulting subsequently in his transfer to a prison in Dehra Dun, which, situated in the Himalayan foothills, enjoyed a more hospitable climate than the plains. Symptoms of tubercular infection also appeared.[175] Roy's defense committee complained of inadequate medical treatment. Nehru wrote at this time, in reference to Roy, that the life of "one of the bravest and ablest of India's sons" was "sliding downhill to the brink." It was a tragedy, he said, "to see the waste of the lives of those who have the ability and capacity to do so much for their country."[176]

Trade-Union Unity

Following the secession of the communists, the president of the AITUC, R. S. Ruikar, a Royist sympathizer, issued a statement heralding the event as removing "the last obstacles in the way of unity" and suggesting an amalgamation of all unions outside the Red TUC on the basis of an agreement on the fundamental principles of trade unionism. Individual unions would be free to support whatever political views they wished.[177] This was essentially the position of Roy and his group, which continued to work within the AITUC during Roy's long confinement. The main thrust of their activity was in behalf of trade-union unity. Their goal was to unite the AITUC with the AIRF and the moderate trade unions which had seceded in 1929 to form the ITUF into a single labor federation.

On May 10, 1931, a meeting attended by representatives of approximately forty unions was held in Bombay under the chairmanship of Jamnadas Mehta, president of the AIRF, who had served as one of Roy's spokesmen at Karachi. Its purpose was to explore possible means of healing the breach in the Indian trade-union movement. Failing to reach consensus, the conference appointed a committee to consider the question further. Two members of the seven-man committee—Tayab Shaikh and Dr. C. Y. Chitnis—were Royists. Jamnadas Mehta also served on the committee.[178]

Trade-union unity was first advanced as a slogan of moderate trade unionists, who wished to lock the door securely behind the secessionist communists and isolate them permanently from the mainstream of Indian labor. The Royists, however, soon appropriated the slogan and adapted it to their own purposes by attaching to it the doctrine of class struggle.[179] Shortly before his arrest, Roy had drafted a Platform of Unity in which he defined a union as an organ of class struggle, set forth a minimum program of economic and political demands, and pledged the trade-union movement to support the nationalist struggle. The platform was broad enough to include communist-dominated unions should their leaders eschew their ultra-left tactics. This document, under the sponsorship of the Royist GKU, was to serve as a focus of unity efforts in the next several years.[180]

Toward the end of the year a unity conference was convened at which Roy's Platform of Unity, with modifications, was endorsed, and a Trade Union Unity Committee appointed to popularize the platform within the labor movement.[181] In May 1932 the AITUC executive committee met at Nagpur to consider proposals which had been put forth by the Unity Committee. At the meeting, the Royists, who enjoyed a temporary majority on the executive due to the arrest of several of its members,[182] sought to find a middle ground between the extremes of the right and the left, both of which were opposed to unity efforts.[183] The Royists were supported in their endeavor by the AITUC President, R. S. Ruikar, who had earlier issued a statement urging all trade unions to put aside party partisanship and "rally round the banner of the TUC . . . [in order] to present a united front to capitalism."[184] Most of the members of the executive were in favor of the Unity Platform in general, although certain provisions evoked considerable opposition.[185]

A few months later, in July 1932, a second trade-union unity conference, attended by representatives of over a hundred unions, was held at Madras. The Royist Platform of Unity, as amended in earlier conferences, again provided the basis around which efforts to secure a working agreement revolved. One of the important clauses in the Platform stated that

> the Indian trade-union movement shall support and actually participate in the struggle for India's freedom from the point of view of the working classes. This would mean the establishment of a socialist state and during the interval, socialization and nationalization of all means of production and distribution as far as possible.

All of the major labor organizations were willing to endorse this plank, with the proviso that the goal of an independent socialist state was to be achieved by nonviolent means and communists would be excluded from the proposed labor federation.[186]

The AITUC was willing to accept these conditions but the attempt at unification failed, at this time, because of a lack of agreement on the question of international affiliation. The ITUF was affiliated with both the International Federation of Trade Unions at Amsterdam and the International Labor Organization at Geneva. The AITUC leaders were opposed to joining either organization, both of which, they claimed, supported the imperialist policies of the European powers. Roy had tried to solve this problem by providing in his original Platform of Unity that the united trade-union movement would not affiliate with either the Amsterdam or Geneva organizations, but that the question of sending representatives to the latter would be decided on an annual basis after the new federation was formed. This was the formula that was eventually adopted when the labor federations merged in 1938.[187]

The ITUF was not willing at the Madras conference, however, to forego its ties with either of the international labor federations as the price for reconciliation. Taking advantage of their majority, its delegates secured the passage of an amendment to the platform calling for participation in both of these organizations. Finally, a six-man committee, which included Jamnadas Mehta and the Royist Dr. C. Y. Chitnis, was appointed to draft a constitution for the proposed united labor federation based on the Platform of Unity as amended.[188]

The twelfth annual session of the AITUC met in Madras the following September with J. N. Mitra presiding in the absence of the president, R. S. Ruikar, who had been arrested. Shortly before the conference was convened, a message from Roy to the delegates was delivered to Mitra by Sudhin Pramanik. The acting president, who was later to join the Royist group and serve as vice-president of Roy's Indian Federation of Labor, incorporated Roy's statement in his presidential address.[189] Attacking both "reformism" and "ultra-leftism" as harmful to the labor movement in that "it overlooks the immediate interests of the working class," he made an impassioned appeal for the adoption of the Platform of Unity sponsored by the GKU "as the basis of uniting, developing and building up the labor movement in India."[190] He also urged Indian labor not to stand aside from the nationalist struggle and called for the creation of a post-independence workers' state. With Mitra's support, a resolution was passed unanimously at this session endorsing the Platform of Unity as the basis for trade-union unity.[191] The Royist Rajani Mukherji was subsequently elected organizing secretary of the AITUC.[192]

Later, however, when the committee appointed at the Madras Unity Conference submitted its proposed constitution, the AITUC refused to accept it as a basis for amalgamation because of the plank calling for affiliation with the Amsterdam and Geneva labor organizations. In contrast, the AIRF and some unaffiliated unions adopted the constitution in February 1933 and formed the National

Federation of Labor (NFL).[193] The ITUF and the NFL decided in April to form a "smaller unity" without the AITUC and the two organizations, effective May 10, were amalgamated to form the National Trade Union Federation (NTUF), which incorporated in its constitution many parts of the Platform of Unity. This new labor federation, with forty-seven unions and a claimed total membership of 135,000, became the largest labor organization in India.[194]

Within the smaller AITUC the Royists continued to consolidate their position. By the end of 1933 they had secured the affiliation of some forty unions located in the industrial centers of Bombay, Calcutta, Madras, and Nagpur, and in scattered towns in the provinces of Assam, the U.P., Bihar, Orissa, Bombay, and the Central Provinces.[195]

In 1935 further steps were taken toward the unification of the Indian trade-union movement. For reasons to be explored later, the Red TUC was dissolved and its unions rejoined the AITUC at its fourteenth annual session at Calcutta in April.[196] The same year, an All-India Joint Labor Board comprised of an equal number of representatives of the AITUC and the NTUF was formed to coordinate the activities of the two organizations.[197] The following year, V. V. Giri, on behalf of the NTUF, proposed a merger with the AITUC for a provisional one-year period on the condition that the AITUC adopt the constitution of the NTUF, which had been based on the Platform of Unity, and a three-fourths majority be required for all political and strike decisions.[198]

The Giri proposals constituted the main item of business at the 1936 AITUC session held at Nagpur in May. The Royist Maniben Kara, as president of the AITUC, played a leading role in the protracted negotiations which eventually broke down over the demand for a three-fourths majority. This would have given the NTUF a virtual veto on certain important issues. The AITUC wanted the NTUF to accept a two-thirds majority on political questions and an ordinary majority in the case of strikes. But the NTUF refused to yield. The atmosphere was cordial, however, and the door was left open for further negotiations.[199] Eventually, in April 1938 the two organizations joined forces at a special session of the AITUC in Nagpur[a] although the NTUF retained its separate identity until September 1940 when it was dissolved and its individual unions were affiliated with the AITUC.[200]

Two factors contributed to the success of the Royist effort on behalf of trade-union unity. Following the Seventh Comintern Congress, to be discussed below, the CPI no longer objected to collaborating with moderate trade unionists. In addition, the newly formed Congress Socialist party gave valuable support to the unity movement. Within a relatively short time of its formation in 1934, it had become a significant force in the Indian labor movement. Such veteran labor leaders as R. S. Ruikar,[b] Sibnath Bannerjee, Hariharnath Sastri, and R. A. Khedgikar joined the party.[201] Nehru, who was sympathetic to the new group, played a leading role in the 1936 negotiations between the AITUC and the NTUF.[202] By 1936 the socialists and the Royists together controlled the AITUC.[203]

The Seventh Comintern Congress

By mid-1932 the Indian communist movement was in serious decline. There was little communist activity outside of Bombay, Calcutta, and Nagpur, and almost no coordination of efforts between these centers. The Bombay group was itself weakened by the intense factional dispute between Ranadive and Deshpande. Moreover, almost all of the former communist unions had fallen under the control of the Royists.

[a] Trade-union unity in India was short-lived. Following the outbreak of World War II the AITUC, divided within itself on the question of supporting the British war effort, adopted a neutral attitude toward the war. The Royists felt that such a stand would, in effect, make India a passive partner of the Axis powers and consequently decided to withdraw from the AITUC to form a separate labor federation. In November 1941 the Indian Federation of Labor was formed with Jamnadas Mehta as president and M. N. Roy as general secretary.

[b] After joining the socialists, Ruikar and the Royists drifted apart.

The Meerut prisoners wrote several memoranda to the Comintern during this period complaining of the weakness of the CPI and suggesting the formation of a provisional Central Committee, the adoption of a new constitution, and the establishment of a regular party apparatus on an all-India basis.[204] Shortly thereafter an article appeared in the *International Press Correspondence* which purported to be an "Open Letter" to the CPI from the communist parties of China, Great Britain, and Germany. It criticized the Indian communists along lines similar to the Meerut critiques and urged them to form an effective underground communist party, while at the same time working through various legal organizations. Although the CPI was advised to continue its exposure of "left national-reformists," the party was warned that it would be "a great mistake to continue the practice of self-isolation from . . . the mass trade-unions which are under the influence of reformists."[205] It is difficult to imagine how both of these aims could be pursued simultaneously. This letter represents the first halting step toward a reversal of the strategy and tactics laid down in 1928-29. The following year the Comintern was in full retreat. The CPI was criticized for isolating itself from the nationalist movement and for failing to understand the need for utilizing "legal and semi-legal forms of mass movements." Both the Chinese and Russian experience had shown, it was said, that "the formation of a mass Communist Party . . . took place and can only successfully take place when the Communist Party participates in and correctly leads all the democratic movements and especially the nationalist movement for independence."

The weakness of the Indian party was ascribed not only to its aloofness from the Congress party, but also to its failure to "take the initiative for the unity of the working class." At the same time, however, the Comintern was careful to make a distinction between this new line and the "economism" of Roy.[206] In November, the CPI was again reminded that opposition to left nationalists did not mean "refusal to work in the reformist trade-unions . . . or even the joining together of the Red and mass national reformist trade-unions."[207]

At first these criticisms had little effect on the CPI, which continued to flounder. The party was not even able to convene the 1933 annual session of the Red TUC, which had been scheduled to be held in Jamshedpur. The situation began to improve, however, from the point of view of the party, in the spring of that year when unfavorable economic conditions produced a resurgence of labor militancy. This was the depth of the economic depression and in Bombay a number of cotton mills were forced to close and thousands of mill workers lost their jobs. Others suffered wage reductions. The CPI called for a general strike of textile workers, but the strike was ineffective. The GKU, under the Royist G. L. Kandalkar, also advocated a general strike, but only after relief funds had been established. In the midst of the dispute, the communists tried, as they had done several times in the past, to regain control of the GKU, but failed.[208]

The first of the Meerut prisoners were freed by mid-August. Dr. Adhikari, who had been released somewhat earlier, convened a conference, attended by communist representatives from various provinces, at Calcutta in November. According to British intelligence, it was at this meeting that a decision was reached to form "the nucleus of the Provisional Central Committee of the Communist Party of India," which would have the task of arbitrating factional disputes and preparing for a conference to establish an all-India party. Dr. Adhikari was appointed temporary chairman.[c]

[c] Muzaffar Ahmed has referred to a secret meeting of the communists held in Calcutta in December 1933, at which time a new party constitution was adopted, a Central Committee elected, and Dr. Adhikari appointed general secretary. A short time later the CPI resumed its affiliation with the Comintern (Muzaffar Ahmed, *The Communist Party of India: Years of Formation, 1921-1933*, p. 40). Despite the discrepancies in date and the title of Dr. Adhikari's position, it would appear that this is the same meeting referred to in the intelligence report.

Shortly after this meeting the dispute between the two rival Bombay groups was settled, and in Calcutta the Bengal Committee of the CPI was reorganized on the basis of an accommodation between the former terrorist groups, led by N. Chakraverty and Dharani Goswami, and the other members of the Bengal party.[209]

By the end of 1933, K. N. Joglekar, S. S. Mirajkar, S. V. Ghate, and R. S. Nimbkar were released from prison. Although they were all assiduously wooed by the Royists, only Nimbkar joined the group. The remainder threw in their lot with the orthodox communists. Less than two months later the CPI formed a united front with the Roy group to exploit the labor unrest in India.

At an All-India Textile Workers' Conference, held in late January, the two groups agreed to call a general strike in the Indian textile industry within the next three months, and a joint Council of Action, or Strike Committee, was formed to make preparations. It was agreed that the strike would begin in Bombay on April 23. Although strikes broke out prematurely in several cities, four Bombay mills were struck on the designated date and by April 27 almost all the mills in the city had been closed and 70,000 workers were on strike.

The strikes soon spread to other locations and the provincial government became sufficiently alarmed to adopt stiff measures to deal with the situation. The Bombay Special (Emergency) Powers Act was invoked and under its provisions many of the strike leaders, including Dr. Adhikari, were arrested, and all meetings and processions were banned. In mid-July the government of India declared the CPI an unlawful organization[d] and the ban was extended to cover a number of its auxiliary groups as well.[210]

[d] The ban on the CPI was not lifted until 1942. The Bombay Trades Disputes Conciliation Act of 1934 was also a direct result of the textile strike. A government spokesman, in introducing the legislation, stated that he wished "to make it clear that . . . it is an open effort on the part of Government to prevent Communists and extremists (labor) from entering the textile affairs of Bombay City." The Act provided for compulsory arbitration of labor disputes and created a labor officer

During the course of the textile strike the orthodox communists tried to convert it into a general strike extending to all industries throughout India. The Royists on the Strike Committee opposed this action and consequently tried to end the strike and negotiate a settlement. The CPI's influence, however, prevailed and the effort failed. Soon thereafter the Roy group was expelled from the Strike Committee by a narrow margin.[211]

The Royists had clearly erred in agreeing to the joint action with the CPI. They were unable to control the situation they had helped to create. As a result of the strike the CPI made considerable headway in regaining the support of the textile workers it had lost in the past several years, and the influence of the Royists declined correspondingly. The following year the AITUC called for fresh elections within the GKU to determine which of its two rival groups was to be awarded recognition. In the ensuing contest the Royist faction, led by V. B. Karnik, in alliance with R. S. Nimbkar, defeated the communist-oriented faction.[211a] Before long, however, the union was recaptured by the communists under the leadership of S. A. Dange.

The Central Committee of the CPI met again in Bombay in late 1934 to review their party's progress during the past year. The committee had good reason to be pleased. Despite the government ban and the arrest of some of its leaders, the size of the party had increased from 20 members at the beginning of the year to 150. Moreover, the party had made significant headway in India's three main railroad systems, the Bombay textile industry, the Bengal jute industry, and the cotton industry in Kanpur.[212] In addition, the Bombay and U.P. branches of the party had established contact with the newly formed Congress Socialist party. Through this association the communists won val-

---

who would represent the workers if they could find no qualified persons to speak on their behalf (Morris David Morris, *The Emergence of an Industrial Labor Force in India*, p. 187).

uable support in the labor movement and gained entry into the Indian National Congress.

The Comintern's gradual change of course was climaxed by its Seventh Congress in 1935. That year Manuilsky, addressing the Moscow branch of the Soviet party, acknowledged that the Comintern had not been infallible in applying its policies "to the concrete conditions of the working class movement" in various parts of the world. In colonial countries, he noted, the Comintern had framed "excellent resolutions," without paying sufficient attention "to the real possibilities of carrying them out." He noted, for example, that communists in dependent areas had been directed to form their "own small unions," with the result that they have been "kept . . . away from the masses."[213]

It was obvious that as a result of the Comintern policy laid down in 1928-29 communist parties throughout the world had been badly weakened. At the same time it was also apparent that the phenomenon of fascism was a force a good deal more tenacious than the final paroxysms of an expiring capitalist system. Consequently, the Seventh Comintern Congress rejected, at least implicitly, its former strategy and tactics. On the colonial question, recommendations were made on the basis of an assessment of the current policy of the CCP. Some weight was given to the efforts of the Chinese party on behalf of the peasantry, but it was held that the party's recent successes were mainly due to its assumption of a nationalist role. The principal Chinese delegate, Wang Ming (Ch'en Shao-yü),[e] argued in a speech before the assembled delegates that the strength of the CCP was derived from its emergence as "the vanguard in the anti-imperialist struggle." He concluded from this experience that it was "inconceivable" that a small communist party could be transformed into a "mass party"

[e] While a political exile in Moscow, Wang Ming published an important article in 1969 condemning Mao Tse-tung's "ten major crimes in China" and "five major crimes in international affairs" (Wang Ming, "China: Cultural Revolution or Counter-revolutionary Coup?" [Moscow: Novosti Press Agency Publishing House, 1969]).

without participating in the national struggle against foreign oppression.[214]

The future policy of the CCP, as outlined by Wang Ming, was based on the above views. The nationalist character of the Chinese communists was to be stressed by spearheading the resistance movement against the Japanese invader. In mobilizing "the broadest masses of the people," the CCP was to alter its policies to give them "a more clearly expressed popular and clearly national character."[215]

Wang Ming criticized the CPI for failing to emulate the Chinese party. Due to its "left sectarian errors," he said, the Indian party had isolated itself from the nationalist movement. Despite the obvious futility of attempting to create an alternative mass nationalist party, it had stubbornly refused to cooperate with the one organization, the Congress party, which was popularly identified with the independence struggle. He exhorted the Indian communists to cooperate with the Congress party and its affiliated organizations while, at the same time, maintaining their own separate organizational and political identity outside the Congress.

Such a policy would obviously require the adoption of a relatively moderate platform. Wang Ming characterized the India party's radical demands for the creation of a Workers' and Peasants' Soviet Republic and the confiscation of zamindari lands without compensation as inopportune. As an alternative he suggested the acceptance of more modest proposals such as opposition to India's "slave constitution," the establishment of democratic liberties, and the abolition of exhorbitant taxes and land rents.[216]

In accordance with these views, the resolution on "The Anti-Imperialist Peoples' Front in the Colonial Areas," adopted by the Seventh Comintern Congress, declared that it was necessary to reconcile the interests of socioeconomic reform and world revolution with the bourgeois-democratic sentiments of nationalist leaders. Communists in colonial areas were instructed to participate actively in the "mass anti-imperialist movements headed by the nationalists-reformists" and to seek joint action with them on the basis of an "anti-imperialist platform." They were warned against the danger of adopting a cavalier attitude toward nationalist aspirations and advised that the support of such goals was consistent with the correct application of "Leninist-Stalinist national policy."[217] With respect to India, communists in implementing this resolution were to strive for the establishment of "a united anti-imperialist front . . . both from within and without the National Congress."[218]

In effect, the Comintern had reverted to Lenin's colonial policy which had sought to utilize nationalist movements for communist ends. Roy and his adherents claimed that the resolutions of the Seventh Comintern Congress had vindicated their stand against the ultra-left tactics of the past several years. But despite the similarities, an important difference remained between the position of the Royists and the orthodox communist point of view. Whereas the Comintern wanted a united front both "from within" and "from without" the Congress party, Roy urged a united front "from within" only. He condemned the CPI's efforts after 1935 to build up separate organizations—such as peasant leagues, trade unions, and youth leagues—outside the Congress party on the grounds that this would only serve to divide and hence weaken the Congress party, the vehicle of Indian nationalism. As one of Roy's followers explained, the Royists regarded the Congress as "*the* organization of the masses, as *the* organization of national revolutionary struggle, as *the* united national front" (italics mine). In contrast, "the official communists . . . condescended to regard the Congress as one of the anti-imperialist organizations in the country," with which "they proposed to form the united front by setting up joint committees which will represent the National Congress as well as" a number of communist-dominated organizations.[219]

Roy maintained that this difference in approach stemmed from an unwillingness on the part of the CPI to accept fully the implications of the new line, and in correspondence with Moscow sought readmission to the Comintern. He contended that there were no longer any differences between himself and orthodox communists on the question of colonial policy.[220] Stalin, however, did not agree. Roy's request for reinstatement was ignored and denunciations of his views continued to emanate from the Comintern.[f]

[f] Wang Ming in his important speech on colonial policy at the Seventh Comintern Congress remarked that "the theory of the Social-Democrats and the renegades—Roy and others—about 'decolonization' has been . . . completely shattered. . . . The position of Social Democracy and of the renegades that evaluate the present situation as the 'beginning of a new era of fascism' and see for the future only the 'prospect of black reaction' is entirely without foundation" (Wang Ming, "The Revolutionary Movement in the Colonial Countries," p. 11).

9. Left-Wing Unity and the Indian Nationalist Movement

THE decade preceding World War II was a crucial period in the history of the Indian nationalist movement. It was at this time that the leadership of Gandhi and the "old guard"—Congress veterans who, with few exceptions, were annually re-elected to the party's Working Committee—faced its most serious challenge for control of the Congress party. The outcome of this internal party struggle determined the nature and scope of the independence movement throughout the war years and until the attainment of freedom in 1947. It also determined the political complexion of the party that was to guide the Republic of India through the early, and critical, formative years of its existence.

The next two chapters focus on the debate between M. N. Roy and Indian socialists in the 1930's on the important question of the relationship between socialism and nationalism in the Indian independence struggle. Failure to resolve this issue contributed in large measure to the inability of the socialists, Royists, communists, and other left-wing groups in India to unite in order to make an effective challenge for the leadership of the Congress party.

The conflict today between the Soviet Union and the People's Republic of China over the correct attitude to adopt toward "bourgeois-nationalist" regimes in the Third World is the latest manifestation of this thorny problem which has agitated communists since the early years of the Comintern. The present dispute between the CPI or "pro-Moscow" party and the CPI (Marxist) or "pro-Peking" party revolves largely around the issue of the role of the national bourgeoisie in the post-independence period. On domestic questions the two parties differ over the extent to which the nationalist leaders can be relied upon to move India's economy in the direction of socialism and ultimately communism. In the area of foreign policy they differ over the extent to which the Congress party is capable of maintaining a strictly neutral foreign policy, free of entangling alliances or economic dependence on the Western powers. For communists in India, as in other former colonial areas, the problem has always been, both before and after independence, how to unite with the national bourgeoisie without being completely absorbed by them.

Both the CPI and the Royists were active within the All-India Socialist party (CSP) during the period under consideration. Information is readily available elsewhere on the alliance between the communists and the socialists at this time.[1] Consequently, there is little need here for a detailed examination of the relationship between these two groups, although for convenience, a summary of the CPI's fractional activities within the socialist party will be provided. In contrast with the CPI, very little is known about the Royists and therefore attention will be concentrated on this group. It will be shown that the Royists played a more important role in the early years of the CSP than has been heretofore suspected and that they made significant contributions to the formulation of socialist policy. Before exploring this question, however, we will first discuss the origins of the CSP and the dissatisfaction of its founders with Gandhi's leadership.

The Congress Socialist Party

In Patna, Bihar, on May 18 and 19, 1934, the All-India Congress Committee (AICC), meeting for the first time since the resumption of the civil disobedience campaign in January 1932, made two important decisions which were to alienate a considerable section of the Congress party. First, formal approval was given to Gandhi's decision to suspend, except for himself, the individual civil disobedience campaign. Second, the proposal of the All-India Swarajya party to contest the forthcoming elections to the central Legislative Assembly was endorsed.[2] Three weeks later the government's ban on the party was lifted.

The decision of the AICC to adopt a new tack was a tacit admission that the civil disobedience campaign had failed. As a result of the government's suppression, the movement had been demoralized. After the first year, the Congress had been put on the defensive and, in the words of a contemporary party spokesman, the campaign had been reduced to "sporadic attempts at defiance of authority by individual Congressmen."[3] After Patna, the Congress secured a new lease on life, not by having vanquished its enemy, but through its sufferance. Its members now had to behave constitutionally or face another round of persecution. To make matters more galling for the nationalists, the government had not granted a full and unreserved amnesty. Its proscription of many organizations affiliated with the Congress, such as the Hindustani Seva Dal and the Khudai Khidmatgars (Khan Abdul Ghaffar Khan's Redshirts in the Northwest Frontier Province), continued, and not all political prisoners were released.[4] When the Congress convened its annual session in October, Jawaharlal Nehru was still in prison and unable to attend.

Also at Patna, on the eve of the AICC meeting, the first All-India Socialist Conference was convened, at which time a decision was taken to organize an All-India Congress Socialist party.[5] Conference delegates were moved to take such action by a common dissatisfaction with the policies of the Congress party, to which they all belonged. The abandonment of the civil disobedience movement had left a residue of bewilderment and disillusionment, especially among the younger and more impatient Congressmen, and had inflamed smouldering doubts about the efficacy of Gandhian tactics. Those who attended the conference vehemently opposed the decision to enter the central Legislative Assembly. To their minds, this was a clear violation of the 1929 Lahore resolution[6] which had called for boycotting the legislatures and had demanded nothing less than complete independence. To the socialists this new policy was further proof that the nationalist movement, under the leadership of Gandhi and the old guard, was drifting inevitably toward constitutionalism and accommodation with the British. Furthermore, they felt that the Congress party had deliberately refrained from adopting programs that would bring any substantial relief to the sufferings and deprivations of India's peasants and workers. They were unhappy with the 1931 Karachi resolution, widely acclaimed as the first public commitment on the part of the nationalist movement on behalf of social and economic reform. Its implementation, they felt, would not alter substantially the inequities endemic to Indian society.[7] The CSP was thus conceived as a party within the Indian National Congress which would press for the adoption of more militant tactics in the nationalist, anti-colonialist struggle and for a more progressive position on the question of social and economic reform.[a]

This was not the first time that a socialist party had been organized in India. Each time there had been a lull in the nationalist movement, discontent had bred new attempts to form separate groups within the Congress party to act as a spur to its leadership. In September 1931 a socialist group had been formed in the northern province of Bihar in response to the suspension of the 1930-31 civil disobedience movement, but it had become moribund with the arrest of its leaders following the partial revival of the movement at the end of the year.[8] In 1932-33 one of the founders of the Bihar Socialist party,[9] Jayaprakash Narayan, was instrumental in forming a socialist group from among fellow Congressmen in Nasik Road Central Prison.[10] Under his leadership, the group formulated a draft constitution for an Indian socialist party as well as a program of action. When in July 1933 Congress leaders decided to sub-

[a] In India, groups which shared one or both of these positions were designated as "left wing." The term "right wing" was given a similarly broad but converse meaning. It is in this dual sense, and in conformity with Indian usage, that these terms are employed throughout this study.

stitute individual "satyagraha" in place of the waning civil disobedience campaign, a group of Congressmen who had attended the meeting and were dissatisfied with this action met separately at Poona to form a socialist opposition group. These men, acting independently of the socialists in prison, appointed a committee to draft a constitution and a program for the new organization.[11]

Socialism at this time was in vogue among young, educated Indians, but it more closely represented an ill-defined sentiment than a distinct ideology. The leadership of the CSP in the 1930's reflected the inchoate nature of Indian socialism. Among the party's ten most influential leaders, no less than three disparate political orientations were to be found. Narayan and Acharya Narendra Deva were Marxists. Minoo R. Masani, a former member of the British Labour party, and Asoka Mehta were democratic socialists. Achyut Patwardhan and Rammanohar Lohia shared Gandhi's faith in governmental and economic decentralization and nonviolent revolution, as applied to both the nationalist struggle and class conflict.[b]

The platform and policies of the party represented a tenuous balance between the various contending points of view of its leaders. The party was described as Marxist, but not Marxist-Leninist—the latter would have implied a commitment, which was not shared by all, to the concept of the dictatorship of the proletariat. As a compromise, the party

[b] How varied were the political views of these early socialist leaders can be seen in tracing their subsequent careers. Narayan came under the influence of Gandhian ideas in the 1940's, and later, in 1954, formally eschewed politics in order to devote himself to work in the Bhoodan Yagna movement of Vinoba Bhave, a disciple of Gandhi. Masani resigned from the CSP in 1939 and in 1959 helped found the Swatantra (Freedom) party, which is a firm advocate of the free enterprise system. Asoka Mehta left the Praja Socialist party (PSP), the successor of the CSP, in 1962 and joined the Congress party. In January 1966, he became planning minister in Prime Minister Indira Gandhi's cabinet. The late Rammanohar Lohia was expelled from the PSP in 1955 because of his views and unaccommodating attitude. Lohia, who died in October 1967, was the founder of the Samyukta Socialist party (SSP).

was not affiliated either with the Second (socialist) or the Third (communist) Internationals.[12] Marxists did not constitute a majority within the leadership cadre, but they were the most influential group among the party rank and file. Consequently, CSP pronouncements were heavily larded with Marxian terms, which gave the party a more radical appearance than was, in fact, the case.

The CSP and Gandhi

Gandhi never dealt systematically with the problem of the nature of Indian society after independence. His views on the subject are interspersed among utterances and writings on a myriad of subjects to which he was forced to give attention in a crowded life. But one of his most explicit statements on the question occurred in an interview he granted with a group of U.P. zamindars in 1934. On that occasion Gandhi observed that he was not in favor of dispossessing the propertied classes. Instead, he said, his object was to reach their hearts and convert them so that they might hold all their private property "in trust" for their tenants and "use it primarily for their welfare." His ultimate aim, he declared, was "the cooperation and coordination of capital and labor and of the landlord and tenant," and, he assured the zamindars, there was "nothing in the Congress creed or policy that need frighten" them. He exhorted them, however, to refrain from squandering their wealth in "luxurious and extravagant living" and to use it instead to promote the well-being of their tenants. Once they "experience a sense of kinship with you and a sense of security that their interests as members of a family will never suffer at your hands," he said, there would be no longer any need to fear class war.[13]

Jayaprakash Narayan, writing in 1936, characterized Gandhism as a mixture of "timid economic analysis, good intentions and ineffective moralizing." Such views, he held, were objectively deceptive in that they masked the fact that the wealth of the landlord and the capitalist was obtained by theft. Gandhi, he continued, was inadvertently giving his seal of approval to a system of "large-scale, organized theft and violence." Moreover, he charged, Gandhism was being used as a "cloak for reaction and conservatism." Gandhi's views had found ready acceptance among the wealthy, he contended, because it made them appear virtuous and at the same time protected their ill-gotten gains. "The acceptance of this philosophy costs them nothing except an occasional donation to a public cause," he wrote, whereas it "strengthens their position . . . by giving it a moral sanction."[14]

Gandhi wanted to transform rather than uproot traditional Indian society and he visualized a revitalized village as the basic social unit. He criticized the socialists for introducing what he regarded to be a foreign system inappropriate to India with its unique problems and heritage. He attacked the socialists not only for popularizing the concept of class war but also for their advocacy of industrialization, which he equated with the introduction of large-scale machinery and its attendant disruption of India's traditional village-based economy, increased suffering for the rural-based population, and the growth of ugly, parasitic cities.

To Narayan and his followers, Gandhi was a "reformist," who offered only palliatives for India's chronic and grievous social ills, when a purgative was required. All Gandhi asked of the landlord and the capitalist, Narayan contended, was that they should "improve their relations with the tenants and laborers," in return for which they could rest assured that nothing disquieting would happen to deny them their favored position in Indian society. He denied Gandhi's claim that, in contrast to the foreign ideas of the socialists, his approach was uniquely Indian. Gandhi's views, Narayan argued, also were imported from the West. Moreover, he likened Gandhi's objections to socialism to those of "Church divines and philosophers of the old order in Europe at the dawn of the industrial revolution," who sought to avoid strife and any sharp reversal of the status quo through the promotion of "common understanding and good will."[15]

William Godwin in his book, *An Inquiry Concerning Political Justice*, argued that the object of all religious morality has been to persuade men "by individual virtue" to repair the injustice of accumulated wealth, and that "the most energetic teachers of religion" have counseled the rich to "hold their wealth only as a trust." In a tract entitled *Why Socialism?* written in 1936, Narayan quoted extensively, and with evident approval, from Godwin's work. He endorsed Godwin's condemnation of this doctrine as exciting man "to palliate" his injustice rather than "to forsake it," and his view that "a gratuitous distribution" by the wealthy was "a very indirect and ineffectual way" of giving every man his due. The result of such a system, Godwin wrote, would be to place the supply of man's wants at the disposal of a few, "enabling them to make a show of generosity with what is not truly their own, and to purchase the gratitude of the poor by the payment of a debt." It endowed the rich with unreasonable pride and the poor with unwarranted servility. Narayan concurred with Godwin's summation that it was "a system of clemency and charity instead of a system of justice."[16]

The CSP and the Congress Party

Many Congress leaders were antagonized by the sharp criticism leveled at them by the socialists. Others were intimidated by the socialists' condoning of violence as a means of resolving class antagonisms. Gandhi was opposed in principle to the use of violence both as a means of settling differences between nations and conflicts between classes.[17] Few shared Gandhi's adherence to nonviolence as a creed; many embraced it as a matter of expedience. It was the most effective weapon available against the British and moreover, to the propertied classes and to others who wished for whatever reason to preserve as far as possible the traditional hierarchical structure of Indian society,

Gandhi's advocacy of class collaboration was more reassuring than the socialist doctrine of class conflict.

It was also feared that the emergence of the CSP might hurt the party at the polls in the forthcoming elections to the central Legislative Assembly.[18] The electorate was restricted to about 1,500,000 persons, representing largely the propertied classes. Consequently, the Congress Working Committee greeted the formation of the CSP in 1934 with a resolution which stated that it was necessary "in view of all the loose talk about confiscation of private property and the necessity of class war, to remind Congressmen" that such ideas were "contrary to the Congress creed of non-violence."[19]

At the same time, the Working Committee advised the various units of the Congress party, in the absence of a program of civil resistance, to concentrate exclusively on Gandhi's constructive program, which involved such varied tasks as the production of *khaddar*,[c] the removal of untouchability, the reconstruction of village life, the establishment of useful small industries, and the promotion of prohibition.[20] Socialists and other dissident groups within the Congress interpreted this move as a suit for peace with their British rulers and as a further retreat from the goal of complete independence as stated at Lahore.

Because of continued resistance to his program, Gandhi announced in September his decision to withdraw from active work in the party. In his announcement he reaffirmed his belief in nonviolence, as well as reform and revolution through conversion, and observed that "one section of the country was running away from these articles of faith and . . . the other was giving no effect to its allegiance to them which it professed."[21] As for the former, he explained that there was "a growing vital difference of outlook between many Congressmen and myself," and added that if the socialists should "gain ascendancy in the Congress," he could not remain a part of it.[22] In a subsequent

[c] Homespun cotton cloth which is also known as *khadi.*

statement he suggested several changes in the Congress constitution which he deemed necessary if the party was to be saved from "disruption." He wanted the Congress creed to be changed from a belief in "peaceful and legitimate" methods to "truthful and non-violent" ones to eliminate any ambiguity as to its meaning. He also urged that spinning be made a requirement of membership, that voting in party elections be restricted to *khaddar* wearers, and that the number of delegates to Congress sessions be reduced from six thousand to one thousand.[23] A few days after this statement was released, a CSP manifesto was issued in Bombay attacking these proposals as an attempt to reduce socialist influence in the Congress party.[24]

Gandhi's "retirement" was postponed until after the annual Congress session, which was held in Bombay in October 1934. This was the first session of the party since the lifting of the government ban in June and the first full-scale session in over three and a half years. Brief, token sessions had been held in Delhi in 1932 and in Calcutta in 1933, but most of the party leaders had been in jail. On the latter occasion nearly half of the elected delegates, including the president, had been arrested en route.[25] The 1934 session was also the first session in which an organized political group within the Congress with a fundamentally different program from that of the leadership participated. Although this occasioned some misgiving, the socialists were unable to prevent amendments to the party constitution along the lines suggested by Gandhi, and their attempt to substitute their own program for Gandhi's constructive program was easily defeated.

In his presidential address at Bombay, the Gandhian Rajendra Prasad defended the constructive program against its critics. He interpreted it as a nonviolent approach to the problem of imperialism and capitalism. "The spinning wheel and *khadi*," he declared, "are symbols of the country's determination to resist all forms of exploitation by non-violent means," and he warned the socialists that coercive techniques would trigger reaction; whereas conversion, though slow, was the surer route to the goal they all shared.[26]

The annual session had been held earlier than usual, despite the fact that October in Bombay is one of the most uncomfortable months of the year, so that the decision of party leaders to contest seats for the central Legislative Assembly could be endorsed in open session before the elections, scheduled for November, were to be held.[27] It also provided a public forum for the leaders of the party to answer the objections of the socialists that the decision to enter the legislative councils was in violation of earlier party resolutions. Finally the pre-election session presented another opportunity for the old guard to allay the fears of the conservative electorate with respect to the party's position on economic and social issues. Evidently this tactic was successful, for the Congress party was able to secure forty-four of the forty-nine elective seats not reserved for special groups.[28]

The CSP and the Royists

Jayaprakash Narayan has acknowledged that while a student in the United States in the 1920's he first imbibed his Marxism through the writings of M. N. Roy. As a member of a communist cell, he was introduced to Roy's works, which he later described as "flaming political tracts, powerfully written, closely reasoned and attempting to tear to shreds the ideology of Gandhi's non-cooperation movement." Roy's book, *India in Transition,*[29] impressed him as "a masterly exposition," and according to his own account, he soon became one of Roy's ardent admirers.[30]

Although there were important differences, the program of the Royists, of all the political groups in India, most closely approximated that of the CSP. Both called for working within the Congress party for the attainment of political independence and ultimately economic and social reform. In addition, they shared a common aversion to Gandhian ideas of nonviolence and trusteeship, which, it was believed, served as a bastion for the conservative wing of the

Congress party, from whose control they wished to wrest the nationalist movement.

The objectives of the CSP, as stated in its constitution, were the attainment of "complete independence . . . and the establishment of a socialist state." The party's "plan of action" called for "work within the Indian National Congress" to secure the acceptance of these objectives.[31] Party leaders believed that there was no alternative to working within the Congress party, which they felt represented the nationalist movement at "the present stage of the Indian struggle . . . that of bourgeois revolution."[32] But at the same time they were determined, according to an official party resolution, to "rescue the Congress from the hands of the right wing by educating and organizing the rank and file on the basis of a clear-cut program of national revolution and to carry on a consistent propaganda for the exposure of the reactionary aims, policies and programs of the right wing."[33]

Upon release from prison in 1936, Roy also joined the Congress party in the interest of both the nationalist and socialist revolution, and he, too, sought to alter Congress policies by working with the rank and file to subvert its leadership. According to Roy's plan, this was to be accomplished by revitalizing and securing control over local party units at the district, *taluka*,[d] and village level, and by working to democratize the Congress constitution to increase the influence of these units in the organizational structure of the party.[34] For Roy, "democratization" was to be "the means to the object of radicalizing the Congress and activization of the rank and file the condition for effective democratic control."[35]

Within the CSP there was an earnest desire to join forces with the communists and the Royists,[36] the two other contemporary Marxian socialist groups with all-India aspirations, and in Jayaprakash Narayan the party had an eloquent exponent of left-wing unity.[37] Narayan was keenly

[d] A *taluka*, also known as a *tahsil*, is a revenue subdivision of a district.

aware that left-wing hegemony over the nationalist movement required that all radical groups learn to work in concert. In his presidential address before the Bengal CSP Conference in 1935, Narayan contended that had the communists not abandoned the Congress party in 1929 on the eve of its launching of the civil disobedience campaign, "the radicalization of the Congress would have gone much further and we would have been much nearer our goal today." Having exposed the folly of political sectarianism, he reaffirmed his conviction that the CSP ought not to remain separate from other socialist forces in India:

> I firmly believe that unless there is a fusion of the forces which I have mentioned, our common objectives will remain unrealized. I . . . exhort you to develop the greatest possible co-operation with the groups that are, except for minor differences, working for the same object as ourselves. . . . I entreat them to work together in the promotion of identical ideals, keeping in mind the day we shall all come closer and merge into one organization.[38]

In view of Narayan's early acquaintance with Roy's writings, the similarities between the goals of Roy's dissident communist group and the CSP, and Narayan's desire for left-wing unity, it is not surprising that efforts were made by the socialists for collaboration with the Royists. In fact, as the CSP has acknowledged, within a few months after the formation of the party, "many members of the Roy group" were taking "a prominent part in the activities of the Party and held leading positions in it. . . . Every known member of the group, with rare exceptions, was absorbed into the Party."[39]

A Royist, Charles Mascarenhas, had been one of the original four members of the socialist group founded by Narayan at Nasik prison.[40] Later, he became one of the founders of the Bombay CSP[41] and, when the CSP was organized on an all-India basis, he was elected to its twenty-one member executive committee.[42] At his prompting, a group of Royists in Calcutta joined the CSP shortly after the 1934 Bihar conference and became co-founders of the Bengal branch of the party. One of them, Rajani Mukherji, was elected general secretary of the Bengal CSP, and Royists at one time constituted a majority of its executive committee.[43] In December 1936, Mukherji, already a substitute member,[44] was elected to full membership in the party's national executive.[45] The Royist Dharma Das Goonavardan also held high office in the Bengal CSP.

The most important unit of the all-India CSP was in the industrial city of Bombay, where many of the party's early leaders, such as Asoka Mehta, Minoo Masani, Purshottam Tricumdas, Achyut Patwardhan, and Yusuf Meherally, were active. Bombay was also a major center of the Royists, many of whom joined the Bombay CSP. Among the most prominent of these, in addition to Mascarenhas, were: Maniben Kara, secretary of the All-India Trade-Union Council (AITUC) in 1936; R. A. Khedgikar, vice-president of the AITUC in 1937 and a member of the Bombay Legislative Assembly in 1937-39; and Dr. M. R. Shetty, a founder of the Bombay Transport and Dock Workers' Union. V. B. Karnik, another prominent Royist in Bombay, did not formally join the CSP, but was active in the trade-union field. Although Tayab Shaikh made his base in Bombay, he was also engaged in organizational efforts on behalf of Roy throughout India. During the years 1933-35, however, he was in prison. Despite their number, Royists in Bombay were continually frustrated in their efforts to exert influence within the CSP due to the unsympathetic attitude displayed toward them by such socialist leaders as M. R. Masani and Purshottam Tricumdas.[46]

Royist groups were also active in the Maharashtra, Gujarat, Punjab, and Sind branches of the CSP. In Maharashtra, Royists were especially prominent in the Poona and Sholapur units of the party. V. M. Tarkunde, who was later to become one of Roy's most trusted associates, was a secretary of the Maharashtra CSP.[47] Other Royists who held important offices in this body were H. R. Mahajani, G. P. Khare, and R. K. Khadelkar, a member of the Maharashtra

Pradesh Congress Committee (PCC).[48] One of the Royist sympathizers in the Maharashtra CSP was a young man by the name of Y. B. Chavan, who became India's defense minister and later home minister in Prime Minister Indira Gandhi's cabinet.[e] In the Gujarat CSP, especially in the city of Ahmedabad, there was a sizable group of Royists, including Thakoresprasad Pandya, a member of its provincial executive committee, and Dasharathlal Mohanlal Thakar of the Ahmedabad Textile Labor Association.[49] Finally, in southern India, A. K. Pillai, one of the founders of the Congress party, and later of the CSP, in the Kerala region, was a staunch supporter of Roy.[50]

The Royists made an important contribution to the shaping of the program and policies of the CSP in its early years. One of the central themes of the Royists was that Indians should demand their right to frame their own constitution by means of a constituent assembly. This was stressed in a manifesto prepared by Roy and first circulated among Congressmen in 1930. About two years later this document was published under the title *Our Task in India.*[51] At the First Conference of the All-India CSP in Bombay in 1934, the Royists were successful in their major effort to push the demand for the convening of a constituent assembly to the forefront of the party's program. The demand was not only incorporated in the "Plan of Action" of the party constitution adopted at the time, but was also the subject of a resolution, which held that the "right of framing the constitution is the sovereign right of the Indian people and . . . the supreme authority which should promulgate the Constitution of India is the National Constituent Assembly." This assembly, according to the constitution and the known views of the Royists, was not to be the result of an accommodation with the British, but was to be

[e] Interview with Justice V. M. Tarkunde, Bombay, November 1, 1961. Chavan broke with the Royists in 1939 on the question of support to the British war effort. To this day, however, he readily acknowledges his intellectual indebtedness to Roy. One of his closest confidants while chief minister of Maharashtra was the noted Sanskrit scholar and Royist, Tarkateertha Laxsmanshastri Joshi.

the culmination of a mass uprising against foreign rule.[52] Substantial parts of the Royist manifesto were incorporated into the CSP platform adopted at Bombay.[53] It will be shown later that the Royists also played an important role in the revision of the CSP program in early 1936.

In a study conducted in India by the U. S. Office of Strategic Services during the war years it was observed that

> there seems little doubt that the Congress Socialist party . . . was considerably influenced by Roy's program. . . . It has been said that both the Royists and the Communists tried to influence the Congress program and that the Royists won.[54]

It is necessary to emphasize this point, since Indian socialists today, because of old animosities, minimize the role the Royists played in the formative years of the CSP.

Roy's Break with the CSP

It was hoped, according to Narayan, that because of their early association with the CSP, the Royists would eventually merge with the party.[55] But this was not to be. When the CSP was first formed, Roy had felt that if its more radical leaders were encouraged, the party might conceivably become, in his words, "the rallying ground of the radical elements of the de-classed intellectuals—the elements objectively heading toward the party of the proletariat." Although he found several of the party's leaders, such as M. R. Masani and Purshottam Tricumdas, "objectionable," he felt that some of them, such as Kamaledevi and Meherally, were "promising." For this reason, he had urged his followers "to meet them half-way and guide them forwards."[56]

He regarded the party as a whole, however, with disdain as representing merely a "vague, heterogeneous radical tendency in the national movement."[57] Given the nature of its politically disparate membership, he suspected that the CSP, if left to its own devices, would very likely "degenerate" into "reformism," i.e., "bourgeois-parliamentarianism."[58] Roy held, however, that nowhere had a strong communist party developed before such "reformist" parties were split. He felt that in China, for example, the nationalist Kuomintang, which he also regarded as "petty-bourgeois," had been the source of the most active cadre of the Chinese Communist party. Consequently, he directed his followers to join the CSP with the object, not of merging with it, but of splitting it and absorbing the "real proletarian elements."[59]

In June 1936, an alleged Royist document was brought to the attention of the CSP executive in which Roy's followers were exhorted to "liquidate" the party. However, the matter was dropped when the two Royist members of the executive, Charles Mascarenhas and Rajani Mukherji, repudiated the document as spurious.[60]

On the eve of Roy's release from jail in late 1936, the CSP, despite growing doubts about Roy's intentions, issued a statement extending to him a "most hearty welcome," and expressing the hope that "this veteran revolutionary" would "utilize every opportunity to unify the anti-imperialist struggle and unite the socialist movement in the country."[61] Soon thereafter Roy received a visit from Narayan, the general secretary of the CSP. Although Roy was critical of certain policies of the CSP, Narayan left the meeting feeling assured of Roy's cooperation and support.[62] Roy's subsequent behavior came as a rude shock to the party.

Soon after the meeting Roy began to issue a series of public statements attacking the policies of the CSP. Finally, at a meeting of Royists in New Delhi in March 1937, a decision was reached to resign from the CSP. Furthermore, Roy instructed his followers to resign in groups at intervals, rather than en bloc, in order to create the impression of a collapse of the party. To secure maximum effect, each group resignation was to be accompanied by a press statement expressing dissatisfaction with CSP policy.[63]

When the CSP executive learned of the Delhi meeting, its members could not agree on a course of action. Masani called for the immediate expulsion of the Royists from the party. The party's only response, however, was the issuance of a circular letter which accused both the Royists and the CPI of "fractionalism" and warned them of the possibility of disciplinary action. "Fractionalism" was defined as including any or all of the following activities: creating a group hostile to the party leadership for the purpose of capturing or splitting the party; libelling the party, the making of statements or committing of acts with the aim of discrediting the party; and attacking members of the party or a section of its leadership in order to cast doubt on their good faith and thus isolate them.[64]

At about the same time, three Royists, Charles Mascarenhas, Madan Shetty, and Dr. M. R. Shetty, were expelled from the Bombay CSP for working in behalf of Congress candidates instead of the CSP's own candidates in the February elections to the Bombay PCC and the AICC.[65] The first two were members of the newly-elected Bombay PCC. The CSP leaders suspected collusion between the Royists and the Congress right wing in an effort to keep socialists out of the AICC, for after the elections, Maniben Kara, a Royist who had resigned earlier from the CSP, was coopted to the AICC with the support of a right-wing Congressman.[66]

From April through August, as planned, groups of Royists located in various provinces of India resigned from the CSP. As a result of these maneuvers Roy and his group earned the undying enmity of the socialists. Narayan felt that Roy had acted in bad faith and that his behavior had constituted a betrayal of the socialist cause. Writing some years later, he commented bitterly on the affair: "After more than a year and a half of close cooperation our Royist friends left us with a parting kick. . . . The entire responsibility," he charged, "for disrupting the measure of unity that had been achieved must be laid at the door of the Royists, and above all of Shri Roy."[67]

By alienating the socialists, Roy denied himself the support of a group that achieved a considerable measure of influence in the Congress party in the latter half of the 1930's.

The CSP had the sympathy of Jawaharlal Nehru, though he steadfastly refrained from joining the party. As we shall see, when Nehru was chosen president of the Congress party in 1936, three of their members were nominated to the Congress Working Committee, and socialists were represented on several important committees. Moreover, a study of the votes taken at the annual Congress sessions and the session of the AICC between 1936 and 1939 has revealed that the socialists were able to attract during this period the support of approximately a third of Congress delegates.[68] Their influence, however, far exceeded their actual numbers. In 1936 the CSP could claim a membership of only two thousand, in contrast to the Congress claim of two million.[69]

The CSP and the CPI

As indicated earlier, the CPI, as well as the Royists, engaged in factional activities within the CSP. Unlike the latter, however, the communists did not leave the CSP until they were forcibly expelled in 1940. The growth of the CPI during this period at the expense of its socialist allies stands in marked contrast to the decline of the political fortunes of the Royists and casts grave doubts on the wisdom of Roy's decision to adopt an independent course. It is a testimony to the foresight of those Royists, such as V. M. Tarkunde, Rajani Mukherji, and A. K. Pillai, who had warned that such a move not only would weaken the nationalist left wing, but also condemn their group to virtual isolation within the Congress.[f]

In obedience to Comintern policies as formulated in the late 1920's, the CPI's initial attitude toward the newly formed CSP was one of unreserved hostility. The CSP, however, looked forward from its inception to cooperation with the communists, and there had been limited coopera-

[f] These three men did not resign at the time of the Royist mass resignations, but withdrew from the CSP when the party began to assail Roy for his actions and impugn his motives (Interview with Justice V. M. Tarkunde, Bombay, November 1, 1961).

tion since 1934 between the two parties in the trade-union field.[70] The CPI, in contrast, had failed to display good faith and as a result the CSP had adopted a resolution later that year expressly barring communists from membership in the party.[71] Anticipating a change in the communist party's attitude toward participation in united fronts as a result of the 1935 Seventh Comintern Congress, the national executive of the CSP at its Meerut conference in January 1936 reversed its previous policy and invited members of the CPI to join their party on an individual basis.[72] The CPI was slow to respond to the Meerut invitation. Ingrained attitudes toward socialist and other "petty-bourgeois" groups, whom they had been taught to loathe as obstacles to the growth of communism, were hard to overcome. Consequently, it was not until April that Indian communists began to enter the CSP.[73] At the same time they were careful to maintain their separate organizational identity.

It was expected that, as a result of the alliance, the position of the communists would be strengthened within the Congress party and the peasant leagues, where the socialists were influential, and, in return, the socialists would gain new adherents in the trade-union fields.[74] It turned out, however, to be a disastrously bad bargain for the socialists. By joining the CSP, the communists, whose party had been banned in 1934, gained an additional legal cover for their activities. They had recently returned to the All-India Trade-Union Congress—an action which enabled them to operate legally within the limited sphere of the trade-union movement. Now with the support of the socialists they were able to work within the broad field of the nationalist movement and in a short time to secure high office in the Congress party. By 1939, twenty members of the AICC were communists.[75] One of their number, Mian Iftikharrudin, became president of the Punjab PCC.[76] Neither the CSP nor the Congress party were able to determine the exact size of their communist membership. Since the CPI was illegal, membership lists were not available and individuals did not always reveal their communist affiliations. Regardless of the exact number, the communists, through the CSP, were able to identify themselves with the nationalist cause. This was an immeasurable boon, for as nationalists they were able to gain the sympathy of a far larger audience than had been the case in the recent past when they had pursued a narrower, sectarian course. Claimed membership in the CPI rose from 150 in 1934 to 5,000 in 1942.[77]

In contrast to the fortunes of the communists, the socialists, as a result of the alliance, nearly lost control of their own party. By 1937, members of the CPI were holding a number of high offices in the CSP. Two of them, E.M.S. Namboodripad and Sajjad Zaheer, were joint secretaries of the CSP, and two others were on its executive committee. In the 1938 elections to the CSP executive committee, the communists, not satisfied with the "official" list of candidates, which allotted them a third of the seats and two of the four joint secretaryships, sponsored an alternative list which would have given them a majority on the executive. The communist list was defeated, but only by a very narrow margin.[78]

In the face of this and similar provocations, members of the CSP executive could not agree among themselves on what to do and consequently matters were allowed to drift. As a result of exposures by M. R. Masani of confidential CPI documents which revealed the communists' intention of either capturing the CSP or destroying it, it had been decided as early as August 1937 to discontinue the policy of admitting communists to the party. However, those who had already joined had been allowed to remain.[79] In an attempt to secure the expulsion of the communists, M. R. Masani, Asoka Mehta, Achyut Patwardhan, and Rammohan Lohia resigned from the CSP executive in May 1939.[80] But it was not until May 1940 that their aim was accomplished. By this time the communists had become so well entrenched in the party that they were able to take with them from one-third to one-half of the party membership in

Bengal and the Punjab, as well as the greater part of the party organization in Travancore-Cochin, Andhra, and Madras, important areas of communist influence today.[81] Moreover, as a result of the split, the CSP eventually lost control of the All-India Students Federation, the All-India Kisan Sabha, and the All-India Trade-Union Congress.[82]

Roy and the CPI

Roy's uncompromising attitude toward the CSP stands in marked contrast to his attitude toward the CPI. He had been expelled from the Comintern in 1929 because of his opposition to Stalin's ultra-left policies and had returned to India in 1930 to oppose the new line. Although he was subjected to vilification and ostracism, he continued to hope for an eventual reconciliation with his old comrades. As the doyen of Indian communists, he regarded them somewhat solicitously, as adolescent children, who, though kindred in spirit, must be sternly rebuked for their errant ways.[83] His behavior was suggestive of the disillusioned communist, as described by Arthur Koestler, who is often uncomfortable in the company of political allies whom he considers right for all the wrong reasons, and in his heart remains faithful to "the addict," who he feels is "wrong for the right reasons."[84]

At this time, the Royists, and the International Right Opposition to which they belonged, were still seeking reinstatement in the Comintern. Consequently, Roy was hopeful of an eventual merger between his group and the CPI. In March 1935, he wrote to his followers urging them, with respect to Indian communists, to "attempt some conciliatory and persuasive move," and advising them to talk with "the most sensible ones and propose fusion." As a step in that direction, he suggested the convening of a unity conference—to be postponed until such time as he could attend personally—to endorse a mutually acceptable program.

Roy recognized the need for unity within their ranks if the communists were to aspire to an influential role in the nationalist movement. Although not self-effacing by temperament, he avowed that he was willing to pay "the very heavy price of personal elimination for the cherished ideal of unity and reinforcement of the revolutionary movement." Should the members of the CPI agree to unification "but insist on having my head," he said,

> please let them have it. The unity would be worth it. Unless the party of the working class can become an effective political force and assume the leadership of the anti-imperialist struggle, not in word but in practice, the political perspective of the country is dark.[85]

The unyielding attitude of the Comintern, and therefore the CPI, was a bitter disappointment to Roy.[86]

Reasons for the Roy-CSP Split

At the time of Roy's defection, CSP leaders generally attributed his behavior to inordinate ambition.[87] Similar motives were also brought forth to explain the disruptive tactics of the CPI. Truth, however, is seldom unidimensional, and narrow ambitions and larger purposes are often inextricably combined. Narayan came closer to understanding the reason for the failure of the left wing to unite when he wrote:

> The basic difficulty in the path of unity was the ridiculous idea held by every miserable little party that it alone was the real Marxist Party, and that every other party had therefore to be exploited, captured or destroyed. The Roy Group was also a votary of this inflated creed. It was natural for it therefore to consider the development of another socialist party as unnecessary and harmful. It was much better to have a left platform which it could animate and dominate.[88]

As a devotee of an exclusive, Marxist creed, Roy felt compelled to resist any individual or group whose policies he considered inconsistent with the historical consummation he envisioned. "Political Messianism," which holds forth the promise of a "preordained, harmonious and perfect scheme of things" toward which society will inevitably evolve,[g] makes no allowance for opposition. Consequently, Roy could not permit his eschatological creed to be sullied by those whom he regarded either as pronounced opponents or misguided supporters. This is not to argue, however, that Roy's motives in seeking to undermine the CSP were altogether selfless. To his way of thinking, the pursuit of the correct political path involved not only the acceptance of his political views but his guidance and leadership as well.

Reinforcing this sense of exclusiveness are certain psychological factors operative in transitional societies such as India. It has been observed that parties in India provide "a source of identification and a new set of values" in place of those of village, caste, and joint family.[89] For many of its members the psychological advantages of maintaining their own party outweigh the political advantage of having a single leftist party and they may be expected to impede any attempt at political consolidation.

[g] J. L. Talmon, in his *Origins of Totalitarian Democracy*, has argued persuasively that all existing political systems are derived from two schools of political thought which can be distinguished in reference to their attitude toward politics. These are the liberal, empirical attitude, which presupposes politics to be "a matter of trial and error, and regards political systems as pragmatic contrivances of human ingenuity and spontaneity," and the totalitarian, absolutist attitude, which posits the existence of "a sole and exclusive truth in politics." These two traditions in political thought may be styled democratic radicalism and liberalism.

Talmon holds that democratic radicalism has its roots in the eighteenth-century beliefs in the rationality, innate goodness, and perfectibility of man, and in the natural order as an "attainable, indeed inevitable and all-solving end." He calls this view "Political Messianism." In the eyes of its adherents, political ideas achieve legitimacy as derivatives of an all-embracing and coherent philosophy. In such a conception the field of political activity is expanded to embrace all human action. Politics becomes "the art of applying this philosophy to the organization of society" with the end of realizing this philosophy in all fields of human endeavor. Such political behavior was characteristic of the English independents, of the French Jacobins, and of modern-day communists. The Calvinists based their faith on God, the Jacobins in nature and reason, and the Marxists on dialectical materialism (J. L. Talmon, *Origins of Totalitarian Democracy* [London: Secker & Warburg, 1952], pp. 1-3, 249, 253).

Roy steadfastly refused, in view of the disparate political orientation of its leaders, to regard the CSP as either socialist or a party. From his point of view, there were very real and important differences between his policies and those of the CSP which stood in the way of merger between the two groups. First, he felt that not only the ideological vagaries of its leaders, but also, paradoxically, its premature emphasis on socialism would condemn the CSP to political impotence. He argued that in the interest of maintaining unity within the nationalist movement, socialists should not press for the adoption of a radical social and economic platform by the Congress party. As a corollary to this, he felt that the socialists were placing undue reliance upon Nehru to help win acceptance of such a program among Congressmen. Second, he considered the socialists mistaken in sponsoring the principle of collective affiliation of labor unions and peasant leagues with the Congress party. Finally, in contrast to the CSP's opposition to either contesting elections or accepting provincial office under the 1935 Constitution of India, Roy was an advocate of both tactics.

Space does not permit a discussion of all the issues over which the Royists and the socialists disagreed. Consequently we will examine only the most important questions —the relationship between nationalism and socialism, collective affiliation of labor and peasant organizations with the Congress party, and the acceptance of office in provincial legislatures. The next chapter will be devoted to the first issue—the degree to which socialist, as opposed to nationalist, goals should be emphasized. It was this question that underlay all of the other disputes between the two groups. Since Jawaharlal Nehru was regarded by the socialists throughout the 1930's as a person who embraced both socialist and nationalist goals and would serve to link the two, it will be convenient first to examine Nehru's role in the Indian nationalist movement.

10. Nationalism and Socialism

Nehru and Socialism

IT WAS largely through Jawaharlal Nehru that the CSP hoped to influence Congress policy. In the early years of the CSP its leaders looked upon Nehru as one of their own and fully expected him to join with them and lead their party. At their CSP conference at Meerut, in January 1936, the socialists adopted a resolution recommending Nehru for the presidency of their party.[1] But Nehru assiduously refrained from joining the socialists, although he was sympathetic to their outlook. This was largely due to Gandhi's skill in handling Nehru and to the latter's devotion to the nationalist cause above all other considerations.

Gandhi revealed his technique in controlling the volatile Nehru and the young and impetuous radical Congressmen he represented when he wrote that the "inexhaustible energy" of India's youth—like steam which is capable of producing tremendous power only if contained in a "strong little reservoir"—must be "imprisoned, controlled and set free in strictly measured and required quantities."[2] Acting in accordance with this principle, Gandhi championed Nehru for president in both 1936 and 1937. In doing so, Gandhi had to overcome considerable opposition from Sardar Patel and others on the Working Committee who looked askance at Nehru's flirtation with the socialists. In 1937 Gandhi had an additional obstacle—the party's traditional reluctance to allow the same person to serve as president for two years in succession. Only once before—in the case of Rash Behari Ghose in 1907 and 1908—had this been done.

Gandhi felt that Nehru's elevation to the presidency would serve to wean him from the socialists, and he assured his colleagues that if placed at the helm, Nehru would act responsibly and impartially in response to majority opinion among party leaders. Members of the Working Committee acceded to Gandhi's wish on both occasions. They knew that if Nehru got too far out of line, they could pull him back. Gandhi's maneuver worked. After Nehru had been asked to lead the party for a second time in succession, M. R. Masani lamented, with justification, that his acceptance had deprived the CSP "of its natural leader, who was so well fitted to lead it, to rally the radical forces."[3]

Contributing to Gandhi's success was Nehru's conviction that national independence must precede socialist reform and his consequent unwillingness to do anything which might disrupt nationalist unity or dislodge Gandhian leadership, which he felt was essential to maintain that unity and achieve independence. Nehru was convinced that the left could not provide an alternative either to Gandhi's leadership or methods. Only Gandhi, he felt, could hold together the disparate groups which together comprised the Congress, and only tactics based on nonviolence offered any prospect of success. He did not interpret nonviolence as broadly as Gandhi, however, to include avoidance of class conflict. Nor was it for him a matter of principle but of practicality. Although he would have preferred "freedom with violence to subjection with non-violence," he felt that the left wing did not offer such a choice. Under Gandhi, a "subservient and demoralized people" had, in the course of little more than a decade, developed a "backbone and power of resistance and an amazing capacity for united action" which had enabled them to challenge "the might of a great and entrenched empire." He compared their accomplishments with those of India's would-be leaders who espoused "a braver ideology" and found the latter decidedly wanting. As for communism, he observed that in most countries it was represented by mutually hostile groups "incapable of united action and often forgetting the common foe in their mutual hatreds."[4]

Except for brief periods, Nehru was in prison from January 1932 until September 1935, when he was allowed to journey to Europe to be with his ailing wife. In March 1936 he returned to India with her ashes, and in his grief, immersed himself in the nationalist cause. The previous January, while still in Europe, he had been elected president of the Congress party.[5] In his presidential address at the Lucknow Congress session in April, Nehru laid bare his socialist views. He told the assembled delegates that socialism was "the only key" to the solution of the problems of India and the world. Socialism, as he defined it, would involve "vast and revolutionary changes" in India's social and political structure, "the ending of private property, except in a restricted sense, and the replacement of the present profit system by a higher ideal of co-operative service." He praised the Soviet Union. Though much that had transpired there had caused him pain, he felt that in the Soviet Union there was a "great and fascinating unfolding of a new order and a new civilization," which constituted "the most promising feature of our dismal age. If the future is full of hope," he said, "it is largely because of the Soviet Union and what it has done."

He avowed that socialism was for him more than an economic doctrine; it was a "vital creed" which he cherished. At the same time, he acknowledged that a majority of Congressmen did not share his views and he assured them that he would not seek "to force the issue." Such action would only serve to impede the independence struggle. For the moment, he said, he was content to work with all groups within the Congress, for he was convinced that independence would lead inevitably to the social and economic change he desired.[6]

At Lucknow, Nehru was eager to bridge the gap between the leadership and the socialist group. On his recent trip to Europe he had become familiar with the idea of popular fronts and visualized the Congress as a broad-based popular front against British imperialism in India. But at Lucknow he began to realize the difficulties which lay in the way. This was the first Congress session since the formation of the CSP in which he participated. But despite his support, most of the socialist proposals were defeated, and he discovered that although he was president, the old guard was firmly in control.

Among the defeated socialist proposals, which Nehru favored, were resolutions calling for: (1) the collective affiliation of labor unions and peasant leagues; (2) refusal to form provincial ministries should the party obtain a majority in any province in the forthcoming elections; and (3) the election of the Working Committee by the AICC by means of proportional representation rather than by nomination of the president.

Nehru was able, however, to assist the socialists in making some gains, but in this he benefited by the desire of the leadership to make some concessions in order to close ranks in preparation for the elections. The socialists' most notable victory was the overturning of an official resolution, adopted by the Subjects Committee by the narrow margin of thirty-seven votes to thirty-two, which would have amended the Congress constitution to abolish the principle of proportional representation in elections to the AICC. If passed, the representation on the AICC of such minority groups as the CSP would have been severely reduced. The socialists were also able to secure representation on a number of important committees.[7]

As president, Nehru was free, theoretically, to choose his own Working Committee. Originally Nehru had wished to have a Working Committee more in tune with his own way of thinking, but when he met resistance, he desisted. On Gandhi's suggestion, three socialists—Jayaprakash Narayan, Acharya Narendra Deva, and Achyut Patwardhan—were invited to join Nehru on the fourteen-man body.[8] Jayaprakash Narayan, however, soon resigned, along with Chakravarti Rajagopalachari, and in August their places were filled by the nominations of Mrs. Sarojini Naidu and Govind Ballabh Pant.[9] The "basic ten," Congress veterans who, with few exceptions, had been on every Working Committee since 1930, were thus left virtually intact.[10] Unwilling to lead a challenge to the old guard for party leadership and dismayed by the "atmosphere of suspicion, bitterness and conflict," Nehru thought of resigning his office, but refrained.[11]

Cooperation among groups of various political persuasion, Nehru felt, did not require a moratorium on the expression of opinions regarding the future shape of Indian society. Consequently, as he toured the country, he spoke freely, as he had done at Lucknow, of his vision of a socialist society. At Lahore he predicted that the capitalist system, along with the British Empire, would disappear within the next ten years.[12] This behavior, in addition to suggestions publicly made that the Working Committee had been forced upon him, led to the resignation of seven of its members toward the end of June. In the interest of party unity in the election campaign, however, the resignations were eventually withdrawn.[13]

This experience convinced Nehru that it would be a serious tactical error to try and wed the cause of socialism with that of national independence. Socialist slogans, he had found, alienated not only many of the leaders of his party but a large section as well of the Congress rank and file, many of whom might be persuaded to support more militant tactics if they were addressed in a nationalist, rather than an alien, socialist idiom. As a result of his own experience within the Congress party, Nehru observed that "even a discussion of socialism" introduced "an element of confusion" and divided party ranks. He concluded that "we must concentrate on political independence and that alone." "We must avoid," he said, any action which would weaken the "joint front against imperialism."[14] It is not surprising that Nehru refused to join the CSP, which he frequently criticized for speaking in "a language borrowed from Western Socialist literature," and which, he claimed, was seldom understood by the average Congressman.[15]

Nehru and Roy

Nehru's assessment of Gandhi, as well as his definition of socialism, differed markedly from that of Roy, but on the question of the relationship between socialism, however defined, and nationalism they held remarkably similar views. This did not go unnoticed by observers of the contemporary scene, one of whom editorialized, shortly after Roy's release from prison, that his views were "almost identical" with those of Nehru and ventured to suggest that Nehru "is likely to find Mr. Roy a valuable and helpful colleague."[16]

But this was not to be the case, One of the reasons Roy felt the CSP could never develop into a revolutionary party was, to his mind, its excessive dependence on Nehru to lead the way. Roy himself sought to utilize Nehru in his efforts to radicalize the Congress, but with some hesitancy and for lack of any feasible alternative. He quickly became disillusioned with this line of approach.

Nehru and Roy first met in Moscow in 1927 and that acquaintance was renewed in India in 1930-31. Nehru had been impressed with Roy's intellectual abilities, but conceded that the admiration evidently had not been reciprocated. Through the years, Nehru recalled with that disarming candor which was characteristic of him, Roy "wrote many an article with bitter criticism of me and my kind when he dubbed me with considerable truth as petty-bourgeois. He used harsh words which stung but . . . I retained a partiality and a soft corner in my heart for him."[17]

Less than twenty-four hours after his release from jail in November 1936, Roy was conferring with Nehru at Bareilly and a few days later was Nehru's guest in his ancestral home, Anand Bhavan.[18] But shortly before his visit Roy, referring to Nehru, had written in a letter to a friend that "great men who are not really great . . . are uncertain qualities. . . . Pseudo-great men [were] a tiresome lot, [and] conceit, covered by false modesty . . . an incurable disease. And when the disease is made into a virtue, and applauded as such even by those who are expected to know better, the problem becomes baffling." He had, however, concluded that in a complex situation it was best to be a realist and work with whatever material is available.[19]

Far from sharing the prevailing opinion which looked upon Nehru as the socialists' natural leader, Roy regarded him, as well as Gandhi, as an unwitting tool of the old guard. Because he considered Nehru's attraction for the socialists beguiling, Roy was unsparing in his criticism of him. Nehru, he railed, is "a thoughtless, vain, egocentric, popularity-hunting demagogue," who "is popular among the Congressmen with a 'modern outlook' because his demagogy rationalizes Gandhi's irrationalism, and supplies a pseudo-socialist veneer to reactionary nationalism." "His modernism," Roy argued, "serves the undemocratic and reactionary purpose of the Congress. Therefore, his present place has been conceded to him by the real bosses of the organization." As for Nehru's professed attachment to socialism, Roy contended that "acceptance of the Marxist philosophy would never allow Nehru to stand in the relation he has always stood to Gandhi. His apparent advance towards Socialism and Marxism is the typical groping of the lonesome individual of the twentieth-century . . . for a vaguely conceived new world."[20]

The Relationship of Socialism to Nationalism

In a series of letters, written in the years 1934 through 1935 and addressed to the CSP, Roy argued that the formation of a separate socialist party within the Congress party would result in the exclusion of the left wing from the Congress leadership and the continued dominance of the Congress machinery by conservative elements.[21] The maintenance of a distinct party, he felt, would have the effect of placing socialists outside the orthodox Congress fold and thus reducing their effectiveness. No amount of protest, he added, would alter the situation.[22] Ultimately, he warned, "insistence upon keeping up the CSP will . . . compel you to leave the Congress."[23]

This prophecy proved ultimately to be correct. In 1939 a specially appointed constitutional subcommittee recommended to the AICC that the party constitution be amended to disallow membership to groups or parties opposed to the policy of the Congress party.[24] But this recommendation was later dropped by the Working Committee.[25] In less than a year after the attainment of independence, however, when there was no longer a common enemy to compel unity, the constitution of the party was altered to deny membership to those belonging to political parties with distinctive constitutions and policies. The socialists, rather than abandon their separate organizational identity, decided at that time to leave the Congress party.

Although both Roy and the CSP subscribed to the goals of national independence and a socialist society, they differed as to their order of priority. Upon his release from prison on November 20, 1936, Roy declared in a press interview that in the interest of national unity he was not prepared to espouse a socialist program. "My message to the people," he said, "is to rally in the millions under the flag of the National Congress and fight for freedom. Socialism or communism," he continued, "is not the issue of the day, and socialists and communists should realize that the immediate objective is national independence." "We should realize," he concluded, "that the National Congress is our common platform."[26] Elaborating on this theme some months later, Roy maintained that socialism was inevitable provided all groups worked in concert to ensure the growth of the "necessary preconditions," the most important of which was the attainment of national independence.[27]

Because of these well-publicized views, Roy was accorded special attention by the Congress leadership on his release from prison. He was met at the prison gate by leaders of the local Congress organization, as well as by some of his followers.[28] The following day, he journeyed to Bareilly to attend the U.P. Provincial Political Conference, where he joined the Congress party and was elected a delegate to the annual party conference to be held at Faizpur in December.[29] The Bareilly Conference passed a special resolution welcoming Roy to the Congress fold. At the end of the month, Roy went to Allahabad. He was met at the station by a member of the Working Committee, Acharya

Kripalani, who escorted him to Nehru's home, where he spent a week recuperating from his long confinement.[30] In December he was given an enthusiastic reception at Kanpur where, accompanied by political workers, he was taken on a grand procession, and according to a contemporary press report, was "profusely garlanded by the public and showered with flowers amidst loud cheers."[31] Later at Faizpur, he was assigned quarters in the leaders' camp next to Nehru's cottage.[32] Roy had been elected a member of the AICC and when it met shortly before the conference as the Subjects Committee he was given a seat on the dais[33]—an honor usually reserved for the most important Congress leaders. Later, in his presidential address before the assembled delegates, Nehru welcomed Roy to the party as a veteran soldier in India's struggle for freedom.[34]

Despite the outward warmth of their greetings, Congress leaders were cautious in their relations with Roy. Gandhi, understandably, would have little to do with his long time critic. When approached by Roy for help in financing his paper, Gandhi replied with a postcard suggesting that he "should render only mute service to the cause of freedom." The very first issue of the paper carried an attack on Gandhi entitled "Science and Superstition," which prompted Gandhi to remark that Roy was his "enemy number one."[35]

Other Congress leaders, however, though suspicious of his motives in joining the party, were willing to suspend judgment. In view of his public statements, he was regarded as a possible counterpoise to the socialists. As Roy was to recall in later years, "there was a distinct desire to patronize me, though, not quite to pamper. It was suspected that the notorious revolutionary might have a joker up his sleeve."[36]

Soon after leaving jail, Roy had a series of meetings in Bombay with a number of Congress leaders, including Sardar Vallabhbhai Patel, Rajendra Prasad, and Archarya Kripalani, to discuss to what extent they might be able to work together. It was reported in the press that the Congress leaders had referred in these private discussions to internal differences within the party resulting from the growth of a radical wing, and that Roy had reaffirmed his opposition to the formation of separate parties within the Congress. It was speculated at the time that the party leadership might find Roy more cooperative than the members of the CSP.[37]

The socialists watched these developments with mounting suspicion. Roy had hoped to combine the forces of nationalism, shorn of Gandhian leadership, with radicalism. But in attempting to do so, he had felt it necessary to repudiate policies and programs which had become synonymous with radicalism in India. Consequently, he came to be regarded by the CSP as a heretic who had capitulated to the right wing.[38]

His insistence on the dismemberment of the CSP was taken by some as evidence of this. Socialists, he counseled, should operate inside the Congress as a nebulous group in imitation of the right wing and outside the Congress as a tightly knit conspiratorial party. They should "function inside the Congress as a class, not as a party," he argued, and outside the Congress with an "organizational form and method of operation suitable for a revolutionary working class party existing under the given conditions of the imperialist terror."[39]

If the immediate goal was national independence, Roy felt, the left wing should temporarily eschew radical socialist demands in favor of more moderate proposals.[40] Consequently, he opposed such CSP-sponsored resolutions as those calling for the confiscation of property without compensation and the collectivization of land. Instead of engaging in such vain efforts to amend the Congress platform, he believed, the left wing should concentrate exclusively on offering an alternative to the Gandhian program of national revolution. The development of such an alternative, he reasoned, had been impeded by the formation of a narrow-based party within the Congress, the majority of whose members, he was convinced, were not prepared to rally under a socialist banner.[41] The existence of the CSP, according to Roy, tended to divide Congressmen into socialists and nonsocialists, when it would be more appropriate to effect a division between militant nationalists on the one hand and Gandhians and "responsivists"[a] on the other.[42]

Roy's suggestion that the CSP function as an amorphous group within the Congress party was interpreted by the socialists as an attempt on his part to destroy what he could not dominate. The CSP executive committee charged that when Roy says there should be no socialist party within the Congress he really means "that there should be only secret parties and caucuses, preferably turning around select individuals. . . . For what Mr. Roy is really attempting to do is to organize a secret party that will work within the Congress under his leadership."[43]

This was not an idle charge. The Royists indeed were operating inside the CSP as a secret party. As noted in Chapter Eight, the Royists were organized into an underground communist party, the RPIWC, with branches in Banares, Baroda, Bombay, Calcutta, Poona, and a few other locations. One of the main functions of the party was to work within the CSP to split it and siphon off its more radical members.[44]

Suspicious of the Royists' motives, the socialists, understandably, could find little merit in their proposal that the CSP be disbanded. In his presidential address to the Gujarat Congress Socialist Conference in June 1935, Acharya Narendra Deva, while agreeing with Roy that the main task was to promote the anticolonialist struggle, maintained that "such a struggle can only develop if we succeed in linking up with the economic demands of the masses and this object can only be achieved if there is a party within the Congress that persistently agitates for the acceptance of an economic programme." "This task," he stated emphatically, "cannot be performed by a diffused group."[45]

[a] Those who were willing to cooperate with the British government in working within the framework of the 1935 Constitution of India.

A few months later, however, the CSP did acknowledge at least indirectly, the validity of Roy's warning that in attempting to give equal stress to both nationalist and socialist goals, they risked the failure of achieving either. Within the Congress party, opponents of socialism frequently sought to defeat CSP-sponsored resolutions, including those which had nothing to do with socialism, by alluding ominously to their source. The bogey of socialism, Narayan was to complain bitterly, was dragged in on every issue.[46]

Consequently, at their annual party conference at Meerut in early 1936, socialist delegates endorsed a resolution which affirmed that the immediate "task of the party was not to convert the Congress into a Socialist Party," but into a multi-class, anti-imperialist front. A clear distinction was thus made between the party's immediate objective and its ultimate goal. The party has conceded that "Royist criticism played a part" in strengthening the view that such a clarification of its program was urgently required.[47] Though the party leaders agreed with Roy that socialism was not the immediate issue, they never accepted his suggestion that they should dissolve the party. Though distinct, the two goals of national independence and socialist reconstruction were interdependent and if socialism were not to be consigned to an historical limbo, they maintained, "the whole conscious direction of the nationalist movement must emanate from a Socialist Party."[48]

Roy, Gandhi, and Indian Nationalism

When Roy emerged from prison in November 1936 he was a potential political force in India. The aura of mystery attached to his name as a former confidant of Lenin and Stalin and as a former agent of the Comintern who had been intimately involved in conspiratorial activities of a global nature assured him an attentive audience among Indian nationalists. His six-year incarceration at the hands of the British for his efforts on behalf of his country, even though many judged them as misguided, assured him a large measure of sympathy as well. A contemporary political figure, Subhas Chandra Bose, has observed in reference to Roy's reputation at this time that "because of his revolutionary past . . . Mr. M. N. Roy was a popular and attractive figure with a halo round his name. Young men flocked to him."[49]

But this advantage was quickly dissipated. Following the rupture between their party and the Royists, the socialists began a systematic attempt to thwart Roy's designs by sowing disaffection between the Royists and the Congress leadership. Due to their influence within the Congress and the suspicions already harbored against Roy by the right wing, the socialists' efforts met with considerable success. Long at odds with the communists, the Royists by their policies soon isolated themselves from virtually all other groups within the Congress party. The right wing, with whom Roy had sought to ingratiate himself, never accepted his profession of kinship with the goals and aspirations of Indian nationalism. A half year after joining the Congress, Roy felt it necessary to disavow explicitly any ulterior motive in joining the party. In a prepared speech before a group of Congressmen, he stated:

> Let me tell you once and for all, very clearly that while I may have certain political ideas . . . I am as loyal a Congressman as any of you. There may be some notion that, being a Communist, it is not possible for me to be in the Congress as a loyal Congressman . . . and [that] I am waiting for an opportunity to spring a surprise on you. . . . I find myself in a rather peculiar position. One section of the Congress looks upon me with suspicion, as a dangerous Communist intriguer trying to press through some insidious scheme, and another section, the Socialists, say that here is a man who is a traitor to Communism. . . . I say these few words because, lately, I have, painfully, found a feeling of distrust and suspicion about me on the part of some people.[50]

Roy was never able to establish his bona fides as an Indian nationalist. His frequent and caustic criticism of

Gandhi and Indian tradition stood in the way. He was unable to play the role of an Indian nationalist, which he had cast for himself, for several reasons. First, he had spent the greater part of his life abroad, as a result of which he had acquired cosmopolitan views and tastes which reinforced the internationalist outlook he had imbibed with his Marxian philosophy. Second, he had embraced Marx's disdain for the rural peasantry and the narrowness of village life as compared with the urban proletariat and metropolitan sophistication. Finally, he shared the attitude, born of the failure of the populist movement, of the Russian Marxists toward the tradition-bound hinterland.

Roy was a persistent critic of Gandhi almost from the time he first appeared on the Indian scene. Gandhi was a nationalist, not only in the sense that he wanted to secure India's political independence but also in his attachment to Indian culture, and he appealed to Hindu religious values to gain support for the nationalist movement. In the debate between Roy and Lenin at the second Comintern Congress in 1920, Lenin had maintained that as a leader of a nationalist, anti-imperialist movement, Gandhi was a revolutionary; whereas Roy had insisted that "as a religious and cultural revivalist, he was bound to be reactionary socially, however revolutionary he might appear politically."[51] In support of this view, Roy had cited Plekhanov's similar judgment of Russian Populist and Social Revolutionary movements, which Roy felt corresponded with Gandhism in that, believing in the special genius of the Slavic race, they had denounced capitalism as a Western vice and championed a return to the village and the revival of the *mirs.*[b]

[b] Plekhanov's early faith in the populist movement was shaken by the resort of a section of its members to terrorism, which he considered irrational and aimless, and by mounting statistical evidence that the village commune was a dying institution. In 1884 he published an attack on populism entitled *Our Differences* in which he held that, contrary to the views of his erstwhile allies, capitalism was the dominant economic force in Russia and that the hope of the future lay with the proletariat rather than the peasantry (Georgii V. Plekhanov,

As was the case with Gandhi's followers in India, the nineteenth-century Russian populist movement had been sustained by a vision of their country's future based on her traditional village unit—the commune. Like Gandhi, the populists had a deep faith in their own unique heritage, which if properly understood and employed, they felt, could enable their country to avoid the Western vice of capitalism. Instead of seeking to liberate proletarian energies, as the Marxists would have them do, the populists sought to identify with the peasantry, the vehicle of tradition, as the source of revolutionary power. Stress was placed on the resuscitation of the traditional village as the basic social, economic and political unit, and on spreading enlightenment throughout the countryside.[52]

Like the Russian Marxists, Roy felt that any attempt at social reconstruction based on traditional social units—with their underlying system of customs, values, behavioral patterns, and forms of organization—was doomed ultimately to failure and in the short run could only succeed in restraining social progress.[53] Consequently, as a member of the Comintern he had failed completely to appreciate either Gandhi's appeal to the Indian people or his revolutionary potentiality. As early as 1922, Roy was prophesizing Gandhi's "impending defeat" on the grounds that he sought to utilize prevailing "mass energy" to revive the same heritage to which "the masses" were "objectively" opposed.[54]

Roy felt that Gandhi's style of political leadership was antithetical to the growth of democratic attitudes and perpetrated the values of subservience, submission and self-abnegation already enshrined in Hinduism. He characterized Gandhi's fasts as a form of moral coercion which impeded the development of habits of rational persuasion and his arrogation of complete discretionary power as authoritarian rather than democratic in outlook. For Roy, Hinduism was a slave ideology and Gandhi another in a

---

Our Differences, in *Selected Works*, I, prepared by the Institute of Philosophy of the Academy of Sciences of the USSR [London: Lawrence & Wishart, 1961], pp. 141-400).

long line of ideological jailers who for centuries had fettered the Indian mind in the name of spirituality. Instead of encouraging man to reach beyond his grasp, he argued, Gandhi would consign man to the suffocating restrictions imposed by the caste system, religious superstition, and village life.

Roy was unsparing in his criticism of India's Hindu-based heritage, which Gandhi—and Indian nationalists of the extremist school, such as Bal Gangadkar Tilak, before him—had utilized to evoke a virile, and sometimes virulent, religionationalist sentiment.[55] In the early 1930's Roy wrote from his jail cell in India to his friends in Europe that he was "living in antiquity and the Middle Ages." He confessed that he found "conditions [in India] quite disgusting," and that he often felt like "cleaning that all up, neat and wholesale."[56] He regarded Hinduism as an "ideology of social slavery." India's so-called spiritual heritage, he contended, had resulted in "political slavery for nearly a thousand years, economic backwardness, intellectual inertia and cultural degradation."[57] Reflecting a sense of despair and frustration, Roy wrote that India's ignorant and repressed people were "the product of a decayed civilization awaiting a much delayed burial." "This country needs a Kemal Pasha," he continued,

> to chop off the ridiculous tufts on the heads; to make the wearing of mustaches punishable as culpable homicide; to drive pampered, idle, gossiping, but outrageously maltreated women out in the streets to work down their fat or cure their anaemia and to free themselves from the malignant curse of suppressed passion; to prohibit the irritating chanting of rigmarole in a language which few understand; and to do many other similar things.[58]

Throughout the years Roy continued to underestimate Gandhi's role in the Indian nationalist movement. He failed to realize the extent to which the nationalist movement was dependent on Gandhi's leadership and never faltered in calling for his replacement. By the 1930's, however, Roy had come to realize the magnitude of Gandhi's accomplishments in having aroused the Indian people, consisting largely of illiterate and tradition-bound peasants with parochial loyalties, to a sense of political involvement. But to him this fell far short of developing genuine "class consciousness" capable of disciplined, sustained, and purposive action. To Roy, Gandhi was merely "the embodiment of the primitive, blind, spontaneous, spirit of revolt of the Indian masses."[59] He deplored Gandhi's hold over his compatriots. Roy was convinced that neither political independence nor the kind of radical social and economic reform he so earnestly desired could be achieved under Gandhi's leadership. Moreover, Roy was aware that in the Indian context appeals to traditional values could only be religious in content, and that a nationalism based on such appeals would ultimately prove divisive in so far as it served to estrange the large Moslem minority. At the time of independence, the Indian subcontinent was divided between a predominantly Hindu India and an Islamic Pakistan. The partition of India, the attendant communal rioting, and Gandhi's assassination at the hands of a Hindu fanatic were viewed by Roy as an indictment of Gandhi's handiwork.[c]

Although he alienated a large segment of Moslem India, Gandhi's use of religious symbols shared by the overwhelming majority of Indians played a positive role in the nationalist struggle. In independent India, however, appeals to separate religious, as well as regional and linguistic, groups constitute one of the gravest threats to the unity of

[c] After Gandhi's death a new respect for him emerged in Roy's thinking. Although he continued to reject Gandhi's religiosity and nationalism, in evolving his philosophy of Radical Humanism Roy came closer to Gandhi in his emphasis on human solidarity, the relation of means to ends, the necessity of some form of economic and political decentralization, and the rejection of party politics.

The extent of Gandhi's responsibility for the breakdown in relations between the Hindu and Moslem communities is a matter of some controversy among those knowledgeable in Indian affairs. On this question, however, Roy never changed his mind. To him Gandhi's appeal to Hindu tradition always remained a major cause for Moslem separatism (from a letter to author, dated September 7, 1967, from Professor Shanti Tangri, Wayne State University, who interviewed Roy in Dehra Dun in 1953).

the country. Political groups, including Indian communists, have not been reluctant to exploit such differences despite the threat to the Indian republic and the difficulty of building a viable all-India party on the basis of such minority appeals.

The successful political broker in the Indian contest is one who, respectful of India's "great tradition,"[60] is able to transfer traditional loyalties to modern political institutions, values, and customs by presenting new ideas in familiar language. Such an approach is open to those political leaders who are not only familiar with Western political institutions and values but also retain a nostalgic attachment for the indigenous culture. Gandhi was such a leader. Exhibiting a form of populism, Gandhi was able to project himself as a living symbol of the Indian masses and to stigmatize his political opponents, whether British administrators or Indian socialists, as cultural aliens objectively hostile to the best interests of his people.[61]

Recognizing the fact that in contemporary Asia nationalism is capable of generating the same level of mass enthusiasm as in nineteenth-century Europe, Roy sought to harness the moral force generated by nationalist revolution in order to convert it into a socialist revolution. But his alienation from Indian culture and society, his distrust of the peasantry, and his atheism caused him to stumble. He sought to appeal to the anti-imperialist aspects of Indian nationalism but was disrespectful of its religiocultural foundations. He recognized the existence in India of a wide social gap between the educated elite and the largely illiterate population and realized that the gap had to be spanned if his vision of society was to be achieved. But, in contrast to Gandhi, he was unable to do so.

According to Mosca,[d] leadership within heterogeneous

[d] Mosca has contended that mankind is divided into social groups each with its distinctive beliefs, sentiments, habits, and interests. Different social types may arise inside a single society where there exist urban centers subject to "rapid flows of ideas" which "agitate the higher classes." For Mosca leadership in such societies flows to those who possess a political formula based on "complexes of belief and sentiment which have the sanction of the ages." Contrary to the

societies accrues to those who are able to devise a political formula based upon "the special beliefs and the strongest sentiments" of the society as a whole. Mosca's theory of legitimacy, in which the political formula serves to rationalize the dominance of the ruling class, suggests how masses of the population in a developing society may be mobilized in the process of creating a nationalist movement. Gandhi, utilizing an appropriate formula, was able to link the relatively small, urban-based political elite with the millions of rural India. Although Roy was aware of the need to modify the Marxian political formula to meet objective conditions, in India that formula was not sufficiently flexible for the task. Roy often spoke of the need for a renaissance in India as a prerequisite for the social revolution he desired. He might well have added that such a change would also be necessary for the acceptance of the ideas he espoused. Roy's radical rejection of traditional Hinduism negated all his best efforts to win the acceptance of either the Congress leadership, its rank and file, or the populace at large.

Marxists, however, Mosca did not believe that the gap between the leaders and the led could ever be fully closed—even in a thoroughly modernized society (Gaetano Mosca, *The Ruling Class* [New York: McGraw-Hill, 1939], pp. 71-72, 106-14. I am indebted to Leonard Binder's paper "National Integration and Political Development" delivered at the Fifty-Ninth Annual Meeting of the American Political Science Association, New York City, September 1963, for suggesting the relevance of Mosca's concepts to the study of political development.

11. Twentieth-Century Jacobinism

THE Congress leadership from an early date sought to utilize peasant unrest for nationalist ends. This effort can be dated from the period 1917-18 when Gandhi led the Champaran peasantry in a struggle against certain privileges which had been granted by the government to indigo planters and had resulted in hardships on the peasantry. The activities of the Congress party among the peasantry were directed toward the creation of additional pressures against British rule, rather than the promotion of class unrest in the countryside. For example, participation in the U.P. no-tax campaign of the early 1930's was deliberately extended to include zamindars as well as tenants to avoid, as far as possible, the exacerbation of class antagonisms.[1]

During the 1933-34 satyagraha campaign, the governor of Bihar encouraged the zamindars of his province to form a party for the purpose of contesting future elections against the Congress party. He advised them, at the same time, to support certain moderate changes in land tenure laws to win the support of the peasantry and immunize them against more radical proposals. Acting on these suggestions, a United party was formed and zamindar members of the Bihar provincial legislative assembly sponsored the Tenancy Amendment Bill.

The Congress leadership was alarmed at the emergence of a potentially powerful rival party in Bihar. Since many Congress leaders were in jail at this time and their party banned, it was decided to encourage the peasant leader, Swami Sahajanand Saraswati, to revive the Kisan Sabha (Peasant League). As a result the Kisan Sabha was activated and a campaign launched to expose the inadequacies of the Tenancy Bill. The maneuver was a success. In the 1937 provincial elections the United party was trounced by the Congress.[2]

But the Congress party had difficulty controlling peasant leagues of the type it had helped to revive in Bihar. A struggle soon developed between the more conservative Congress leaders and the young militant and radical wing of the party for control of the peasant movement. The former group visualized the Kisan Sabha primarily as ancillary to the nationalist movement and wanted the Sabha to conform to the Gandhian principle of class collaboration. The latter group viewed the peasant organization not only as a weapon aimed at their British rulers, but as an instrument of class struggle as well. From the latter point of view the Kisan Sabha was regarded as a vehicle for pressing the exclusive class demands of the peasantry.

The socialists took the lead in organizing the All-India Kisan Sabha, which was founded at a convention of Kisan workers held in conjunction with the annual conference of the CSP at Meerut in January 1936.[3] Under the guidance of both the CSP and the CPI, the All-India Kisan Sabha championed proposals for agrarian reform more drastic than those espoused by the Congress party, to which both the socialists and communists belonged. Consequently, in some rural localities, Kisan organizations began to rival the primary Congress committees for the support of the peasants rather than to serve merely as their adjuncts. This was a development welcomed by the socialists and communists, who anticipated that in developing the Kisan Sabhas into a powerful class organization they would be securing for themselves a power base within the nationalist party. In furtherance of this strategy, they pressed for the adoption of an amendment to the Congress constitution which would provide for the collective affiliation of both peasant leagues and trade unions. They hoped that by thus broadening the base of the Congress party they could secure sufficient strength to win control of the nationalist movement.

Collective Affiliation

When the question of collective affiliation first began to be debated, Roy had been in favor of the proposal. He was not opposed, he wrote in 1934, to the representation of the "masses" through "local and functioning bodies as well as individual members."[4] By the following year, however, he had changed his mind and had become an opponent of the idea. He now felt that the formation of separate class organizations within the Congress party would lead to the fragmentation and weakening of the nationalist movement. "A federated body," he argued, "composed of autonomous organizations . . . cannot lead the revolutionary struggle for the capture of power."[5]

This did not mean that Roy minimized the importance of the peasantry in formulating his revolutionary strategy for India. On the contrary, he instructed his followers that "the battle of the Indian revolution will have to be fought and won in the villages. . . . The struggle for the leadership of the peasantry is the critical task."[6] Since the peasantry constitutes the greatest part of the population, he argued, "the movement of freedom will never be successful, unless it secures the active support of the peasantry."[7] This can be done by formulating a program which meets the immediate needs of the peasants. It was unnecessary, he felt, for the peasantry to have their own separate class organizations, for all they seek—private rights in land—can be achieved by working within the nationalist movement.[8] "For the peasants," he contended, "the national revolution means the agrarian revolution—the expropriation of the princes and the landlords."[9]

In order for the Congress party to attract and hold the allegiance of the peasantry, Roy argued, it must champion the demands of the peasants for ownership of land. Consequently, the Royists pressed for the adoption by the Congress of an agrarian program which included the following provisions: the abolition of landlordism, nationalization of land,[a] abolition of all charges on the peasantry except a

[a] Under this provision, the peasant would continue to possess the land insofar as he would be allowed to retain the entire proceeds of his labor, but he would no longer be able to sell or transfer his land.

unitary land-tax, abolition of indirect taxes, exemption from taxation for peasants living on uneconomic holdings, liquidation of peasant indebtedness, and control of usury (interest not to exceed six percent per annum).[10]

Such a program, Roy reasoned, would not only secure the support of the peasantry, but also provide the basic conditions for the transformation of India into a modern industrial society. The solution of the agrarian problem was to him "the essential condition for India's becoming an industrial country."[11] Industrial development was dependent upon a sound agricultural base, which would provide for "the release of labor for the less productive employment on the land, conversion of the accumulated wealth into fluid productive capital and development of the purchasing power of the masses."[12]

Roy's agrarian program approximated that of Lenin rather than Mao Tse-tung's. Despite his sympathetic approach to the peasantry, it would be a serious mistake to confuse Roy's approach to the peasant problem with that of the Chinese leader. While in Germany in the late 1920's, Roy published a number of articles in the Communist Opposition press on the situation in China, in addition to writing a book on the Chinese revolution. He therefore gave a great deal of attention to the peasant question. It was his opinion at the time that "anyone who once claims to industrialize China must in the first place accomplish the agrarian revolution, . . . but at the same time the proletariat must retain its hegemony even over a program of bourgeois revolution, if it is to go on to its successful conclusion."[13] Following the bolshevik example, Roy felt that although the peasants should be used as a "vast reserve of revolutionary energy," it was necessary for communists to focus their attention on "the political and industrial nerve centres of the country." Observing that the bulk of the membership of the CCP were drawn from the peasantry,

---

This measure was designed to prevent the reconcentration of land in individual hands. It was similar to Lenin's Decree on Land, which was enacted shortly after he came to power.

he remonstrated that "the peasants could never make a revolution by themselves unless it [the communist party] functions as the vanguard of the proletariat not only in theory but in actual practice." This was a direct criticism of Mao Tse-tung's revolutionary strategy and tactics which stressed the importance of first securing rural areas, as opposed to industrial centers, and relied heavily on the peasantry rather than the proletariat to provide a mass base for the party.

Roy frequently quoted Lenin on the necessity of gaining the support of the peasantry if revolution in precapitalistic areas was to succeed.[b] In a letter, for example, written in 1934, Roy reminded his followers that "the appreciation of the revolutionary role of the peasantry in an industrially backward country is one of the basic conditions of Leninism insofar as it is anything more than Marxism. It is not known how much the success of the Russian revolution depended upon Lenin's appeal to act to the peasant question."[14] But Roy also shared Lenin's view that separate peasant organizations were not only unnecessary, but undesirable.

In seeking to establish a dictatorship of the proletariat with hegemony over the peasantry, rather than a democratic dictatorship of the proletariat and the peasantry, Lenin had operated on the principle that parties representing peasant interests were not to be encouraged, but weakened and eventually destroyed. The peasantry and the entire petty-bourgeois class were to look to a single party

[b] In the debate on the national and colonial question at the Second Comintern Congress in 1920, Lenin stated his views on the importance of the peasantry to the success of revolution in colonial and semicolonial areas. He argued that "the peasantry is usually the support of . . . national revolutionary movements. . . . The struggle of agricultural toilers against landlord exploitation is the basis upon which you can build an organization of toilers even in backward countries. In such countries it is quite possible to build a Soviet authority" (*Pravda*, July 28, 1920, translated in United States, Department of State, *The Second Congress of the Communist International as Reported and Interpreted by the Official Newspapers of Soviet Russia*, pp. 38-39).

in which the self-proclaimed spokesmen of the proletariat were to dominate. Thus, when Lenin finally succumbed to pressures to form a coalition government with the Social Revolutionaries shortly after coming to power, he did so only with a section of the party—the Left Social Revolutionaries. In this way he split the bolsheviks' most serious rival. Similarly Lenin sought to pit the peasants who lived by their own labor against the Kulak who used hired labor —a policy which divided the loyalties of the countryside between the Social Revolutionaries and the bolsheviks.[15]

Roy shared Lenin's aversion to separate organizations for nonproletarian classes. He sought to convert the Congress into a three-class organization—a party of the petty bourgeoisie and the peasantry under the hegemony of the proletariat. Concretely this meant that only communists were to be allowed to organize independently outside the Congress party, while retaining their membership inside the nationalist organization. Consequently, Roy opposed the efforts of the CSP and the CPI to organize peasants into their own separate class organization. He felt that "it should not be difficult for a Marxist to grasp that nothing could be a greater obstacle to Socialism than a peasantry organized in their independent class organization."[16]

Shortly after leaving jail, Roy was made a member of the Mass Contacts Committee of the Congress party.[17] This committee had been formed at the Lucknow Congress session the previous April. At this session the socialists had sponsored a resolution, supported by Nehru, calling for the affiliation of workers' and peasants' organizations with the party. The resolution was defeated and in its place the formation of a Mass Contacts Committee was authorized. This committee was to seek ways to strengthen the mass base of the party.[18]

The Mass Contacts Committee met in December to formulate recommendations on how to achieve closer contact with the peasantry. The committee membership was divided between advocates of collective affiliation and those who would concentrate exclusively on strengthening the primary Congress committees. The latter point of view was held, for different reasons, by Roy and the conservative members of the committee. Their position was bolstered by the results of a poll which indicated that a majority of the Congress PCC's, while stressing the need for broadening party membership, were also opposed to collective affiliation.[19]

The stage was thus set for a major clash over this issue between the socialists and the communists on the one hand and Roy and the more conservative members of Congress on the other hand at the annual Congress session at the end of the month. On Gandhi's suggestion the party met for the first time in a village, Faizpur, to symbolize its aim of identification with the peasantry.[20]

At Faizpur the socialists reintroduced their resolution on collective affiliation, which would extend to affiliated organizations the right to seat a certain number of representatives on various Congress committees. The proposal again received the support of Nehru,[21] but Roy once more supported the position of those who would channel peasant unrest through the primary Congress committees. On the basis of discussions which he had held in Bombay with the Congress leaders, Rajendra Prasad, Sardar Patel, and Bhulabhai Desai, Roy had come to Faizpur with a scheme for rallying the countryside under the banner of the Congress party and with concrete proposals for democratizing the party constitution.[22] In interviews with Gandhi and Nehru after his arrival, he pressed his views on the question of widening the social base of the nationalist struggle.[23]

Following these talks, Roy sent to the Working Committee a number of recommendations for amending the party constitution. Among other proposals he suggested that each Congress member be required to pay dues of one anna to be collected monthly. The collection process, he felt, would keep the active party cadre in close touch with its rank and file members and provide an opportunity for agitation and propaganda among them. He also recommended that membership meetings be conducted on a weekly basis to discuss current political events and economic problems facing the locality and to explore the connection between local demands and the independence struggle. He felt that primary Congress committees should become the forum for the expression of local grievances and that consequently they should be allotted the right to submit draft resolutions to the AICC, via the PCC's. He proposed a procedure whereby such resolutions, to be received by the AICC at least two months before the annual Congress session, would be circulated, along with official Working Committee proposals, among all units of the party to provide an opportunity for a thorough study of all proposals by the entire party membership before they were to be voted on at the annual party session.[24]

The resolution on collective affiliation was again defeated at Faizpur. In its place a resolution on mass contacts was adopted which expressed "the desirability of increasing association of the masses with the Congress organization and of giving opportunities to primary members to initiate and consider the Congress policies and programme." The PCC's were directed to establish primary committees in all villages and wards and it was suggested that such committees should meet at least twice a year to consider local problems and grievances and to formulate recommendations on party policy and program. A subscription of four annas per year was to be collected locally. The Working Committee was authorized to appoint an organizing secretary and the various PCC's to appoint provincial organizing secretaries. Finally a committee was appointed—comprised of Rajendra Prasad, Jairamdas Doulatram, and Jayaprakash Narayan—to consider the findings of the Mass Contacts Committee and to make recommendations on changes in the party constitution.[25]

When at Faizpur Roy sought the newly-created post of organizing secretary for himself, he was rebuffed. Both Nehru and Gandhi advised him to eschew active politics at least for the time being and devote himself to his writings. Roy was later to wonder if that might not have been the better course.[26] Although the resolution on mass contacts was less than he had hoped for and he failed to secure the office he had sought, Roy was satisfied that the Congress party had taken a step in the right direction at Faizpur. In retrospect, however, some of the Royists felt that the group had erred in its attitude toward the Kisan Sabhas. One important member of the group, S. R. Sunthankar, wrote to Roy in 1940 that from his experience in his own district (Belgaum) he had concluded that the peasantry could not be organized within the Congress party because "everything we accomplish with them will be undone by the leadership." He argued that the Royists might have been able to capture the Congress had it formed separate peasant organizations to serve as a "mass basis."[27]

Roy opposed the idea of collective affiliation because he felt the Congress left wing should concentrate its efforts on gaining control of the primary units of the party, broadening the mass base of the party by enrolling large numbers of peasants at the local level, and working to democratize the Congress constitution to give the party rank and file an increased voice in the formulation of party policy. The Kisan Sabhas, he felt, could not help but rival the primary Congress committees in the rural areas. As the Royists expressed their aim, they wished to transform the Congress committees into peasant committees to convert them into democratic bodies reflecting the will of the masses.[28]

Roy's fear that the Kisan Sabhas might become rivals of the primary Congress committees for the support of the peasantry was well founded. The Congress party could not function as a national organization and an organization of the Kisans at the same time. There were bound to be times when the Kisan Sabhas would be opposed to the Congress party on issues related to the welfare of the peasants. The situation became particularly acute at the time of the provincial Congress ministries in 1937-39. During this period Swami Sahajanand, in a presidential address before the All-India Kisan Sabha, complained that there was "no material difference between the ameliorative measures adopted by the Congress and the non-Congress ministries. At every step the former seemed to be more anxious to enter into agreements with the zamindars and other vested interests than to improve the lot of the peasants."[29]

Nehru became increasingly aware of the problems separate Kisan organizations posed for the nationalist movement. In mid-1937, he wrote that the peasants were becoming "a temporary home for recalcitrants of the Congress" and their platform "a handy weapon to attack the local Congress Committees." Observing that some Kisan conferences had been deliberately organized to conflict with district political conferences, he objected to the tendency to treat the red flag of the All-India Kisan Sabha "as a kind of rival of the national flag."[30] He opposed the formation of Kisan Sabhas in areas where Congress committees had already been established. "The Congress," he held, "is usually considered by the peasantry as their organization and that is as it should be."[31]

The situation in Bihar was particularly disturbing to the Congress leadership. The Bihar provincial Congress ministry had worked out an agreement between the zamindars and the Bihar Kisan Sabha with respect to amendments to the tenancy law. As a result tenants secured a reduction of rent, the right to transfer land, and a few other concessions. However a new problem soon arose. Zamindars were reluctant to settle peasants on recently acquired land, for under the amended tenancy law, such persons would acquire inalienable tenancy rights. The landlords preferred either to till such land themselves or to allow it to remain uncultivated. When the Kisan Sabhas launched an agitation to compel the landlords to release this land, the provincial Congress government was forced to intervene to uphold law and order.[32] The Kisan Sabhas charged that the Bihar Congress ministry was more sympathetic to the landlords than to the poor peasants. In support of this view they observed that most of the local Congress committees in the rural areas were dominated by the landlords.[33] Subsequently, Kisan Sabha activity became more violent and more anti-Congress in nature.

At the same time the Congress party's attitude toward Kisan agitation hardened. Referring to developments in Bihar, the Congress Working Committee in January 1938 adopted a resolution which warned the leaders of the Bihar Kisan Sabha that if they continued to violate the party's creed of nonviolence they would be subject to disciplinary action.[34] As a result of this criticism Swami Sahajanand resigned from the Working Committee of the Bihar PCC.[35] In an interview with Calcutta Congressmen a few months later, Gandhi voiced the opinion that separate Kisan organizations had been formed "only with a view to capturing the Congress organization." He felt that the Kisan Sabhas were weakening the Congress rather than strengthening it. He observed that if the Sabha was "a rival organization and a Congress organization only in name, its strength and energy will be utilized in resisting the Congress and those of the Congress will be utilized in resisting the Kisan Sabha."[36]

Finally, at its annual session at Haripura in February 1938, the Congress party passed a resolution which directed its members not to associate with Kisan Sabhas to the detriment of local party organizations and advised them to devote their energies instead to the strengthening of Congress committees in the villages. It was declared that the Congress itself must champion the claims of the "kisan masses" and that it was therefore essential "that kisans should be invited to join it in ever larger numbers and organized to carry on the struggle under its banner." It was thus "the duty of every Congressman," the resolution concluded, "to work for the spread of the Congress organization in every village in India and not do anything which weakens this organization in any way."[37] The alienation between the Congress party and the All-India Kisan Sabha contributed to the capture of the peasant organization by the CPI during World War II.

Office Acceptance

Under the terms of the 1935 Constitution of India, provincial autonomy was to come into force on April 1, 1937 and the general elections for provincial legislative seats under the new constitution were scheduled for February 1937. At this time the franchise was to be extended to include about ten percent of the population or about thirty million persons.[38] The question of whether the Congress should participate in the elections, and if so whether if should form ministries in those provinces where it succeeds in winning a majority of seats, was a subject of considerable debate within the party. The issue as stated by the AICC was as follows: "Shall the country take to an evolutionary political program and accept and work the new reforms? Or would it prefer to encourage and organize forces of discontent with a view to an early bid for absolute freedom?"[39]

Roy's position on the question of collective affiliation cannot be fully understood without reference to his position on this second important political issue. His views on office acceptance were first expressed in connection with the revival of the Swaraj party in 1934 at the instigation of Dr. Mukhtar Ahmad Ansari. The party was formed, with Gandhi's blessing, for the purpose of contesting the forthcoming elections to the Central Legislative Assembly.[40]

Like its namesake of the 1920's, the new party was formed in the wake of the abandonment of a civil disobedience campaign and represented an attempt to revitalize the nationalist movement through council entry. But the two parties were quite dissimilar in terms of their political orientation. The earlier group, under the leadership of C. R. Das, was known as the "pro-changers" because it was opposed to the continuance of the policies of Gandhi and his supporters, the "no-changers." Dr. Ansari, in contrast, was considered a member of the old guard. In the 1920's he was the leader of a Center party which attempted to moderate between the two groups. A decade later his revived Swaraj party was regarded by the left wing as a vehicle of the more conservative forces of the Indian National Congress. Jawaharlal Nehru, for example, complained at the time that Dr. Ansari's group exhibited "a tender solicitude for every vested interest."[41]

In his manifesto "Whither Congress?" sent to selected members of the Congress party in 1934, Roy interpreted the decision to revive the Swaraj party as a "definite turn of Congress politics toward the Right" and as a manifestation of "neo-colonialism." He characterized a Congress resolution calling for the rejection of constitutional changes recently proposed in a British White Paper as merely "an empty gesture." He reasoned that a return to parliamentary tactics would ultimately lead to compromise with the British government and acceptance of the new Constitution. According to Roy, the formation of the Swaraj party was tantamount to a repudiation of the Lahore Congress resolution which had demanded nothing less than complete independence. There were many in the party, most notably the socialists, who agreed with this interpretation.

In his manifesto, Roy warned Congressmen that "a great betrayal" was in the making and he suggested that they take steps to "frustrate" it. He rejected the notion that this could be done by calling for a continuation of the civil disobedience campaign and Gandhi's "constructive program." Such a program of "political passivity," he felt, "could only help the Old Guard." The right-wing policy of compromise and capitulation, he argued, could be combatted only by expropriating the slogan of council entry and diverting it toward more militant ends. The tactic of parliamentary maneuver, he continued, must be made part of "a comprehensive program of action" which would consist largely of "extra-parliamentary mass action." He did not regard the legislatures as the primary political arena—a view he had ascribed to the old guard—but "as so many available instruments for developing a mass struggle."

Roy envisioned that the elections would provide an excellent vehicle for popularizing a more radical program of action. Such a program, he suggested, might properly include the development of mass agitation in support of a number of concretely formulated minimum demands and the "organization of a mass opposition to the White Paper Constitution" in favor of the election of a Constituent Assembly. By imposing upon legislative candidates a radical platform, he argued, it would be possible to prevent the policy of council entry from degenerating into "reformism" and compromise.[42]

Shortly before his manifesto appeared in the spring of 1934, Roy wrote to Jawaharlal Nehru, upon the latter's release from prison, and urged him to support the suspension of civil disobedience and the policy of council entry for the purpose of stealing the platform of the right wing and transforming it into an effective form of mass action. The elections, he contended in the letter, could be used to launch an essentially extra-parliamentary program on an all-India scale.[43] Nehru continued, however, during his brief period of freedom, to oppose the tactic of council entry. After he was returned to prison, the field was clear once more for the more moderate forces within his party. Roy was later to contend that if Nehru had adopted the Royist scheme it might well have succeeded.[44]

Nehru's aversion to Roy's plan was shared by members of the newly formed CSP. According to one of the leading Royists of this period, V. B. Karnik, Roy's suggestions were "contemptuously dismissed" when they were broached in discussions with the socialists. For their efforts in promoting this line of action the Royists were castigated by both the CSP and the CPI as "shirkers, renegades, reformists, and reactionaries."[45] When it later became clear that the Congress party would contest the elections, the CSP shifted its position from opposition to the contesting of elections to opposition to the formation of ministries.[46] When, despite their opposition, Congress governments were finally formed in several provinces, the socialists refused to accept office. As a result of its stand the CSP cut itself off from positions of influence which the party might have utilized to push forward its program both within the various provincial governments and within the Congress party itself.

Largely because of the opposition of Nehru and the socialists, the final decision on the question of office acceptance had to be postponed on several occasions when the subject came up for consideration—at a Working Committee meeting in August 1935 and at both the Lucknow and Faizpur Congress sessions.[47] At Lucknow, a motion urging the nonacceptance of ministerial office was defeated by a vote of 487 to 225.[48] At Faizpur the CSP pressed a demand for a nationwide *hartal* to begin the following April when the new Constitution was to go into effect rather than contest elections under its auspices.[49]

All these efforts having failed, the socialist leader Jayaprakash Narayan took the lead in opposing a resolution before the Subjects Committee calling for the postponement of a decision on office acceptance until after the elections. Narayan sponsored a counterproposal urging an immediate decision on the matter. He assumed that if a vote were taken before the elections a majority would oppose the acceptance of office, but that once Congressmen had tasted electoral victory they would be reluctant to deny themselves the fruits of office. Following a heated six-hour debate, the socialist maneuver failed.[50]

Narayan's assumption was correct. Following the elections in which the Congress party obtained 711 out of a total of 1585 seats in the provincial assemblies, the AICC met in March 1937 and agreed, after a lengthy debate, to accept office provided governors would forego their special powers of interference. The vote was 127 to 70. At the same time the AICC reminded Congress parliamentarians that they must adhere to "the fundamental Congress policy of combatting the new Constitution"—one of the policies on the basis of which they had sought and secured the support of the electorate. A socialist-sponsored resolution asserting that the acceptance of office was inconsistent with a policy of combatting the new constitution was defeated by a margin of 135 to 78.[51] This decision was followed by lengthy negotiations between the government and the Congress party on the extent of the governors' powers. During this period interim governments were formed. Finally in July, upon receipt of assurances by the viceroy that governors would not intervene in ministerial matters except as a last resort, the Working Committee, at Gandhi's urging, agreed to accept offices in provinces where the party enjoyed a majority.[52] Congress ministries were eventually formed in eight of the eleven provinces of British India.

In supporting the policies of mass contacts, council entry, and office acceptance, as well as in advocating the slogan of Constituent Assembly, Roy sought to reformulate what he considered to be essentially bourgeois-democratic programs in such a way as to make them compatible with the goal of democratic dictatorship. Just as the French Jacobins, the Russian bolsheviks, and the English Independents had utilized the Jacobin Clubs, the Soviets, and the New Model Army and Independent Churches respectively, Roy sought to use the Congress party as a steppingstone to political power. He believed that the acceptance of governmental responsibility by Congressmen would facilitate the capture of the party by the dissidents; for once the burdens of political office were assumed, attention of the party's leaders would be deflected from organizational matters. Moreover, he reasoned, the inability of the Congress ministries, given their class character and the constitutional restrictions under which they would have to operate, to satisfy the demands of the workers and peasants would serve to discredit the party leadership and advance the political fortunes of their more radical rivals ensconced in the local party apparatus. Had this not been the fate of the Girondists in France and the mensheviks in Russia?

With the French revolution obviously in mind, Roy hoped that with the establishment of a Constituent Assembly these local party committees would be converted into the basic units of a parallel government, which, in the course of a protracted struggle, would gradually displace the government in power. But whereas the leadership of the French Jacobins had come from the urban middle class, Roy conceived of his group, whom he styled "twentieth-century Jacobins," as a multi-class group of workers, peasants, and the petty bourgeoisie under proletarian hegemony.[53] He hoped that his followers, although "objectively" the representatives of the proletariat, would become the "driving force" behind the nationalist movement by functioning "as the vanguard of the agrarian revolution, which is the social content of the movement for political freedom" in colonial areas.[54] It is not surprising that Roy's support of various policies sponsored by the party leadership —such as the mass contacts program, council entry, and office acceptance—was misunderstood by the left wing. His advocacy of these various courses of action can be comprehended only when viewed as the components of a single, interlocking scheme by which he hoped that it might be possible for a radical minority to capture the Congress party from an entrenched majority and transform it into a parallel government capable of challenging the authority of the British *raj*.

As Roy had expected, the mass base of the Congress party was broadened as a result of its participation in the elections. Party membership grew from 600,000 in 1936 to over 3,000,000 in early 1938 and over 5,000,000 in 1939.[55] As also anticipated, the subsequent formation of Congress ministries did serve to crystallize class antagonisms within the nationalist movement.

The success of the Congress party at the polls was largely due to its identification with the nationalist struggle, its extensive party organization, and the appeal of its election manifesto to the poor and downtrodden. The manifesto, drafted by Nehru, stated that, although the Congress party "rejected in its entirety the Constitution imposed upon India" by the British Parliament, its leaders had nevertheless decided to contest the elections "not to cooperate in any way" with the new constitution, but "to combat it and seek to end it."[56] The manifesto reaffirmed the Fundamental Rights resolution adopted at Karachi and put the party on record as favoring, among other measures, "a reform of the system of land tenure, and revenue and rent," the granting of "immediate relief to the smaller peasantry by a substantial reduction of agricultural rent and revenue," and the exemption of "uneconomic holdings from payment of rent and revenue."[57]

Congress ministries did make a modest effort at social reform during their brief two-year existence. Attempts were made to reduce rents, curb the power of money lenders, relieve peasant indebtedness, improve famine relief methods, and increase educational opportunities. But these efforts did not satisfy the left wing, which accused the Congress party of failing to live up to its campaign promises. Furthermore, in exercising governmental responsibility, Congressmen in office were sometimes obliged to urge force against their more radical compatriots who were bent on disrupting law and order in the pursuit of national independence and socioeconomic reform. In Bihar a Congress ministry fired on peasant processions and in Bombay severe restrictions were imposed on the right to strike. The Congress ministry in Madras sentenced S. C. Batliwala, a communist member of the CSP, to six months' imprisonment for sedition under section 124A of the Indian Penal Code. This section had been a weapon of the British government against Congressmen and its employment in a similar manner by Rajagopalachari, the Congress chief minister of Madras, resulted in bitter dissension within the party.[58] Some professed to see little difference between Congress rule and the British *raj*. Distressed by these developments, Nehru wrote to Gandhi in April 1938 that the Congress ministries were "not doing much that they could do" and were "trying to adopt themselves far too much to the old order." He warned that, as a result, the party was in danger of "losing the high position" it had won "in the hearts of the people."[59]

The formation of Congress ministries, as Roy had hoped, brought into sharp focus the differences between the radicals and the more conservative forces within the nationalist movement and led to a confrontation between the two wings which culminated in the events of 1939. But due to various errors of strategy and tactics, some of which have already been discussed, the inability of the left wing to work in unison, and the political skill of Gandhi and the old guard, the conflict led to defeat, rather than to victory for the left wing. Congress leaders in assuming provincial office recognized that the winning of independence would ultimately depend on the strength and unity of the party organization and they were careful to take steps to ensure that the acceptance of ministerial posts did not result in any weakening of the nationalist movement.

Dissolution of the Left

It was feared by some and hoped by others that Congress officeholders might become so engrossed with their new responsibilities and so enamored of their new status and prestige that they would be lost to the nationalist movement. To maintain party unity in the face of the temptations of office, it was felt necessary to enforce strict party discipline. Consequently a Parliamentary Subcommittee was formed.

This subcommittee, later called the Parliamentary Board, consisted, during this period, of three persons—Sardar Vallabhbhai Patel (chairman), Maulana Azad, and Rajendra Prasad.[60] It should also be noted that the Congress president, who from 1936 to 1939 was a person sympathetic to the left wing, was not then a member of this body.

The Parliamentary Board was charged with the responsibility for coordinating and regulating parliamentary activities of all the Congress legislative parties. In addition to maintaining a solid front against the British, the board served to keep the party under the firm control of the old guard. This body selected all party candidates for the provincial legislative seats and, in provinces where Congress cabinets were formed, it chose the ministers and dictated their policies. Each Congress candidate was obliged to take a pledge that he would conform to the principles and policies of the party, obey the rules and regulations to be issued from time to time, and resign his seat whenever directed to do so by a competent Congress authority.[61] In most cases party luminaries were not allowed to assume ministerial office. Only secondary party figures were allowed ordinarily to direct their attention to such matters. This procedure not only reserved the major talent for party work, but helped to prevent the party from splitting into a ministerial and organizational wing. Presumably the second echelon leadership would be more tractable than the top party bosses.

With the establishment of the Congress ministries, lines between the dissident groups, on the one hand, and Gandhi and the old guard, on the other, were more clearly drawn. Although dissatisfied with the policies of the provincial ministries, the left wing found that it had little influence over their actions. The complaints of the Royists and the other radical groups that the Parliamentary Board was circumventing the control of local Congress legislative parties and was acting in an authoritarian manner were ineffectual.[62]

By mid-1938 Gandhi was reported to be under a "spiritual cloud." He was despondent over the incessant "petty bickerings" among Congressmen and "the spirit of violence" he sensed "in the air."[63] In July he complained that persons with no faith in nonviolence as a creed had infiltrated the party and that "the evil has continued to grow." To date, he observed, the Working Committee had made only feeble attempts "to purge the Congress of the evil" due to an understandable reluctance to deplete the nationalist ranks. But he added, signifying a change of mood, "I myself believe in quality rather than quantity."[64]

By early September, following a two-week period of silence, Gandhi had determined on an uncompromising stance against the left wing. In *Harijan* he wrote that the paramount question was "how to preserve the purity of the organization." His "prescription" was that all those who did not believe "in the necessity for observing truth and nonviolence as conditions of attainment of Swaraj . . . should automatically cease to belong to the Congress." He concluded:

> With all the earnestness I can command, I therefore plead with every Congressman who believes in his pledge to make his choice; either to apply the purge I have suggested, or if that is not feasible, because of the Congress being already overmanned by those who have lost faith in its creed . . . to secede from it.[65]

Indications of an offensive against the left were already in evidence. The day before the above article appeared, Dr. Z. A. Ahmed, of the Economics Department, AICC, and Dr. Rammanohar Lohia, secretary, Foreign Department of the AICC, were forced by the Working Committee to resign their posts on the basis of a newly established policy that active socialists were to be excluded from the AICC Secretariat.[66] But the attack was intensified following the tempestuous AICC meeting held in New Delhi in late September.

At this meeting there was a direct confrontation between the opposing forces within the Congress party. They were divided on every issue before the committee—on the action to be taken against a Congress minister who had violated party discipline, and on the questions of civil liberties, Indian federation, and the party's stance towards the war in Europe. For the purposes of this study, we shall be concerned only with the ministerial crisis and the related issue of civil liberties.

Dr. Khare, the Congress premier of the Central Provinces (C.P.), along with two members of his cabinet, had resigned from office the previous July. The remaining three ministers, having refused to resign, had been subsequently dismissed by the governor. Shortly thereafter, the governor had called on Dr. Khare to form a new ministry. The former premier had complied with this request without consulting the Parliamentary Board.[67] There was a strong indication of collusion between the governor and Dr. Khare, for this action had enabled the latter, a Brahman from the Marathi-speaking areas of the C.P., to remove from office his political rivals, two of whom were Kanja Kubja Brahmans who represented the Hindu-speaking region of the province.[68] At a Working Committee meeting held in late July, Dr. Khare was found guilty of gross indiscipline and was held to be unworthy of holding office. Subsequently, the C.P. Congress Parliamentary party met and elected a new leader.[69]

At the New Delhi AICC meeting Dr. Pattabhi Sitaramayya moved a resolution of censure against Dr. Khare. He asked how such undisciplinary behavior could be condoned by a party which had been erected as "the Central Government of the country parallel to the British Government." Addressing himself to critics within the party who were accusing the leadership of dictatorial practices, he added that those who believed that the party structure "ought to be subordinated to flimsy notions of democracy and parliamentary conventions" should remember that "we are in a state of transition," which calls for emergency measures.[70] The resolution as finally adopted not only censured Dr. Khare, but recommended that disciplinary action be taken against him.

Roy attended the AICC meeting in New Delhi. In opposing the above resolution, he asserted that both Dr. Khare and the Working Committee were partly responsible for the crisis and he called for a judicial inquiry into the case. Roy charged that the purpose of the resolution was to sanction the expulsion of Dr. Khare and "those who sympathized and associated with him." He asked, "If those who today regarded the Congress as a pocket borough wish to turn out all inconvenient men as undesirable, who would be left?"[71] But such views did not prevail. Subsequently the Working Committee disqualified Dr. Khare from party membership for a two-year period and he was directed to resign from all Congress organizations as well as from the C.P. Legislative Assembly.[72] The action taken against Dr. Khare was regarded by the left wing as a harbinger of things to come.

Gandhi came to the Delhi AICC meeting armed with a number of proposals, which, as he announced, were intended to purify the Congress and strengthen party discipline.[73] It was he who offered the resolution on civil liberties,[74] which precipitated the only walkout in the history of the AICC. Observing that some Congressmen "in the name of civil liberties" were advocating violence and "class war by violent means," his resolution warned that "civil liberty does not cover acts of incitement to violence or promulgation of palpable falsehood." The admonition was clearly directed at the left wing, whose spokesmen had complained of action taken against them by Congress ministries to curb their activities among peasants and workers. The resolution affirmed the AICC's support of all measures taken by Congress governments in "the defence of life and property," and reiterated its confidence in Gandhi and the creed of nonviolence.[75]

In the four-hour debate on the civil liberties resolution, Roy held that it was not as innocuous as it appeared. He contended that it would prevent those who did not believe in the Gandhian creed of nonviolence from carrying out the Congress program of socioeconomic reform as expressed in the Karachi resolution and the Election Manifesto and he predicted that, if the resolution was passed, persons like himself would be forced out of the party. Those who supported the resolution relied largely on the argument that although the Congress ministries were sympathetic to the interests of workers and peasants, they had the duty to uphold law and order.

After all attempts to defeat the resolution had failed, fifty members of the AICC, including the socialists, communists, Royists, and Kisan Sabhaites, staged a walkout amidst shouts of "Down with the Right Wing" and other slogans.[76] In private correspondence Roy later confided that the idea for the demonstration had originated with a member of the Royist group, Bhuben Sanyal.[77]

The Delhi walkout convinced Gandhi that the time had come for a showdown with the party left wing. In an article in *Harijan*, Gandhi condemned the demonstration as an "unfortunate and hasty act," which had served no purpose except to point up the disunity within the AICC. He now declared that within the Congress there was room only for those "who willingly and wholeheartedly subscribed to its creed."[78] Answering to charges of authoritarianism on the part of the Congress high command, Gandhi had earlier likened the party to an army. Until victory is achieved, "the Congress, conceived as a fighting machine," must "centralize control and guide every department and every Congressman, however highly placed, and expect unquestioned obedience."[79] Gandhi now set out to enforce this principle.

Subhas Chandra Bose, president of the Indian National Congress in 1938, did not believe in the Gandhian creed of nonviolence, and was impatient for a showdown with the British. On many concrete issues related to the freedom struggle—such as collective affiliation, civil liberties, and the proposed Indian federation—he found himself in conflict with Gandhi and the old guard. In spite of Gandhi's opposition, Bose was reelected as Congress president by the narrow margin of 1,580 to 1,375 votes in January 1939. Although suspected by the left of fascist leanings, he could conceivably have rallied dissident groups within the Congress against the present leadership. Moreover he proved himself to be more intractable than his predecessor in office, Jawaharlal Nehru. For these reasons Gandhi was determined to remove him from office.

One of the principal points of dispute between Bose and the Congress high command was the attitude the party should take toward the proposed Indian federation. The 1935 Constitution provided for a union of the princely states with the provinces of British India on a federal basis. This was to take place after a certain number of states had indicated their willingness to join. This part of the constitution never came into effect for it failed to secure the assent of the required number of princes, but nevertheless the question of its acceptance in principle was hotly debated for some time within the party.

In opposing federation, Bose spoke for many within the Congress party. He argued that under the terms of the constitution the princes would have one-third of the seats in the lower house although they represented only one-fourth of India's population. Moreover, they would nominate their own representatives, whereas legislators from British India, the nominees of various political parties, would not be equally united. Consequently, he reasoned, the princely states would have a reactionary influence on Indian politics.[80] Following his election for a second term of office, Bose had charged that some members of the Working Committee were willing to compromise on this issue. Incensed at this allegation, all but three of the fifteen members of the Working Committee resigned. The exceptions were Nehru, Bose himself, and his brother Sarat. There was no longer any hope for reconciliation between the dissidents and the old guard.

The climax of the crisis occurred at the annual Congress session held at Tripuri in March. This was the third year in a row that the Congress party had chosen a village as the site for the annual meeting. But the choice of Tripuri had a special significance, for the village had once been the capital of the Talchuri kings who had ruled in the tenth century A.D. Gandhi did not attend the session. He was recuperating from a fast recently undertaken against the ruler of Rajkot. In his absence, Pandit Pant introduced a resolution which reaffirmed the delegates' faith in Gandhian principles and practices and required that the president accept the wishes of Gandhi in the formation of a Working Committee. It also expressed confidence in the previous Working Committee and criticized attacks that had been leveled against it.[c] The resolution was adopted

[c] The resolution was as follows: "This Congress declares its firm adherence to the fundamental policies which have governed its program in the past years under the guidance of Mahatma Gandhi and is definitely of the opinion that there should be no break in these policies and that they should continue to govern the Congress program in the future. This Congress expresses its confidence in the work

both by the Subjects Committee and later in open session, but not before Bose's supporters had unleashed one of the most disruptive demonstrations in the history of the Congress party.[81]

The passage of the Pant resolution was in effect a vote of no-confidence in Bose, who had disagreed with both Gandhi and the Working Committee's conduct of the nationalist struggle and had made this a central issue in his campaign for the presidency. Although the socialists agreed with Bose on this important question, they remained neutral on the Pant resolution and abstained from voting. The communists actually voted in favor of the resolution.[82]

This behavior on the part of the socialists and communists requires some explanation. Although the CSP had moved closer to the Royists on the question of dampening socialist slogans in the interest of national unity, the two groups had moved further apart in their evaluation of the importance of Gandhi's leadership to the nationalist movement. Until 1936 the socialists and Royists had shared the slogan of alternative leadership, which symbolized their intention of replacing Gandhian dominance of the Congress party with left-wing hegemony. In 1936 the socialists abandoned this aim in favor of a composite leadership in which the left wing was to participate but not necessarily to dominate. They now felt that they could continue their former policy only at the risk of splitting the nationalist movement and seriously jeopardizing the nationalist cause. Henceforth the CSP was logically committed to supporting Gandhi's position within the Congress party, even if faced with the necessity, at the expense of the left wing. When Gandhi

---

of the Working Committee which functioned during the last year and regrets that any aspersions should have been cast against any of its members.

"In view of the critical situation that may develop during the coming year and in view of the fact that Mahatma Gandhi alone can lead the Congress and the country to victory during such crisis, the Congress regards it as imperative that its executive should command his implicit confidence and requests the President to appoint the Working Committee in accordance with the wishes of Gandhiji."

adroitly forced such a choice in 1939, by compelling Congressmen to choose between his leadership and that of Bose, the result was catastrophic for the left wing.

In defense of the socialist position on the Pant resolution, Jayaprakash Narayan argued at Tripuri that although the CSP had voted for Bose in the presidential election the party was now withholding support out of fear of creating a schism in the Congress party. He felt that unless Gandhi continued to lead the party and a Working Committee was appointed which met with his approval, it would not be possible to maintain nationalist unity.[83] The communists in voting for the Pant resolution had come to a similar conclusion.

Bose has maintained that if the socialists had voted against the Pant resolution, it would have been defeated.[84/d] The socialist leader, Madhu Limaye, in retrospect felt that the Tripuri stand of the CSP had been a mistake.[85] Roy agreed with Bose's analysis. Following the latter's victory in the presidential election, Roy had counseled him to stand firm "with courage and conviction" against any possible challenge from Gandhi and the old guard. He had urged Bose not to weaken in the face of the threat of a split in the party. He had expressed confidence that the left wing could shoulder the responsibility of providing an alternative leadership.[86] He had argued that Bose should hold out for a Working Committee in which the left wing would enjoy a majority of at least sixty percent.[87] At Tripuri the Royists voted against the Pant resolution and sponsored a compromise amendment which expressed confidence in both Gandhi and Bose. It urged Gandhi and Congress leaders to cooperate with Bose in the discharge of his duties. The proposal received only thirty-eight votes.[88] Needless to say, the Royists roundly condemned the socialists for abandoning the slogan of alternative leadership and for failing to maintain left-wing unity at Tripuri.

[d] Michael Brecher in his distinguished political biography of Nehru has also concluded that the vote of the CSP had been decisive (*Nehru: A Political Biography*, p. 250).

Because of the failure of the socialists and communists to unite behind Bose, the left wing suffered a debacle at Tripuri. The two groups had signalled their intention to cooperate with the Congress high command on the basis of a united leadership, but they were rebuffed. Following the Tripuri session Gandhi refused to cooperate with Bose in the formation of a composite Working Committee, thereby forcing his resignation. Bose proposed a compromise formula by which he would nominate seven members of the Working Committee and Sardar Patel would choose a like number. The general secretary of the party was to be nominated by Bose. Gandhi rejected the proposal and suggested that Bose should form a "homogenous cabinet" of his own choice.[89] Since such a procedure would not have complied with the Pant resolution which required the president to pick a Working Committee "in accordance with the wishes of Gandhiji" and would not have had the confidence of the AICC, Bose had little choice but to resign. In his place the AICC chose the Gandhian Rajenda Prasad, despite protests from the left that the procedure adopted was unconstitutional.

Encouraged by their victory at Tripuri, the resignation of Bose, and the demonstrated inability of the dissidents to unite in their common defense, Gandhi and the old guard pressed their campaign to purge the party. In a meeting at Calcutta the following May, the AICC appointed a subcommittee to consider reforms of the Congress constitution. The acknowledged purpose of the new body was "to recommend measures for the purification of the Congress."[90]

The constitutional subcommittee met in early June to frame proposals which were to be submitted to the AICC for its consideration. The committee recommended that the Working Committee be granted the authority to declare ineligible for membership of any elective committee the members of any organization whose objectives were in conflict with those of the Congress party. This issue was debated at great length when the AICC met in Bombay in late June. Nehru led the opposition to it. He argued that disciplinary action, when necessary, should be taken against individuals, not groups. The proposed constitutional amendment was subsequently dropped.[91]

Despite the failure of this proposal, control over the party was tightened at the Bombay meeting. Two important resolutions were adopted. The first prohibited Congressmen from organizing any form of Satyagraha without the permission of the AICC. The second placed the Congress provincial ministries more directly under the authority of the Congress high command, bypassing the local provincial Congress committees. Both resolutions had been vehemently opposed by the party left wing, which interpreted them as further efforts to reduce its influence within the party.[92]

Following the Tripuri session, the Royists met together with a few other like-minded Congressmen and decided to form a separate organization within the Congress party to be known as the League of Radical Congressmen (LRC) with the object of "combatting the Gandhist ideology" and of raising "the historic banner of Jacobinism."[93] According to Roy, the program of the LRC was to be that of "national democratic revolution," which found ideological expression in philosophical radicalism and political expression in Jacobinism. Since philosophical radicalism was the precursor of Marxism, he argued, it could be considered Marxism "as applied to precapitalist and capitalist conditions" such as to be found in contemporary India.[94]

After resigning from the Congress presidency, Bose formed a separate group known as the Forward Bloc, which it was hoped would serve as a focus for dissent within the nationalist movement. The CSP, the Royist LRC, and the CPI declined offers to merge with the Forward Bloc, but they did agree to cooperate with Bose's group in a loose organization known as the Left Consolidation Committee (LCC) for the purpose of coordinating their activities.[95]

The LCC, at Bose's instigation, organized an All-India protest day against the two resolutions adopted by the AICC at its June meeting in Bombay despite a warning from the Congress president that such a move would be considered a breach of party discipline. Rather than risk expulsion from the party, Roy decided to dissociate his group from the demonstration and withdraw from the LCC, even though his representative on the Consolidation Committee had earlier agreed to participate in the demonstrations. Roy held that Bose's action amounted to a blatant breach of discipline and openly charged that Bose was a fascist sympathizer who was merely exploiting "the left wing groups for his personal purpose."[96] By October the socialists had also broken away from the organization to be followed in November by the communists. For this action, Bose was disqualified from serving as president of the Bengal PCC and debarred from membership in any Congress committee for a three-year period.[97] Gandhi acknowledged the authorship of the resolution removing Bose from party office. Without his insistence, he felt, the Working Committee would have "shirked its duty" and refrained from such drastic action in fear of the "steady opposition" it was certain to provoke.[98]

At Tripuri the socialists and communists chose nationalist unity under Gandhi rather than left-wing hegemony under Bose. In retreat and disarray, the left wing never again reached the level of influence within the Congress party it had attained by the late 1930's. The socialists, Royists, and communists, in failing to combine their talents and aspirations, were unable to integrate their dual goals of social revolution and national independence. Myron Weiner, in his pioneering study, *Party Politics in India*, has suggested that "had the entire left wing remained in the Congress, it might have been possible to dislodge the conservative leadership."[99] But the important question remains, what would have happened to the nationalist movement if they had succeeded? On this issue the Royists and socialists disagreed and it is impossible to come to any firm conclusion.

India at War

England declared war on Germany on September 3, 1939. Without consulting Indian opinion, India was proclaimed a belligerent country, a restrictive Defense of India ordinance was imposed, and special powers were granted to the central government.[100] The Congress party was divided on the question of an appropriate response. Some nationalists, like Nehru, viewed the war in broad terms as a contest between democracy and fascist totalitarianism and were anxious to defend the principles of freedom and democracy provided the British government declared that they would be made applicable to India. In accordance with this view, the AICC adopted a resolution the following October condemning fascism and offering assistance in the prosecution of the war on the condition that India be declared "an independent nation . . . and present application [was] . . . given to this status to the largest possible extent."[101] In the absence of a satisfactory response to the request for a declaration of war aims, the Working Committee, meeting later in the month, declared its inability to cooperate in the prosecution of the war and called upon all Congress provincial ministries to resign.[102]

Gandhi opposed participation in the war on pacifist grounds. Moreover, he became convinced that England would lose the war and could see little value to India in drawing a post-dated check on a failing bank.[e] Gandhi's views on nonviolence, however, were in a minority. The CSP, for example, had no compunction about counselling violence and felt that England's predicament should be freely exploited in the interest of achieving Indian independence. The socialist leader, Jayaprakash Narayan, drew a distinction between Gandhi's views and those of the Working Committee and the AITUC. "We are therefore justified," he wrote, "to fight Britain with arms. If this does not accord with Gandhiji's principles, that is not my fault."[103]

In the early years of the war, the CPI also opposed supporting the British war effort. In their opinion the war was an internecine struggle within the imperialist camp and should be utilized to force the pace of anticolonial revolu-

[e] The phrase is Gandhi's own. It refers to promises of freedom after the war in return for Congress cooperation.

tion. This was the declared policy of the CPI until the end of 1941, approximately six months after the invasion of the Soviet Union by Nazi Germany.

The Royists, as we shall see, supported the war effort. They wished to defer the nationalist struggle until the conclusion of the war. What would India gain, they reasoned, if she secured her freedom from England and fascism were to triumph throughout the world?

Following the abandonment of the provincial ministries, the Congress Working Committee in November resolved to embark on a course of civil disobedience once internal party discipline had been achieved.[104] In order to obtain this goal, all Congressmen were required to sign a Satyagraha pledge if they wished to retain party office. At the annual party session at Ramgarh in March, only one resolution was adopted—on Satyagraha. It directed Congressmen not to aid the war effort in any way and warned that the party would resort to civil disobedience "as soon as the Congress organization is considered fit for the purpose."[105]

The price of Gandhi's leadership was to be unquestioned obedience to his creed of nonviolence. In a speech before the Subjects Committee, Gandhi stated that "the General who has to lead the fight must let his army know his conditions for leading them," and warned that he would not launch a civil disobedience movement until all his conditions were met. Strict discipline would be required, for the British, engaged in war, would be less patient than in the past and the Congress itself was a divided house. He said:

> When we march as an army we are no longer a democracy. As soldiers we have got to take orders from the General and obey them implicitly. His word must be law. . . . You must fulfill the conditions set down in the Independence Pledge. If you do not fulfill them it will be impossible for me to launch a struggle. You will have to find another General.

In a speech before the open session, Gandhi continued this theme. If they wished his leadership, he told the delegates, they must honor his commitment to truth and nonviolence, the essence of Satyagraha. "Without full faith in truth and the *Charkha*,"[f] he said, "you cannot be my soldiers."[106] Gandhi was determined not to start a struggle for the leftists to exploit and develop as they like.

At the Ramgarh session, Roy made a bid for the Congress presidency. He was defeated by Maulana Abdul Kalam Azad by a vote of 1,854 to 183. Roy's poor showing can be attributed to a number of factors: the symbolic character of his candidature (he had not actively campaigned in his own behalf[107]); the disqualification of the Bengal PCC, where Roy enjoyed a large measure of support; and the opposition of the CSP and the CPI to his candidacy. Although Roy's action had been intended to demonstrate opposition to Gandhian leadership and tactics, his heavy defeat only served to highlight the disunity of the left and the isolation of the Royists within the nationalist movement.

Shortly after the Ramgarh session, an article appeared in *Harijan* in which Gandhi urged every Congress committee to become a Satyagraha committee. Only those Congressmen who believed in Satyagraha and pledged not to interfere with the struggle by acting independently were to be enrolled. Following its publication, the general secretary of the party issued a circular to all Congress committees directing them to convert themselves to Satyagraha committees and prescribing a pledge for all Satyagrahis to take.[108] In this manner, Satyagraha committees superseded local Congress committees. The following month the Working Committee recommended that all those unwilling to take the pledge resign from all executive positions.[109] The Royists and all others who refused to acquiesce in Gandhi's leadership or to attest falsely to faith in nonviolence as a creed were forced out of all positions of influence within the party.

[f] Gandhi employed the *Charkha*, or spinning-wheel, to symbolize truth and *ahimsa* (nonviolence).

At Ramgarh, Roy presented his resolution on the constituent assembly for the last time. Although Roy must be given a large share of the credit for introducing this slogan into Congress party parlance, as was noted in the discussion of the CSP, it must be recognized that in the process of its adoption by the Congress it was altered beyond recognition. Roy had conceived of the constituent assembly as the apex of an extra-legal government which would supplant the British regime in a final, violent struggle for power; whereas the Congress leadership envisioned it as a body to be convened under the auspices of the British government and as a means of avoiding revolutionary conflict.[g]

Roy proposed before the Subjects Committee at Ramgarh that specially elected "People's Councils" serve as the collective electorates for the constituent assembly, which was to be convened in defiance of British authority.[110] After he had concluded his speech the presiding officer, Rajendra Prasad, observed that the party continued to place its faith in the Gandhian constructive program, rather than the Royist constituent assembly, as the best means of capturing power. He also observed that the Congress preferred that the constituent assembly be elected by universal adult suffrage rather than by "People's Councils." He added that Roy's resolution visualized a picture of independent India entirely different from that of the Congress party.[111]

The Royists now abandoned all hope of transforming the Congress into a revolutionary "People's Party." The assumption on which it had been based—that it would be possible to capture the party machinery through work in the primary Congress committees—had proved to be invalid. At a discussion of Satyagraha and the potentialities of the Congress held by the LRC in May-June 1940 the opinion was expressed by one of the leading Royists that

[g] According to Gandhi "all sources must . . . be exhausted to reach the Constituent Assembly before direct action is thought of. A stage may be reached when direct action may become the necessary prelude to the Constituent Assembly. That state is not yet" (Gandhi, "The Only Way," *Harijan* [Poona], Nov. 25, 1939, pp. 352-53).

the Congress machinery in the villages was in the hands of middle and rich peasants. The poorer peasants and agricultural workers, he complained, had no political influence. Consequently, all attempts to start partial struggles for removal of grievances of the poorest strata against the upper strata of peasants was squashed by the "party bosses" in the interest of "unity."[112] Roy agreed. However much we work, he observed, the party leaders "do not allow us to come anywhere near our goal."[113] Although the Congress had acquired a mass base, it had been shown that this was "no guarantee for the triumph of the revolution. . . . Objectively revolutionary masses can be utilized for the purposes of counter-revolution by reactionary leaders armed with a powerful organizational machinery."[114]

At the conference the LRC decision not to sign the Satyagraha pledge and to combat Gandhi's present policies was reconfirmed. Royists were directed to resign from all executive committees of the Congress and to prepare to leave the party altogether should this become necessary. Not all agreed with this recommendation. V. M. Tarkunde voiced a minority opinion. He argued that the LRC ought to participate in the Satyagraha movement while insisting at the same time that it be linked with economic demands and pointing out its limitations. Not to take part in the Satyagraha movement, he warned, will isolate the Royists and condemn them to a long period of inactivity. The alternative course of staying away from Satyagraha committees and pursuing a policy of local struggles for partial demands, he felt, would be futile. "This means we would hand over the control of local Congress organizations to the Gandhists."

If the struggle is not launched, he continued, the Royists will be charged with having abandoned their posts when struggle and self-sacrifice were in the offing. Again, if a struggle is begun and fails, "those who took no part in it will have little right to criticize it." The disillusioned workers will swell others' ranks, not the LRC's. Royists should welcome the opportunity presented by the Satyagraha movement of exposing by practical experience the limits of reforms. The present policy of the LRC, he argued, was based on the misguided hope that the Congress organization can be radicalized "by purely rational criticism." To Roy's claim that his followers constituted "the only sane group in the lunatic asylum of Indian politics," Tarkunde replied that instead of leading "the conscious and semi-conscious revolutionaries step by step to the path of revolution," the LRC had failed to gain their support. "Leaders should . . . be ahead of their following, but if they are so far ahead that the followers lose sight of them, they can serve no useful purpose. We have taken a stand beyond the intellectual range of the Congress rank and file."[115] The Royists, Tarkunde charged, were suffering from "ultra-leftism," but instead of being the "infantile disorder" of which Lenin spoke, it was the result of "over-rationalism." The Royists were sacrificing their movement "on the altar of rationalist purity."[116/h]

Linked to the decision of the LRC to combat current Congress policy was the Royist attitude toward the war. When war first broke out in Europe, the LRC adopted a neutral policy and called for the early termination of hostilities. At this time the Royists shared the prospect held out by the Comintern of an eventual joint attack by imperialist England and fascist Germany against the Soviet Union, the citadel of communism. But long before the Nazi invasion of the USSR in 1941, the LRC altered its position. Roy interpreted Russian diplomacy in the period 1939-41, including the Stalin-Hitler pact, as maneuvering to capture strategic positions before striking. By 1940 Roy was advocating the formation of coalition governments in the provinces and unconditional cooperation with the British in the common anti-fascist cause. He predicted that Britain's victory, if achieved, would be at the expense of her capitalist rulers and her empire and that a greatly weakened England

[h] Despite his misgivings, Tarkunde was willing to abide by the decision taken. He was later to serve as general secretary of Roy's new party, the Radical Democratic party.

would inevitably go socialist. After the war, he said, "the people of Britain," as opposed to the British "imperialists, will be there to cooperate with us."[117] Consequently, India could join the fight against fascism without sacrificing her chance for freedom.

The Royists organized a number of anti-fascist meetings throughout India on September 1, 1940 in which a demand was made for India's unconditional participation in the war. At one of these rallies Roy warned that it would be a delusion to think that "the destruction of democracy in Europe" would "help its establishment in India."[118]

The previous month the government of India had for the first time acceded to the nationalist demand that Indians be allowed to draft their own constitution, but this was to be postponed until after the war. In the meantime the viceroy had offered to expand the Executive Council. Having been disappointed with the constitutional advances granted after the first world war, many Congress leaders lacked faith in Britain's pledges. Consequently, the party rejected the proposals and decided to launch a Satyagraha campaign in defense of the freedom to preach war resistance. It was a novel form of protest, which, although limited in scope at first, culminated in the All-India Quit India movement inaugurated in August 1942.

Following this decision a press statement issued by Roy appeared in the *Statesman* (Calcutta) and other Indian newspapers in which the Congress party's rejection of the viceroy's offer and its decision to embark on an aggressive anti-British course was condemned as a betrayal of democratic and progressive forces. Roy publicly invited "more realistic politicians . . . to form popular ministries in the provinces."[119]

The acting secretary of the U.P. PCC characterized Roy's action as not merely indiscipline, but "an invitation to revolt against the Congress and to organize anti-Congress elements for that purpose." "Under the cover of fighting fascism," he charged, "it is an attempt to help British imperialism at a moment when that imperialism is determined to crush Indian nationalism and our movement for freedom."[120]

Two days after the appearance of the article, the Council of the U.P. PCC resolved to suspend Roy from membership in all elective organizations of the Congress. Roy at the time was a member of the AICC and the Working Committee of the U.P. PCC. The resolution charged Roy with a "grave breach of discipline" in conducting "persistent propaganda" against the Congress party and its policies. A few days later the Council removed Roy's name from the list of primary members for a one-year period.[121/i]

The Central Executive Committee of the LRC, meeting on October 26 and 27 declared "Congress membership" had "become incompatible with anti-fascist conviction," and resolved to form an independent political party with the name Radical Democratic People's party.[122] The inaugural conference of the party was held in Bombay, December 20-22, 1940, and was attended by 109 delegates representing about 3,500 members. The program of the new party was declared to be "the same as should have been adopted by the Congress, if the latter could be transformed into the political party of the people."[123]

Within a year, the Royists had also broken away from the Indian labor federation, the AITUC. Trade-union unity, for which the Royists among other groups had worked so hard in the 1930's, had proved to be short-lived. After England's entry into the war, the labor movement had been divided on the issue of support to the war effort. As a result, N. M. Joshi, the general secretary of the AITUC, secured the adoption of a neutral policy toward the war on the part of organized labor.[124]

Feeling that such a policy would, in effect, make India a passive partner of the axis powers, the Royists decided to

[i] The Congress Working Committee, meeting at Wardha, October 11-13, considered Roy's appeal against the disciplinary action that had been taken against him and upheld the decision of the U.P. PCC. It recommended however, that the resolution of suspension be cancelled and that Roy be allowed to resign instead (Indian National Congress, *Report of the General Secretaries, March 1940-September 1946*, p. 95).

withdraw from the AITUC and form a separate labor organization. In November 1941, Roy convened an All-India Anti-Fascist Labor Conference in Lahore. At the conference the Royists and a number of other trade unionists —such as Jamnadas Mehta of the All-India Railwaymen's Federation, Aftab Ali of the Calcutta Seaman's Union, and Mohammed Arab Khatib[j] of the Karachi Dockworkers' Union—formed the Indian Federation of Labor[k] with Jamnadas Mehta as president and Roy as general secretary.[125]

The decision of the Royists to abandon the nationalist movement and compromise with the colonial power was a complete reversal of the policies pursued by the group since the early 1930's. It was a highly unpopular stand to take in the emotionally-charged atmosphere of the war years. The decision not only created hardships in the personal lives of individual members of the group, but resulted ultimately in the political demise of the Royist movement. Roy's new party failed to gain a political foothold and was disbanded after the war. Roy failed to live up to Bagehot's

[j] M. A. Khatib in the 1960's was the president of the West Pakistan Federation of Labor (WPFL) and of the All-Pakistan Confederation of Labor (APCL). The WPFL is a descendant of the IFL unions which fell on the Pakistan side of the border following the 1947 partition of the Indian sub-continent. This organization still uses the former symbol of the defunct IFL—a lighted torch (Interview with C. P. Dave, Assistant general secretary of the WPFL and the APCL, Karachi, Oct. 10, 1961).

[k] The following year the IFL challenged the AITUC's claim to be the most representative Indian labor organization. Rather than examining the claims of the two bodies, the government of India from 1943 until 1946 followed the principle of allowing both the IFL and the AITUC—on alternate years—to send delegates to International Labor Organization conferences. The strength of the IFL declined when its receipt of a government subsidy was publicly revealed in 1944. In December 1948 the IFL amalgamated with the socialist Hind Mazdoor Panchayat to form the Hind Mazdoor Sabha (Government of India, Department of Labor, *Report Regarding the Representative Character of the All-India Trade Union Congress and the Indian Federation of Labour* [1946]; and V. B. Karnik, *Rupees 13,000 X-Rayed* [Delhi: IFL, 1945]. See also Government of India, Legislative Assembly Debates, III, 6 [1944]: 1915-16; IV, 2 [1944]: 111-14; and 3 [1944]: 220-21; V, 2 [1944]: 792, 850-51).

definition of a democratic leader—"an uncommon man with common opinions."

Over the years Roy had become increasingly disenchanted with Russian communism as a progressive force in the world. As World War II progressed, nationalist themes became more and more pronounced, to the exclusion of revolutionary zeal. Roy has related that in the early years of the war, as he listened to Radio Moscow, "the stirring music" of the "International" had restored his faith "in the ultimate outcome of the war." But one evening in 1942 "the message of hope" had failed to come. He continued: "At the same hour the bells in the Kremlin tower began playing the new Russian national anthem instead of the 'International'—a period of history was over. I lost my faith in the liberating significance of the Russian revolution."[126] The following year, on May 22, 1943, the Comintern was dissolved.

Despite the above passage, however, Roy's faith in his spiritual homeland was not completely dispelled until some years later. It was still possible for him to excuse Stalin's faults as due to the exigencies of war and as the heavy price the USSR had to pay for skipping the stage of bourgeois-democracy. The tradition of the old Russian aristocracy—autocracy, bureaucracy, and political and cultural conformity—had managed to survive the defeat of its class bearers. Roy had hoped that after the war these defects could be remedied by closer contact between the USSR and Europe, where humanist traditions were more firmly rooted, just as Rome had succumbed to the culture of Greece. Consequently, he had initially welcomed the establishment of Soviet rule over Eastern Europe. But as Stalin drew the "iron curtain" and embarked on the "cold war," Roy's final hopes died.[127]

After the war, Roy left politics altogether and devoted himself to developing the Radical Humanist movement. He abandoned the teleological aspects of Marxism, such as the concepts of economic determinism and historical necessity, and placed increased emphasis on Marxist humanism.[128] He came to regard the idea that the means of production determine the whole course of human history as the most serious defect of Marxism. It negates, he argued, Marx's humanist predilections and was inconsistent with the view, to which Roy subscribed, that "man is the root of mankind." In his later years, Roy attached supreme importance to the potentiality of ideas.[129] According to Roy:

> Man, the creator of machines, is greater than the means of production. Man did not emerge from the process of evolution with a hammer in his hand, but with a distinctive brain. The human brain, itself a kind of "means of production," is more powerful than the most powerful machine.[130]

Through all the modifications he made in his political philosophy over the years, runs one consistent theme—the quest for human freedom and dignity—to which Roy devoted his entire life.

Notes

Introduction

[1] Interview with Nripendranath Chakravarty, Calcutta, Dec. 1, 1962. As a member of Juguntar, Chakravarty knew Roy as a youth. In 1962 he was still living near Roy's village of Kodalia.

[2] Gene D. Overstreet and Marshall Windmiller, *Communism in India* (Berkeley: University of California Press, 1959), p. 20, cite the year of Roy's birth as 1886 or 1887. Ellen Roy based her conclusion on the expressed belief of Roy's personal physician, who had treated him during the last sixteen years of his life, that he could not possibly have been 67 or 68 years of age at the time of his death on January 25, 1954. She has also recalled that in a letter written to her in 1933 or 1934 he observed that according to the saying "life begins at forty," his life was only just about to begin (Ellen Roy, "Comments on the First Seven Chapters of Overstreet and Windmiller's *Communism in India*"). A copy of this typewritten manuscript, dated May 18, 1957, was given to the author by Philip Spratt.

[3] Evelyn Roy, "French Persecution of Indian Political Exiles," *Inprecor*, v, 20 (1925): 288, and A. K. Hindi [Tayab Shaikh], *M. N. Roy—The Man Who Looked Ahead* (Allahabad: The Modern Publishing House, 1959), p. 8.

[4] A. K. Hindi [Tayab Shaikh], p. 14.

[5] Richard L. Park, "The Rise of Militant Nationalism in Bengal: A Regional Study of Indian Nationalism" (Ph.D. dissertation, Harvard University, 1950), p. 257.

[6] A. K. Hindi [Tayab Shaikh], pp. 16-19.

[7] *Ibid.*, pp. 23-24.

[8] *San Francisco Chronicle,* Dec. 14, 1917.

[9] A. K. Hindi [Tayab Shaikh], p. 21, and Hiren Mukherjee, *India's Struggle for Freedom,* 3rd ed. rev. (Calcutta: National Book Agency, 1962), p. 132. The latter book was first published in 1946 under the title, *India Struggles for Freedom.*

[10] A. K. Hindi [Tayab Shaikh], pp. 20-23.

[11] *San Francisco Chronicle*, April 13, 1918.

[12] A. K. Hindi [Tayab Shaikh], pp. 20-23.

[13] Editorial on M. N. Roy, *Hindustan Standard* (Calcutta), Jan. 28, 1954.

[14] A. K. Hindi [Tayab Shaikh], pp. 24-36.

[15] U.S. Department of Justice, File 9-10-3, Part III, entry no. 54272/105, dated May 12, 1917. See also M. N. Roy, "Across the Pacific," *Radical Humanist* (Calcutta), XVII, 8 (1953): 91.

[16] *San Francisco Chronicle*, Dec. 15, 1917.

[17] U.S. War Department Files, 10640-690, M. I. 5. Report on M. N. Roy's activities in Mexico by the United States Military Attaché in Mexico in 1918.

[18] *Ibid.*

[19] *Ibid.*

[20] M. N. Roy, "The Quest of the Golden Fleece," *Radical Humanist* (Calcutta), XVI, 23 (1952): 56.

[21] *Ibid.*; and M. N. Roy, "End of the Mexican Sojourn," *Radical Humanist* (Calcutta), XVII, 8 (1953): 414-16.

[22] M. N. Roy, "In the Land of Liberty," *Radical Humanist* (Calcutta), XVII, 7 (1953): 79-80.

[23] U. S. War Department Files.

[24] *San Francisco Chronicle*, Jan. 9, 1917 and July 7, 1917. There is no transcript available in the United States of the 1917 San Francisco trial, known as the Hindu Conspiracy Case. There is a stenographic report in the India Office Library of the Ministry of Commonwealth Relations in London. The *San Francisco Chronicle* (May 9, 1917-June 12, 1918) offered fairly complete coverage of the trial, but tended to emphasize its more sensational aspects. The National Archives contains a great deal of information on the case. At the Archives I have found the following sources to be most helpful: Record Group 85, Immigration and Naturalization Service, Files 52903/110D, 53854, 53854/133A, and 53854/133B; Record Group 60, Department of Justice, File 193424; Record Group 118, Records of the U.S. Attorney; Records of the Department of State Relating to World War I and its Termination, 1914-29, 763.72111H58-763.72111M45, Hindu Political Plots in the U.S. and 763.72111/AC-763.72111An7, Retention of the vessels *Academy* and *Annie Larsen*.

[25] Manuel Gomez, "Roy and Borodin in Mexico," *Radical Humanist* (Calcutta), June 6, 1965, pp. 267-76. This is a reprint of Theodore Draper's interview with Manuel Gomez which appeared in *Survey*, Oct. 1964, under the title, "From Mexico to Moscow."

[26] Carleton Beals, *Glass Houses: Ten Years of Free-Lancing* (Philadelphia: Lippincott, 1938), pp. 43-53.

[27] M. N. Roy, "An Emissary of the International," *Radical Humanist* (Calcutta), XVII, 32 (1953): 379.

[28] Gomez, "Roy and Borodin in Mexico."

[29] Roy, "End of the Mexican Sojourn."

[30] Beals, pp. 43-53.

[31] *Ibid.*

Chapter 1

[1] M. N. Roy, "First Meeting With Lenin," *Radical Humanist* (Calcutta), XVI, 23 (1952): 268.

[2] "The Situation in India—Report of Comrade Roy," *Petrograd Pravda* (July 29, 1920), quoted in U. S. Department of State, *The Second Congress of the Communist International, as reported and interpreted by the official newspapers of Soviet Russia* (Washington: Government Printing Office, 1920), p. 43.

[3] Jane Degras, ed., *The Communist International: 1919-1920 Documents*, I (London: Oxford University Press, 1954): 138. Degras reports that although the vote on Lenin's thesis was marred by three abstentions, Roy's supplementary thesis was adopted unanimously. However, Edward H. Carr, *The Bolshevik Revolution: 1917-1923*, III

(New York: Macmillan, 1953): 252-57, states that the Italian delegate Serrati opposed both theses. Carr also has noted that Roy's original draft thesis erroneously appeared as the final version in most official Soviet documents until 1934. For Roy's thesis in its modified form as adopted by the Second Congress, see *The Second Congress of the Communist International Proceedings* (Moscow: Communist International, 1920), pp. 114-17.

[4] Compare Vladimir I. Lenin's "Preliminary Draft Theses on the National and Colonial Questions," *Selected Works*, x (New York: International Publishers, 1938): 236, with "Theses on the National and Colonial Questions" (adopted at the Second Comintern Congress), *Theses and Statutes of the Third (Communist) International* (Moscow: Publishing Office of the Communist International; reprinted by the United Communist Party of America, 1920), p. 70.

[5] Vladimir I. Lenin, "The Report on the National and Colonial Questions at the Second Congress of the Communist International," July 26, 1920, *Selected Works*, x: 240-41.

For studies of Roy's contribution to the Comintern colonial policy, see John P. Haithcox, "The Roy-Lenin Debate on Colonial Policy: A New Interpretation," *Journal of Asian Studies*, xxiii, 1 (1963): 93-101; and Claude Hamel, "Un Débat au second Congres du Komintern (1920)," *Est et Ouest* (Paris), xiv, 281 (1962): 9-12. For contrasting views on this subject, see Allen S. Whiting, *Soviet Policies in China 1917-1924* (New York: Columbia University Press, 1954), pp. 50-55, 93-95; and Gene D. Overstreet and Marshall Windmiller, *Communism in India*, pp. 29-36.

[6] Robert C. North and Xenia J. Eudin, *M. N. Roy's Mission to China: The Communist-Kuomintang Split of 1927* (Berkeley: University of California Press, 1962), p. 1.

[7] A. K. Hindi [Tayab Shaikh], *M. N. Roy—The Man Who Looked Ahead*, p. 22. See also M. N. Roy, "Across the Pacific."

[8] For a study of the differences between the moderates and the radicals within the Congress party before the advent of Gandhi, see Stanley A. Wolpert, *Tilak and Gokhale* (Berkeley: University of California Press, 1962).

[9] R. C. Majumdar, *History of the Freedom Movement in India*, ii (Calcutta: K. L. Mukhopadhyay, 1963): 328.

[10] A. K. Hindi [Tayab Shaikh], p. 22. See also Roy, "Across the Pacific."

[11] T. Walter Wallbank, *A Short History of India and Pakistan: From Ancient Times to the Present* (New York: The New American Library, 1965), pp. 116-17, 132. This is the abridged paperback edition of the author's *India in a New Era*, published in 1951 by Scott Foresman and Co.

[12] U. S. Department of State, p. 41.

[13] "Theses on the National and Colonial Questions," p. 74.

[14] Vladimir I. Lenin, "Report on the Current Moment," made at the Fourth Conference of the Trade Union and Factory Committees, Moscow, June 27, 1918, *Sochineniia*, xxiii (Moscow-Leningrad, 1926-32, 30 vols.): 82, as translated by Alfred G. Meyer, *Leninism* (Cam-

bridge: Harvard University Press, 1957), p. 30. For a discussion of Lenin's concept of "spontaneity," see Meyer, pp. 29-30.

[15] Overstreet and Windmiller, p. 22, quoting from Alfred Rosner, "In Moscow in Lenin's Days: 1920-21," *The New International*, XXI (Summer, 1955): 109.

[16] "Theses on the National and Colonial Questions," p. 70.

[17] *Ibid.*, p. 75.

[18] Alfred G. Meyer, *Marxism: The Unity of Theory and Practice* (Cambridge: Harvard University Press, 1954), pp. 109-13. I am indebted to Professor Meyer for his excellent description of the maximum and minimum programs.

[19] "Theses on the National and Colonial Questions," p. 73.

[20] M. N. Roy, *India in Transition* (Geneva: J. B. Target, 1922), p. 29. Except for the date, the publication details are fictitious.

[21] M. N. Roy, "An Attempt to Interpret Indian History by the Marxist Method," *Radical Humanist* (Calcutta), 33 (1954): 390-91; and 34 (1954): 398-407.

[22] Roy, *India in Transition*, p. 29.

[23] *Ibid.*, p. 40.

[24] Gangadhar M. Adhikari, *Communist Party and India's Path to National Regeneration and Socialism* (New Delhi: New Age Printing Press, 1964), pp. 55-57.

Chapter 2

[1] Muzaffar Ahmed, *The Communist Party of India and Its Formation Abroad* (Calcutta: National Book Agency Private Ltd., 1962), p. 65.

[2] F. Walter Wallbank, *A Short History of India and Pakistan* (New York: The New American Library, 1965), pp. 154-58.

[3] This account of the Indian Moslems at India House in Tashkent, and later at the Communist University of Toilers of the East in Moscow, is a composite drawn from several sources. These include: the memoirs of one of the *muhajirun*, Rafiq Ahmed, which appears in Muzaffar Ahmed, pp. 11-55; further details supplied by Muzaffar Ahmed in his book, pp. 56-97; and Roy, *M. N. Roy's Memoirs*, pp. 411-76, 525-32. The two memoirs complement each other in most respects, although there are a few discrepancies concerning details.

[4] Abdul Qadir Khan, "The Road to Moscow," Part I of a three-part series entitled "Pupil of the Soviet," *The Times* (London), Feb. 25, 26, and 27, 1930. Khan's British sympathies can be seen in his concluding article in which he expresses his conviction that "Indian progress and contentment" can be secured only "by the steady development of those liberalizing forces to which the British government is pledged."

[5] Government of India, Home Department, *Communism in India 1924-27* (Calcutta: Government of India Press, 1927), pp. 5-14, 31. This confidential document was prepared under the supervision of Sir David Petrie, Director, Intelligence Bureau, Government of India.

[6] *Ibid.*, pp. 7-8, 31.

[7] A. K. Hindi [Tayab Shaikh], *M. N. Roy—The Man Who Looked Ahead*, pp. 16-19.

[8] P. C. Ghosh, *The Development of the Indian National Congress, 1892-1909* (Calcutta: Firma K. L. Mukhopadhyay, 1960), pp. 184-85.

[9] Nirad C. Chaudhuri, *The Autobiography of an Unknown India* (London: Macmillan and Co., 1951), p. 245.

[10] Banki Bihari Misra, *The Indian Middle Classes: Their Growth in Modern Times* (London: Oxford University Press, 1961), pp. 393-95. For a discussion of the *bhadralok* in terms of Max Weber's concept of a status group and an account of their futile efforts after 1912 to retain their socioeconomic dominance, see J. H. Broomfield, *Elite Conflict in a Plural Society: Twentieth-Century Bengal* (Berkeley: University of California Press, 1968).

[11] Great Britain, *Parliamentary Papers*, VIII, "Sedition Committee Report," Cmnd. 9190 (1918): 11-12. This report—also known as the Rowlatt Report after the chairman of the committee, Sir S. A. T. Rowlatt—is a major source of information on the Bengali revolutionary movement.

[12] Richard L. Park, "The Rise of Militant Nationalism in Bengal: A Regional Study of Indian Nationalism" (Ph.D. dissertation, Department of Government, Harvard University, 1950), pp. 240-41. See also P. C. Ray, *The Life of C. R. Das* (London: Oxford University Press, 1927), pp. 52-53.

[13] *Juguntar* (Calcutta), May 30, 1908, quoted in P. C. Ghosh, p. 194. Passages such as this were frequently employed in equating religious sacrifice with political assassination.

[14] Sir Charles A. Tegart, "Terrorism in India," a speech delivered before the Royal Empire Society in London, November 1, 1932, and published in pamphlet form by the society. At the time of the speech he was a member of the Secretary of State's India Council. He was a former commissioner of police in Calcutta.

[15] Subhas Chandra Bose, *The Indian Struggle, 1920-34* (London: Wishart and Co., 1935), p. 337.

[16] Interview with Jibanlal Chatterjee, Calcutta, Dec. 3, 1962; and Government of India, Home Department, 1927, pp. 64, 83.

[17] Government of India, Home Department, 1927, pp. 33, 64-68; and Muzaffar Ahmed, pp. 114-16.

[18] Philip Spratt, *Blowing Up India: Reminiscences and Reflections of a Former Comintern Emissary* (Calcutta: Prachi Prakashan, 1955), p. 44.

[19] K. S. Bhat, "The Workers' Welfare League of India," *Labour Monthly* (London), XIII, 12 (1931): 777-79 (the author was president of the League); and Government of India, Home Department, 1927, pp. 20-21, 33, 124, 134-35.

[20] Government of India, Home Department, 1927, p. 12.

[21] M. N. Roy, *Origins of Radicalism in the Congress* (Lucknow: New Life Union, 1942), pp. 16-17, 74.

[22] Government of India, Home Department, 1927, pp. 17-18.

[23] V. B. Karnik, *Indian Trade Unions: A Survey* (Bombay: Labour Education Service, 1960), p. 34.

[24] M. N. Roy's comments on the "Theses on the Eastern Question," in *International Press Correspondence* (English edition), II, 109 (1922): 894; *Inprecor*, II, 116 (1922): 988; and J. Degras, ed., *The Communist International: 1919-1922*, p. 382. The name of the official organ of the Comintern was changed in June 1938 from *International Press Correspondence* to *World News and Views.* It will be cited hereafter as *Inprecor.*

[25] Government of India, Home Department, 1927, p. 16.

[26] J. Degras, ed., "Theses on the Eastern Question—Fourth Comintern Congress," Part V: "The General Task of the Communist Parties of the East," pp. 388-89.

[27] *Ibid.*, Part VI: "The United Anti-Imperialist Front," pp. 390-91.

[28] Gregory Zinoviev, Opening Speech to the Central Committee at the Fourth Comintern Congress, quoted in Government of India, Home Department, 1927, p. 16.

[29] Government of India, Home Department, 1927, p. 16.

[30] Kermit E. McKenzie, *Comintern and World Revolution: 1928-43: Shaping of Doctrine* (New York: Columbia University Press, 1964).

[31] "The Enlarged Executive, Opening Session," *Inprecor*, III, 45 (1923): 438.

[32] Ahmed, pp. 34-51.

[33] *Ibid.*, p. 87.

[34] Spratt, *Blowing Up India*, p. 34.

[35] Government of India, Home Department, 1927, pp. 23, 26-27, 31-32.

[36] Ahmed, pp. 90-93.

[37] M. N. Roy, "The Labour Government in Action," *Inprecor*, IV, 24 (1924): 226.

Chapter 3

[1] Government of India, Home Department, *Communism in India*, 1927, pp. 17-18.

[2] Letter from M. N. Roy to S. A. Dange, Nov. (exact date not given) 1922, quoted in *ibid.*, pp. 13, 19-20.

[3] Letter from M. N. Roy to Muzaffar Ahmed, May 1923, quoted in *ibid.*, p. 25.

[4] See Chapter 2.

[5] M. N. Roy, "Debate on the National Question" (Fifth Comintern Congress, Twentieth Session, July 1, 1924), *Inprecor*, IV, 50 (1924): 518-19.

[6] *From the Fourth to the Fifth World Congress* (London: Communist Party of Great Britain, 1924), p. 68.

[7] Roy, "Debate on the National Question."

[8] Letter from Evelyn Roy, quoted in Government of India, Home Department, 1927, p. 6.

[9] Dmitry Manuilsky, "Concluding Speech on the National Question" (Fifth Comintern Congress, July 8, 1924), *Inprecor*, IV, 57 (1924): 608.

[10] "Theses on Tactics" (Fifth Comintern Congress), *Inprecor*, IV, 62 (1924): 62.

[11] M. N. Roy, "Fifth World Congress" (Speech by Roy, June 20, 1924), *Inprecor*, IV, 42 (1924): 418.

[12] Vladimir I. Lenin, *Collected Works*, XVIII, 4th ed. rev. (London: Lawrence and Wishart, 1960): 358.

[13] Vladimir I. Lenin, *Selected Works*, IX: 398-400.

[14] "The Situation in India—Report of Comrade Roy," *Petrograd Pravda* (July 29, 1920), quoted in U.S. Department of State, *The Second Congress of the Communist International as reported and interpreted by the official newspapers of Soviet Russia*, pp. 42-44.

[15] *Ibid.*

[16] *Theses and Statutes of the Third (Communist) International*, p. 73.

[17] Dmitry Manuilsky, "Report on the National Question," *Inprecor*, IV, 54 (1924): 569.

[18] "Theses and Resolutions Adopted by the Fifth World Congress of the Communist International," *Inprecor*, IV, 62 (1924): 647.

[19] M. N. Roy, *The Future of Indian Politics* (London: R. Bishop, 1926). This book was written to show "the historic necessity for a People's Party in India" (p. 7).

[20] Government of India, Home Department, 1927, pp. 49-50.

[21] This account of Satya Bhakta and the formation of the CPI is based primarily on the following sources: Government of India, Home Department, 1927, pp. 53-54; and Muzaffar Ahmed, *Communist Party of India: Years of Formation, 1921-1933* (Calcutta: National Book Agency Private Ltd., 1959), pp. 16-21.

[22] Ahmed, *Communist Party of India: Years of Formation, 1921-1933*, pp. 22-23.

[23] Muzaffar Ahmed, *The Communist Party of India and its Formation Abroad*, p. 161.

[24] Government of India, Home Department, Intelligence Bureau, *Communism in India*, revised up to January 1, 1935 (Simla: Government of India Press, 1935), p. 239. This report was prepared by J. F. Cowgill under the direction of H. Williamson, Director, Intelligence Bureau.

[25] Government of India, Home Department, 1927, p. 71.

[26] Ahmed, *The Communist Party of India and its Formation Abroad*, pp. 153-62.

[27] Ahmed, *Communist Party of India: Years of Formation, 1921-1933*, p. 20.

[28] Letters from M. N. Roy, quoted in Government of India, Home Department, 1927, pp. 54-55.

[29] *Ibid.*, pp. 38-40, 51, 58, 63.

[30] *Ibid.*, p. 58.

[31] Letter from M. N. Roy to J. P. Bergerhotta, March 1926, quoted in Government of India, Home Department, 1927, p. 54.

[32] Letter from M. N. Roy, December 1926, quoted in *ibid.*, p. 60.

[33] "From Gaya to Gauhati," *Masses of India*, quoted in *ibid.*, p. 104.

[34] M. N. Roy, "Elections in India," *Inprecor*, VI, 84 (1926): 84-85.

[35] Government of India, Home Department, 1927, p. 154. See also George M. Kahin, *Nationalism and Revolution in Indonesia* (Ithaca: Cornell University Press, 1952), pp. 71-72. The argument presented here—that Roy's views had altered in favor of working within the Congress party before his departure for China—contrasts sharply with that presented by Gene D. Overstreet and Marshall Windmiller in *Communism in India.* These authors contend (pp. 104, 108 and 120-21) that Roy's attitude toward the Indian nationalist movement did not change until after the Sixth Comintern Congress, held in mid-1928.

[36] Philip Spratt, *Blowing Up India*, p. 24. See also Henry Pelling, "The Early History of the Communist Party of Great Britain, 1920-29," *Transactions of the Royal Historical Society* (London), VIII (1958): 45-46.

[37] Rajani Palme Dutt, *Modern India*, 2nd ed. rev. (London: Communist Party of Great Britain, 1927).

[38] *The Times* (London), June 25, 1929, p. 15; and Dec. 4, 1929, p. 13.

[39] Government of India, Home Department, 1935, p. 114.

[40] Spratt, *Blowing Up India*, p. 29.

[41] Government of India, Home Department, 1927, p. 145.

[42] *Ibid.*, p. 124.

[43] Interviews with Philip Spratt, Bangalore, Nov. 20-22, 1962.

[44] Government of India, Home Department, 1927, p. 123.

[45] Great Britain, *Parliamentary Papers*, XXIII (Accounts and Papers, VIII) Cmnd. 2682, 1926, "Communist Papers," 77-83.

[46] "Communist Plotting in India," *The Times* (London), Jan. 18, 1933, p. 9. This is a summary of the decision of the Sessions Judge, R. L. Yorke, at the Meerut Conspiracy Trial.

[47] Government of India, Home Department, 1927, pp. 10-11.

[48] *Ibid.*, pp. 52, 137-38.

[49] *Ibid.*, pp. 56-57, 73; Government of India, Home Department, 1935, p. 114; and Spratt, *Blowing Up India*, p. 32.

[50] Vasant Bhagwant Karnik, *Indian Trade Unions*, pp. 34-35.

[51] Hugh Lester Hutchinson, *Conspiracy at Meerut* (London: Allen and Unwin, 1935), p. 50. Hutchinson had sought to capitalize not only on the name of the famous paper of the Russian Social Democrats, *Iskra* (*The Spark*), but also on that of a famous Bombay weekly, *The Spark*, which had been edited by M. G. Desai.

[52] Interviews with Philip Spratt, Bangalore, Nov. 20-22, 1962; and Government of India, Home Department, 1935, p. 115.

[53] *The Times* (London), June 26, 1929, p. 14; Dec. 11, 1929, p. 11; and Jan. 16, 1930, p. 11.

[54] Spratt, *Blowing Up India*, p. 29.

[55] Ahmed, *Communist Party of India: Years of Formation, 1921-1933*, p. 21.

[56] Spratt, *Blowing Up India*, p. 35.

[57] Philip Spratt, "Eighteen Months in India," *Independent India* (New Delhi), VIII, 52 (1942): 627-28.

[58] Government of India, Home Department, 1927, p. 73. See also Meerut, District Court, p. 249.

[59] Karnik, *Indian Trade Unions*, p. 37.

[60] *Ibid.*, pp. 35-36.

[61] "The Indian Labour Movement," *Inprecor*, XIII, 22 (1933): 490. This is confirmed in Government of India, Home Department, 1927, p. 73.

[62] Government of India, Home Department, 1927, p. 58.

[63] *Ibid.*, pp. 60-62.

[64] "Meerut Trial," *The Times* (London), Dec. 5, 1929, p. 14.

[65] Ahmed, *The Communist Party of India and Its Formation Abroad*, p. 95.

[66] Spratt, *Blowing Up India*, pp. 30 and 38.

[67] *Ibid.*, p. 37.

[68] Government of India, Home Department, 1935, p. 118.

[69] *The Times* (London), March 21, 1929, p. 16.

Chapter 4

[1] Gregory Zinoviev, "The Epoch of Wars and Revolutions," *Inprecor*, v, 55 (1925): 745-47.

[2] Government of India, Home Department, *Communism in India*, 1927, p. 99.

[3] For a detailed account of the events in China during the period 1925-1927, see Harold R. Isaacs, *The Tragedy of the Chinese Revolution*, 2nd ed. rev. (Stanford: Stanford University Press, 1961).

[4] Joseph V. Stalin, *Marxism and the National and Colonial Question: A Collection of Articles and Speeches*, 4th ed. (London: Lawrence and Wishart, 1947), p. 237.

[5] "Theses on the Situation in China by the Seventh Extraordinary Plenum of the Executive Committee of the Communist International, November 22-December 16, 1926," Robert C. North and Xenia J. Eudin, *M. N. Roy's Mission to China: The Communist-Kuomintang Split of 1927*, p. 132. All the documents cited from this book, except the present one, were translated from *Kitaiskaia revoliutsiia i kommunisticheskii internatsional.* Copies of this latter book, published in Moscow in 1929, were discovered only a few years ago in the libraries of the University of California at Berkeley and The Hoover Institution on War, Revolution, and Peace at Stanford University. It is believed that these are the only copies of the book available outside of the Soviet Union. North and Eudin have pointed out (pp. 4-5) that they did not attempt in their introductory chapters (pp. 12-128) to present a complete analysis of the translated documents (pp. 131-376), which contained a wealth of previously unavailable material concerning communist strategy and tactics in China in the 1920's. Consequently, where this source has been cited the present author is solely responsible for the interpretations placed thereon.

[6] *Ibid.*, p. 142.

[7] *Ibid.*, p. 138.

[8] Joseph V. Stalin, "The Revolution in China and the Tasks of the Comintern: Speech Delivered at the Tenth Sitting, Eighth Plenum of

the ECCI, May 24, 1927," *Works*, II (Moscow: Foreign Languages Publishing House, 1952): 291-92.

[9] "Theses on the Situation in China by the Seventh Extraordinary Plenum," pp. 140-41.

[10] Nikolai I. Bukharin, *Problems of the Chinese Revolution* (London: Communist Party of Great Britain, 1927), p. 36. This report appeared in *Pravda*, April 19 and 20, 1927.

[11] "The Agenda and Preparation of the Enlarged Executive of the Communist International," *Inprecor*, VI, 12 (1926): 181; and *Inprecor*, VI, 17 (1926): 255.

[12] United States Department of State, Division of Biographic Information, Office of Libraries and Intelligence Acquisition, *Far Easterners in the Communist Structure*, OIR Report No. 5226 (Washington: U. S. Government Printing Office, 1950), p. 19.

[13] "Seventh Meeting of the Enlarged ECCI," *Inprecor*, VI, 83 (1926): 1432.

[14] "Election of the Presidium and the Secretariat of the ECCI," *Inprecor*, VI, 93 (1926): 1646.

[15] "Seventh Plenum of the Enlarged ECCI," *Inprecor*, VI, 83 (1926): 1432. See also M. N. Roy, "Discussion of the Report on the Situation in China," *Inprecor*, VI, 91 (1926): 1603-4. Bukharin, Bubnov and Roy drafted the thesis on the Chinese revolution adopted by the Seventh Plenum (Robert C. North, *Moscow and the Chinese Communists* [Stanford: Stanford University Press, 1963], p. 90).

[16] Home Department, Government of India, 1927, pp. 110-17.

[17] Gene D. Overstreet and Marshall Windmiller, *Communism in India*, pp. 93-94.

[18] *Ibid.*, pp. 105-109.

[19] Letter from Louise Geissler to author, Zurich, March 23, 1966. Louise Geissler, a Swiss citizen, was a parliamentary stenographer of the Comintern Congresses between 1920 and 1926. She accompanied Roy to China in late 1926.

[20] Bukharin, *Problems of the Chinese Revolution*, p. 30.

[21] Isaacs, pp. 111-86.

[22] C. Martin Wilbur and Julie Lien-ying How, eds., *Documents on Communism: National and Soviet Advisers in China, 1918-1927: Papers Seized in the 1927 Peking Raid* (New York: Columbia University Press, 1956), p. 381.

[23] Isaacs, p. 202.

[24] "Resolution on the Chinese Question" (Eighth Plenum of the ECCI, May 18-30, 1927), *Inprecor*, VII, 35 (1927): 737-41.

[25] "The Questions of the Chinese Revolution: Theses of Comrade Stalin for Propagandists, Approved by the CC of the CPSU," *Inprecor*, VII, 27 (1927): 543-45.

[26] Nikolai I. Bukharin, "The Results of the Plenary Session of the ECCI," *Inprecor*, VII, 39 (1927): 879-84.

[27] North and Eudin, p. 76.

[28] M. N. Roy, *My Experiences in China* (Calcutta: Renaissance Publishers, 1949), pp. 30-41. It is a little known fact that this book first appeared in India in the early 1930's under the title *China in*

Revolt. Roy had only recently returned to India surreptitiously, and to escape detection, he employed the *nom de plume*, S. K. Vidyarthi. This book was published in Bombay by the Vanguard Publishing Company.

[29] Letter from Louise Geissler to author, Zurich, March 23, 1966.

[30] "Resolution on the Continuation of the Northern Campaign: Adopted by the Central Committee of the Chinese Communist Party in Hankow, April 16, 1927," as translated by North and Eudin, pp. 176-77.

[31] Note by Roy appended to the "Resolution on the Continuation of the Northern Campaign," in North and Eudin, p. 177.

[32] "Theses on the Political Situation and the Tasks of the Chinese Communist Party" (adopted by the Fifth Congress of the CCP, May 9, 1927), as translated by North and Eudin, pp. 243-53.

[33] Isaacs, pp. 234-36.

[34] Roy, *My Experiences in China*, p. 45.

[35] *Ibid.*, p. 53. For a translation of the telegram, see North and Eudin, pp. 106-107.

[36] For Borodin's reaction, see Conrad Brandt, *Stalin's Failure in China, 1924-1927* (Cambridge: Harvard University Press, 1958), p. 135. For Roy's reactions, see Roy, *My Experiences in China*, p. 45.

[37] M. N. Roy, *Our Task in India* (Calcutta: Committee for Action for Independence of India, 1932), p. 22.

[38] Bukharin, *Problems of the Chinese Revolution*, p. 41.

[39] André Malraux, *Man's Fate* (New York: Random House, 1934), p. 152.

[40] Roy, *My Experiences in China*, pp. 49-53. For an account of this meeting between Roy and Wang Ching-wei, see T'ang Leang-li, *The Inner History of the Chinese Revolution* (London: G. Routledge and Sons, Ltd., 1930), p. 280; also Robert C. North, *Moscow and the Chinese Communists*, pp. 107-108.

[41] Letter from Chang Kuo-t'ao (Chang T'e-li) to the Enlarged Conference of the CCP, *Central Newsletter* (Shanghai), No. 13, Nov. 30, 1927, pp. 63-72, translated by C. Martin Wilbur, "The Ashes of Defeat: Accounts of the Nanchang Revolt and Southern Expedition, August 1-October 1, 1927, by Chinese Communists Who Took Part," *China Quarterly*, April-June 1964.

[42] Pavel Aleksandrovich Mif, *Kitaiskaya Revolutsia* (Moscow, 1932), p. 139, as cited in Isaacs, p. 251.

[43] Roy, *My Experiences in China*, p. 49.

[44] North and Eudin, p. 122.

[45] Letter from Louise Geissler to author, Zurich, March 23, 1966.

[46] Edgar Snow, *Red Star Over China* (New York: Random House, 1938), p. 147.

[47] The quotations are from Earl Browder's review of *M. N. Roy's Mission to China*, *Political Science Quarterly*, 79, 2 (1964): 311. Comments on Browder's personal relationship with Roy and Borodin are based on two sources: Harriet Cohen Ringel, "A Look at Earl Browder's Mission to China," *Scope* (New York), Dec. 1965 (based on a

personal interview); and a letter from Browder to author, Princeton, July 31, 1967.

[48] The nationalist character of the demand of the Malayalam-speaking people for a separate linguistic state of Kerala and the rise to power of the Kerala communists as champions of this demand is revealed in E.M.S. Namboodripad, *The National Question in Kerala* (Bombay: People's Publishing House, 1952), pp. 154-56; and A. K. Gopalan, *Kerala-Past and Present* (London: Lawrence and Wishart, 1959), pp. 75-78. See also Selig Harrison, *India: The Most Dangerous Decades* (Princeton: Princeton University Press, 1960), pp. 193-99.

[49] Chalmers A. Johnson, *Peasant Nationalism and Communist Power: The Emergence of Revolutionary China, 1937-1945* (Stanford: Stanford University Press, 1962), p. 13. As Johnson has acknowledged (p. 195), the concept of peasant nationalism was first used by George E. Taylor, *The Struggle for North China* (New York: International Secretariat, Institute of Pacific Relations, 1940), pp. 41-42.

[50] M. N. Roy, *Some Fundamental Principles of Mass Mobilization*, a report of the lectures and discussions in the All-India Political Study Camp, Dehra Dun, May 1940, held under the auspices of the All-Indian League of Radical Congressmen (Dehra Dun: Indian Renaissance Institute, 1940[?]), pp. 35-36.

[51] For the distinction between mass nationalism and other forms of nationalism, see E. H. Carr, *Nationalism and After* (London: Macmillan and Co., 1945).

[52] Johnson, pp. 4-5, 23-26.

[53] Letter from Leon Trotsky to Max Schachtman, Dec. 10, 1930, cited in Leon D. Trotsky, *Problems of the Chinese Revolution*, p. 19.

[54] Conrad Brandt, *Stalin's Failure in China, 1924-1927*, pp. 154-61.

[55] Leon D. Trotsky, "O lozunge sovetov v Kitze," p. 6, a manuscript dated April 16, 1927, cited by Brandt, p. 160.

[56] "Theses on the Situation in China by the Seventh Extraordinary Plenum."

[57] "Resolution on the Chinese Question" (Eighth Plenum).

[58] See below, Chapter 6.

[59] Ellen Roy, "Comments on Overstreet and Windmiller's *Communism in India.*" This unpublished statement, a copy of which is in the possession of the author, is dated Dehra Dun, May 18, 1957. Ellen Roy's opinion in this matter is corroborated by a letter to the author from Louise Geissler, Zurich, March 23, 1966.

[60] North and Eudin, *M. N. Roy's Mission to China*, p. 128.

[61] Roy, *My Experiences in China*, p. 53.

[62] *New York Times*, July 1, 1964, p. 5.

[63] Joseph V. Stalin, "Concerning Current Questions," *Inprecor*, VII, 45 (1927): 999-1006.

[64] Franz Borkenau, *World Communism: A History of the Communist International* (Ann Arbor: University of Michigan Press, 1962), pp. 279-83.

Chapter 5

[1] A. K. Hindi [Tayab Shaikh], *M. N. Roy—The Man Who Looked Ahead*, p. 103.

[2] Letter from Louise Geissler to author, Zurich, March 23, 1966.

[3] Saumyendranath Tagore, *Historical Development of the Communist Movement in India* (Calcutta: Red Front Press, 1944), pp. 10-11. A copy of this rather obscure publication can be found at the library of the University of California at Berkeley.

[4] *Ibid.*, pp. 18, 28. Tagore is also the author of an earlier diatribe against Roy, *Bourgeois-Democratic Revolution and India* (Calcutta: Ganavani Publishing House, 1939).

[5] Details about Saumyendranath Tagore have been gathered from the following sources: interview with Saumyendranath Tagore by the author, Calcutta, Dec. 2, 1963; Muzaffar Ahmed, *The Communist Party of India and Its Formation Abroad*, pp. 155-77; Gene D. Overstreet and Marshall Windmiller, *Communism in India*, pp. 96-117, 141-42; and written "Comments" on Overstreet and Windmiller's book by Ellen Roy, Dehra Dun, May 18, 1957.

[6] Franz Borkenau, *World Communism: A History of the Communist International*, pp. 359-60.

[7] Ellen Roy's "Comments."

[8] Government of India, *Legislative Assembly Debates*, 1944, Vol. III, pp. 1915-16; Vol. IV, pp. 111-14, 220-21; and Vol. V, pp. 793, 850-51, 935.

[9] Ironically, Roy was partially supported during this period by the General Motors Corporation in whose office in Berlin Louise Geissler found employment (letter from Louise Geissler to author, Zurich, March 23, 1966).

[10] Letter from M. N. Roy to Louise Geissler, Moscow, Feb. 5, 1928.

[11] *Ibid.*

[12] Borkenau, pp. 322-23.

[13] Letter from M. N. Roy to Louise Geissler, Moscow, Feb. 10, 1928.

[14] Harold R. Isaacs, *The Tragedy of the Chinese Revolution*, p. 357.

[15] Borkenau, pp. 334-35.

[16] Letters from M. N. Roy to Louise Geissler, Moscow, Feb. 19 and 26, 1928.

[17] *Resolutions Adopted at the Ninth Plenary Session of the ECCI*, pp. 47-51, as cited in Benjamin I. Schwartz, *Chinese Communism and the Rise of Mao* (Cambridge: Harvard University Press, 1951), p. 110.

[18] *Ibid.*, p. 111. This analysis of the Ninth Plenum's discussion on the China question is based on Schwartz, pp. 109-13.

[19] Letter from M. N. Roy to Louise Geissler, Moscow, March 1, 1928.

[20] *Ibid.*, March 15, 1928.

[21] Letter from Louise Geissler to author, Zurich, March 23, 1966.

[22] Letter from M. N. Roy to Louise Geissler, Moscow, March 17, 1928.

[23] This account of Roy's flight from Moscow is based on a letter from Louise Geissler to the author, Zurich, March 23, 1966.

[24] Details of Roy's stay in Germany were provided by Louise Geissler in correspondence with the author.

[25] M. N. Roy, *Revolution und Konterrevolution in China*, trans. Paul Frölich (Berlin: Soziologische Verlagsanstalt [1931(?)]). A revised and enlarged English edition of this work was published in 1946: M. N. Roy, *Revolution and Counterrevolution in China* (Calcutta: Renaissance Publishers, 1946). To the later English edition were added two final chapters written in 1938-39 and an epilogue written in 1945.

[26] Vladimir I. Lenin, "Report on the National and Colonial Questions at the Second Congress of the Communist International," *Selected Works*, x: 240-41.

[27] M. N. Roy, *My Experience in China*, p. 18.

[28] M. N. Roy, "Imperialism and Indian Nationalism," *Inprecor*, VIII, 1 (1928): 1-3.

[29] Government of India, Home Department, *Communism in India*, 1927, pp. 47-48.

[30] R. N. Carew-Hunt, "Willi Muenzenberg," *St. Anthony's Papers Number* IX, pp. 72-87.

[31] Jawaharlal Nehru, Speech delivered at the International Congress Against Imperialism, Brussels, February 10, 1927, in Nehru, *Nehru on War Danger, Independence and Imperialism* (Lahore: Allied Publishers, 1944), p. 22.

[32] Government of India, Home Department, 1927, p. 48.

[33] *Indian Quarterly Register*, I (1927): 207, as quoted in Michael Brecher, *Nehru: A Political Biography* (London: Oxford University Press, 1959), p. 111.

[34] Jawaharlal Nehru, *Soviet Russia* (Bombay: Chetana, 1929), p. 6.

[35] M. N. Roy, "Imperialism and Indian Nationalism."

[36] Jawaharlal Nehru, *Toward Freedom: The Autobiography of Jawaharlal Nehru*, 2nd ed. (Boston: Beacon Press, 1958), pp. 129-30.

[37] D. G. Tendulkar, *Mahatma: Life of Mohandas Karamchand Gandhi* (Bombay: by the author and V. K. Jhaveri, 1951-54), II: 402.

[38] Nehru, *Toward Freedom*, pp. 129-30.

[39] V. P. Menon, *The Transfer of Power in India* (Princeton: Princeton University Press, 1957), p. 35.

[40] M. N. Roy, "On the Constituent Assembly," *Independent India* (New Delhi), February 11, 1940, p. 65.

[41] Speech delivered by Jawaharlal Nehru at the All-Parties Conference at Lucknow on the resolution dealing with dominion status for India, August 29, 1928, in Nehru, *Nehru on War Danger*, pp. 12-17.

[42] Brecher, pp. 130-31.

[43] Clemens Dutt, "The Indian League for Independence," *Labour Monthly* (London), XI, 1 (1929): pp. 22-28.

[44] Sardul Singh Caveeshar, *Within or Without the British Empire?* (Lahore: Independence of India League, Punjab Branch, 193[?]). This is a small, twenty-four page pamphlet.

[45] Jawaharlal Nehru, *Nehru in the Punjab* (Lahore: Allied Indian

Publishers, 1944), p. 10. This is an English version of the Presidential Address delivered in Hindustani at the Punjab Provincial Conference of the Congress party held on April 11, 1928.

[46] Motilal Nehru, Presidential Address. Forty-third session of the Indian National Congress, Calcutta, December 29, 1928 (Allahabad: AICC, 1929).

[47] Charles A. Myers, *Labor Problems in the Industrialization of India* (Cambridge: Harvard University Press, 1958), p. 60.

[48] Philip Spratt, *Blowing Up India*, pp. 36-37.

[49] Government of India, Home Department, 1927, p. 144.

[50] V. B. Karnik, *Indian Trade Unions*, p. 38.

[51] Great Britain, *Royal Commission on Labour In India* (London: His Majesty's Stationery Office, 1931), I: 318. This Commission, under the Chairmanship of John H. Whitley, was appointed in July 1929. Its eleven-volume report, commonly referred to as the Whitley Report, constitutes the single most valuable source on labor conditions in India before 1930.

[52] Labor Office, Government of Bombay, *Labour Gazette* (Bombay), VII, 4 (1927): 330-32.

[53] *All-India Trade Union Bulletin* (Bombay: AITUC), VI, 6-8 (1927-28): 76-83.

[54] *Royal Commission*, pp. 7 and 246: and Morris David Morris, *The Emergence of an Industrial Labor Force in India: A Study of the Bombay Cotton Mills* (Berkeley: University of California Press, 1965), p. 183.

[55] Morris, p. 34.

[56] *The Indian Year Book and Who's Who, 1935-36* (Bombay: The Times of India Press, n.d.), XXII, "Labour in India," 479-80.

[57] *Royal Commission*, p. 318.

[58] *Ibid.*, p. 320.

[59] "Communism in the Labour Movement in Bombay City," Appendix B, *Labour Gazette* (Bombay), IX, 6 (1930): 571-72.

[60] *Ibid.*, p. 103; *The Indian Year Book*, p. 480; and "The Present Strike Movement in India," *Labour Monthly* (London), x, 6 (1928): 369-74.

[61] S. D. Punekar, *Trade Unionism in India* (Bombay: New Books Co., 1948), p. 326.

[62] Meerut, District Court, *Judgment Delivered by R. L. Yorke, Additional Sessions Judge, Meerut, on 16th January, 1933 in the Meerut Conspiracy Case* (Simla: Government of India Press, 1932-33), I: 249-56.

[63] *Royal Commission*, pp. 104-105.

[64] *Labour Gazette* (Bombay), VII, 9 (1928): 752.

[65] *Ibid.*, VIII, 2 (1928): 148.

[66] "The World of Labour," *Labour Monthly* (London), x, 7 (1928): 439-41, and 11 (1928): 698-700; *The Indian Year Book*, p. 480; and Karnik, p. 39.

[67] *Labour Gazette* (Bombay), VIII, 2 (1928): 149.

[68] "The World of Labour," *Labour Monthly* (London), x, 7 (1928): 439-41.

[69] *Labour Gazette* (Bombay), VIII, 2 (1928): 151.

[70] *The Times* (London), May 28, 1928, p. 9.

[71] Meerut, District Court, *Judgment Delivered by R. L. Yorke*, I: 249-56.

[72] *Royal Commission*, p. 104; and Punekar, pp. 93-107.

[73] Karnik, p. 39; "The World of Labour," *Labour Monthly* (London), X, 11 (1928): 699-700; and *Labour Gazette* (Bombay), VIII, 2 (1928): 164-66.

[74] *Royal Commission*, p. 309.

[75] Karnik, p. 40; and Government of India, Home Department, 1935, p. 126.

[76] *Royal Commission*, pp. 104-105. This union was registered on October 5, 1928.

[77] Punekar, p. 326.

[78] Government of India, Home Department, 1935, p. 126.

[79] *All-India Trade Union Bulletin* (Bombay), V, 7-11 (1929): 65-68.

[80] *Labor Unity* (New York: Trade Union Unity League), II, 12 (1929), and III, 2 (1929).

[81] Karnik, p. 38; and Nehru, *Toward Freedom*, p. 141.

[82] *All-India Trade Union Bulletin* (Bombay), V, 7-11 (1929): 70-81.

[83] Government of India, Home Department, 1935, p. 119.

Chapter 6

[1] "Draft Programme of the Communist International," adopted by the Program Committee of the ECCI, May 25, 1928, *Inprecor*, VIII, 30 (1928): 549-59.

[2] *The Communist International Between the Fifth and Sixth World Congresses* (London: Communist Party of Great Britain, 1928), p. 469.

[3] *Ibid.*, pp. 473-76.

[4] Nikolai I. Bukharin, "The International Situation and the Tasks of the Comintern," Report of the ECCI, *Inprecor*, VIII, 41 (1928): 733-34.

[5] Otto V. Kuusinen, "The Revolutionary Movement in the Colonies," *Inprecor*, VIII, 68 (1928): 1230-31.

[6] Gregory Zinoviev, "The Results of the Sixth Session of the Enlarged ECCI," *Inprecor*, VI, 45 (1926): 744.

[7] "Resolution on the Situation in Great Britain," *Inprecor*, VI, 40 (1926): 643.

[8] "Continuation of the Discussion on the First Part of the Agenda," *Inprecor*, VI, 89 (1926): 1560.

[9] G.A.K. Luhani, "Discussion on the Colonial Question," *Inprecor*, VIII, 78 (1928): 1472; and Saumyendranath Tagore, *Historical Development*, pp. 9-11.

[10] Robin Page Arnot, "Continuation of the Discussion on the Questions of the Revolutionary Movement in the Colonies," *Inprecor*, VIII, 76 (1928): 1420-24.

[11] Letter from Louise Geissler to author, Zurich, March 23, 1966.

[12] M. N. Roy, "Trotsky and the Third World Congress of the Communist International, II," *Radical Humanist* (Calcutta), XVIII, 31 (1954): 366-67.

[13] This document was never published by the Comintern, but is quoted at length by M. N. Roy in his book, *Our Differences* (Calcutta: Saraswaty Library, 1938), pp. 32-33.

[14] M. N. Roy, "Left Social Democrats as Defenders of Imperialism," *Inprecor*, VIII, 2 (1928): 44-45; and Roy, "The Indian Constitution," *Inprecor*, VIII, 54 (1928): 954-55.

[15] M. N. Roy, "Imperialism and Indian Nationalism," *Inprecor*, VIII, 1 (1928): 1-3.

[16] Eugene Varga, "Economics and Economic Policy in the Fourth Quarter of 1927," Section 2: "India, the Focus of the British Empire," *Inprecor*, VIII, 15 (1928): 287-94.

[17] Arnot, "Continuation of the Discussion of the Revolutionary Movement in the Colonies."

[18] "Notes of the Month," *Labour Monthly* (London), X, 6 (1928): 323-41.

[19] Arnot, "Continuation of the Discussion of the Revolutionary Movement in the Colonies."

[20] Otto V. Kuusinen, "The Revolutionary Movement in the Colonies."

[21] "Concluding Speech of Comrade Kuusinen on the Colonial Question," *Inprecor*, VIII, 81 (1928): 1519-28.

[22] Kuusinen, "The Revolutionary Movement in the Colonies."

[23] Nikolai I. Bukharin, "Speech in Reply to the Discussion on the International Situation," *Inprecor*, VIII, 70 (1928): 863-72.

[24] Nikolai I. Bukharin, "Report on the Results of the Sixth Comintern Congress to Party Functionaries of the Moscow Organization of the CPSU," *Inprecor*, VIII, 70 (1928): 1267-77.

[25] A. J. Bennet [D. Petrovsky], "Questions on the Revolutionary Movement in the Colonies," *Inprecor*, VIII, 72 (1928): 1320-22.

[26] A. J. Bennet [D. Petrovsky], *Inprecor*, VIII, 76 (1928): 1425.

[27] Bennet [Petrovsky], "Questions on the Revolutionary Movement in the Colonies."

[28] Andrew Rothstein, "Questions on the Revolutionary Movement in the Colonies," *Inprecor*, VIII, 72 (1928): 1323-24.

[29] Clemens Dutt, "Continuation of the Discussion of the Revolutionary Movement in the Colonies," *Inprecor*, VIII, 76 (1928): 1424-25.

[30] Statement by Andrew Rothstein, *Inprecor*, VIII, 78 (1928): 1471-72.

[31] "Concluding Speech of Comrade Kuusinen on the Colonial Question."

[32] Declaration of Andrew Rothstein, *Inprecor*, VIII, 81 (1928): 1592; and "Declaration of the British Delegation on the Theses on the Colonial Question," *Inprecor*, VIII, 91 (1928): 1743-44.

[33] *Inprecor*, VIII, 81 (1928): 1529-30.

[34] Otto V. Kuusinen, "Report of the Colonial Commission," *Inprecor*, VIII, 81 (1928): 1542.

[35] "Theses on the Revolutionary Movement in the Colonies and Semi-Colonies," Part A: "On Communist Strategy and Tactics in China, India and Similar Colonial Countries," *Inprecor*, VIII, 88 (1928): 1665-73.

[36] "The International Situation and the Tasks of the Communist International," Part V: "Colonial Countries and the China Revolution," *Inprecor*, VIII, 83 (1928): 1571-72.

[37] "Theses on the Revolutionary Movement in the Colonies and the Semi-Colonies."

[38] Report of the Credentials Committee, *Inprecor*, VIII, 81 (1928): 1531-32; and Muzaffar Ahmed, *The Communist Party of India and Its Formation Abroad*, p. 94.

[39] Ahmed, *The Communist Party of India and Its Formation Abroad*, pp. 91-92, 109, 167.

[40] *Ibid.*, p. 164.

[41] M. N. Roy, *M. N. Roy's Memoirs*, pp. 489-91.

[42] Ahmed, *The Communist Party of India and Its Formation Abroad*, pp. 93, 167.

[43] Philip Spratt, *Blowing Up India*, p. 41.

[44] Ahmed, *The Communist Party of India and Its Formation Abroad*, pp. 90-91.

[45] Narayan [Saumyendranath Tagore], "Continuation of the Discussion on the Report of Comrade Bukharin on the Draft Program of the Comintern," *Inprecor*, VIII, 66 (1928): 1203.

[46] Narayan [Saumyendranath Tagore], "Continuation of the Discussion on the Questions of the Revolutionary Movement in the Colonies," *Inprecor*, VIII, 76 (1928): 1390-91.

[47] *Ibid.*

[48] "Declaration of Luhani," *Inprecor*, VIII, 78 (1928): 1472.

[49] Sikander Sur [Shaukat Usmani], "Discussion on the Report of Comrade Bukharin," *Inprecor*, VIII, 44 (1928): 775.

[50] Sikander Sur [Shaukat Usmani], "The Development in India," *Inprecor*, VIII, 68 (1928): 1247-48.

[51] Karl Marx, "The British Rule in India," *New York Daily Tribune*, June 25, 1853.

[52] Karl Marx, "The Future Results of British Rule in India," *New York Daily Tribune*, Aug. 8, 1853.

[53] Sikander Sur [Shaukat Usmani], "Concluding Speech," *Inprecor*, VIII, 78 (1928): 1472-74.

[54] Sikander Sur [Shaukat Usmani], "The Development of India."

[55] Sikander Sur [Shaukat Usmani], "Concluding Speech."

[56] Sikander Sur [Shaukat Usmani], "Discussion on the Report of Comrade Bukharin."

[57] "Election of the Presidium," *Inprecor*, VIII, 39 (1928): 706. Shaukat Usmani has recorded his experience at the Sixth Comintern Congress in a pamphlet entitled, *I Met Stalin Twice* (Bombay: K. Kurian, 1953).

[58] Spratt, *Blowing Up India*, p. 42; Ahmed, *The Communist Party*

of India and Its Formation Abroad, pp. 94-95. Spratt mistakenly has reported that all three of Usmani's companions were killed in Moscow.

59 Solomon A. Lozovsky, "Continuation of the Discussion on the Reports of Comrades Kuusinen and Manuilsky," *Inprecor*, IX, 48 (1929): 1037-39.

60 "Open Letter of the Y.C.I. to the All-India Youth Congress and to All Young Workers and Peasants of India," *Inprecor*, X, 1 (1930): 25.

61 P. Sch. [?], "The Conference of the Workers' and Peasants' Party of India," *Inprecor*, IX, 16 (1929): 319-20; and *Inprecor*, 17 (1929): 347-48.

62 Vyacheslav Molotov, "Report on the Activities of the Delegation of the CPSU in the ECCI," *Inprecor*, IX, 33 (1929): 589-95.

63 Dmitri Manuilsky, *Inprecor*, IX, 48 (1929): 1140.

64 Henry Pelling, "Early History of the Communist Party of Great Britain."

65 Ruth Fischer, *Stalin and German Communism: A Study on the Origins of the State Party* (Cambridge: Harvard University Press, 1948), p. 603.

66 Interviews with Philip Spratt, Bangalore, Nov. 20-22, 1962.

67 Franz Borkenau, *World Communism: A History of the International*, pp. 221-73; and Fischer, pp. 215-31, 287, 313-73.

68 Comments by Philip Spratt on Saumyendranath Tagore's *Historical Development of the Communist Movement in India* (Calcutta: Red Front Press, 1944). These handwritten notes are in the possession of Robert C. North, Stanford University.

69 Government of India, Home Department, *Communism in India*, 1935, p. 162.

70 Otto V. Kuusinen, "The International Situation and the Tasks of the Communist International."

71 S. A. Lozovsky, "Continuation of the Discussion on the Reports of Comrades Kuusinen and Manuilsky."

72 "Declaration of G.A.K. Luhani," *Inprecor*, IX, 48 (1929): 1039.

73 A. K. Hindi [Tayab Shaikh], *M. N. Roy—The Man Who Looked Ahead*, p. 176.

74 Gene D. Overstreet and Marshall Windmiller, *Communism in India*, p. 142. These articles, in the original German, are in the library of the University of California at Berkeley.

75 "Expulsion of Roy from the Comintern," *Inprecor*, IX, 69 (1929): 1470.

76 *Bolshaia Sovietskaia Entsiklopediia*, as cited in R. Sorich, "Fragments in the Biography of M. N. Roy" (research paper at the Hoover Library, Stanford, California, 1953), p. 7.

77 *New York Times*, Aug. 29, 1967, p. 16.

78 See above, Chapter 4, "The China Episode."

79 M. N. Roy, *Our Differences*, p. iv.

80 Irving Howe and Lewis Coser, *The American Communist Party: A Critical History*, 2nd ed. rev. (New York: Frederick A. Praeger, 1962), p. 164; and Robert C. Tucker and Stephen F. Cohen, eds., *The Great Purge Trials* (New York: Grosset and Dunlap Publishers, 1965), pp. 697 and 701.

[81] Tucker and Cohen, p. 712.

[82] Roy, *M. N. Roy's Memoirs*, p. 498.

[83] Kermit E. McKenzie, *Comintern and World Revolution, 1928-1943: The Shaping of Doctrine*, p. 30.

[84] Joseph V. Stalin, "The Danger of the Right Deviation," Speech delivered before the Central Committee of the CPSU, April 1929, *Problems of Leninism*, p. 244ff.

[85] Dmitri Manuilsky, "Questions on the Plenary Sessions of the ECCI," *Inprecor*, IX, 29 (1929): 629-32.

[86] For an account of the Right Opposition in America, see Howe and Coser, pp. 98 and 163-73; and Theodore Draper, *American Communism and Soviet Russia: The Formative Period* (New York: The Viking Press, 1960), pp. 386-430.

[87] "Report of Comrade Bukharin," *Inprecor*, VIII, 70 (1928): 1267-77.

[88] "Resolution of the Joint Session of the Politburo of the Central Committee and the Presidium of the Central Control Commission," *On Intra-Party Affairs*, Feb. 9, 1929 (CPSU Resolutions, II, 558-62), translated in Robert V. Daniels, ed., *A Documentary History of Communism*, I (New York: Vintage Books, 1962): 319.

[89] "Resolution of the Tenth Plenum of the ECCI on Comrade Bukharin," *Inprecor*, IX, 45 (1929): 964-65.

[90] Tucker and Cohen, p. xviii.

[91] *Ibid.*, pp. xxxiv-xxxviii, 717.

[92] *Revolutionary Age* (New York), I, 3 (1929): 16-17; and 15 (1930): 3, 7. It was the official organ of the Communist party of the USA (Majority Group) and was described by its editors as "an organ of Marxism-Leninism in the U.S. for communist unity in the revolutionary class struggle." It began publication November 1, 1929. In addition to Jay Lovestone, Benjamin Gitlow, the editor, and Bertram D. Wolfe, the associate editor, its editorial board consisted of J. O. Bixby, Ellen Dawson, Will Herberg, Bert Miller, William Miller, R. Pires, Jack Rubinstein, Frank Vrataric, Ed Welsh, W. J. White, Herbert Zam, and Charles S. Zimmerman.

[93] Howe and Coser, pp. 152-59 and 173.

[94] K. K. Sinha, "Dynamics of Roy's Ideals," *Radical Humanist* (Calcutta), XVIII, 8 (1954): 88.

[95] Letter from M. N. Roy to European Associates, June 10, 1933 in Roy, *Fragments of a Prisoner's Diary*, Vol. III: *Letters From Jail* (Dehra Dun: Indian Renaissance Association, 1943), p. 58.

[96] M. N. Roy, "The Conference of the German Communist Opposition," *Revolutionary Age* (New York), I, 3 (1929): 16-17.

[97] Letter from M. N. Roy to European Associates, July 14, 1933, Roy, *Letters From Jail*, p. 60.

[98] Tucker and Cohen, pp. xxi, 688-89, 697.

[99] Roy, *Our Differences*, pp. 42-43.

[100] *Ibid.*

[101] Letter from Louise Geissler to author, Zurich, March 8, 1966.

[102] Letter from Chitnis to Roy, Bombay, Nov. 11, 1939, League of Radical Congressmen, General Files No. 8, Roy Archives.

[103] M. N. Roy, *Fragments of a Prisoner's Diary,* Vol. III: *Letters From Jail,* p. 168.

[104] Letter from Louise Geissler to author, Zurich, March 8, 1966.

[105] M. N. Roy, "The Death of Stalin," *Radical Humanist* (Calcutta), XVII (1953): 121, 132.

[106] Benjamin Gitlow, *I Confess: The Truth About American Communism* (New York: E. P. Dutton and Co., 1940), p. 560.

[107] Draper, p. 430.

[108] Borkenau, p. 346.

[109] Letter from M. N. Roy to European Associates, Dehra Dun, April 21, 1934; Roy, *Letters From Jail,* p. 87.

[110] Letter from M. N. Roy to European Associates, Dehra Dun, Oct. 29, 1934, File No. 111/2, Roy Archives.

[111] Interview with Joseph Starobin, New York, May 16, 1967.

[112] Draper. Three of the principal members of the Communist party, USA (Majority Group), were Jay Lovestone, Bertram D. Wolfe, and Benjamin Gitlow. In 1943 Lovestone became international affairs director of the Ladies Garment Workers Union and, in 1963, international affairs director of the AFL-CIO. In the latter position he has gained wide attention and become the object of some controversy for his vigorous prosecution of anti-communist activities. Bertram D. Wolfe is the author of the distinguished study of Lenin, Trotsky, and Stalin, *Three Who Made A Revolution.* Gitlow, at the time of his expulsion from the Comintern, had been the general secretary of his party. In both 1924 and 1928 he had been the communist candidate for vice-president and had promised, if elected, to convert the White House into "apartments for the workers and poor peasants." He was the defendant in the historic Supreme Court case of the 1920's, *Gitlow vs. New York,* in which the Court for the first time included freedom of expression under the protection of the due process clause of the fourteenth amendment. He died in 1965 (*New York Times,* July 20, 1965, p. 33).

Chapter 7

[1] M. V. Ramana Rao, *A Short History of the Indian National Congress* (Delhi: S. Chand & Co., 1959), p. 127.

[2] Vapal P. Menon, *The Transfer of Power in India,* p. 38.

[3] AICC, *Indian National Congress: Report of the 44th Annual Session Held at Lajpat Rai Nagar, Lahore on December 25-31, 1929* (Lahore: Dr. Gopi Chand Bhargava, 1930), Appendix I, p. xvi.

[4] Winston Leonard Spencer Churchill, "Dominion Status," *Daily Mail* (London), Nov. 1929, in Churchill, *India: Speeches and an Introduction* (London: Thorton Butterworth, 1931), pp. 32-33.

[5] Menon, pp. 40-41.

[6] *Report of the 44th Annual Session,* p. 130.

[7] *Ibid.,* p. 39.

[8] *Young India* (Bombay), Jan. 9, 1930.

[9] *Report of the 44th Annual Session,* pp. 87-88 and 95.

[10] AICC, *Congress Bulletin,* No. 3, Feb. 7, 1930, p. 19.

[11] *Ibid.*, No. 5, March 7, 1930, pp. 41-48.

[12] Sarvepalli Gopal, *The Viceroyalty of Lord Irwin 1926-1931* (London: Oxford University Press, 1957), pp. 56-57.

[13] AICC, *Congress Bulletin*, No. 6, March 27, 1930, p. 56; and No. 7, April 25, 1930, pp. 63-65.

[14] Gopal, pp. 58-62, 69-71.

[15] T. N. Lahiri, *Our Patriots of Wax, Iron and Clay: Moderate Revolutionary and Intermediate Strains in the Indian Struggle for Freedom* (Calcutta: C. K. Bhattacharjee, 1954[?]), pp. 117-21; and Kalpana Dutt, *Chittagong Armoury Raiders: Reminiscences* (Bombay: People's Publishing House, 1945), pp. 5-13. The author participated in the raid as a young girl of eighteen.

[16] Daniel A. Thorner, "India and Pakistan," *Most of the World*, ed. Ralph Linton (New York: Columbia University Press, 1949), pp. 548-643.

[17] Gopal, pp. 67-82.

[18] T. Walter Wallbank, *A Short History of India and Pakistan*, p. 168.

[19] Gopal, pp. 79-87.

[20] "The Political Situation in India: Thesis of the Workers' and Peasants' Party of India," *Labour Monthly* (London), XI, 3 (1929): 151-61.

[21] Government of India, Home Department, *Communism in India*, 1935, pp. 133-35.

[22] S. A. Lozovsky, "Continuation of the Discussion on the Reports of Comrades Kuusinen and Manuilsky," *Inprecor*, IX, 48 (1929): 1037-39.

[23] Otto V. Kuusinen, "The International Situation and the Tasks of the Communist International," *ibid.*, IX, 40 (1929): 837-51.

[24] Vyacheslav Molotov, "Report of the Activities of the Delegates of the CPSU in the ECCI," Speech delivered at the Sixteenth Party Congress of the Soviet Party, *ibid.*, XI, 33 (1929): 589-95.

[25] Clemens Dutt, "The Class Struggle in India," *Labour Monthly* (London), XI, 7 (1929): 405-16.

[26] Letter from Virendranath Chattopadhyaya to Jawaharlal Nehru, Dec. 4, 1929, quoted in Michael Brecher, *Nehru: A Political Biography*, p. 114.

[27] Brecher, p. 115.

[28] Clemens Dutt, "The Role and Leadership of the Indian Working Class," *Labour Monthly* (London), XI, 12 (1929): 742-51.

[29] Molotov, pp. 589-95.

[30] "Draft Platform of Action of the C.P. of India," *ibid.*, X, 58 (1930): 1218-22.

[31] Government of India, Home Department, 1935, pp. 169-70.

[32] *Ibid.*, pp. 130-33; *The Times* (London), August 18, 1929, p. 9; and Sept. 11, 1929, p. 11.

[33] *The Times* (London), Sept. 17, 1928, p. 12.

[34] *Ibid.*, Sept. 11, 1928, p. 11; and Feb. 6, 1929, p. 3.

[35] *Ibid.*, Sept. 25, 1928, p. 14.

[36] *Ibid.*, Feb. 7, 1929, p. 13.

[37] Charles A. Myers, *Labor Problems in the Industrialization of India*, p. 61.

[38] *The Times* (London), April 9, 1929, p. 16.

[39] *Ibid.*, April 13, 1929, p. 12.

[40] Philip Spratt, *Blowing Up India*, p. 49.

[41] *The Times* (London), March 21, 1929, p. 16; and March 22, 1929, p. 8.

[42] *Ibid.*, March 21, 1929, p. 16; June 13, 1929, p. 16; and June 15, 1929, p. 13; Meerut District Court, II: 448.

[43] *The Times* (London), Jan. 13, 1930, p. 12.

[44] *Ibid.*, Nov. 28, 1929, p. 13.

[45] Government of India, Home Department, 1935, p. 141.

[46] "The Speech of the Prosecutor in the Meerut Case," *Labour Monthly* (London), I (1930): 24-29.

[47] Saumyendranath Tagore, *Historical Development of the Communist Movement in India*, pp. 20-21.

[48] *The Times* (London), Jan. 17, 1933, p. 9.

[49] *Ibid.*, August 3, 1933, p. 9.

[50] Government of India, Home Department, 1935, p. 140.

[51] *Labour Gazette* (Bombay), IX, 1 (1929): 52-54.

[52] *The Indian Year Book & Who's Who, 1935-36*, XXII: 481.

[53] *Labour Gazette* (Bombay), IX, 1 (1929): 57-59.

[54] "Communism in the Labor Movement in Bombay City," pp. 571-72.

[55] V. B. Karnik, *Indian Trade Unions*, p. 46.

[56] Great Britain, *Royal Commission on Labour in India*, I: 339.

[57] S. D. Punekar, *Trade Unionism in India*, p. 95.

[58] *Labour Gazette* (Bombay), IX, 4 (1929): 380-82.

[59] Karnik, pp. 49-50.

[60] *The Times* (London), Dec. 2, 1929, p. 11.

[61] Punekar, p. 326.

[62] *Labour Monthly* (London), IX, 4 (1929): 381; and Meerut, District Court, I: 227.

[63] J. S. Mathur, *Indian Working Class Movement* (Allahabad: J. S. Mathur, 1964), p. 27.

Chapter 8

[1] Minutes of a talk by Ruth Fischer at a seminar of the Russian Research Center (mimeo.), Harvard University, July 11, 1952, p. 6.

[2] *Independent India* (Delhi), April 1, 1942, p. 2.

[3] Murray T. Titus, *Islam in India and Pakistan*, 2nd ed. rev. (Calcutta: YMCA Publishing House, 1959), pp. 106-10. The Khojahs are located principally in the Punjab, Sind, Gujarat, and in the area around Bombay City and Poona. The sect's most prominent member was the late Mohammed Ali Jinnah, the chief architect of Pakistan.

[4] Interview with K. K. Sinha, Dehra Dun, May 19, 1962.

[5] Letter from M. N. Roy to Louise Geissler, Bombay, Dec. 17, 1930.

[6] Report on Tayab Shaikh by a subcommittee comprised of S. S. Pirachi, V. P. Jain, A. K. Mukherji, Ram Singh, and M. N. Roy, dated August 7, 1942, Radical Democratic Party Central File No. 4, Roy Archives.

[7] Letter from M. N. Roy to V. G. Kulkarni, Dehra Dun, May 28, 1942, Radical Democratic Party Files No. 5, Roy Archives.

[8] Resolution of the Central Executive Committee of the Radical Democratic Party, August 7, 1942, Radical Democratic Party Files No. 5, Roy Archives. Shaikh lives today in London but has evaded all efforts on the part of the author to contact him. In the 1950's Shaikh was active in the co-operative and trade-union fields in England and was a member of the London Co-operative party and the Union of Democratic Control (see Tayab Shaikh, *More Powerful Than the Hydrogen Bomb* [London: Union of Democratic Control, 1953]).

[9] Letter from Louise Geissler to author, Zurich, March 23, 1966.

[10] Interview with Samaren Roy, Calcutta, Dec. 13, 1962. Dr. Bhaduri is now deceased.

[11] A. K. Hindi [Tayab Shaikh], pp. 223-25. See also *Independent India* (Delhi), April 1, 1942, p. 2.

[12] The manifesto appeared in *Revolutionary Age* (New York), I, 15 (1930): 3, 7.

[13] *Ibid.*, I, 4 (1930): 1.

[14] *Ibid.*, I, 16 (1930): 1.

[15] M. N. Roy, "The Indian National Congress," *Inprecor*, VIII, 91 (1928): 1732-33.

[16] M. N. Roy, "The Ways of the Indian Revolution," *Inprecor*, IX, 4 (1929): 64-65.

[17] M. N. Roy, "The Conference of the Workers' and Peasants' Party of India," *Inprecor*, IX, 6 (1929): 93-94. See also the following articles in *Inprecor* by Roy: "The Bourgeoise and the National Revolution in India," IX, 9 (1929): 149-52; and "Indian Communists in the Election Struggle," IX, 12 (1929): 203-4.

[18] M. N. Roy, *Our Differences*, p. 38.

[19] M. N. Roy's manifesto to the CPI, July 1930, quoted in A. K. Hindi [Tayab Shaikh], *M. N. Roy—The Man Who Looked Ahead*, p. 233; and M. N. Roy, *My Defense* (Pondicherry: Committee for Indian Independence, 1932), pp. 113-14.

[20] Interview with K. K. Sinha, Dehra Dun, May 19, 1962.

[21] Letter from M. N. Roy to Ellen Gottschalk, Agra, March 25, 1931.

[22] Roy's itinerary was reconstructed through his correspondence with Ellen Gottschalk and Louise Geissler during this period.

[23] Interview with V. B. Karnik, Maniben Kara, and J.B.H. Wadia, Bombay, Oct. 20, 1961. Roy wrote to Ellen Gottschalk (Lucknow, March 16, 1931) that she would be amused to see his uniform: "I go about as a 300 per cent Gandhiist dressed all in homespun."

[24] Interview with Dharitri Ganguly, Calcutta, Dec. 8, 1962.

[25] Government of India, Home Department, *Communism in India*, 1935, p. 163.

[26] This portion of Roy's manifesto is quoted in A. K. Hindi [Tayab Shaikh], *M. N. Roy—The Man Who Looked Ahead*, p. 233.

[27] *Ibid.*, pp. 198-219. The article is reproduced on the pages cited.

[28] M. N. Roy, *Some Fundamental Principles of Mass Mobilization* (Dehra Dun: Indian Renaissance Institute, 1940), p. 36. This is a report of the lectures and discussions of a political study camp held in Dehra Dun in May 1940 under the auspices of Roy's League of Radical Congressmen (LRC).

[29] *Ibid.*, pp. 4 and 35.

[30] Letter from M. N. Roy to Political Associates, Dehra Dun, Oct. 29, 1934, File No. 111/1, Roy Archives.

[31] Crane Brinton, *The Anatomy of Revolution*, 2nd ed. rev. (New York: Prentice-Hall, 1952), p. 189.

[32] Letter from Roy to Political Associates, *loc. cit.*

[33] *Ibid.*

[34] Letter from M. N. Roy to V. B. Karnik, Dehra Dun, May 6, 1940, LRC Central Party Files No. 10, Roy Archives.

[35] M. N. Roy, *Our Task in India*, pp. 95-96.

[36] Ruth Fischer, *Stalin and German Communism: A Study in the Origins of the State Party*, pp. 138-40.

[37] Brinton, pp. 150, 177-78.

[38] M. N. Roy's Report to Political Associates in Bombay, Dehra Dun, May 25, 1938, LRC Central Party Files No. 1, Roy Archives.

[39] *Independent India* (Bombay), April 3, 1938, p. 4.

[40] Speech by M. N. Roy at Serempore, Bengal, *ibid.*, Feb. 2, 1938, p. 8.

[41] *Independent India* (Bombay), May 9, 1937, p. 8.

[42] M. N. Roy, *Our Task in India*, p. 93.

[43] Letter from August Thalheimer to M. N. Roy, Paris, May 24, 1934.

[44] Letter from M. N. Roy to August Thalheimer, Dehra Dun, Nov. 4, 1934.

[45] "Repairing the Ruins in India" (an anonymous letter from India), *Revolutionary Age* (New York), Nov. 22, 1930, p. 10.

[46] Letter from M. N. Roy to Louise Geissler, Merano, Italy, Nov. 16, 1930.

[47] Letter from M. N. Roy to Ellen Gottschalk, Bombay, Jan. 10, 1931.

[48] Interview with V. B. Karnik, Maniben Kara and J.B.H. Wadia, Bombay, Oct. 20, 1961.

[49] Interview with Maniben Kara, Bombay, Nov. 16, 1961; and Great Britain, *Royal Commission on Labour in India*, I: 551-53.

[50] *Tribune* (Lahore), July 2, 1932, p. 1.

[51] Interview with Maniben Kara, Bombay, Nov. 16, 1961.

[52] Meerut, District Court, I: 243-44.

[53] Philip Spratt, *Blowing Up India*, p. 46.

[54] Interview with Maniben Kara, Bombay, Oct. 31, 1961.

[55] M. N. Roy, "Some Reminiscences," *Independent India* (Bombay), IX, 13 (1936): 142-44.

[56] Interview with Dharitri Ganguly and Janardin Bhattacharya, Calcutta, Dec. 8, 1962.

[57] Roy, *Some Fundamental Principles*, p. 15.

[58] Letter from Political Associates to M. N. Roy, Bombay, Dec. 12, 1934, File No. 111/1, Roy Archives.

[59] M. N. Roy, "Plan of Action and Organization" (1934[?]), File No. 111/1, Roy Archives. This is a hand-written statement calling for "the formation of a Revolutionary Party of the Indian Working Class."

[60] Interview with C. T. Daru and Dashrathlal Thakar, Ahmedabad, Nov. 13, 1962 and Dharitri Ganguly and Janardin Bhattacharya, Calcutta, Dec. 8, 1962.

[61] Interview with Maniben Kara, V. B. Karnik, and J.B.H. Wadia, Bombay, Oct. 20, 1961.

[62] Roy, "Some Reminiscences."

[63] Government of India, Home Department, 1935, p. 164; and letter from Tayab Shaikh to Bombay Political Associates, Calcutta, June 8, 1932, File No. 111/1, Roy Archives.

[64] References to many of these early papers can be found in V. Basak, *Some Urgent Problems in the Labour Movement in India* (London: Modern Books, Ltd., 1932[?]).

[65] Letter from M. N. Roy to Louise Geissler, Bombay, Jan. 9, 1931.

[66] Letter from M. N. Roy to Louise Geissler, Bombay, Jan. 29, 1931.

[67] Government of India, Home Department, 1935, pp. 158-62.

[68] *Labour Gazette* (Bombay), x, 5 (1931): 436.

[69] Government of India, Home Department, 1935, p. 164.

[70] Letter from M. N. Roy to Louise Geissler, Bombay, Dec. 31, 1930, Bombay, Jan. 23, 1931; Agra, March 25, 1931; and Karachi, March 30, 1931.

[71] Government of India, Home Department, 1935, pp. 176-77.

[72] A. K. Hindi [Tayab Shaikh], *M. N. Roy—The Man Who Looked Ahead*, p. 226.

[73] Letter from M. N. Roy to Ellen Gottschalk, Bombay, Jan. 1, 1931.

[74] M. N. Roy, "Letter to the Communist International" (1935), quoted in Roy, *Our Differences*, pp. 118-19.

[75] V. B. Karnik, *Indian Trade Unions*, pp. 51-53.

[76] *Ibid.*, pp. 58-59.

[77] K. Milani, "The Tactics of the Counter-Revolutionary Indian Bourgeoisie," *Inprecor*, xi, 50 (1931): 912-13; "The Immediate Tasks of the Rival Trade Union Movement in India" (Resolution adopted by the Eighth Session of the Red International Labor Union Central Council), *Inprecor*, xii, 10 (1932): 194-200; and Government of India Home Department, 1935, p. 114.

[78] *Labour Gazette* (Bombay), x, 7 (1931): 702.

[79] "M. N. Roy Found in Bombay," *Statesman* (Calcutta), July 21, 1931, p. 1.

[80] Letter from M. N. Roy to Louise Geissler, Bombay, Jan. 15, 1931.

[81] Letter from M. N. Roy to Louise Geissler, Bombay, Dec. 31, 1930.

[82] *Labour Gazette* (Bombay), ix, 6 (1930): 560-61; and ix, 9 (1930): 875.

[83] V. Basak, *Some Urgent Problems*, pp. 13, 16, 42; "The Indian Labour Movement," *Inprecor*, xiii, 22 (1933): 490-94; and Karnik, pp. 51-52.

[84] Minocheher R. Masani, *The Communist Party of India*, pp. 51-52.

[85] Karnik, pp. 59-60.

[86] "The New Party of Bose and What Should Be Our Attitude Toward It," *Inprecor*, XIII, 52 (1933): 1179-89; and V. Basak, "The Present Situation in India," *Inprecor*, XIII, 42 (1933): 927-28.

[87] Basak, *Some Urgent Problems*, pp. 17, 29. For the text of this appeal see *Independent India* (Bombay), I, 8 (1937): 11, 14.

[88] *Tribune* (Lahore), July 8, 1931, p. 4; and Ahmad Mukhtar, *Trade Unionism and Labor Disputes in India*, p. 163.

[89] *Tribune* (Lahore), July 8, 1931, p. 4.

[90] *Pioneer* (Allahabad), July 9, 1931, p. 12.

[91] *Tribune* (Lahore), July 8, 1931, pp. 2 and 4.

[92] *Labour Gazette* (Bombay), x, 11 (1931): 1096-98.

[93] *Ibid.*

[94] S. D. Punekar, *Trade Unionism in India*, p. 335.

[95] Letter from M. N. Roy to Ellen Gottschalk, Bombay, July 10, 1931, p. 4.

[96] *Pioneer* (Allahabad), July 10, 1931, p. 12.

[97] *Labour Gazette* (Bombay), x, 11 (1931): 1096-98.

[98] *Tribune* (Lahore), July 10, 1931, p. 4.

[99] Basak, *Some Urgent Problems*, p. 31; and The Young Workers' League, Madras, "Mr. Roy's Services to Counterrevolution," *Inprecor*, XI, 55 (1931): 296.

[100] Dr. Pattabhi B. Sitaramayya, *The History of the Indian National Congress*, I (Allahabad: Congress Working Committee, 1935), 431-33.

[101] Jagdish S. Sharma, *Indian National Congress: A Descriptive Bibliography of India's Struggle for Freedom*, p. 537. For the text of the settlement see Sitaramayya, pp. 437-42.

[102] Sarvepalli Gopal, *The Viceroyalty of Lord Irwin 1926-1931*, pp. 107-14.

[103] Michael Brecher, *Nehru: A Political Biography*, pp. 172-73.

[104] Jawaharlal Nehru, *Toward Freedom*, pp. 192-94.

[105] Jawaharlal Nehru, *Toward Freedom*, p. 134; and Brecher, pp. 174-75.

[106] *Tribune* (Lahore), March 26, 1931, p. 1; and *The Times* (London), March 26, 1931, p. 14.

[107] Nehru, *Toward Freedom*, pp. 192-94.

[108] *Tribune* (Lahore), March 24, 1931, p. 9.

[109] *Ibid.*, March 28, 1931, p. 12.

[110] *Ibid.*, March 27, 1931, p. 1; and *The Times* (London), March 26, 1931, p. 14.

[111] *The Times* (London), March 27, 1931, p. 14.

[112] *Tribune* (Lahore), March 24, 1931, p. 9.

[113] Interview with D. B. Karnik, New Delhi, Nov. 23, 1961. D. B. Karnik, a brother of V. B. Karnik, assisted Roy in his activities at Karachi.

[114] Letter from M. N. Roy to Louise Geissler, Karachi, March 30, 1931.

[115] Letter from M. N. Roy to Louise Geissler, Lucknow, March 16, 1931.

[116] Letter from M. N. Roy to Ellen Gottschalk, Karachi, March 30, 1931.

[117] *Ibid.*

[118] *Tribune* (Lahore), March 30, 1931, p. 6.

[119] Letter from M. N. Roy to Ellen Gottschalk, Karachi, March 30, 1931.

[120] *The Times* (London), March 30, 1931, p. 12.

[121] *Tribune* (Lahore), April 1, 1931, pp. 1-2.

[122] *Ibid.*

[123] Letter from M. N. Roy to Ellen Gottschalk, Karachi, March 30, 1931.

[124] *The Times* (London), April 1, 1931, p. 14.

[125] Nehru, *Toward Freedom*, p. 196.

[126] *The Times* (London), March 26, 1931, p. 14.

[127] *Ibid.*, March 28, 1931, p. 12; and *Tribune* (Lahore), March 29, 1931, p. 9.

[128] *Tribune* (Lahore), March 30, 1931, p. 6.

[129] For the text of the resolution as adopted at Karachi see *Indian National Congress, 1930-34: Resolutions of the AICC and Working Committee Between January 1930 and September 1934* (Allahabad: AICC, n.d.), pp. 66-68.

[130] *Tribune* (Lahore), April 2, 1931, p. 3.

[131] *Congress Bulletin*, No. 1, April 10, 1931, pp. 7-9; and *Tribune* (Lahore), April 2, 1931, p. 9.

[132] *Ibid.*

[133] Government of India, Home Department, 1935, p. 165.

[134] Interview with V. B. Karnik, Maniben Kara, and J.B.H. Wadia, Bombay, October 20, 1961.

[135] Jawaharlal Nehru, *Toward India*, p. 197.

[136] D. G. Tendulkar, *Mahatma: Life of Mohandas Karamchand Gandhi*, Vol. III, p. 111; and *Tribune* (Lahore), April 2, 1931, p. 9.

[137] M. N. Roy, "The Karachi Resolution," reprinted in *Independent India* (Bombay), Oct. 3, 1937, pp. 7, 10.

[138] M. N. Roy, "Whither Congress?" A manifesto dated April 15, 1934, File No. 111/2, Roy Archives.

[139] "Conservative Differences in India," Speech delivered by Sir Winston Churchill at Winchester House, Feb. 23, 1931, in Winston Churchill, *India: Speeches and an Introduction*, pp. 87-97.

[140] Great Britain, *Parliamentary Papers*, XVIII (Accounts and Papers, v), Cmnd. 4014, 1931-32, "East India (Emergency Measures): Measures Taken to Counteract the Civil Disobedience Movement and to Deal With the Terrorist Movement in Bengal," pp. 5-6.

[141] *Ibid.*, pp. 3-6.

[142] *Ibid.*, pp. 7-10, 18-19.

[143] Letter from M. N. Roy to Ellen Gottschalk, Agra, March 25, 1931.

[144] Letter from M. N. Roy to Ellen Gottschalk, Lucknow, April 15, and May 4, 1931.

[145] Government of India, Home Department, 1935, pp. 165-66.

[146] Address by Sir Malcolm Hailey to the Legislative Council, July 20, 1931, quoted in "East India (Emergency Measures)," p. 10.

[147] Roy, *Our Task in India*, pp. 58-72.

[148] "East India (Emergency Measures)," pp. 12-16.

[149] Government of India, Home Department, 1935, pp. 165-66.

[150] Sharma, p. 545.

[151] Government of India, Home Department, 1935, p. 167.

[152] *Tribune* (Lahore), July 23, 1931, p. 1; and *The Times* (London), July 22, 1931, p. 11.

[153] Letter from M. N. Roy to Louise Geissler, Bombay, Dec. 25, 1930.

[154] *Ibid.*, Agra, March 25, 1931.

[155] *Ibid.*, Karachi, March 30, 1931. The same information is contained in a letter Roy wrote to Ellen Gottschalk on the same day.

[156] *Statesman* (Calcutta), July 23, 1931, p. 1.

[157] M. N. Roy to Ellen Gottschalk, Bombay, July 3, 1931.

[158] *Ibid.*

[159] Letter from Louise Geissler to author, Zurich, March 23, 1966.

[160] *Ibid.*; and *Tribune* (Lahore), Aug. 2, 1931, p. 1.

[161] Letter from M. N. Roy to Louise Geissler, Allahabad Prison, April 23, 1933.

[162] Government of India, Home Department, 1935, p. 168.

[163] Sachin K. Roy, "How M. N. Roy Helped Indian Revolution From Abroad," *Radical Humanist* (Calcutta), Jan. 25, 1963, pp. 49-50.

[164] Letter from M. N. Roy to Louise Geissler, Kanpur Prison, Nov. 15, 1931; and Roy, *Letters From Jail*, pp. 4, 9.

[165] Letter from M. N. Roy to Louise Geissler, Central Jail, Bareilly, Jan. 18, 1932.

[166] Letter from M. N. Roy to Louise Geissler, Central Jail, Bareilly, March 20, 1932.

[167] Government of India, Home Department, 1935, p. 169.

[168] Letter from M. N. Roy to Louise Geissler, Allahabad Prison, April 23, 1933.

[169] Sachin K. Roy, *loc. cit.*

[170] M. N. Roy, *Letters From Jail*, pp. 53-54, 61-64, 91, 100, 119-20, 228.

[171] A copy of this document is in File No. 111/1, Roy Archives.

[172] Interview with V. B. Karnik, Maniben Kara, and J.B.H. Wadia, Bombay, Oct. 20, 1961.

[173] Letters from M. N. Roy to Louise Geissler, Kanpur Prison, Sept. 1, 1931; and Central Jail, Bareilly, March 20, 1932.

[174] Letter from M. N. Roy to Robert C. North, Dehra Dun, March 26, 1952.

[175] Letter from M. N. Roy to Louise Geissler, Allahabad Prison, April 23, 1933.

[176] Jawaharlal Nehru, *Manabendranath Roy* (Poona: Young Socialist League Pamphlet No. 4, n.d.).

[177] Government of India, Home Department, 1935, p. 168.

[178] *Tribune* (Lahore), May 13, 1931, p. 2; and letter from Tayab

Shaikh to Bombay Associates, Nagpur, June 20, 1932, File No. 111/1, Roy Archives.

[179] Letter from Tayab Shaikh to Bombay Associates, Nagpur, June 20, 1932.

[180] Karnik, p. 60; and M. N. Roy, "Open Letter to the Communist International," 1935, File No. 111/1, Roy Archives.

[181] Karnik, p. 60; and Roy, "Open Letter to the Communist International."

[182] Letter from Tayab Shaikh to Bombay Associates, Nagpur, June 20, 1932.

[183] Basak, *Some Urgent Problems*, p. 27.

[184] *Tribune* (Lahore), May 2, 1932, p. 2.

[185] *Ibid.*, May 12, 1932, p. 16.

[186] *Ibid.*, July 18, 1932, p. 16; and July 21, 1932, p. 3.

[187] Karnik, pp. 60 and 214.

[188] *Tribune* (Lahore), July 18, 1932, p. 16.

[189] Interview with Jatindra Nath Mitra, Calcutta, Dec. 14, 1962.

[190] Sharma, p. 96.

[191] *Labour Gazette* (Bombay), XII, 2 (1932): 114.

[192] Interview with Rajani Mukherji, Calcutta, Dec. 13, 1961.

[193] Ahmad Mukhtar, *Trade Unionism and Labour Disputes in India*, p. 165.

[194] *Tribune* (Lahore), April 23, 1933, p. 1; Karnik, p. 61; and *Labour Gazette* (Bombay), XII, 12 (1933): 920.

[195] Government of India, Home Department, 1935, pp. 211-12.

[196] K. B. Panikkar, *An Outline History of the AITUC* (New Delhi: All-India Trade-Union Congress, 1959). This is a nineteen-page pamphlet.

[197] *Tribune* (Lahore), Aug. 5, 1935, p. 16.

[198] *Ibid.*, May 19, 1936, p. 1.

[199] *Ibid.*, pp. 1, 3; and Punekar, p. 333.

[200] Karnik, pp. 61-62.

[201] *Ibid.*, p. 69.

[202] *Tribune* (Lahore), May 17, 1936, p. 4; and May 19, 1936, p. 1.

[203] S. A. Dange, *On the Indian Trade Union Movement* (Bombay: Communist Party of India, 1952), p. 33.

[204] Government of India, Home Department, 1935, pp. 182-83.

[205] "Open Letter," *Inprecor*, XI, 10 (1932): 347.

[206] V. Basak, "The Situation in India," *Inprecor*, XIII, 41 (1933): 896-97.

[207] Communist Party of China, Central Committee, "Open Letter to the Indian Communists," *ibid.*, XIII, 51 (1933): 1153.

[208] Government of India, Home Department, 1935, p. 186.

[209] *Ibid.*, pp. 188-90.

[210] *Ibid.*, pp. 195-204.

[211] *Ibid.*, p. 214.

[211a] *Tribune* (Lahore), Aug. 5, 1935, p. 4; and Aug. 8, 1935, p. 13.

[212] *Ibid.*, pp. 208-9.

[213] D. Manuilsky, "The Work of the Seventh Congress of the Communist International," *The Communist International, Seventh Con-*

gress, Moscow, 1935: Reports, Resolutions and Speeches (New York: Workers Library Publishers, 1935), pp. 68-71.

[214] Wang Ming (Ch'en Shao-yü), "The Revolutionary Movement in the Colonial Countries," *ibid.*, p. 50.

[215] *Ibid.*, p. 48.

[216] *Ibid.*, pp. 40-43.

[217] "Resolutions, Seventh Congress of the Communist International," *The Communist International, Seventh Congress, Moscow, 1935*, pp. 32 and 35.

[218] Wang Ming, pp. 42-43.

[219] V. B. Karnik, "On Royism," Part II of Roy, *Our Differences*, pp. 167-74.

[220] Roy, *Our Differences*, p. iv.

Chapter 9

[1] See, for example, Gene D. Overstreet and Marshall Windmiller, *Communism in India*, pp. 161-66.

[2] Indian National Congress, *General Secretaries Report, 1933-34* (Bombay: AICC, 1934), p. 9.

[3] Address of K. F. Nariman, Chairman of the Reception Committee, Oct. 26, 1934, at the 48th Session of the Indian National Congress, Bombay.

[4] *AICC Newsletter*, No. 38, Feb. 27, 1936, p. 3.

[5] Acharya Narendra Deva, *Socialism and the National Revolution* (Bombay: Padma Publications Ltd., 1946), p. xii.

[6] Address of K. F. Nariman, Chairman of the Reception Committee, Oct. 26, 1934, at the 48th Session of the Indian National Congress, Bombay.

[7] Jayaprakash Narayan, *Why Socialism?* (Benares, CSP, 1936), pp. 25-26.

[8] *Congress Socialist Party: Constitution, Programme and Resolutions, 1934*, adopted at the First Conference of the All-India Congress Socialist Party, pp. 27-32.

[9] Thomas A. Rusch, "Role of the Congress Socialist Party in the Indian National Congress, 1941-42" (unpublished Ph.D. dissertation, Department of Political Science, University of Chicago, 1955), p. 145.

[10] Minocheher R. Masani, *The Communist Party of India* (New York: Macmillan, 1954), p. 53.

[11] Rusch, p. 148.

[12] Masani, pp. 53-54. See also Thomas A. Rusch, "Dynamics of Socialist Leadership in India," in Richard L. Park and Irene Tinker, eds., *Leadership and Political Institutions in India* (Princeton: Princeton University Press, 1959), p. 189.

[13] *The Leader*, Aug. 3, 1934, quoted in Jayaprakash Narayan, *Why Socialism?*, pp. 87-88.

[14] Narayan, pp. 74, 89-93. Since writing this tract, Narayan's views have altered considerably. As indicated earlier, he later came under the influence of Gandhi's ideas.

[15] *Ibid.*, pp. 70 and 84-87.

[16] *Ibid.*, pp. 86-87. Narayan is here quoting from William Godwin, *An Inquiry Concerning Political Justice* (Dublin: Printed for Luke White, 1793), Vol. II, pp. 330-33.

[17] Gandhi, "Is Violence Creeping In?," *Harijan* (Poona), Aug. 13, 1938, p. 216. Gandhi here cites as an example of violence to which he is opposed the reviling of capitalists as a class and "inciting people to loot them."

[18] "Proceedings of the Working Committee, June 12-13, 1934," in Nripendra Nath Mitra, ed., *The Indian Annual Register: An Annual Digest of Public Affairs in India* (Calcutta: The Annual Register Office, 1935), I: 283-84.

[19] *Congress Bulletin* (Allahabad), June 27, 1934, p. 13.

[20] Indian National Congress, *General Secretaries Report, 1933-34*, p. 11.

[21] Quoted in Presidential Address of Rajendra Prasad, Oct. 26, 1934, at the 48th Session of the Indian National Congress, Bombay.

[22] Quoted in Hiren Mukherji, *Gandhiji: A Study*, 2nd ed. rev. (New Delhi: People's Publishing House, 1960), p. 109.

[23] Meeting of the Working Committee, Wardha, Sept. 9-11, 1934, as referred to in Presidential Address of Rajendra Prasad, p. 15.

[24] Jagdish S. Sharma, *Indian National Congress: A Descriptive Bibliography of India's Struggle for Freedom* (Delhi: S. Chand, 1959), p. 565.

[25] Indian National Congress, *General Secretaries Report, 1933-34*, pp. 1-2.

[26] Presidential Address of Rajendra Prasad.

[27] Address by K. F. Nariman, Chairman of the Reception Committee, Oct. 26, 1934, at the 48th Session of the Indian National Congress, Bombay.

[28] Michael Brecher, *Nehru: A Political Biography* (London: Oxford University Press, 1959), p. 207.

[29] M. N. Roy, *India in Transition.*

[30] Jayaprakash Narayan, "M. N. Roy," dated May 1954. This is a testimonial to Roy written shortly after his death. A copy is in the possession of the author. In this document Narayan makes the interesting observation that, after a long period of disagreement, the political thought of the two men converged once again in the early 1950's on the concept of partyless democracy. Narayan wrote: "We had moved closer together at the end just as I was close to him at the beginning. . . . Both of us, each in his own way, had moved away from Marxism in the same direction and to the same goals." Narayan felt that Roy "had done more thinking" on the question of non-party democracy than anyone else and visited him twice, just before his death, to discuss the topic with him, but on both occasions Roy was too ill to speak. Narayan's writings on the subject are well known. Roy's pertinent essays have been gathered together in a volume entitled *Politics, Power and Parties* (Calcutta: Renaissance Publishers, 1960).

[31] *Congress Socialist Party*, pp. 5, 9-10.

[32] Presidential Address of Acharya Narendra Deva at the First All-India Congress Socialist Conference, Patna, May 1934, quoted in Deva, p. 4.

[33] *Congress Socialist Party*, p. 14.

[34] Roy's report to associates in Bombay Province, Dehra Dun, May 25, 1938, League of Radical Congressmen Files No. 1, Roy Archives.

[35] *Independent India* (Bombay), April 3, 1938, p. 4.

[36] Masani, p. 67.

[37] See Jayaprakash Narayan, *Socialist Unity and the Congress Socialist Party* (Bombay: The Congress Socialist Party, 1941), pp. 3-4.

[38] Jayaprakash Narayan, "Presidential Address at the Bengal Congress Socialist Party Conference (1935)," in Jayaprakash Narayan, *Towards Struggle* (Bombay: Padma Publications, 1946), pp. 132-35.

[39] "CSP Reply to the Royists," *Congress Socialist* (Bombay), Aug. 28, 1937, pp. 7-9, 14.

[40] Rusch, "Role of the Congress Socialist Party in the Indian National Congress, 1931-42," p. 147. The other three members were: Jayaprakash Narayan, M. R. Masani, and C. K. Narayanswamy.

[41] Interview with Rajani Mukherji, Calcutta, Dec. 13, 1962.

[42] *Congress Socialist Party: Constitution, Programme and Resolutions, 1934*, p. 3.

[43] Interview with Rajani Mukherji, Calcutta, Dec. 13, 1962.

[44] *Congress Socialist* (Bombay), Jan. 25, 1936, p. 16.

[45] *Ibid.*, Jan. 9, 1937, p. 20.

[46] Letter from Bombay associates to Roy, Bombay, Dec. 12, 1934, File No. 111/2, Roy Archives.

[47] *Congress Socialist* (Bombay), May 1, 1937, p. 18; and May 8, 1937, p. 17.

[48] *Independent India* (Bombay), June 20, 1937, p. 2.

[49] *Congress Socialist* (Bombay), Aug. 7, 1937, p. 13, and interview with Thakar, Ahmedabad, Nov. 13, 1962.

[50] *Independent India* (Bombay), *loc. cit.*, and interview with M. Govindan, Madras, Nov. 29, 1962. Pillai was a member of the Legislative Council under the system of dyarchy and was for ten years a member of the AICC. He met Roy in 1928 on a trip to Germany.

[51] M. N. Roy, *Our Task in India.*

[52] *Congress Socialist Party*, pp. 9-10, 20.

[53] Interview with Minocheher R. Masani, July 1953, cited in Rusch, "Role of the Congress Socialist Party," p. 335.

[54] U.S. Department of State, Office of Strategic Services, *The Radical Democratic Party of India* (Washington, D.C., U.S. Government Printing Office, 1945), pp. 4-6. The source for this statement was apparently Government of India, Home Department, *Communism in India*, 1935, p. 225.

[55] Narayan, *Socialist Unity and the Congress Socialist Party*, p. 4.

[56] Letter from Roy to Bombay associates, Dehra Dun, May 5, 1935, File 111/3, Roy Archives.

[57] *Ibid.*, Oct. 29, 1934, File No. 111/2, Roy Archives.

[58] *Ibid.*, March 12, 1935, File No. 111/3, Roy Archives.

[59] *Ibid.*, Oct. 29, 1934, File No. 111/2, Roy Archives.

[60] "CSP Reply to the Royists," *loc. cit.*

[61] *Congress Socialist* (Bombay), Nov. 21, 1936, p. 11.

[62] *Ibid.*

[63] Minocheher R. Masani, "General Secretary Indicts M. N. Roy," *Congress Socialist* (Bombay), June 26, 1937, pp. 18-19. See also *Independent India* (Bombay), July 4, 1937, p. 9.

[64] *Congress Socialist* (Bombay), April 10, 1937, p. 17.

[65] Minocheher R. Masani, "Good Riddance of Bad Rubbish," *Congress Socialist* (Bombay), March 13, 1937, p. 18.

[66] *Ibid.*, March 6, 1937, p. 6.

[67] Narayan, *Socialist Unity and the Congress Socialist Party*, pp. 6-8.

[68] Susanne Hoeber Rudolph, "The Working Committee of the Indian Congress Party: Its Powers, Organization and Personnel" (Paper No. D/55-2, Center for International Studies, Massachusetts Institute of Technology, Cambridge, Mass., 1955), p. 33.

[69] Rusch, "Role of the Congress Socialist Party," p. 169.

[70] Masani, *The Communist Party of India*, pp. 54-55.

[71] Rusch, "Role of the Congress Socialist Party," p. 343.

[72] Narayan, *Socialist Unity and the Congress Socialist Party*, p. 34.

[73] *Ibid.*

[74] Acharya Narendra Deva, p. 117.

[75] R. Palme Dutt, *India Today* (Bombay: People's Publishing House, 1949), p. 397; cited in Overstreet and Windmiller, *Communism in India*, p. 167.

[76] Masani, *The Communist Party of India*, p. 74.

[77] P. C. Joshi, "Report to the Central Committee," *People's War*, I (Oct. 4, 1942), p. 5; cited in Overstreet and Windmiller, p. 166.

[78] Masani, pp. 68-71.

[79] Narayan, *Towards Struggle*, p. 175.

[80] Rusch, "Role of the Congress Socialist Party," p. 354.

[81] *Ibid.* Before the CSP-CPI split, these last three areas were already under the control of E.M.S. Namboodripad, P. Sundarayya, and P. Ramamurti respectively.

[82] Rusch, "Role of the Congress Socialist Party," p. 356.

[83] Roy frequently used such epithets as "adolescents" and "noisy youngsters" in referring to Indian communists. See, for example, "An Open Letter to the Executive Committee of the Communist International," 1935, File No. 111/1, Roy Archives.

[84] Arthur Koestler, *The Yogi and the Commissar and Other Essays* (New York: Collier Books, 1961), p. 12.

[85] Letter from Roy to Bombay associates, Dehra Dun, March 12, 1935, File No. 111/3, Roy Archives.

[86] Letter from Roy to European associates, Dehra Dun, April 22, 1936, in Roy, *Letters From Jail*, pp. 185-87.

[87] See, for example, Masani's comment that Roy left the CSP because it did not lend itself "to the personal leadership of would-be dictators." Masani, "General Secretary Indicts M. N. Roy," *loc. cit.*

[88] Narayan, *Socialist Unity and the Congress Party*, pp. 5-6.

[89] Myron Weiner, *Party Politics in India: The Development of a Multi-Party System* (Princeton: Princeton University Press, 1957), pp. 158, 163.

Chapter 10

[1] *Congress Bulletin*, Feb. 13, 1936, p. 19.

[2] D. G. Tendulkar, *Mahatma: Life of Mohandas Karamchand Gandhi* (Bombay: by the author and V. K. Jhaveri, 1951-1954), Vol. II: 489-90.

[3] Minoo R. Masani, "From Lucknow to Faizpur," *Congress Socialist* (Bombay), Dec. 5, 1936, p. 6.

[4] Jawaharlal Nehru, *Whither India?*, 2nd ed. rev. (Allahabad: Kitabistan, 1933), pp. 35-40. The first edition was published in November 1933, the second in December.

[5] *AICC Newsletter* (Allahabad), No. 26, Sept. 5, 1935; No. 36, Feb. 13, 1936; and No. 40, March 3, 1936.

[6] "Presidential Address by Jawaharlal Nehru, 49th Session of the Indian National Congress, Lucknow, April 1936," Appendix B, in Jawaharlal Nehru, *Toward Freedom*, pp. 400-401.

[7] Jawaharlal Nehru, *The Unity of India: Collected Writings, 1937-1940* (New York: The John Day Co., 1948), pp. 97-98; Nripendra Nath Mitra, ed., *Indian Annual Register*, I (1936): 280-94; and Jagdish S. Sharma, *Indian National Congress*, p. 573.

[8] Jawaharlal Nehru, *Eighteen Months in India* (Allahabad: Kitabistan, 1938), pp. 6-8; and Rajendra Prasad, *Autobiography* (Bombay: Asia Publishing House, 1957), p. 420.

[9] *AICC Newsletter*, No. 7, Sept. 10, 1936, p. 2.

[10] This leadership core consisted of Maulana Abul Kalam Azad, Rajendra Prasad, C. Rajagopalacharia, Jawaharlal Nehru, Sardar Vallabhbhai Patel, Acharya J. B. Kripalani, Jamnalal Bajaj, Mrs. Sarojini Naidu, Khan Abdul Ghaffar Khan, and Jairamdas Doulatram (Susanne Hoeber Rudolph, "The Working Committee of the Indian Congress Party," pp. 28-29).

[11] Nehru, *Toward Freedom*, p. 358.

[12] *AICC Newsletter*, No. 2, June 18, 1936, p. 3.

[13] For letters of resignation, dated June 29 and July 1, 1936, see Jawaharlal Nehru, *A Bunch of Old Letters* (Bombay: Asia Publishing House, 1958), pp. 184-87.

[14] Jawaharlal Nehru, "Congress and Socialism," July 15, 1936, in Nehru, *Eighteen Months in India*, pp. 28-40.

[15] Nehru, *The Unity of India: Collected Writings, 1937-40*, p. 95.

[16] *Tribune* (Lahore), Dec. 4, 1936, p. 8.

[17] Jawaharlal Nehru, *Manabendranath Roy* (Poona: Young Socialist League Pamphlet, No. 4, n.d.). See also Nehru, *Jawaharlal Nehru, An Autobiography, With Musings on Recent Events in India* (London: John Lane, The Bodley Head, 1936), pp. 153-54, 161.

[18] *Tribune* (Lahore), Nov. 24, 1936, p. 6 and Dec. 3, 1936, p. 9.

[19] Letter from Roy to a friend, Dehra Dun, Feb. 24, 1936, in M. N.

Roy, *Fragments of a Prisoner's Diary*, Vol. III: *Letters From Jail* (Dehra Dun: Indian Renaissance Association, Ltd., 1943), pp. 168-69.

[20] M. N. Roy, *Jawaharlal Nehru* (Delhi: Radical Democratic Party, 1945), pp. 12-13, 41, 51.

[21] Letter from Roy to the CSP, May 1934, in M. N. Roy, *Letters by M. N. Roy to the Congress Socialist Party* (Bombay: Renaissance Publishers, 1937), p. 4. This is a collection of three letters—dated May 1934, May 1935, and February 1936—which Roy claims he wrote to the CSP. The CSP contends, however, that only the 1936 letter was ever received ("Resolutions of the Central Committee of the CSP, Calcutta, Oct. 26-Nov. 1, 1937," *Congress Socialist* [Bombay], Nov. 13, 1937). Whatever might be the case, it is clear from the record that the CSP leaders were aware of Roy's views on the subject from the inception of the party. See, for example, Narayan's refutation of this view at the Bombay Conference in 1934 (*Congress Socialist Party: Constitution, Programme and Resolutions, 1934*, p. 32).

[22] Letter from Roy to the CSP, Feb. 1936, *ibid.*, p. 52.

[23] Letter from Roy to the CSP, May 1935, *ibid.*, p. 29.

[24] *AICC Newsletter* (Allahabad: Foreign Department, AICC, 1940), No. 5, June 15, 1939, pp. 3-4.

[25] *Ibid.*, No. 6, June 30, 1939, p. 1.

[26] *Tribune* (Lahore), Nov. 23, 1936, p. 16.

[27] *Independent India* (Bombay), Sept. 19, 1937.

[28] *Tribune* (Lahore), Nov. 21, 1936, p. 1.

[29] *Ibid.*, Nov. 24, 1936, pp. 6 and 16.

[30] *Ibid.*, Nov. 30, 1936, p. 8.

[31] *Ibid.*, Dec. 6, 1936, p. 9.

[32] *Ibid.*, Dec. 24, 1936, p. 2.

[33] *Ibid.*, Dec. 27, 1936, p. 3.

[34] Presidential Address by Jawaharlal Nehru at the Fiftieth Session of the Indian National Congress, Faizpur, Dec. 1936. Appendix C in Nehru, *Toward Freedom*, pp. 416-31.

[35] M. N. Roy, "Some Reminiscences," *Independent India* (Delhi), April 1, 1945, pp. 142-44.

[36] *Ibid.*

[37] *Tribune* (Lahore), Dec. 10, 1936, p. 3.

[38] V. B. Karnik, "One Year," *Independent India* (Bombay), Nov. 21, 1937, p. 2.

[39] Letter from Roy to CSP, Feb. 1936, in M. N. Roy, *Letters by M. N. Roy to the Congress Socialist Party*, p. 54.

[40] *Ibid.*, p. 36.

[41] *Ibid.*, p. 42.

[42] Letter of resignation of Bengal Royists from CSP, *Congress Socialist* (Bombay), July 17, 1937, pp. 21-22.

[43] "CSP Reply to the Royists."

[44] Interviews with C. T. Daru and Dashrathlal Thakar, Ahmedabad, Nov. 13, 1962, and Dharatri Ganguly and Janardan Bhattacharya, Calcutta, Dec. 8, 1962.

[45] Presidential Address, Gujarat Congress Socialist Conference

(1935), Ahmedabad, June 23-24, 1935, in Acharya Narendra Deva, *Socialism and the National Revolution*, pp. 65-87.

[46] Jayaprakash Narayan, "Issues Before and After Lucknow," *Congress Socialist* (Bombay), May 16, 1936, p. 8.

[47] "CSP Reply to the Royists."

[48] *Ibid.* See also the resolution adopted on the subject at the All-India CSP Conference, Faizpur, Dec. 1936, quoted in *Congress Socialist* (Bombay), Jan. 9, 1937, p. 26.

[49] Subhas Chandra Bose, *The Indian Struggle, 1935-42* (Calcutta: Chuckervertty, Chatterjee and Co., 1952), p. 14.

[50] Address by Roy to the Madras DCC, July 27, 1937, *Independent India* (Bombay), Aug. 19, 1937, p. 12.

[51] M. N. Roy, "Disagreement with Lenin," *Radical Humanist*, XVI, 25 (1952): 292.

[52] See Leopold H. Haimson, *The Russian Marxists and the Origins of Bolshevism* (Cambridge: Harvard University Press, 1955).

[53] It should be noted that Marx himself, toward the end of his life, was unable to discount altogether the Russian commune as a basis for social reconstruction. In 1881 Marx wrote to Vera Zasulich that "the analysis in *Das Kapital* offers no argument either for or against the vitality of the rural commune (mir), but . . . [I am convinced] that this commune is the *point d'appui* for the social regeneration of Russia." However, he added that this could come about only after a general revolution based on the urban proletariat. The isolation of the Russian commune rendered it incapable of serving as a revolutionary catalyst. (See David Mitrany, *Marx Against the Peasant: A Study in Social Dogmatism* [New York: Collier Books, 1961], pp. 56-57.)

[54] M. N. Roy, *India in Transition*, p. 207.

[55] B. G. Tilak (1856-1920), "the father of Indian unrest," alarmed Indian Moslems by his glorification of the seventeenth-century Hindu patriot, Sivaji, the scourge of the Moslem Mughal rulers, and by his sponsorship of "cow-protection societies." One of the arguments of Congress moderates such as G. K. Gokhale (1866-1915) against Tilak's tactics was that, however useful they might be in the short run, ultimately they would divide the country into two hostile religious camps.

[56] M. N. Roy, *Fragments of a Prisoner's Diary*, Vol. III: *Letters From Jail*, pp. 16, 69-70.

[57] *Ibid.*, Vols. I and II: *Crime and Karma: Cats and Women*, 2nd ed. rev. (Calcutta: Renaissance Publishers, 1957), pp. 66-67.

[58] *Ibid.*, Vol. III: *Letters From Jail*, pp. 69-70.

[59] *Independent India* (Bombay), Oct. 16, 1938. In formulating my views on the relationship between the thought of Roy and Gandhi I have benefited by conversations with Philip Spratt in Bangalore in November 1962.

[60] For a discussion of the interrelationship between the "great tradition" of a peasant society and the culture and local communities of which it is composed, see Robert Redfield, *Peasant Society and Culture* (Chicago: University of Chicago Press, 1956).

[61] For a discussion of populism in transitional societies, see Edward Shils, *Political Development in the New States* (The Hague: Mouton & Co., 1962), p. 21.

Chapter 11

[1] Jawaharlal Nehru, *Toward Freedom*, p. 176.

[2] Rajendra Prasad, *Autobiography*, pp. 360-61, 454.

[3] Acharya Narendra Deva, *Socialism and the National Revolution*, p. xiii.

[4] Letter from M. N. Roy to the CSP, May 1934, in Roy, *Letters By M. N. Roy to the Congress Socialist Party*, p. 17.

[5] *Ibid.*, p. 17n.

[6] *Independent India* (Bombay), May 22, 1938, pp. 120-21.

[7] A. K. Hindi [Tayab Shaikh], *M. N. Roy—The Man Who Looked Ahead*, p. 208.

[8] M. N. Roy's address at a labor rally in Saharanpur, quoted in *Independent India* (Bombay), June 26, 1938, p. 210.

[9] M. N. Roy, "The Course of the Indian Revolution: The Anti-Communist Line of the Party Leadership," *Revolutionary Age* (New York), June 1930, p. 1.

[10] M. N. Roy, *Our Task in India*, pp. 71-77, 110-11.

[11] *Ibid.*, p. 75.

[12] A. K. Hindi [Tayab Shaikh], *M. N. Roy—The Man Who Looked Ahead*, p. 204.

[13] *Ibid.*, pp. 235-38. Tayab Shaikh is here quoting passages from Roy's writings during the period 1928-1930.

[14] Letter from M. N. Roy to Political Associates, Dehra Dun, Oct. 29, 1934, File No. 111/2, Roy Archives.

[15] Ruth Fischer, *Stalin and German Communism*, pp. 158, 205-206, 224-25, 237.

[16] *Independent India* (Bombay), April 9, 1939, pp. 240-41.

[17] *Tribune* (Lahore), Dec. 6, 1936, p. 9.

[18] *The Times* (London), April 11, 1936, p. 11.

[19] *Tribune* (Lahore), Dec. 9, 1936, p. 2; and Dec. 13, 1936, p. 2.

[20] *Harijan* (Poona), Jan. 9, 1937, p. 379.

[21] *Tribune* (Lahore), Dec. 24, 1936, p. 9.

[22] *Ibid.*, Dec. 23, 1936, p. 2.

[23] *Ibid.*, Dec. 24, 1936, p. 15; Dec. 25, 1936, p. 1; and Dec. 27, 1936, p. 9.

[24] *Ibid.*, Dec. 25, 1936, p. 1.

[25] *Ibid.*, Dec. 27, 1936, p. 1.

[26] Interview with Ram Singh, New Delhi, Dec. 1, 1961.

[27] Letter from S. R. Sunthankar to M. N. Roy, Dharwar, Jan. 21, 1940, File No. 2, Maharashtra League of Radical Congressmen, Roy Archives.

[28] V. B. Karnik, "Collective Affiliation," *Independent India* (Bombay), Dec. 19, 1937, p. 14.

[29] *Independent India* (Bombay), May 22, 1938, p. 121.

[30] Jawaharlal Nehru, "Labor and Peasant Organizations," June 28, 1937, in Nehru, *Eighteen Months in India*, pp. 213-17.

[31] *Congress Socialist* (Bombay), July 10, 1937, pp. 18-20.

[32] Prasad, pp. 455-59.

[33] Letter from Ellen Roy to V. B. Karnik, Benares, April 27, 1938, V. B. Karnik Files, Roy Archives.

[34] Resolution passed by the Congress Working Committee, Bombay, June 2-4, 1938, quoted in *Harijan* (Poona), Jan. 8, 1938, p. 411.

[35] *Harijan* (Poona), Jan. 29, 1938, p. 434.

[36] *Ibid.*, April 23, 1938, pp. 85-86.

[37] *Ibid.*, Feb. 26, 1938, p. 25.

[38] *AICC Newsletters*, No. 2, June 18, 1936, pp. 6-7.

[39] *Ibid.*, No. 3, July 2, 1936, p. 2.

[40] *Tribune* (Lahore), Dec. 25, 1936, p. 1.

[41] Letter from Jawaharlal Nehru to Gandhi, August 13, 1934, quoted in D. G. Tendulkar, *Mahatma*, VIII: 379-84.

[42] M. N. Roy, "Whither Congress?," April 15, 1934, File No. 111/2, Roy Archives.

[43] *Ibid.*

[44] Letter from M. N. Roy to Sharma, a member of the U.P. PCC, n.d., File No. 111/1, Roy Archives. Roy sent another letter to Nehru in 1936 at the time of the Lucknow Congress session urging a similar course of action (*Hindustan Standard* [Calcutta], June 24, 1939).

[45] V. B. Karnik, "The LRC Line," *Independent India* (Bombay), August 18, 1940, pp. 403-4.

[46] Subhas Chandra Bose, *The Indian Struggle, 1935-42*, p. 14.

[47] Jagdish S. Sharma, *Indian National Congress*, pp. 570, 573, 576.

[48] *The Times* (London), April 14, 1936, p. 9.

[49] *Tribune* (Lahore), Dec. 24, 1936, p. 9.

[50] *Ibid.*, Dec. 27, 1936, p. 1.

[51] *AICC Newsletters*, No. 14, March 25, 1937, p. 1.

[52] *Ibid.*, No. 22, July 15, 1937, p. 1; and Sharma, p. 578.

[53] V. B. Karnik, "On Royism," in M. N. Roy, *Our Differences*, p. 2.

[54] *Independent India* (Bombay), July 10, 1938, p. 232.

[55] Daniel A. Thorner, "India and Pakistan," in Ralph Linton, ed., *Most of the World*, pp. 598-646.

[56] *AICC Newsletters*, No. 7, Sept. 10, 1936.

[57] "Congress Election Manifesto: 1936," adopted by the AICC at Bombay, August 22, 1936, Appendix A in Jawaharlal Nehru, *The Unity of India*, pp. 401-5.

[58] Jawaharlal Nehru, *The Unity of India*, pp. 103-4.

[59] *Ibid.*, pp. 105-6.

[60] Prasad, p. 427.

[61] *AICC Newsletters*, No. 4, July 16, 1936, p. 1.

[62] *Independent India* (Bombay), August 21, 1938, p. 32.

[63] *Harijan* (Poona), May 21, 1938, p. 123.

[64] Gandhi, "How Non-Violence Works," *ibid.*, July 23, 1938, pp. 192-93.

[65] Gandhi, "Choice Before Congressmen," *ibid.*, Sept. 3, 1938, pp. 242-43.

[66] *Tribune* (Lahore), Sept. 3, 1938, p. 16.

[67] Indian National Congress, *Indian National Congress Resolutions: February 1938-January 1939* (Allahabad: All-India Congress Committee, 1939), pp. 50-58.

[68] Prasad, pp. 474-77.

[69] *AICC Newsletters*, No. 3, August 4, 1938.

[70] *Tribune* (Lahore), Sept. 25, 1938, pp. 1-2, 9.

[71] *Ibid.*, Sept. 26, 1938, pp. 1 and 9; and Sept. 27, 1938, p. 14.

[72] *Indian National Congress Resolutions*, p. 58.

[73] *Tribune* (Lahore), Sept. 24, 1938, p. 3; and Sept. 26, 1938, p. 1.

[74] *Harijan* (Poona), Dec. 10, 1938, p. 365.

[75] *Tribune* (Lahore), Sept. 27, 1938, pp. 8-10.

[76] *Ibid.*, Sept. 28, 1938, p. 3; and Sept. 29, 1938, p. 5.

[77] Letter from M. N. Roy to V. B. Karnik, New Delhi, Sept. 28, 1938, League of Radical Congressmen Files No. 2, Roy Archives. In this letter Roy also noted that among the socialists, neither M. R. Masani nor Kamaladevi participated in the walkout.

[78] Gandhi, "That Unfortunate Walk Out," *Harijan* (Poona), Oct. 15, 1938, p. 287.

[79] Gandhi, "Functions of the Working Committee," *ibid.*, August 6, 1938, pp. 208-9.

[80] *AICC Newsletters*, No. 1, June 23, 1938, p. 2.

[81] *Ibid.*, No. 1, March 23, 1930, pp. 1-6.

[82] V. B. Karnik, "Congress Socialists and the Pant Resolution," *Independent India* (Bombay), March 26, 1939, pp. 203-5. For a detailed account of the Tripuri crisis and its aftermath, see Indian National Congress, *Report of the General Secretaries, March 1939-February 1940* (New Delhi: All-India Congress Committee, 1940), pp. 6-27, 51-65.

[83] *Tribune* (Lahore), March 13, 1939, pp. 2, 5.

[84] Letter from Bose to Gandhi, dated March 25, 1939, in Jawaharlal Nehru, *A Bunch of Old Letters*, pp. 184-87, 355-56.

[85] Madhu Limaye, *Evolution of Socialist Policy*, p. 1.

[86] *Amrita Bazar Patrika* (Calcutta), Feb. 6, 1939.

[87] *Ibid.*, Feb. 7, 1939.

[88] *Tribune* (Lahore), March 10, 1939, pp. 1, 14-15; and March 11, 1939, pp. 1, 15. See also "Roy's Speech on the Pant Resolution," *Independent India* (Bombay), March 26, 1939, p. 221.

[89] *Report of the General Secretaries, March 1939-February 1940*, p. 6.

[90] *Harijan* (Poona), May 6, 1939, p. 116.

[91] *Report of the General Secretaries, March 1939-February 1940*, p. 11.

[92] *Ibid.*, pp. 19-20.

[93] Roy, "League of Radical Congressmen," *Independent India* (Bombay), March 26, 1939, p. 198; and M. N. Roy, "Lessons of the Tripuri Congress," *ibid.*, pp. 213-17.

[94] *Independent India* (Bombay), May 12, 1940, p. 247.

[95] Bose, *The Indian Struggle, 1935-42*, pp. 87-90.

[96] Circular Letter from Roy to members of the LRC, July 20, 1939, LRC Files No. 4, Roy Archives.

[97] *Report of the General Secretaries, March 1939-February 1940*, p. 23.

[98] Gandhi, "The Two Resolutions," *Harijan* (Poona), August 26, 1939, pp. 248-49.

99 Myron Weiner, *Party Politics in India*, p. 54.

100 *AICC Newsletters*, No. 1, Feb. 1, 1940.

101 AICC Resolution, Oct. 10, 1939, quoted in Vapal Pangunni Menon, *The Transfer of Power in India*, p. 66.

102 *AICC Newsletters*, No. 1, Feb. 1, 1940.

103 Statement issued by Jayaprakash Narayan in 1942 entitled "To All Fighters of Freedom," quoted in Great Britain, *Parliamentary Papers*, IX (Sessional Papers of House of Commons), Cmd. 6430, "Statement Published by the Government of India on the Congress Party's Responsibility for the Disturbances in India, 1942-43," pp. 60-64.

104 *Report of the General Secretaries, March 1939-February 1940*, p. 40.

105 Indian National Congress, *Report of the General Secretaries, March 1940-October 1946* (New Delhi: AICC, 1940), p. 1.

106 *AICC Newsletters*, No. 4, March 28, 1940, p. 1-4.

107 *The Times* (London), Feb. 19, 1940, p. 5; and *Times of India* (New Delhi), Feb. 2, 6, 12, 13, 14, and 15, 1940.

108 *AICC Newsletters*, No. 5, April 5, 1940, pp. 1-2.

109 *Report of the General Secretaries, March 1940-October 1946*, p. 2.

110 *Independent India* (Bombay), March 31, 1940, p. 179.

111 *Ibid.*, p. 177.

112 Minutes of the LRC Study Camp, Dehra Dun, May 20-June 5, 1940, LRC Files No. 13, Roy Archives.

113 M. N. Roy, *Some Fundamental Principles of Mass Mobilization* (Dehra Dun: Indian Renaissance Assoc., 1940), p. 10. Reports of the lectures and discussions of the LRC Study Camp, Dehra Dun, May-June 1940.

114 *Ibid.*, p. 25.

115 *Independent India* (Bombay), May 19, 1940, pp. 257-58.

116 Letter from Tarkunde to Roy, Poona, April 15, 1940.

117 Speech by Roy, "Discussions on Satyagraha and the Potentialities of the Congress," LRC Files No. 14, Roy Archives.

118 U.S. Department of State, Office of Strategic Services, *The Radical Democratic Party of India* (Washington, D.C.: U.S. Government Printing Office, 1945), p. 173.

119 *Statesman* (Calcutta), Sept. 20, 1940, quoted in letter from Lal Bahadur, acting secretary, U.P. PCC, to Roy, Allahabad, Sept. 23, 1940. Letter reprinted in *Independent India* (Bombay), Oct. 6, 1940, p. 486.

120 *Independent India* (Bombay), Oct. 6, 1940, pp. 487-92.

121 *Ibid.*

122 Radical Democratic Party, *The Radical Democratic Party, An Introduction* (New Delhi: Radical Democratic Party, 1944), p. 10.

123 Manifesto issued by the Inaugural Conference of the Radical Democratic Party, quoted *ibid.*, p. 11.

124 V. B. Karnik, *Indian Trade Unions*, pp. 106-7.

125 U.S. Department of State, Office of Strategic Services, p. 14.

[126] M. N. Roy, "The Matriarch of Bolshevism," *Radical Humanist* (Calcutta), Nov. 29, 1953, pp. 570-71.

[127] Interview with A. K. Mukherjee, Delhi, Sept. 7, 1962.

[128] M. N. Roy, "The Twenty-Two Theses of Radical Democracy" (A speech concluding the discussion of the draft theses at the third All-India Conference of the RDP, Dec. 27, 1946), *Radical Humanist* (Calcutta), Jan. 5, 1958, p. 1.

[129] M. N. Roy, *New Orientation*, Lectures delivered at the Political Study Camp, Dehra Dun, May 8th to 18th, 1946 (Calcutta: Renaissance Publishers, 1946), p. 117.

[130] Roy, "The Twenty-Two Theses of Radical Democracy."

Selected Bibliography†

Books and Pamphlets

Adhikari, Gangadhar M. *Communist Party and India's Path to National Regeneration and Socialism.* New Delhi: New Age Printing Press, 1964.

Ahmed, Muzaffar. *The Communist Party of India and Its Formation Abroad.* Translated by Hirendranath Mukerjee. Calcutta: National Book Agency, 1962.

———. *Communist Party of India: Years of Formation, 1921-1933.* Calcutta: National Book Agency Private, Ltd., 1959.

Azad, Maulana Abul Kalam. *India Wins Freedom.* London: Orient Longmans, 1959.

Bannerjee, Benoy N., Parikh, G. D., and Tarkunde, V. M. *People's Plan for Economic Development.* Delhi: Indian Federation of Labor, 1944.

Basak, V. *Some Urgent Problems of the Labour Movement in India.* London: Modern Books, Ltd. [1932?].

Black, Cyril E., and Thornton, Thomas P., eds. *Communism and Revolution.* Princeton: Princeton University Press, 1964.

Boersner, Demetrio. *The Bolsheviks and the National and Colonial Question (1917-1928).* Geneva: Librairie E. Droz, 1957. Etudes d'Histoire Economique, Politique et Sociale Sous la direction de Jacques Freymond et Jacques L'Huillier.

Borkenau, Franz. *World Communism: A History of the Communist International.* Ann Arbor: University of Michigan Press, 1962. This book was first published by Norton in 1939.

Bose, N. S. *The Indian Awakening.* Calcutta: Mukhopadhyay, 1960.

Bose, Nirmal Kumar. *Modern India.* Institute of Interna-

† Items in the bibliography preceded by an asterisk indicate that an original, microfilm, or mimeograph copy is in the possession of the author.

tional Studies. Reprint No. 10. Berkeley: University of California, 1959.

Bose, Subhas Chandra. *The Indian Struggle, 1920-34.* London: Wishart and Co., 1935.

———. *The Indian Struggle, 1935-42.* Calcutta: Chuckerverty, Chatterjee and Co., 1952.

Brandt, Conrad. *Stalin's Failure in China 1924-27.* Cambridge: Harvard University Press, 1958.

Brecher, Michael. *Nehru: A Political Biography.* London: Oxford University Press, 1959.

Bukharin, Nikolai I. *Problems of the Chinese Revolution.* London: Communist Party of Great Britain, 1927.

Carr, Edward H. *Studies in Revolution.* New York: Universal Library Edition, 1964.

Caveeshar, Sardul Singh. *Within or Without the British Empire?* Lahore: Independence of India League, Punjab Branch [193?].

Chaudhuri, Bhawani Prasad, and Chakrabarty, Deb Ranjan. *Leftist Leaders of India.* Calcutta: Calcutta Book Store, 1947. Chapter I on "M. N. Roy."

*Churchill, Winston Leonard Spencer. *India: Speeches and an Introduction.* London: Thorton Butterworth, 1931.

Coatman, John. *India in 1927-28.* Calcutta: Government of India, 1928.

Communist Party of Great Britain. *The Communist International Between the Fifth and the Sixth World Congresses.* London: Communist Party of Great Britain, 1928.

———. *From the Fourth to the Fifth World Congress.* London: Communist Party of Great Britain, 1924.

Dange, Shripat Amrit. *On the Indian Trade Union Movement.* Bombay: Communist Party of India, 1952. A report to a convention of Communist party members working in the trade-union movement, Calcutta, May 20-22, 1952.

Das, Ramyansu Sikhar. *M. N. Roy—The Humanist Philosopher.* Calcutta: R. S. Das, 1956.

Degras, J., ed. *The Communist International: 1919-1922.* Vol. I. London: Oxford University Press, 1956.

Deva, Acharya Narendra. *Socialism and the National Revolution.* Bombay: Padma Publications, Ltd., 1946.

Draper, Theodore. *American Communism and Soviet Russia: The Formative Period.* New York: The Viking Press, 1960.

Druhe, David N. *Soviet Russia and Indian Communism.* New York: Bookman Associates, 1959.

*Dutt, Kalpana. *Chittagong Armoury Raiders: Reminiscences.* Bombay: People's Publishing House, 1945.

Dutt, Rajani Palme. *Modern India.* 2nd ed. rev. London: Communist Party of Great Britain, 1927.

Fischer, Ruth. *Stalin and German Communism: A Study in the Origins of the State Party.* Cambridge: Harvard University Press, 1948.

Ghosh, P. C. *The Development of the Indian National Congress, 1892-1909.* Calcutta: Firma K. L. Mukhopadhyay, 1960.

Giri, V. V. [Venkatagiri, Varahagiri]. *Labour Problems in Indian Industry.* 2nd ed. New York: Asia Publishing House, 1960.

Gitlow, Benjamin. *I Confess: The Truth About American Communism.* New York: E. P. Dutton & Co., 1940.

Gopal, Sarvepalli. *The Viceroyalty of Lord Irwin 1926-1931.* London: Oxford University Press, 1957.

Haimson, Leopold H. *The Russian Marxists and the Origins of Bolshevism.* Cambridge: Harvard University Press, 1955.

Hindi, A. K. [Tayab Shaikh]. *M. N. Roy—The Man Who Looked Ahead.* Allahabad: The Modern Publishing House, 1938.

Hobsbawn, Eric J. *Social Bandits and Primitive Rebels: Studies in Archaic Forms of Social Movements in the 19th and 20th Centuries.* Glencoe: The Free Press, 1959.

Howe, Irving, and Coser, Lester. *The American Commu-*

nist Party: A Critical History. 2nd ed. rev. New York: Frederick A. Praeger, 1962.

Hutchinson, Hugh Lester. *Conspiracy at Meerut*. London: Allen and Unwin, 1935.

**India, the Commission and the Conference*. London: The Times Publishing Co., 1931. A reprint of leading articles on the Indian question from the return of the statutory commission to the conclusion of the Round Table Conference in London.

The Indian Year Book and Who's Who, 1935-36. XXII. Bombay: The Times of India Press, n.d.

Isaacs, Harold R. *The Tragedy of the Chinese Revolution*. 2nd ed. rev. Stanford: Stanford University Press, 1961.

Johnson, Chalmers A. *Peasant Nationalism and Communist Power: The Emergence of Revolutionary China, 1937-1945*. Stanford: Stanford University Press, 1962.

Karnik, Vasant Bhagwant. *Indian Trade Unions: A Survey*. Bombay: Labour Education Service, 1960.

———. *The New India: A Short Account of the RDP, Its Programme and Policy*. London: Twentieth Century Press Ltd., 1944.

———. *Rupees 13,000—Controversy X-Rayed*. Delhi: Indian Federation of Labour, 1945.

Lenin, Vladimir I. *Collected Works*. Vols. I, II, III, IV, VIII, and XVIII. Prepared by the Institute of Marxism-Leninism, Central Committee of the CPSU. 4th ed. rev. London: Lawrence and Wishart, 1960.

———. *Selected Works*. Vols. III, IX, and X. New York: International Publishers, 1938.

Limaye, Madhu. *Evolution of Socialist Policy*. Hyderabad: Prakashan Ltd., 1952.

McKenzie, Kermit E. *Comintern and World Revolution: 1928-43: Shaping of Doctrine*. New York: Columbia University Press, 1964.

Majumdar, Ramesh Chandra. *History of the Freedom Movement in India*. Vols. I, II, and III. Calcutta: K. L. Mukhopadhyay, 1963.

Malraux, André. *Man's Fate*. New York: Random House, 1934.

**Manifesto of the Workers' and Peasants' Party to the Indian National Congress, Madras, December, 1927.* Calcutta: Peasants' and Workers' Party of Bengal, 1927.

Marx, Karl. *Articles on India.* 2nd ed. Bombay: People's Publishing House, Ltd., 1951. These articles originally appeared in the *New York Daily Tribune* in 1853.

———, and Engels, Friedrich. *Letters to Americans 1848-95.* New York: International Publishers, 1953.

Masani, Minocheher Rustom. *The Communist Party of India.* New York: Macmillan, 1954.

Mathur, A. S., and Mathur, J. S. *Trade Union Movement in India.* Allahabad: Chaitanya Publishing House, 1957.

Menon, Vapal Pangunni. *The Transfer of Power in India.* Princeton: Princeton University Press, 1957.

Meyer, Alfred G. *Leninism.* Cambridge: Harvard University Press, 1957.

———. *Marxism: The Unity of Theory and Practice.* Cambridge: Harvard University Press, 1954.

Misra, B. B. *The Indian Middle Classes: Their Growth in Modern Times.* London: Oxford University Press, 1961.

Mitra, Nripendra Nath, ed. *The Indian Annual Register: An Annual Digest of Public Affairs of India.* Calcutta: The Annual Register Office, 1919-1947.

Morris, Morris David. *The Emergence of an Industrial Labor Force in India: A Study of the Bombay Cotton Mills.* Berkeley: University of California Press, 1965.

Mukerjee, Hiren. *Gandhiji: A Study.* 2nd ed. rev. New Delhi: People's Publishing House, 1960.

———. *India's Struggle for Freedom.* 3rd ed. rev. Calcutta: National Book Agency, 1962. This book was first published in 1946 under the title *India Struggles for Freedom.*

Mukherjee, Haridas, and Mukherjee, Uma. *"Bande Mataram" and Indian Nationalism, 1906-1908.* Calcutta: Firma K. L. Mukhopadhyay, 1957.

Mukhtar, Ahmad. *Trade Unionism and Labour Disputes in India.* London: Longmans, Green and Co., 1935.

Myers, Charles A. *Labor Problems in the Industrialization of India.* Cambridge: Harvard University Press, 1958.

Narayan, Jayaprakash. *Socialist Unity and the Congress Socialist Party.* Bombay: Congress Socialist Party, 1941.

———. *The Socialist Way.* Lucknow: Dulabeylal Bhargava, 1946.

———. *Towards Struggle.* Bombay: Padma Publications, 1946.

*———. *Why Socialism?* Benares: Congress Socialist Party, 1936.

Nehru, Jawaharlal. *A Bunch of Old Letters.* Bombay: Asia Publishing House, 1958.

———. *Eighteen Months in India 1936-1937.* Allahabad: Kitabistan, 1938.

*———. *Manabendranath Roy.* Poona: Young Socialist League Pamphlet No. 4, n.d. Internal evidence indicates that this pamphlet was written between 1932 and 1936.

*———. *Nehru in the Punjab.* Lahore: Allied Indian Publishers, 1944. This is an English version of the presidential address delivered in Hindustani at the Punjab Provisional Conference of the Congress party held on April 11, 1928.

*———. *Nehru on War Danger, Independence and Imperialism.* Lahore: Allied Publishers, 1944.

*———. *Report Submitted to the AICC by Jawaharlal Nehru,* Haripura, 1938.

———. *Soviet Russia.* Bombay: Chetana, 1929.

———. *Toward Freedom: The Autobiography of Jawaharlal Nehru.* New York: John Day Co., 1941. This book was first published in 1936 under the title *Jawaharlal Nehru, an Autobiography, with Musings on Recent Events in India.* London: John Lane, The Bodley Head, 1936. A revised edition, containing an additional chapter, was published by the same company in 1945.

———. *The Unity of India: Collected Writings, 1937-1940.* New York: John Day Co., 1948.

———. *Where Are We?* Allahabad: Kitabistan, 1939. Articles written and published in the *National Herald* of Lucknow during the ten days preceding the Tripuri session of the Indian National Congress in March 1939.

———. *Whither India?* 2nd ed. rev. Allahabad: Kitabistan, 1933.

North, Robert C. *Moscow and the Chinese Communists.* Stanford: Stanford University Press, 1953.

———, and Eudin, Xenia J. *M. N. Roy's Mission to China: The Communist-Kuomintang Split of 1927.* Berkeley: University of California Press, 1963.

Ornati, Oscar A. *Jobs and Workers in India.* Prepared under the auspices of the Institute of International Industrial and Labor Relations. Ithaca: Cornell University Press, 1955.

Overstreet, Gene D., and Windmiller, Marshall. *Communism in India.* Berkeley: University of California Press, 1959.

Pattabhi, Sitaramayya, Bhogaraju. *The History of the Indian National Congress.* Vol. I. Allahabad: Congress Working Committee, 1935.

Pelling, Henry. *The British Communist Party: A Historical Profile.* London: Adam and Charles Black, 1958.

Prasad, Rajendra. *Autobiography.* Bombay: Asia Publishing House, 1957.

Punekar, S. D. *Trade Unionism in India.* Bombay: New Books Co., 1948.

Radical Democratic Party. *The Radical Democratic Party, an Introduction.* New Delhi: Radical Democratic Party [1944?].

Rao, M. V. Ramana. *A Short History of the Indian National Congress.* Delhi: S. Chand and Co., 1959.

Ray, P. C. *The Life of C. R. Das.* London: Oxford University Press, 1927.

Ray, Sibnarayan. *M. N. Roy—Philosopher Revolutionary.* Calcutta: Renaissance Publishers, 1959.

The Second Congress of the Communist International Proceedings. Moscow: Communist International, 1920.

Sen, Niranjan. *Bengal's Forgotten Warriors.* Bombay: People's Publishing House, 1945.

Seton-Watson, Hugh. *Nationalism and Communism: Essays 1946-1963.* New York: Frederick A. Praeger, 1964.

———. *Neither War nor Peace: The Struggle for Power in the Post-war World.* New York: Frederick A. Praeger, 1960.

Sharma, G. K. *Labour Movement in India: Its Past and Present.* Jullundur: University Publishers, 1963.

Sharma, Jagdish S. *Indian National Congress: A Descriptive Bibliography of India's Struggle for Freedom.* Delhi: S. Chand, 1959.

Sitaramayya. See Pattabhi, Sitaramayya, Bhogaraju.

Smith, Vincent A. *The Oxford History of India.* 3rd ed. rev. Edited by Percival Spear. Oxford: Clarendon Press, 1958.

Snow, Edgar. *Red Star Over China.* New York: Random House, 1938.

Spratt, Philip. *Blowing Up India: Reminiscences and Reflections of a Former Comintern Emissary.* Calcutta: Prachi Prakashan, 1955.

———. *Communism and India.* Eastern Economist pamphlets, No. 16. Edited by E. P. W. da Costa. New Delhi: 1952.

Stalin, Joseph. *Marxism and the National and Colonial Question: A Collection of Articles and Speeches.* 4th ed. London: Lawrence and Wishart, 1947.

Tagore, Saumyendranath. *Bourgeois-Democratic Revolution and India.* Calcutta: Ganavani Publishing House, 1939.

———. *Historical Development of the Communist Movement in India.* Calcutta: Red Front Press, 1944.

T'ang Leang-li. *The Inner History of the Chinese Revolution.* London: G. Routledge & Sons, Ltd., 1930.

*Tegart, Sir Charles A. "Terrorism in India." Speech delivered before the Royal Empire Society and published under its auspices. London, 1932.

Tendulkar, D. G. *Mahatma: Life of Mohandas Karamchand Gandhi.* Bombay: By the author and V. K. Jhaveri, 1951-54. Vols. II and III.

Theses and Statutes of the Third (Communist) International. Moscow: Publishing Office of the Communist International. Reprinted by the United Communist Party of America, 1920.

Trotsky, Leon D. *The Permanent Revolution.* Translated by Max Schachtman. New York: Pioneer Publishers, 1931.

———. *Problems of the Chinese Revolution.* 3rd ed. New York: Praeger, 1966.

———. *The Stalin School of Falsification.* New York: Pioneer Publishers, 1937.

Tucker, Robert C., and Cohen, Stephen F. *The Great Purge Trials.* New York: Grosset and Dunlap Publishers, 1965.

Wallbank, T. Walter. *A Short History of India and Pakistan.* New York: The New American Library, 1965. This is the abridged paperback edition of the author's *India in the New Era* published in 1951 by Scott Foresman and Company.

Whiting, Allen S. *Soviet Policies in China 1917-1924.* New York: Columbia University Press, 1953.

Wilber, C. Martin, and How, Julie Lien-ying, eds. *Documents on Communism: Nationalism and Soviet Advisers in China, 1918-1927.* Papers seized in the 1927 Peking Raid. New York: Columbia University Press, 1956.

Articles (exclusive of *Inprecor*)

Degras, Jane. "United Front Tactics in the Comintern 1921-1928." *St. Antony's Papers Number* IX: *International Communism.* Edited by David Footman. Carbondale: Southern Illinois University Press, 1960.

Deutsch, Karl W. "Social Mobilization and Political Development." *American Political Science Review*, September 1961, pp. 493-514.

Haithcox, John P. "The Roy-Lenin Debate on Colonial Policy: A New Interpretation." *Journal of Asian Studies*, November 1963.

———. "Nationalism and Communism in India; The Impact of the 1927 Comintern Failure in China." *Journal of Asian Studies*, May 1965.

Hamel, Claude. "Un debat au second Congres du Komintern (1920)." *Est et Quest* (Paris). xiv, 281 (1962).

Hunt, R. N. Carew. "Willi Muenzenberg." *St. Antony's Papers Number* ix: *International Communism.*

Kautsky, John H. "An Essay in the Politics of Development." *Political Change in Underdeveloped Countries: Nationalism and Communism.* Edited by John H. Kautsky. New York: John Wiley and Sons, 1962.

Khan, Abdul Qadir. "Pupil of the Soviet." *The Times* (London), Feb. 25, 26, and 27, 1930.

Lenin, Vladimir I. "Preliminary Draft Theses on the National and Colonial Questions." *Selected Works.* Vol. x. New York: International Publishers, 1938, p. 236.

———. "The Report on the National and Colonial Questions at the Second Congress of the Communist International." *Selected Works.* Vol. x: 240-41.

Lowenthal, Richard. "Communism and Nationalism." *Problems of Communism.* xi, 6 (1962): 37-44.

Manuilsky, Dmitry. "The Work of the Seventh Congress of the Communist International." Speech delivered at a meeting of the Moscow organization of the Communist party of the Soviet Union, September 14, 1935. *The Communist International, Seventh Congress, Moscow, 1935 (Reports, Resolutions and Speeches).* New York: Workers Library Publishers, 1935.

Mao Tse-tung. "Report of an Investigation into the Peasant Movement in Hunan," to the Central Committee of the Chinese Communist party, February 1927, in Jacobs, Dan N., and Baerward, Hans H., eds. *Chinese Commu-*

nism: Selected Documents. New York: Harper and Row, 1963.

North, Robert C. "M. N. Roy: The Revolution in Asia." *Soviet Survey*, April-June 1960, pp. 102-8.

Park, Richard L. "Labor and Politics in India." *Far Eastern Survey.* xviii, 16 (1949).

*Pelling, Henry. "The Early History of the Communist Party of Great Britain, 1920-29." *Transactions of the Royal Historical Society.* London. viii, 1958.

Plekhanov, Georgii V. "Our Differences." *Selected Philosophical Works.* Vol. i. Prepared by the Institute of Philosophy of the Academy of Sciences of the U.S.S.R. London: Lawrence and Wishart, 1961.

Punekar, S. D. "Trade Union Movement in India." *Industrial Labour in India.* Edited by V. B. Singh. New York: Asia Publishing House, 1963.

"Resolutions, Seventh Congress of the Communist International." *Communist International, Seventh Congress, Moscow, 1935.* New York: Workers Library Publishers, 1935.

Roy, Sachin K. "How M. N. Roy Helped Indian Revolution from Abroad." *Radical Humanist* (Calcutta), January 25, 1963.

Rusch, Thomas A. "Dynamics of Socialist Leadership in India." *Leadership and Political Institutions in India.* Edited by Richard L. Park and Irene Tinker. Princeton: Princeton University Press, 1959.

*S. D., "A Mystery Man." *Modern Review* (Calcutta), Feb. 1937, pp. 185-87.

Samra, Chattar Singh. "Subhas Chandra Bose: An Indian National Hero." *Leadership and Political Institutions in India.*

Sinha, K. K. "Dynamics of Roy's Ideals." *Radical Humanist* (Calcutta). xviii, 8 (1954): 88.

Stalin, Joseph. "The Revolution in China and the Tasks of the Comintern: Speech Delivered at the Tenth Sitting, Eighth Plenum of the ECCI, May 24, 1927." *Works.* Vol.

x. Moscow: Foreign Languages Publishing House, 1952, pp. 291-92.

Thorner, Daniel A. "India and Pakistan." *Most of the World.* Edited by Ralph Linton, New York: Columbia University Press, 1949.

Wang Ming (Ch'en Shao-yü). "The Revolutionary Movement in the Colonial Countries." *Communist International, Seventh Congress, Moscow, 1935.* New York: Workers Library Publishers, 1935.

Articles from Inprecor (arranged chronologically)

"The Enlarged Executive, Opening Session." III, 45 (1923): 438.

Manuilsky, Dmitry. "Report on the National Question." IV, 54 (1924): 569.

———. "Concluding Speech on the National Question." (Fifth Comintern Congress, July 8, 1924). IV, 57 (1924): 608.

"Theses on Tactics." (Fifth Comintern Congress). IV, 62 (1924): 62.

"Theses and Resolutions Adopted by the Fifth World Congress of the Communist International." IV, 62 (1924): 647.

Roy, Evelyn. "French Persecution of Indian Political Exiles." V, 20 (1925): 288.

Zinoviev, Gregory. "The Epoch of Wars and Revolutions." V, 55 (1925): 745-47.

"The Agenda and Preparation of the Enlarged Executive of the Communist International." VI, 12 (1926): 181.

"Resolution on the Situation in Great Britain." VI, 40 (1926): 643.

Zinoviev, Gregory. "The Results of the Sixth Session of the Enlarged ECCI." VI, 45 (1926): 744.

"Seventh Meeting of the Enlarged ECCI." VI, 83 (1926): 1432.

"Continuation of the Discussion on the First Point of the Agenda." VI, 89 (1926): 1560.

"Election of the Presidium and the Secretariat of the ECCI." vi, 93 (1926): 1646.

"The Question of the Chinese Revolution: Theses of Comrade Stalin for Propagandists, Approved by the CC of the CPSU." vii, 27 (1927): 543-45.

Statement by the Secretariat of the ECCI on the Work of the Eighth Plenum of the ECCI. vii, 34 (1927): 706-7.

"The Fifth Party Conference of the Communist Party of China." vii, 34 (1927): 716-17. "The Political and Organizatory Report of the Central Committee."

"Resolution on the Chinese Question." (Seventh Plenum of the ECCI), May 18-30, 1927. vii, 35 (1927): 737-41.

Bukharin, Nikolai. "The Results of the Plenary Session of the ECCI." vii, 39 (1927): 879-84. The report given at the Plenum of the Moscow Committee of the CPSU, June 4, 1927.

———. "An Abrupt Turn in the Chinese Revolution." vii, 41 (1927): 897.

"Resolution of the ECCI on the Present Situation of the Chinese Revolution." vii, 44 (1927): 983-85.

Stalin, Joseph. "Concerning Current Questions." vii, 45 (1927): 999-1006.

"The R.I. L.U. to the Eighth All-India Congress of Trade Unions." vii, 68 (1927): 1539.

Varga, Eugene. "Economics and Economic Policy in the Fourth Quarter of 1927." viii, 15 (1928): 287-94.

"Draft Programme of the Communist International." Adopted by the Programme Commission of the ECCI, May 25, 1928. viii, 30 (1928): 540-59.

Proceedings of the Sixth World Congress of the Communist International. viii, 38-91 (1928).

"Election of the Presidium." viii, 39 (1928): 706.

Bukharin, Nikolai. "The International Situation and the Tasks of the Comintern." viii, 41 (1928): 733-34. Report given at the Second Session of the Sixth World Congress of the Communist International.

Sikander Sur [Shaukat Usmani]. "Discussion on the Report of Comrade Bukharin." viii, 44 (1928): 775.

Narayan [Saumyendranath Tagore]. "Continuation of the Discussion on the Report of Comrade Bukharin on the Draft Programme of the Comintern." VIII, 66 (1928): 1203.

Kuusinen, Otto V. "The Revolutionary Movement in the Colonies." VIII, 68 (1928): 1230-31.

Sikander Sur [Shaukat Usmani]. "The Development in India." VIII, 68 (1928): 1247-48.

Bukharin, Nikolai. "Speech in Reply to the Discussion on the International Situation." VIII, 70 (1928): 863-72.

———. "Report on the Results of the Sixth Comintern Congress to Party Functionaries of the Moscow Organization of the CPSU." VIII, 70 (1928): 1267-77.

"Report of Comrade Bukharin." VIII, 70 (1928): 1267-77.

Bennet, A. J. [D. Petrovsky]. "Questions on the Revolutionary Movement in the Colonies." VIII, 72 (1928): 1320-22.

Rothstein, Andrew. "Questions on the Revolutionary Movement in the Colonies." VIII, 72 (1928): 1323-24.

Dutt, Clemens. "Continuation of the Discussion of the Revolutionary Movement in the Colonies." VIII, 76 (1928): 1323-24.

Narayan [Saumyendranath Tagore]. "Continuation of the Discussion of the Revolutionary Movement in the Colonies." VIII, 76 (1928): 1390-91.

Arnot, Robin Page. "Continuation of the Discussion on the Questions of the Revolutionary Movement in the Colonies." VIII, 76 (1928): 1420-24.

Bennet, A. J. [D. Petrovsky]. VIII, 76 (1928): 1425.

Statement of Andrew Rothstein. VIII, 78 (1928): 1471-72.

"Declaration of Luhani." VIII, 78 (1928): 1472.

Luhani, G.A.K. "Discussion on the Colonial Question." VIII, 78 (1928): 1472.

Sikander Sur [Shaukat Usmani]. "Concluding Speech." VIII, 78 (1928): 1472-74.

Kuusinen, Otto V. "Concluding Speech of Comrade Kuusinen on the Colonial Question." VIII, 81 (1928): 1519-28.

"Statements by Remmele, Chairman." VIII, 81 (1928): 1529.

"Declaration of Comrade Rothstein." VIII, 81 (1928): 1529.

"Declaration of Comrade Murphey." VIII, 81 (1928): 1530.

Report of the Credentials Committee. VIII, 81 (1928): 1531-32.

Kuusinen, Otto V. "Report of the Colonial Commission." VIII, 81 (1928): 1542.

"The International Situation and the Tasks of the Communist International." VIII, 83 (1928): 1571-72.

"Theses on the Revolutionary Movement in the Colonies and Semi-Colonies." Adopted by the Sixth World Congress. VIII, 88 (1928): 1665-70.

"Declaration of the British Delegation on the Theses on the Colonial Question." VIII, 91 (1928): 1743-44.

Sch., P. [?]. "The Conference of the Workers' and Peasants' Party of India." IX, 16 (1929): 319-20.

———. "The Conference of the Workers' and Peasants' Party of India." IX, 17 (1929): 347-48.

Manuilsky, Dmitry. "Questions on the Plenary Sessions of the ECCI." IX, 29 (1929): 629-32.

Molotov, Vyacheslav. "Report on the Activities of the Delegates of the CPSU in the ECCI." IX, 33 (1929): 589-95. A speech delivered at the Sixteenth Party Congress of the CPSU.

Kuusinen, Otto V. "The International Situation and the Tasks of the Communist International." IX, 40 (1929): 837-51. Speech given at the First Session of the Tenth Plenum of the ECCI, July 3, 1929.

"Resolution of the Tenth Plenum of the ECCI on Comrade Bukharin." IX, 45 (1929): 964-65.

Lozovsky, S. A. "Continuation of the Discussion on the Reports of Comrades Kuusinen and Manuilsky." IX, 48 (1929): 1037-39. Tenth Plenum of the ECCI, July 8, 1929.

"Declaration of G.A.K. Luhani." IX, 48 (1929): 1039.

Speech by Manuilsky. IX, 48 (1929): 1140.

"Expulsion of Roy from the Comintern." IX, 69 (1929): 1470.

"Open Letter of the Y.C.I. to the All-India Youth Congress and to All Young Workers and Peasants of India." X, 1 (1930): 25.

Radek, Karl. "Problems of the Revolution in India." X, 30 (1930): 545.

"Solidarity with the Working Masses of India." X, 35 (1930): 666.

"Draft Platform of Action of the C.P. of India." X, 58 (1930): 1218-22.

"Draft Platform of the C.P. of India." X, 81 (1930): 1218.

Milani, K. "The Tactics of the Counter-Revolutionary Indian Bourgeoisie." XI, 50 (1931): 912-13.

The Young Workers League, Madras. "Mr. Roy's Services to Counter-Revolution." XI, 55 (1931): 296.

"The Immediate Tasks of the Revolutionary Trade Union Movement of India." XII, 10 (1932): 194-200. Resolution adopted by the Eighth Session of the Red International Labor Union Central Council.

"The Indian Labour Movement." XIII, 22 (1933): 490-94.

Basak, V. "The Situation in India." XIII, 41 (1933): 896-97.

———. "The Present Situation in India." XIII, 42 (1933): 927-28.

Communist Party of China, Central Committee. "Open Letter to the Indian Communists." XIII, 51 (1933): 1153.

"Open Letter to the Indian Communists from the C.C. of the C.P. of China." XIII, 51 (1933): 1153.

"The New Party of Bose and What Should be Our Attitude to It." XIII, 52 (1933): 1179-89.

M. N. Roy: Books and Pamphlets

This does not constitute an exhaustive list of Roy's works, but merely those of his numerous writings which are most relevant to this book. For further references, see Patrick Wilson, "A Preliminary Checklist of the Writings of M. N. Roy" (Modern India Project: University of

California, Berkeley. Bibliographic Study Number 1, 1955); and "List of Writings by M. N. Roy," *Radical Humanist* (Calcutta), Vol. xix, Nos. 4/5, 1955, p. 50.

*Roy, M. N. *The Communist International.* Bombay: The Radical Democratic Party, 1943.

———. *Die internationalen Verbündeten der Opposition in der KPDSU.* Hamburg: C. Hoym Nachf., 1928.

———. *Fragments of a Prisoner's Diary.* Vol. i: *Memoirs of a Cat, 1940*; Vol. ii: *Ideal of Womanhood,* 1941; Vol. iii: *Letters From Jail,* 1943. Dehra Dun: Indian Renaissance Association, Ltd., 1940-43.

———. *The Future of Indian Politics.* London: R. Bishop, 1926. Also published in German under the title *Indiens politische Zukunft.* Hamburg, Berlin: Verlag Carl Hoym Nachf. [1927?].

———. *Heresies of the Twentieth Century.* Bombay: Renaissance Publications, 1943.

———. *India in Transition.* Geneva: J. B. Target, 1922. Imprint fictitious—(cf. *Roy's Memoirs, Radical Humanist* [Calcutta]. xviii, 34 [1954]: 398). Written in collaboration with Abani Mukherji and published in German under the title *Indien.* Autorisierte Übersetzung aus dem Englischen von Willi Schulz. Hamburg: Verlag der Kommunistischen Internationale, 1922. A Russian version appeared in 1921.

*———. *Jawaharlal Nehru.* Delhi: Radical Democratic Party, 1945.

———. *Letters by M. N. Roy to the Congress Socialist Party.* Bombay: Renaissance Publishers, 1937. This is a collection of three letters—dated May 1934, May 1935, and February 1936—which Roy wrote to the organizers of the CSP.

———. *My Defense.* Pondicherry: Committee for Indian Independence, 1932. This is a statement Roy prepared in his own defense at his trial at Kanpur, November 3, 1931 to January 9, 1932. This book also appeared under the title *"I Accuse": From the Suppressed Statement of Manabendra Nath Roy on Trial for Treason Before Ses-*

sion Court, Cawnpore, India. New York: Roy Defense Committee of India, 1932.

———. *My Experiences in China.* 2nd ed. Calcutta: Renaissance Publishers, 1945. First published under this title in 1938. It had appeared several years earlier under the pseudonym of S. K. Vidyarthi with the title **China in Revolt.* Bombay: Vanguard Publishing Co. [1932?].

———. *New Humanism: A Manifesto.* Calcutta: Renaissance Publishers, 1947.

———. *New Orientation.* Calcutta: Renaissance Publishers, 1946. Lectures delivered at the Political Study Camp, Dehra Dun, May 8 to 18, 1946.

———. *On the Congress Constitution.* Calcutta: M. Sarkar, 1936.

———. *Origins of Radicalism in the Congress.* Lucknow: New Life Union, 1942.

———. *Our Differences.* Calcutta: Saraswaty Library, 1938.

*———. *Our Task in India.* Calcutta: Committee for Action for Independence of India [1932?]. Foreword by Rajani Mukherji. "The programme submitted by Manabendra Nath Roy for National Workers of India and as adopted by the Revolutionary Working Class Party, The Communist Party of India."

———. *Reason, Romanticism and Revolution.* Calcutta: Renaissance Publishers, 1955.

*———. *The Relation of Classes in the Struggle for Indian Freedom.* Patna, Bihar: Bihar Radical Democratic People's Party [1940?].

———. *Revolution and Counterrevolution in China.* Calcutta: Renaissance Publishers, 1946. First published in German with the title *Revolution und Konterrevolution in China.* Übersetzung aus dem englischen Manuskript von Paul Frölich. Berlin: Soziologische Verlagsanstalt [1931?]. To the English edition were added two final chapters written in 1938-39 and an epilogue written in 1945. In this last revision Roy included a number of citations and quotations taken, without acknowledge-

ment, from the first edition of Harold R. Isaacs, *The Tragedy of the Chinese Revolution.* Although one may object to Roy's Marxist interpretation of Chinese history, his analysis of events in 1927, based in large part on firsthand experience, is of considerable value.

———, and Sinha, K. K. *Royism Explained.* Calcutta: Saraswaty Library, 1938.

———. *The Russian Revolution.* Calcutta: Renaissance Publishers, 1949.

———. *Satyagraha and the Potentialities of the Congress.* Ajmer: Dr. J. N. Mukherjea on behalf of the RDP, 1941.

———. *Scientific Politics.* Dehra Dun: The Indian Renaissance Association, 1942. Lectures in the All-India Political Study Camp, Dehra Dun, May and June 1940.

*———. *Some Fundamental Principles of Mass Mobilisation.* Dehra Dun: Indian Renaissance Association [1940?]. Reports of the lectures and discussions in the All-India Political Study Camp, Dehra Dun, May 1940, held under the auspices of the All-India League of Radical Congressmen.

———. *Tripuri and After.* Nasik: M. R. Dalvi for Radical Congressmen's League [1939?].

M. N. Roy: Articles from Inprecor (arranged chronologically)

M. N. Roy. "Communism on Trial in India." IV, 23 (1924): 214-15.

———. "The Labour Government in Action." IV, 24 (1924): 226.

———. "Fifth World Congress" (Speech by Roy, June 20, 1924). IV, 42 (1924): 418.

———. "Debate on the National Question—Roy." Twentieth Session, July 1, 1924. IV, 50 (1924): 518-19.

———. "Elections in India." VI, 84 (1926): 84-85.

———. "Discussion of the Report on the Situation in China." VI, 91 (1926): 1604. Seventh Enlarged Executive of the Communist International, November-December 1926.

———. "The Indian National Congress." VII, 5 (1927): 99-100.

———. "The Fifth Congress of the Communist Party of China." VII, 41 (1927): 909-10. Article is dated Hankow, May 13, 1927.

———. "Revolution and Counter-Revolution in China." VII, 42 (1927): 926. Written in Wuhan, June 1927.

———. "On the Eve of Chiang Kai-shek's Return." VII, 53 (1927): 1188-89. Article is dated Moscow, September 3, 1927.

———. "Imperialism and Indian Nationalism." VIII, 1 (1928): 1-3.

———. "Left Social Democrats as Defenders of Imperialism." VIII, 2 (1928): 44-45.

———. "The Indian Constitution." VIII, 54 (1928): 954-55.

———. "The Indian National Congress." VIII, 91 (1928): 1732-33.

———. "The Conference of the German Communist Opposition." IX, 3 (1929): 16-17.

———. "The Ways of Indian Revolution." IX, 4 (1929): 64-65.

———. "Conference of the Workers' and Peasants' Party of India." IX, 6 (1929): 93-94.

———. "The Bourgeoisie and National Revolution in India." IX, 9 (1929): 149-52.

———. "Indian Communists in the Election Struggle." IX, 12 (1929): 203-4.

M. N. Roy: Articles

(exclusive of communist publications in which his articles appeared regularly and his own journals)

M. N. Roy. "The Communist Problem in Asia: An Asian View." *Pacific Affairs.* XXIV, 3 (1951).

———. "The Crisis in the Comintern." A series of articles which appeared in *Gegen den Strom*, the theoretical journal of the Communistische Partie Deutschlands (Opposition) in 1929-30.

———. "The Crisis of Our Times: An Asian View." *Pacific Spectator.* VII, 1 (1953).

———. "Democracy and Nationalism in Asia." *Pacific Affairs.* XXV, 2 (1952).

———. "Heroic Struggle of the Indian Proletariat." *Daily Worker* (New York), March 6, 1929, p. 6.

———. "Mao Tse-tung: A Reminiscence." *New Republic,* September 3, 1961.

———. "Memoirs." Published serially in *Amrita Bazar Patrika* (Calcutta), February 1952 to August 1953. These articles also appeared in *Radical Humanist* (Calcutta) from February 1, 1953 to September 5, 1954. They have been compiled and published in book form under the title *M. N. Roy's Memoirs* (Bombay: Allied Publishers, 1964).

———. "Perspectives of the Situation in China." *Daily Worker* (New York), March 28, 1929, p. 6.

———. "The Situation in India—Report of Comrade Roy." Petrograd *Pravda* (July 29, 1920), quoted in *The Second Congress of the Communist International as Reported and Interpreted by the Official Newspapers of Soviet Russia.* Washington, D. C.: Government Printing Office, 1920.

———. "The State of Socialism in Asia—Rangoon and After." *Pacific Affairs.* XXVI, 2 (1953).

Government Documents

*Government of Bombay. Labor Office. *Labour Gazette.* Bombay: Government Central Press. Vols. VII-XII, 1927-33.

Government of India. Department of Labor. *Report Regarding the Representative Character of the All-India Indian Federation of Labour.* Report prepared by S. C. Joshi, Chief Labour Commissioner. Simla: Government of India Press, 1946.

*———. Home Department. *Communism in India, 1924-27.* Calcutta: Government of India Press, 1927. This confidential document was prepared under the supervision

of Sir David Petrie, Director, Intelligence Bureau, Government of India. It includes a summary of an earlier document entitled *Communism in India* prepared in 1925 by Sir Cecil Kaye, a former director of intelligence. Kaye provides an account of communist activities in India from 1920 to the end of 1924. The present report brings the account forward to September 1927.

———. Home Department (Intelligence Bureau). *Communism in India* (Revised up to January 1, 1935). Simla: Government of India Press, 1935. This report was prepared by J. F. Cowgill under the direction of H. Williamson, Director, Intelligence Bureau.

———. Legislature. *Legislative Assembly Debates.* Vols. III, IV, and V. 1944.

Great Britain. Parliament. *Parliamentary Papers* (House of Commons and Command), 1918. VIII (*Reports*). Cmnd. 9190. "Sedition Committee Report." This report is also known as the Rowlatt Report after the chairman of the committee, S.A.T. Rowlatt. It constitutes the most important source of information on the Bengal revolutionary movement.

———. Parliament. *Parliamentary Papers* (House of Commons and Command). XXIII (*Accounts and Papers,* VIII). Cmnd. 2682, 1926. "Communist Papers." 77-83.

———. Parliament. *Parliamentary Papers* (House of Commons and Command). XVIII (*Accounts and Papers,* V). Cmnd. 4014, 1931-32. "East India (Emergency Measures): Measures Taken to Counteract the Civil Disobedience Movement and to Deal with the Terrorist Movement in Bengal."

———. Parliament. *Sessional Papers* (House of Commons). IX. Cmnd. 6432. "Statement Published by the Government of India on the Congress Party's Responsibility for the Disturbances in India, 1942-43."

———. Royal Commission on Labor in India. *Report of the Royal Commission on Labour in India.* Cmnd. 3883. Presented to Parliament June 1931. London: His Majesty's Stationery Office, 1931. This document is also known as the Whitley Commission Report after the chairman of the commission, John H. Whitley. Its eleven-volume report constitutes the most valuable study of labor conditions in India up to the end of 1930.

Meerut, District Court. *Judgment Delivered by R. L. Yorke, Additional Session Judge, Meerut, on 16th January, 1933, in the Meerut Conspiracy Case.* Simla: Government of India Press, 1932-33. Vol. I.

United States, Department of State, Division of Biographic Information, Office of Libraries and Intelligence Acquisition. *Far Easterners in the Comintern Structure.* OIR Report No. 5226. Washington, D. C.: U.S. Government Printing Office, 1950.

———. Department of State. Office of Strategic Services. *The Radical Democratic Party of India.* Washington, D.C.: U.S. Government Printing Office, 1945.

———. Department of State. *The Second Congress of the Communist International, as reported and interpreted by the official newspapers of Soviet Russia.* Washington, D.C.: U.S. Government Printing Office, 1920.

Newspapers, Journals, Party and Non-Government Publications

With the exception of *International Press Correspondence (Inprecor)*, articles cited in the text and appearing in the publications listed below have not been listed separately in the bibliography.

**All-India Trade Union Bulletin* (Bombay). Vols. 1-6, July 1924-November 1929.

Amrita Bazar Patrika (Calcutta).

**Congress Socialist* (Bombay). Vols. I and II, 1935-37. Organ of the All-India Congress Socialist Party.

Congress Socialist Party: Constitution, Programme and Resolutions, 1934. Adopted at the First Conference of the All-India Congress Socialist Party.

Harijan (Poona). Edited by Mahadev Desai, under the auspices of the Harijan Sevak Sangh. Vols. IV-VII, 1936-40.

Hindustan Standard (Calcutta).

Independent India (Bombay). An early version of the paper appeared in 1931 with Charles Mascarenhas serving as editor. It has been published continuously in India since April 4, 1937 when the paper was revived under the editorship of V. B. Karnik. Beginning in 1943 the paper was published in New Delhi under the name *Vanguard.* Since independence it has been published in Calcutta under the title *Radical Humanist.*

*Indian National Congress. *AICC Newsletters.* May 2, 1935-April 2, 1936; June 4, 1936-February 3, 1938; June 23, 1938-October 5, 1940. Allahabad: Foreign Department, AICC.

———. "Address of Sjt. K. F. Nariman," Chairman of the Reception Committee, 48th Session of the Indian National Congress, Bombay, October 26, 1934.

*———. Agrarian Distress in the United Provinces. Allahabad: Shri Prakasa, 1931. "Being the Report of the Committee appointed by the Counsel of the UPPCC to Inquire into the Agrarian Situation in the province."

*———. *Congress Bulletin* (Allahabad: AICC). Jan. 15, 1929-42.

*———. *Constitution of the Indian National Congress as Amended at the Bombay Session, October 1934.*

*———. *Constitution of the Indian National Congress (As Amended at the Bombay Meeting of the AICC, June 1939).* Allahabad: AICC, 1939.

*———. "Presidential Address of Motilal Nehru." 43rd Session of the Indian National Congress, Calcutta, Dec. 29, 1928.

*———. "Presidential Address of Sardar Vallabhbhai Patel." 45th Session of the Indian National Congress, Karachi, March 1931.

*———. "Presidential Address of Babu Rajendra Prasad." 48th Session of the Indian National Congress, Bombay, Oct. 26, 1934.

*———. "Presidential Address of Shri Subhas Chandra Bose." 51st Session of the Indian National Congress, Haripura, Feb. 19, 1938.

*———. "Presidential Address of Abul Kalam Azad." 53rd Session of the Indian National Congress, Ramgarh, March 1940.

*———. *Report of 44th Annual Session.* Lahore, December 1929.

*———. Reports of the General Secretaries, 1933-34; 1939-40; 1940-46. New Delhi: AICC, 1934, 1940, 1946.

———. *Resolutions of the AICC and Working Committee Between January, 1930 and September, 1934.* Allahabad: AICC, 1934.

———. *Resolutions, March, 1940-September, 1946.* Allahabad: AICC, n.d.

Indian Social Reformer (Bombay).

International Press Correspondence (English Edition) (Moscow).

Labour Monthly (London).

Labor Unity. New York: Trade Union Unity League, II and III.

**Masses of India* (Paris). Vols. I-IV, January 1925-April 1928. This communist propaganda organ, founded and edited by M. N. Roy, was published from various locations in Europe between May 1922 and 1928. Smuggled into India in large quantities, it played a major role in the development of the Indian communist movement.

Mysindia (Bangalore).

New York Times.

Pioneer (Allahabad). Place of publication changed to Lucknow in 1933.

Radical Humanist (Calcutta).

Revolutionary Age (New York). Organ of the Communist party of the USA, Majority Group. Edited by Ben Gitlow and Bertram D. Wolfe.

Statesman (Calcutta).

The Times (London).

Tribune. This Indian newspaper was formerly published in Lahore, but since independence has been published in Ambala.

Vanguard of Indian Independence.

Unpublished Material

Roy Archives, Dehra Dun, U.P. India. The Archives, under the management of the Board of Trustees of the Indian Renaissance Institute, contains the extensive correspondence of Roy dating from the early 1930's until his death in 1954, in addition to the official files of Roy's political and trade-union organizations—The Revolutionary party of the Indian Working Class, The League of Radical Congressmen, The Radical Democratic party of India, The Indian Federation of Labor, and the National Democratic Union. Also located here are files of newspaper clippings, stenographic copies of Roy's unpublished speeches, microfilms of material on Roy at the National Archives in New Delhi, and a large collection of published material, including a complete run of *Independent India* (Bombay).

*Biographical sketch by Philip Spratt.

*Minutes of a talk by Ruth Fischer on "The Indian Communist Party" at the Russian Research Center (mimeo.), Harvard University, July 11, 1952.

*Narayan, Jayaprakash. "M. N. Roy." Poona, May 24, 1954. Testimonial written in May 1954 after Roy's death.

Park, Richard L. "The Rise of Militant Nationalism in Bengal: A Regional Study of Indian Nationalism." Ph.D. dissertation, Harvard University, 1950.

*Rhodes, Henry. "The Eastern Philosophy of M. N. Roy." Senior Thesis, Princeton University, 1956.

*M. N. Roy's correspondence with Louise Geissler, February 5-March 17, 1928; November 3, 1930-April 18, 1931; July 19, 1931-April 23, 1933. Louise Geissler first met Roy in November 1926. She accompanied him to China in 1927 and helped him to escape from the Soviet Union the following year. She followed Roy to India in 1931 and was subsequently arrested and deported.

M. N. Roy's correspondence with Ellen Gottschalk (the late Mrs. M. N. Roy), November 1930 to July 1931. She was born in Paris on August 15, 1904. Her mother was German, but her father was a naturalized American citizen who worked for the U.S. Consular Service. She lived in Germany from the age of two until she fled the country in 1933 to escape from the Gestapo. Her association with the communist movement in Germany dates from 1923. In 1929 she joined the German Communist Opposition and her apartment in Berlin soon became a gathering place for its members. It was during this period that she met Roy. They were married in December 1936 at a civil ceremony in Bombay. She died in Dehra Dun on December 13, 1960, the victim of a burglary. For further bibliographic information, see the following articles by her brother, Robert Gottschalk in *Radical Humanist* (Calcutta): "Ellen Roy," December 17, 1961, p. 613; and "My Sister Ellen: Some Recollections," January 25, 1962, pp. 26 and 43.

*Roy, Ellen. "Comments on the First Seven Chapters of Overstreet and Windmiller's *Communism in India*." Dated May 18, 1957.

*Roy, M. N. "The Manifesto of the Central Committee of the Revolutionary Party of the Indian Working Class (The Communist Party)." 1935. This Manifesto with a forwarding letter was submitted to the Seventh World Congress of the Communist International held at Moscow in 1935.

*Rudolph, Susanne Hoeber. "The Working Committee of the Indian Congress Party: Its Powers, Organization and Personnel." Paper, No. D/55-2, Center for International Studies, Massachusetts Institute of Technology, Cambridge, Mass., 1955.

*Rusch, Thomas A. "Role of the Congress Socialist Party in the Indian National Congress, 1931-42." Ph.D. dissertation, Department of Political Science, University of Chicago, 1955.

*Sorich, R. "Fragments in the Biography of M. N. Roy." Research paper at the Hoover Library, Stanford, California, 1953.

*A Critique of Masani's *The Communist Party of India* by Philip Spratt.

*Selected List of Interviews**

Ahmedabad, Gujerat

Bakulshai B. Bhatt. Joined Royists in early 1930's.

C. T. Daru. Joined Royists in late 1930's. He is general secretary of the Ahmedabad Mill Mazdoor Mandal—a textile workers' union—and a leading advocate.

Dashrathlal M. Thakar. A Royist since the early 1930's. He was one of the publishers of A. K. Hindi [Tayab Shaikh], *M. N. Roy—The Man Who Looked Ahead*, and is a founding member of the Ahmedabad Mill Mazdoor Mandal.

Andhra

Coconada

M. V. Sastry. Joined Royists in late 1930's. He was a member of the Central Executive Committee of the RDP. In the mid-1960's he was a member of the Swatantra party.

Tenali

Avula Gopalakrishna Murty, advocate. He was a general secretary of the Andhra unit of the RDP in the 1940's. He was a leader of the backward classes amelioration movement in Andhra Pradesh and a leading member of the Tenali Municipal Council. He died in 1968.

M. V. Ramamurty, advocate. A Royist since 1942.

Dr. G. V. Krishna Rao. A Royist since 1937.

P. V. Subbarao, lawyer. One of the early Royists in Andhra.

K. Subramanyan. Considered the founder of the Royist group in Andhra. He joined the League of Radical Congressmen in 1938.

* In the biographic sketches accompanying the list of interviews, the abbreviations RDP and IFL stand for two Royist organizations of the World War II period, the Radical Democratic party of India and the Indian Federation of Labor.

Bangalore, Mysore

Philip Spratt. Joined the CPGB in 1924 and two years later was sent to India as a party emissary. He was arrested in March 1929 in connection with the Meerut Conspiracy Case. Released in September 1935 he was arrested the following November and interned until January 1936. He did not rejoin the communist movement after release. He joined the RDP in 1943. For many years he worked for the English weekly *Mysindia* (Bangalore). He is now editor of *Swarajya*, with which C. Rajagopalachari is closely associated.

Bihar

Ankhori, Shahabad District

Ram Lal Verma. Formerly member of the RDP. He has worked as a Kisan leader in his district for over forty years.

Sassaram, Shahabad District

Sheopujan Singh Shastri. A peasant leader in Bihar since the early 1930's when he was a member of the provincial PCC. He was later a member of the Central Executive Committee of the RDP. In the 1960's he was vice-president of the Bihar Committee of the Hind Mazdoor Sabha, and vice-president of the Shahabad district Panchayat Parishad. As a leader of the *Radical Maanavaadii Aandoolan* (Radical Humanist Movement) in his district, he and his associates have helped found a number of village schools and libraries and established a number of cooperatives. He has written five social dramas and a number of booklets to convey Roy's ideas to villagers. In 1967 he was elected to the Lok Sabha (the Lower House of the Indian Parliament).

Bombay

Nissim Ezekiel. Joined Royists as a student at Bombay University in 1942. He edited the Royist-oriented *Students World* in early 1940's and for a brief period in 1946 served as Secretary of the Bombay branch of the

RDP. He was editor of *Quest* and *Poetry India.* His poems, in English, have appeared in many leading magazines. He is also a Professor of English Literature.

Maniben Kara. Joined Royists in 1931. Ex-president of IFL and member of the Central Executive Committee of the RDP. In the 1960's she was president of the Western Railwaymen's Employees Union, vice-president of the All-India Confederation of Railwaymen, and vice president of the Hind Mazdoor Sabha, one of India's leading trade-union federations.

Vasant Bhagwant Karnik. One of the earliest members of the Roy group, having joined in 1930. He served as editor of the Royist journal *Independent India* from its inception in 1937 until the 1940's. He was general secretary of Roy's League of Radical Congressmen and, until 1944, of the RDP. Active since the early 1930's in the Indian labor movement, he was one of the organizers of the Royist IFL and was its general secretary from 1944 until its disbandment in 1948. He is currently associated with Minoo R. Masani in the Democratic Research Service, an organization devoted to the exposure of communist activities in India. He is also an advocate of the Bombay High Court and editor of *Freedom First,* a publication of the Democratic Research Service.

Govardhan D. Parikh. He served as a member of the Central Executive Committee of the RDP and of the Executive Committee of the IFL. He was co-author of the book *People's Plan for Economic Development* (Delhi: Indian Federation of Labour, 1944). He was rector of Bombay University from 1958-68. Currently, he is editor of *Humanist Review* and chairman of Nachiketa Publications, Ltd.

Sibnarayan Ray. Rose to prominence in the Royist group after 1946. He is the author of several books on Roy's political philosophy and a former editor of *Radical Humanist* (Calcutta). He is presently head of the Department of Indian Studies, University of Melbourne (Australia).

A. B. Shah. Joined the Royists in the 1940's. In the 1960's he was principal of South Indian Educational Society College, Sion West, Bombay. Currently, he is the Indian representative of the International Association for Cultural Freedom, and president of the Indian Secular Society.

Justice V. M. Tarkunde. At the time of joining the Royists in the mid-1930's, he was secretary of the Maharashtra CSP and a member of the AICC. He served as general secretary of the RDP from 1944 until 1948. He was a justice of the Bombay High Court for nearly twelve years. At present he practices in the Supreme Court of India, New Delhi.

J.B.H. Wadia. A Royist since the late 1930's and one of Roy's financial contributors. He is a film producer in Bombay.

Calcutta

Abu Sayeed Ayyub. Did not join Royists but was attracted to Roy's attacks on nationalist shibboleths and Indian tradition and his idea of founding a party based on rational politics. He is a noted Bengali essayist, and in 1961-62 was head of the Department of Indian Studies at the University of Melbourne (Australia). In the 1960's he was editor of *Quest*.

Anil Banerjee. Joined Royists in the early 1940's. He served as secretary and organizer for the Bengal branch of the RDP. In the 1960's he was secretary of the Calcutta branch of the Maritime Union of India.

Sadananda Bannerjea. Former member of Juguntar. He joined the Royists while a student at Vidyasagar College in 1936. He served as secretary of the 24 Parganas District unit of the RDP and was assistant secretary of the Bengal provincial unit of the IFL after 1944.

Sibnath Bannerjee. Knew Roy in Moscow in the 1920's.

He is a former president of the Hind Mazdoor Sabha and in the 1960's was a member of its general council.

S. Bhadra. Active in Royist group in 1940's. He was for some time on the management committee of *Radical Humanist* (Calcutta).

Janardhan Bhattarcharya. Active in Bengal provincial unit of the RDP during period of World War II.

Lalit Bhattacharjee. The brother of M. N. Roy.

Probodh Bhattacharjee. Joined Royists while a student at Vidyasagar College in 1936. He was manager of Renaissance Publishers until 1951, and was for some years publisher of *Radical Humanist* (Calcutta).

Jagannath Bose. Joined Royists while student at Vidyasagar College in 1936. He was active in the League of Radical Congressmen and the Calcutta branch of RDP. He was for some years on the management committee of *Radical Humanist* (Calcutta).

Basudha Chakravarty. He served as the *de facto* editor of *Janata*, an organ of the Bengal provincial unit of the RDP, between 1940 and 1942. A free-lance journalist, he now writes the regular West Bengal newsletter for *Thought* (Delhi).

Nripendranath Chakravarty. A former member of Juguntar he lives near the village of Kodalia, West Bengal, where Roy was born and spent his early youth. He is a close friend of the late Harikumar Chakravarty, a Juguntar leader under whom Roy served before leaving India in 1915. He was secretary of the 24 Parganas unit of the RDP.

Gauranga Dev Chatterjee. Joined Royists in 1940's. He was for some time a member of the management committee of the *Radical Humanist* (Calcutta).

Jibanlal Chatterjee. Former Juguntar leader of Munshiganj district in eastern Bengal. He came under the influence of Roy in the 1920's. Imprisoned between 1923-28 and 1930-38, he joined the Royists after his release in 1938, but broke with Roy in late 1941. He is presently general secretary of the Workers party of

India (formerly the Democratic Vanguard—a Marxist-oriented party which believes in the necessity of violent revolution. He is editor of the party's organ *Gana Biplav* (*People's Revolution*), and one of the founders of the Bata Workers' Employees Union, Calcutta.

Sitangshu Chatterjee. Joined Royists in 1946. He helped edit *Radical Humanist* (Calcutta) for a number of years.

Debabrata Sur Choudhury. Member of Juguntar in the early 1930's. He joined the Royists while a student at Vidyasagar College in 1937, and was one of the founder members of the All-India Students Federation. He is presently a Bengali playwright.

Swadesh Ranjan Das. Former member of Juguntar (1925-30). He joined the CPI in 1933, but later left the party to join the Royists.

Amlan Datta. Royist sympathizer since 1944. He is an occasional contributor to *Radical Humanist* (Calcutta), a professor of Economics at Calcutta University and was for many years joint editor of *Quest.*

Dharitri Ganguly. Joined Royists in 1931. He was one of the founders of the All-India Students Federation and a member of the Central Executive Committee of the RDP.

Jatindra Nath Mitra. A Royist sympathizer since 1932, he actively joined the group in 1936. He was vice-president of the AITUC in 1930 and its president in 1932. From 1943 to 1946, he was deputy welfare adviser in the Department of Labor. He joined the Indian Labor Federation, the Hind Mazdoor Sabha, in 1948, and subsequently became president of its All-India Council. He died in April 1965.

Rajani Mukherji. Joined Royists in 1932. He had formerly been a member of the Red Trade-Union Congress. He was general secretary of the Bengal CSP and a member of the executive committee of the All-India CSP in the 1930's. Later he became general secretary of the

Bengal Provincial Committee of the IFL. He served on the executive committees of both the IFL and the RDP. Currently he is general secretary of the Confederation of Free Indian Unions.

Sachin Roy. A Royist since 1941. He is an advocate of the Bombay High Court.

Samaren Roy. Joined Royists in the early 1940's. In the 1960's he was a political adviser at the American Consulate, Calcutta.

K. K. Sinha. Joined Royists in 1935. He is a former member of the Executive Committee of the IFL and a member of the Central Executive Committee of the RDP. He was for some years secretary of the Calcutta Center of the Indian Committee for Cultural Freedom and is presently director of the Institute of Political and Social Studies, Calcutta.

Saumyendranath Tagore. The grandson of Rabindrath Tagore's eldest brother, Dwijendranath Tagore. He was a member of the Bengal Workers' and Peasants' party in the late 1920's and a delegate to the Sixth World Congress of the Comintern. He broke with the CPI in 1934 to form the Communist League, later called the Revolutionary Communist Party of India.

Dehra Dun, U.P.

R. L. Nigam. Joined Royists in 1940's. He is presently professor of English Literature, D.A.V. College, in Dehra Dun. He is also in charge of the Roy Archives and was till recently editor of *Radical Humanist* (Calcutta).

Jaipur, Rajasthan

Professor Chandmull. Member of the Philosophy Department, University of Jodhpur. He has been a Royist sympathizer since 1941.

Karachi

C. P. Dave. Presently assistant secretary of both the West Pakistan Federation of Labor and the All-Pakistan

Confederation of Labor. The nucleus of the former organization is composed of those unions within the defunct IFL which fell on the Pakistan side of the border after the 1947 partition. The West Pakistan Federation still uses the former symbol of the Royist trade-union federation—a lighted torch.

Madras

M. Govindan. Joined Royists in 1938. He is a prominent Malayalam writer and is presently editor and publisher of *Sameeksha* (Madras), a quarterly of arts and ideas.

New Delhi

Prem Nath Bazaz. Joined Royists in the 1940's. He was one of the founders of the National Conference, Kashmir and was jailed for three years, 1947-50, and again in 1955-56 for advocating a plebiscite in Kashmir. He was editor of *Voice of Kashmir* in 1954-55, and is the author of several books on Kashmir.

S. N. Chakravarty. Formerly in charge of Patna district unit of RDP. He is presently secretary of the Hindustan General Insurance Society, New Delhi.

Professor M. K. Haldar. Member of Department of Philosophy, Delhi University. He organized the material at the Roy Archives with the assistance of the National Archives of India.

Vimal Prasad Jain. Implicated in plot to assassinate the viceroy, Lord Irwin, in 1931. He was imprisoned for seven years. He served as a member of the AICC, 1937-40. He was a member of the Central Executive Committee of the RDP, 1940-48. He is presently proprietor of Naya Hindustan Press.

D. B. Karnik. A brother of V. B. Karnik, he assisted Roy with activities at the Karachi session of the Indian National Congress in 1931. In the 1960's he was editor of the *Maharashtra Times*, a Marathi language publication of the *Times of India*.

S. C. Malik. Advocate, Delhi High Court and Supreme

Court of India. He was a member of the RDP and is today an active member of the Radical Humanist movement.

A. K. Mukherjee. While a student at Bombay University in 1934, he left the communist camp to join the Royists. He served as secretary of the IFL and on the executive committee of the RDP. He was a joint editor of the influential English language weekly, *Thought* (Delhi) for some time. He died in 1968.

Balraj Puri. Editor of *Kashmir Affairs.*

C.R.M. Rao. Joined Royists in 1947. He was with the Asian Office of the International Association for Cultural Freedom before assuming the editorship of *China Report* (New Delhi) in 1963.

Ram Singh. Joined Royists in late 1930's. He was a member of the Central Executive Committee of the RDP and editor of the Royist journal *Vanguard* (New Delhi). He is presently editor of the influential English language weekly, *Thought* (Delhi) and was, until early 1969, diplomatic and international writer for the *Hindustan Times* (New Delhi).

S. H. Vatsyayan. Well-known Hindi writer. He was a member of the RDP.

Index

INDEX

Communism and Nationalism in India: M. N. Roy and Comintern Policy, 1920-1939, appears in a series of studies sponsored by the Research Institute on Communist Affairs of Columbia University, New York City. The Institute promotes studies on international communism and on various aspects of Marxist theory and practice. While the Institute does not assume responsibility for the views of the authors, it feels that these studies contribute to a better understanding of the role of communism in the world today.

Books Published by the Research Institute on Communist Affairs

Diversity in International Communism. Alexander Dallin, ed., in collaboration with the Russian Institute. Columbia University Press, 1963.

Political Succession in the USSR. Myron Rush. Published jointly with the RAND Corporation, Columbia University Press, 1965.

Marxism in Modern France. George Lichtheim. Columbia University Press, 1966.

Power in the Kremlin: Khrushchev to Kosygin. Michel Tatu. Published by Grasset, 1966, and by Viking Press, 1969.

Vietnam Triangle. Donald S. Zagoria. Pegasus Press, 1968.

The Soviet Bloc: Unity and Conflict. Zbigniew Brzezinski. Revised and enlarged edition. Harvard University Press, 1967.

Communism in Malaysia and Singapore. Justus van der Kroef. Nijhoff Publishers, 1968.

Radicalismo Cattolico Brasiliano. Ulisse Alessio Floridi. Instituto Editoriale Del Mediterraneo, 1968.

Marxism and Ethics. Eugene Kamenka. Macmillan, 1969.

Stalin and His Generals. Seweryn Bialer, ed. Pegasus Press, 1969.

Dilemmas of Change in Soviet Politics. Zbigniew Brzezinski, ed. Columbia University Press, 1969.

The USSR Arms the Third World: Case Studies in Soviet Foreign Policy. Uri Ra'anan. MIT Press, 1969.

Communists and Their Law. John N. Hazard. University of Chicago Press, 1969.

The Fulcrum of Asia. Bhabani Sen Gupta. Pegasus Press, 1970.

Le Conflit sino-soviétique et l'Europe de l'Est. Jacques Levesque. Les Presses de l'Université de Montreal, 1970.

Between Two Ages. Zbigniew Brzezinski. Viking Press, 1970.